Blue Ice

To Charlie.
Best friends and
c ya there!.
from
Teddy

Blue Ice

The Story of Michigan Hockey

John U. Bacon

Ann Arbor

THE UNIVERSITY OF MICHIGAN PRESS

Published in the United States of America by
The University of Michigan Press
Manufactured in the United States of America
⊗ Printed on acid-free paper

2004   2003   2002   2001   4   3   2   1

A CIP catalog record for this book is available from the British Library.

Library of Congress Cataloging-in-Publication Data

Bacon, John U., 1964–
    Blue ice : the story of Michigan hockey / John U. Bacon.
        p.   cm.
    Includes bibliographical references (p.   ) and index.
    ISBN 0-472-09781-4 (alk. paper) — ISBN 0-472-06781-8 (Pbk. : alk.
paper)
    1. University of Michigan—Hockey—History.   I. Title.
GV847.75.U53 B33   2001
796.962'63'0977435—dc21   2001001086

Preface

A professor of mine once said nothing exists in a vacuum. She was talking about the history of Western art, but the theory applies just as well to the history of the Michigan hockey team. By exploring the trials and triumphs of the Michigan hockey program, it's easy to recognize the impact eight decades of unprecedented changes on campus and around the country have had on a small band of college hockey players.

With that in mind, I've tried to avoid presenting one of those simple year-by-year chronologies, which usually are little more than glorified laundry lists of the big names and the big games, in favor of a broader story, one that includes the historical context of the pivotal moments in the program's growth—and sometimes its survival—and the individual experiences of a wide variety of players, not all of them stars.

I was also guided by the belief that the many successes and occasional disappointments of the Michigan hockey program were not inevitable, nor were they simply the result of broad trends carrying the team along. I believe that a few remarkable individuals have made a huge difference—from famed athletic director Fielding Yost in the 1920s to fourth-line player Kent Brothers in the 1990s—and that the outcomes of certain events—including big games, byzantine recruiting trips, and even administrative gambles—were crucial to the program's surviving, and thriving.

If coach Joseph Barss hadn't won Michigan's first game, which attracted a big crowd for the second; if coach Eddie Lowrey and Fielding Yost hadn't installed artificial ice before the Depression; if Vic Heyliger hadn't organized the first NCAA tournament in a New York hotel room; if Al Renfrew hadn't persuaded Red Berenson and his Regina buddies to eschew Fargo, North Dakota for Ann Arbor; or if Mike Legg hadn't scored his magical goal, still the most miraculous in hockey history—well, things would have been very different for the Michigan hockey program.

Other college teams didn't have such men performing such feats, and things *were* very different.

One night in 1996, I went down to see some old friends who owned Rick's American Cafe, when I noticed the Michigan hockey players quietly celebrating their first NCAA title in 32 years. While I watched them, I realized there was something special going on there. They didn't attract the insipid entourages or gawkers the basketball players did, but they seemed to savor their achievements on a deeper level than the Fab Five ever could.

After having spent so much time with big-time athletes and their big-time ways, I found it refreshing, to say the least. And when I tried to buy a few of them some huevos rancheros at the Fleetwood Diner at four A.M., and they refused because they didn't want any potential trouble with the NCAA to spoil their celebration, I knew I was onto something. Five years and 400-some pages later, I'd say I was right.

A couple notes:
In the program's first decades, most quotes from newspapers are identified only as a 'local paper,' because in the Michigan athletic archives it is usually impossible to determine if a particular story appeared in the *Michigan Daily* or the *Ann Arbor News*. Where I have been able to determine the source, I've listed it accordingly.

Also, I have chosen to refer to individual All-American players as just that, "All Americans." I refuse to use the sobriquet "All-America," as in, "He was a three-time All-America," simply because it sounds so stupid and snobbish. I hope the authors of the style guides will forgive me.

Acknowledgments

All authors need lots of help, of course, but I've probably needed more than most just to get my brain around the sprawling subject of the Michigan hockey program.

First, thanks to Jim Russ, my former editor at the *Detroit News*, who gave me the green light to write a Sunday feature story on the 1996 Michigan hockey players' "undercover" status on campus, a week after they won Michigan's eighth NCAA title. In doing so, Russ broke a number of unwritten rules at the paper, including: we don't cover college hockey; we don't write big Sunday features about it; and we definitely don't do any of those things a week after the season's over. As was so often the case, however, Russ didn't care, placing a higher value on the story's merits than its demographics.

In 1997, two editors who had already produced a book on Michigan State's hockey team asked me if I was interested in doing a similar book on Michigan's program. I was too busy at the time, but when they asked again a year later I remembered how much I enjoyed writing the feature story on the 1996 team, and decided a book would be easy and fun to do. Well, it has been fun, even more fun than I expected. But easy? To paraphrase Rick in *Casablanca,* if I thought it was going to be easy, I was misinformed. This project has required much more time and effort than I had anticipated. Coach Berenson once told me that if he knew what he was getting into when he took the Michigan job, he might have thought twice—but he's glad he didn't, because then he might have missed out on a great opportunity. That describes my feelings about this project exactly.

By the time I finished a 300-page draft in the fall of 1999, however, the publisher had gone out of business, but had failed to notify me of this development. Enter the University of Michigan Press and its heroic interim director, Mary Erwin. She not only understood what I was trying to do—write a professionally researched and written book that just happened to be about a college hockey team, instead of cranking out one of those hastily produced "buff books" written only for die-hard fans—she also was smart enough to give the project to her first-rate editor, Kelly Sippell, whose passion for accuracy is matched only by her passion for sports.

Kelly believed in this project from the outset and fought many internal battles for it over the past year—and I have since learned that she fought a lot more battles than I was aware of at the time. Where the University of Michigan Press's more academically minded writers turn in their work well in advance of deadlines and make few, if any, revisions, I was in the habit of getting everything in at the last second—if that—and making each page bleed red every time they gave me a chance to revise my work. After a while most of them got wise and quit letting me look at it, but Kelly always afforded me the chance to make one more "final" revision if it meant improving the book, and even though it invariably meant more work for her. The highest praise I can give her is that she cared about this book as much as I did, and proved it by working more than a few weekends and late nights to help me get it right. She infused the project with consummate good cheer and exceptional editorial savvy, making enough good catches to earn a gold glove, maybe two. I simply couldn't have had a better editor.

Thanks also to Kevin Rennells and the many other people at the University of Michigan Press who work in copyediting, production, marketing, and distribution for all of their important work on behalf of this book. My agent, Carol Mann, helped me switch publishers without a headache.

The biggest reason this project was hard was the complete lack of books already out there on Michigan hockey—but that's also what made it fun, because almost everything had to be learned from scratch. This heightened the sense of discovery at each turn, and allowed me to meet over a hundred memorable guys, ranging in age from 18 to 93, and to hear thousands of great stories, some of which I could actually print. Unlike many jaded modern athletes, the Michigan men were unfailingly open, honest, and self-effacing.

First and foremost were Michigan's former coaches, all of whom endured endless interviews and follow-up questions without complaint. Michigan's first coach, Dr. Joseph Barss, passed away years ago, but his son, Dr. Joseph Andrew Barss, filled in wonderfully and repeatedly for his late father, providing hard-to-find facts, stories, and insights about his father.

Vic Heyliger, Al Renfrew, Dan Farrell, and Red Berenson all patiently painted vivid portraits of their tenures behind Michigan's bench. Since four of them also served as Michigan captains, they had to perform double-duty by discussing their playing days, too. Renfrew, Farrell, and Berenson endured the longest interviews of any of the books' hundred-plus subjects, and plenty of second-round questions, too.

I feel compelled to point out that Coach Farrell first performed yeoman duty on my behalf when I was a talkative 14-year-old boy, long before this book was a twinkle in my eye. He agreed to drive me from his hockey camp in Traverse City back to Ann Arbor, and along the way found himself enduring an impromptu interview at the hands of a junior reporter. It's said that the truest test of a man's character is how he behaves when he thinks no one's watching, and there goes your proof.

I would also like to give Coach Berenson special recognition for giving me far more time than I asked of any other subject. Without his complete cooperation, this book simply would not have been possible.

Coach Berenson often says the head coach of any team gets too much credit, and the assistants not enough. So too was it with this book. The assistant coaches I interviewed provided the kind of insider information, perspective, and anecdotes I could not have gotten from either the head coaches or the players. Mark Miller, another former Wolverine captain, Mel Pearson, Rob Palmer, Dave Shand, and Billy Powers were all immensely helpful.

Of course, the heart of this book is the players' experience. The list here is very long, but the conversations were often longer because I enjoyed them so much. Listening to someone recount the happiest years of his life is a pleasure—and even more pleasurable when he tells you so many great stories off the record. Suffice it to say, if any of the players I interviewed becomes president, I'll be able to pick any cabinet post I wish.

In alphabetical order, the players who shared their stories included: John Arnold, Bubba Berenzweig, Russ Blanzy, Roger Bourne, Rob Brown, Justin Clark, Greg Daddario, Dave Debol, Don Dufek, Chris Fox, Wally Grant, Steve Halko, David Harlock, Bobby Hayes, the brothers Helber (Tim and Mike), Matt Herr, Connie Hill, Les Hillberg, Kevin Hilton, Dan Hoene, Alex Hood, Pat Hughes, Dave Huntzicker, Willard Ikola, Billy Jaffe, Wayne Kartusch, Ben Kawa, Mike Knuble, Jerry Kolb,

Mike Legg, Joe Lockwood, Warren Luhning, Joe Lunghamer, Kris Manery, Wilf Martin, Kip Maurer, the May family (Dennis, Doug, and their father, Ed), Brad McCaughey, Mark Miller, Angie Moretto, Brendan Morrison, Billy Muckalt, Myles O'Connor, Ryan Pardoski, Mark Perry, Marty Read, Rudy Reichert, Sean Ritchlin, Alex Roberts and his cousin David, Mark Sakala, Harold Schock, Steve Shields, Mark Sorenson, Ted Speers, Don and Mike Stone, Ed Switzer, Marty Turco, Jeff Urban, Mel Wakabayashi-san, Frank Werner, Bill White, Bob White, Gordon Wilkie, Ricky Willis, and last, but far from least, Brian Wiseman. Thanks to their candor, I learned of the qualities that make the Michigan hockey team unique among college athletic programs.

It simply would not be possible to produce a book on the history of the Michigan hockey program without the constant help, and prior research, of Michigan's Sports Information Department. Having worked with several dozen such departments around the country, I can tell you unequivocally that Michigan's is by far the best in the business. Bruce Madej is the department's director, but he wasn't afraid to roll up his sleeves to help me with my research when I needed it most. Jim Schneider gave me a lot of great quotes, stories, and documents from his time as the hockey S.I.D., which spanned from the end of Farrell's tenure through the beginning of the Berenson era.

Easily the saddest day of this journey was Friday, January 8, 1999, when I learned that former hockey sports information director Brian Fishman had died the day before due to a faulty circulation system in his apartment. Brian had worked as the hockey team's S.I.D. from 1995 to 1998, before leaving to work with the USA Hockey program in Ann Arbor. That didn't stop him, though, from compiling a one-foot-high stack of photocopied newspaper clips from 1911 through the 1960s, and giving it to me with no strings attached. He didn't ask for money, or even credit, but suffice it to say, the copious work he'd done provided the backbone of this book's research, without which I wouldn't have even considered embarking on the project in the first place. Brian was one of those great spirits who poured his whole self into his work, and it is my sincere hope that some of his incredible energy and enthusiasm lives on in these pages.

Jason Gerdom had the unenviable task of following the popular Fishman as both Michigan's hockey S.I.D., and the principle research resource for this project, and he did so with exemplary professionalism, remarkable responsiveness, and equally endless patience with my endless requests for materials and access. In short, I put the poor boy through hell, and he never so much as squealed. To you, Jason, a heartfelt thank you.

No one exhibited more good humor more often than the lovely De Aronson, the hockey team's secretary. Her warmth never flagged despite weekly, and sometimes daily, phone calls over the better part of three seasons. I now know the coaches' secret, that day in and day out De Aronson is the most indispensable person on that floor.

The book also benefited from the perspectives of many people who touched the Michigan athletic program in other ways. These include former CCHA Commissioner Bill Beagan; NHL legend Scotty Bowman; former U-M athletic director Don Canham; unofficial team attorney Paul Gallagher, who first suggested using the winged helmet; equipment manager Ian Hume; current Michigan hockey radio announcer Jim Hunt; former radio announcer Ken Kal; current athletic director Bill Martin; Bo Schembechler (if you don't know who he is, you should kindly put this book down and select another); Kip Taylor, who scored the first touchdown in Michigan Stadium and later managed the Coliseum; Nate Weinberg, son of the Coliseum's founder; long-time public address announcer Glen Williams; and arena manager Craig Wotta, who told me some things about the House that Yost built I never learned in my books.

There were still others outside the program who provided special knowledge of the people and places mentioned in this book. I list them here in the order of their appearance. Dr. Al Cain, Dr. David Dickinson, and Dr. John Segall helped with one of the most difficult profiles, that of the late Dr. Eddie Kahn, because Dr. Kahn was so loathe to talk about himself. The Schlanderer family trusted me with letters, documents, and other keepsakes of Art Schlanderer, '31, the team's first Ann Arbor captain. Ted Heusel and Sister Yvonne Gelese offered some interesting takes on Dr. Rudy Reichert. Barton Hills golf pro Doug White chipped in some valuable information on the golf course architects at the University of Michigan and the Broadmoor Hotel. William John Foster, Wally and Mickey Grant, and Rhonda Collins assisted me on the sections covering the Upper Peninsula, Minnesota's Iron Range and Regina, Saskatchewan, respectively. NHL Hall of Famer Ted Lindsay told me some good stories about the old Wolverine–Red Wing exhibition games, and Joy Berenson shared some biographical information about the current head coach that only she could have known.

Forbes magazine once calculated that Yoshiaki Tsutsumi-san was the richest man in the world, but he still took time out of his busy schedule to grant me a very rare interview, and a 30-minute one at that. His handlers were as surprised as I was, but the guy loves hockey and Mel Wakabayashi so much, he couldn't help himself. To him, a sincere domo arigoto gozaimas. (And thanks also to Hiroko Hara for translating for this baka gaijin.) George and Florence Cavender, Dave Finn, and John Wilkins answered my many questions about Michigan's heralded hockey pep band, while Chuck Legg, Mike's dad, told me some things about his son's well-publicized Miracle Goal that, incredibly, had never been printed before.

A few coaches from other schools contributed unique insights, including Michigan State's Ron Mason, former Ferris State and Michigan Tech coach Bob Mancini, and coaching legend Herb Brooks, who led Minnesota to three NCAA titles in the 1970s, the U.S. Olympic team to the gold medal in 1980, and several NHL teams in the eighties, nineties, and aughts. He'll be wearing the whistle again for the U.S. Olympic team in 2002. Likewise, a handful of Wolverine opponents offered a view from the "other side," including Michigan State's Brian "Sandy" McAndrew, Denver's great Keith Magnuson, Wisconsin's all-time leading scorer Mike Eaves, and North Dakota's Justin Duberman.

I also enlisted the aid of numerous professional researchers, including the outstanding reference librarians at the Ann Arbor Public Library, the University of Michigan Graduate Library, especially Holde Borcherts, and the University of Michigan's Medical Library, who answered my arcane questions in minutes, again and again. (And I promise to return Dr. Kahn's autobiography this week. Honest.) The research staffs of the Halifax Maritime Museum; the University of Michigan Hospital; St. Joseph Mercy Hospital; Albert Kahn and Associates; Minnesota's Mayo Clinic (especially Renee Ziemer); the Broadmoor Hotel in Colorado; the United States Hockey Hall of Fame in Eveleth, Minnesota; the Saskatchewan Sports Hall of Fame in Regina; the chambers of commerce of Eveleth, Regina, Houghton, and Halifax; the NCAA, the WCHA, the CCHA, the ECAC and Hockey East; and some two dozen college athletic departments have earned my gratitude for their considerable help to ensure the accuracy of this text. MSU's hockey S.I.D. Nate Ewell deserves special mention.

Special thanks to the Bentley Historical Library, particularly Diane Hatfield, who pitched in from her posts as both an archivist and a Deker devotee, and Greg Kinney, who is simply the nation's best sports archivist in charge of the nation's best sports archive. I benefited greatly from the work others painstakingly performed in that library decades before this book was conceived. I also relied on the Bentley and the Michigan sports information department for numerous photos, available nowhere else, which you see in these pages. I also solicited photos from Wally and Mickey Grant, Alex Roberts, the Schlanderer family, and the late Bob Kalmbach.

A few professional journalists saved me days of fruitless searching by directing me to exactly what I needed. Ed Swift (better known as E.M. Swift to *Sports Illustrated* readers) is not only one of the very best in the business, he's one of the field's nicest guys, too. He pointed me toward some valuable information on Hobey Baker, Minnesota high school hockey, and the 1980 U.S. Olympic Hockey team, on which he wrote the memorable Sportsmen of the Year cover story. Former *Ann Arbor News* beat reporters Doug Hill and Marty Frank gave some colorful material for the sections on the CCHA. A few civilian researchers pitched in with crucial kernels of data, including Steve Armstrong on Pioneer high school hockey records, Andreea Marinescu on Ploesti, Romania, and Eddie Pocock on Albert Kahn.

My writing friends were generous enough to read some very rough drafts of the manuscript, tough enough to be honest about it, and kind enough to encourage me anyway. Rick Ratliff and Dave Stringer had the toughest job—slogging through the first edition—while my former editor Jim Russ and my former players Peter Uher and Ryan White fine-tuned the later drafts. Many other coaches, players, and insiders read part or all of the manuscript for accuracy, leaving the judgment calls to me. To all of them, a hearty thank you for performing a vital task with vigor.

I must also thank the Fraser's Institute of Sporting Research (FISR) and its outstanding staff of research assistants, who provided an excellent forum for discussing the history of Michigan hockey, and, unlike so many research institutes these days, also provided cooling beverages for my interview subjects and me for a nominal fee.

Finally, thanks to my Canadian grandparents, my parents, and former Michigan goalie Ross Childs for cultivating my love for this great game at any early age. Because of them, I grew up spending just about every winter weekend playing and watching hockey at Yost Field House. When I had to wait for my brother's games to end, I liked to roam the concourse, gazing at the framed photos of the Deker Hall of Fame players and reading their biographies, again and again. I was captivated by their peculiar hair styles, their antiquated equipment, and their confident, clear-eyed expressions staring back at me. I wondered how they played the game, and what their lives were like. Now I know their stories are far more fascinating than anything I could have imagined then.

John U. Bacon
Ann Arbor, Michigan
May 2001

Contents

Contents

Contents

What Is Michigan Hockey?

After spending over two years researching and writing this book, I have become convinced there is something special about hockey in general, and Michigan hockey in particular.

Hockey is not easy. Just to play it, you have to endure the biting cold and withstand unusual levels of pain, which is enough to scare most athletes off to other sports. To play it well, you must have the lungs of a runner and the strength of a gymnast, the balance of a skier and the hands of a hoopster. Until they start playing water polo with lacrosse sticks or golf on roller blades, there is no sport that requires its players to master as many foreign elements as does hockey.

The nature of the sport ensures that no single player can dominate a game the way, say, a basketball player can. It's impossible to hang onto the puck for very long, and the game is too exhausting to play more than a couple minutes at a stretch. You need teammates.

All these things make hockey players a tough but humble breed.

The fact that most Michigan players have hailed from small, cold-weather towns has also added to the character of the program. They didn't come to Ann Arbor with big reputations from New York or Chicago; they arrived as unknowns from the Upper Peninsula; Eveleth, Minnesota; and Regina, Saskatchewan. Most came to Ann Arbor with little, and they didn't ask for much after they arrived, either. Blessed is he who expects little, as they say, for he will never be disappointed.

Michigan didn't start giving out hockey scholarships until the sixties and still does not bestow on its hockey players the kind of adulation its football and basketball players receive. So be it. Michigan hockey comes as close to the ideal of the student-athlete as any college team in any sport in the country.

Unlike football and basketball, hockey developed first as a pro sport, not as a college game, which forced the NHL to create its own minor league system long before the NCAA sponsored its first ice hockey championship in 1948. Football and basketball, on the other hand, blossomed first as college games and later as pro sports; thus, the NFL and NBA have always had colleges willing to train their prospects for free. Bottom line: Today there are still no viable minor leagues for football and basketball players, but there are three times more minor league hockey teams than college programs; therefore, the only people playing college hockey in Ann Arbor are those who have actively chosen to be college students.

The game's basic innocence hasn't been tarnished over time, either. In the 1990s, the Michigan hockey team quietly won five league titles, two NCAA crowns, and more games than any other college team, all while graduating 91 percent of its players—a rate 7 percent higher than the student body at large. When Red Berenson led the Wolverines to their eighth NCAA hockey title in 1996, their first in 32 years, they had become the famous National Champions as a team, but individually they were still a bunch of nameless students, caught somewhere between big-time celebrity and small-sport anonymity. While college basketball and football players now seem to live in a world apart from their classmates, the Michigan hockey team is a refreshing throwback to an era when championships were won by your classmates sitting in the next seat.

"These guys are real people," Berenson says. "That's what I like best about them. They're the kids down the street who'll wash their dad's car, go out and play top-notch hockey, then come home and take out the trash—and not think anything of it."

Unlike winning the national title in college basketball or football, winning the hockey trophy does not confer wealth or fame on the victor, just a slab of wood. That never concerned Mark Sakala, a defenseman and engineering major on that 1996 team. "We really wanted to win it," he said, "just to win it."

In 1999 and 2000 the Wolverines failed to get past the quarterfinals. As of this writing, just two of the seniors from either class has made it to the NHL, and only for a few games thus far. But all 11 graduated on time with degrees from the University of Michigan, and all 11 say their four years at Michigan were the best years of their lives.

That was the idea, wasn't it?

The young men who have played hockey at Michigan over the past eight decades weren't motivated by fame or fortune. They did it because they loved it. And as a happy by-product, they created something bigger than any of them dared imagine it could become.

So, what *is* Michigan hockey?

It's a bunch of guys born before the turn of the twentieth century playing a game of shinny on the Huron River.

It's Josh Langfeld slipping the puck past the Boston College goalie in overtime to win Michigan's ninth NCAA title in 1998.

It's Ross Childs, a year after losing the national goals-against title because he had played one period too few, volunteering to play forward the next year because that's what the team needed, and then scoring a goal on his first shift.

It's Red Berenson's first team being swept by lowly Ferris State, 9-7 and 9-0, then beating an All-Star Soviet squad the following night on a breakaway goal by local hero Joey Lockwood, right in front of a potential recruit named Myles O'Connor.

It's Wally Grant, hopping on a train from Duluth to Ann Arbor one afternoon because he had nothing better to do, then calling athletic director Fritz Crisler when he arrived to get the hockey coach's number, and going on to become Michigan's first three-time All-American.

It's Dan Farrell's vaunted class of '77 jumping over the fence at his house on a steamy summer evening to skinny-dip in his pool.

It's Eddie Kahn scoring Michigan's first goal in 1923 and graduating from Michigan's medical school the next year. And it's Chris Fox, winning an NCAA ring in 1998 for Michigan's ninth title, then following in Kahn's footsteps at the same medical school the next fall.

It's Rudy Reichert, an Ann Arbor kid who had never played a game of organized hockey in his life, skating in both the freshman and varsity practices each day during World War II, just to become good enough to put on the Michigan sweater for the first time as a junior.

It's Brendan Morrison, seconds after hoisting Michigan's first NCAA trophy since 1964, spontaneously saying, "This is for all the guys who never had a chance to win it"—and it's all the guys who never had a chance to win it tearing up when he said that.

This is the story of Michigan hockey.

Part I

Lighting the Torch
1911–27

1

The Start of Something Special

In the beginning, Fielding Yost said, "Let there be ice."

And there was.

But like the other Almighty, Yost didn't make his decisions lightly.

Hockey historians say the game began in Windsor, Nova Scotia, sometime in the 1860s, then crossed the border at a tennis tournament in Niagara Falls in 1894 when teams of Canadian and American college tennis players there compared notes on their winter pastimes. Hockey soon caught on in eastern U.S. colleges, Minnesota mining towns, and the frozen outposts of the Upper Peninsula, but it didn't enter the American mainstream until a man named Hobart Amory Hare Baker arrived on Princeton's campus in 1910.

The star of both the football and hockey teams, Hobey Baker was Princeton's undisputed "big man on campus," thrilling the national press and classmates like F. Scott Fitzgerald with his skill and sportsmanship. Among Baker's many feats, he scored an astounding 92 points as a sophomore, almost four per game, and recorded an incredible 30 shots in one game against Yale. The *New York Times* reported that Baker "carried the puck to every part of the ice surface without being stopped." And he did all this while picking up only two penalties in his entire college career. After each game he would visit the opposing team's locker room to shake their hands, win or lose.

"It became a cliché to compare him to Sir Galahad," writes David Brooks in the *Atlantic Monthly*, "the solitary knight charging bravely into the breach. . . . [Baker] personified the ideals of the age—manly courage, duty, courtesy, honor, and service."

Baker was a nattily attired, tow-headed All-American boy who rose to become hockey's first American star. After graduating in 1914, he had the nerve to turn down the Montreal Wanderers to play amateur hockey in New York City, which boosted the game's profile among the Gatsby set the same way Wayne Gretzky's arrival in L.A. did among the Hollywood crowd. Baker worked by day for J.P. Morgan, but Wall Street bored him, so he jumped at the chance to fly combat missions over France during World War I. He shot down three enemy planes, and was soon promoted to squadron commander with 206 men and two dozen planes under his command.

Hobey Baker, and the trophy named for him
(Courtesy of the U-M Athletic Department.)

"There was no finer man, nor a better pilot," said U.S. Major Charles Biddle, a long-time friend and flying companion. "He was very skillful and particularly fearless."

Baker was visibly disappointed when the Great War ended, according to an account in *Sports Illustrated.* Six weeks after the 1918 Armistice, Baker decided to take one final flight, over the vehement objections of his peers and in direct defiance of a deep-seated pilots' superstition. On December 21, 1918, Baker took a recently repaired plane up to 2,000 feet, where the engine sputtered and died. Although he could have crash-landed a few miles away from the airport—which he and most of his peers had done safely during the war—he apparently decided to turn back to the airport to spare the plane. But as he turned, the aircraft fell nose-first to earth. On the way to the field hospital, Baker bled to death.

Although he was only 26 years old when he died, Baker left a longer legacy than all but a few of those who have lived three times longer. The memory of Hobey Baker lives on in Fitzgerald's novel *This Side of Paradise,* for which Baker served as the inspiration for Allenby, the "slim and defiant" football captain who embodies manly grace. Many of Baker's Princeton classmates named their sons after their fallen campus hero. And, of course, Baker is now remembered as the namesake for the award given each year to the nation's best college hockey player. In the words of one of Baker's college classmates, "the aura of Hobey Baker permeated the campus," as it still does the game of college hockey.

Hockey at Michigan began humbly enough when a band of students called the Huron Hockey Club started organizing games of shinny—the hockey equivalent of stickball—on the Huron River a few years into the twentieth century. If you flip through a Michigan yearbook from that era, you'll see pictures of the club members playing their games and wearing coats and ties, highcollared shirts and bowler hats. They played a primitive game, using clip-on blades; one-piece sticks often made by Nova Scotia's Mi'Kmaq Indians for about 50¢ each; and tin cans, wooden blocks, frozen fruit, and even packed horse manure, for pucks. Hockey players throughout North America eventually graduated to a ball, but when they found it too hard to control, they sliced off two sides of it to make it into what we call a puck. They didn't play the sport quite the way we do today—shooters weren't allowed to lift the puck, goalies weren't permitted to drop to their knees, and forward passing was illegal—but they knew they had a game good enough to grow. The trick was convincing other people of hockey's potential.

In 1911, the Huron Hockey Club asked the members of the University's Board in Control of Intercollegiate Athletics to recognize hockey as an intercollegiate sport. They didn't.

The Huron Hockey Club
In 1911, the Huron Hockey Club players petitioned for varsity status but were rejected in favor of cross-country, swimming, wrestling, golf, and even soccer, rifle shooting, and bowling. Twelve years later, the hockey players finally succeeded in obtaining varsity status. The game was on.
(Courtesy Bentley Historical Library, University of Michigan.)

In 1913, the club asked the board representatives for a small stipend so the team could play games in Detroit during winter break. They said no.

In 1914, the club asked the board members to consider giving hockey varsity status. They refused. Snakebit, the boys didn't risk asking the board for anything else for six years.

At the time, the University of Michigan sponsored only five varsity teams: baseball, football, track, tennis, and basketball. But while the Huron Hockey Club members stewed on the sidelines, screwing up their courage to ask the board to add men's ice hockey to that list, they had to watch the board grant varsity status to virtually every other team that asked, including cross-country, swimming, wrestling, golf, and even soccer, rifle shooting, and bowling.

In the board's defense, they had reason to be suspicious of ice hockey. Unlike the other sports the board considered, most of which were well-known Olympic events, hockey was new and exotic, and known only to younger generations. It's very likely that no one on that board had ever played a hockey game and, because the Red Wings didn't join the young National Hockey League until 1926, probably none of them had ever watched an organized contest, either.

Thanks to figure skating's immense popularity and hockey's infectious appeal, however, the ice sports began to capture the students' imagination on their own. A *Michigan Daily* article from January 1916 reported that "skating is rapidly becoming just as important and popular on the Michigan campus as it is throughout the United States, with hundreds and hundreds of students crowding the single rink here in Ann Arbor."

The "single rink" in question was the Weinberg Coliseum, still located on the corner of Hill and Fifth. Michigan hockey has been touched by serendipity many times over its 80-year history, but its first stroke of luck was the unlikely creation of its birthplace. The Weinbergs settled in Ann Arbor in the late 1800s on the corner of Seventh Street and Jefferson Court. Although the house is now surrounded by the cozy homes of Ann Arbor's Old

West Side, when the Weinbergs built the modest dwelling it served as the center of the old Weinberg farm.

Frederick Weinberg got out of the farming business around the turn of the century to open up two new operations, an auto repair shop and a construction company. Because Weinberg knew how to start and run a business, he decided to create a third enterprise on the side in 1901 by building a swimming pool, where the Coliseum parking lot is today. To draw swimmers Weinberg built a tall slide and a precarious wooden diving platform 30 or 40 feet high, but the dirt-floored pool was so rustic, local boys could earn a little extra money by pulling frogs from the water. When winter came Weinberg froze the pool to attract skaters, who were entertained by Weinberg's brother-in-law, Louis Otto, and his eight-piece band. They played in a small hut in the middle of the rink, occasionally closing the windows to warm up.

Weinberg decided to expand his success in 1913 by creating a new building adjacent to the pool for roller skating. Weinberg's workers put the old building together out of hand-formed concrete blocks, and did the job well enough that the building is still structurally sound nine decades later.

Weinberg soon realized he could double his revenue during winter by moving the roller-skating rink to the building's overhanging balcony and hosing down the floor—which was considered an "innovation" by the local paper—to pull in the ice-skaters. Still, the ice was so unreliable that Weinberg had to post special flags in front of State Street stores to tell local skaters when the ice was good enough to skate on.

"You're going back a looong time," says Weinberg's youngest son, Nate, who was 5 years old when his father's rink opened and is now a 93-year-old resident of Ann Arbor. "But I can remember a lot of things about the old rink. My father put that big electric organ in for the skaters. It was a Wurlitzer, just a wonderful organ, a wonderful instrument." The organ worked like a player piano, and could imitate the sounds of an entire orchestra, serenading the skaters with songs like the "Blue Danube Waltz," the "Poet and Peasant Overture," and, naturally enough, the "Skater's Waltz." The songs could be heard several blocks away, especially when the Coliseum's windows were kept open to freeze the ice. "But when the weather was real cold," Weinberg says, "the organ pipes'd freeze up, silent."

Being privately owned, however, the Coliseum didn't have to cater to the players in the Huron Hockey Club, who continued to conduct their games on the river. Just as serendipity has often spurred the growth of Michigan hockey, so has tragedy. The first occurred in 1916, when a student skater died after falling through the ice of the Huron River. The accident sparked an outcry for a university-run rink to get the players off the dangerous river. The university initially tried to meet that need by flooding the tennis courts on Ferry Field, but the quantity and quality of the ice wasn't sufficient to satisfy the skating-mad student body, so the university started renting out the Coliseum.

Unlike the anything-goes environment on the Huron River, however, the Coliseum didn't afford the college students free rein. Nate Weinberg remembers his father as "a very serious person. He had lots of rules and regulations on how to operate the rink, very strict. The bouncers had a big job on their hands when I was a kid."

Sadly, Nate didn't get to know his father very well. In 1917, when Nate was just nine years old, his father was driving his car along Packard past Stone School Road when a streetcar collided with his vehicle and killed him. He is buried in the Forest Hills cemetery on Geddes, not far from the final resting place of Fielding Yost.

Frederick Weinberg's rink lived on, however, and served as Nate's second home for years. "I sort of grew up with the rink," he says. While attending the old Ann Arbor High School on State Street, which is now the university's Frieze Building, Nate worked as a bouncer at the rink ("Anyone who'd go too fast or create a disturbance, I'd throw 'em out"), a goal judge, the ice plant operator, and the driver of a prehistoric Zamboni, which entailed sitting atop an ice scraper pulled by a horse, like a chariot racer. "We cleared the ice with six or eight snowplows, then flooded it overnight, if it was cold enough."

"I remember them days," Nate Weinberg says, "and how different everything was."

The memories of the Huron Hockey Club's repeated rejections were still fresh in the players' minds, but they were sufficiently encouraged by the growing popularity of their sport to approach the board in the fall of 1920 with the most modest of requests: to grant the squad "informal team" status.

The board members took their time to consider the petition and review the squad's meager schedule—but, to the club's surprise, they eventually granted this minor wish. The young men were heartened by the concession, however small, and a few months later they felt brave enough to ask for the moon: varsity status.

The board members didn't say yes, as usual, but for the first time they didn't say no, either.

Humble Beginnings

While the board pondered the question, the hockey team made the most of its new status. In 1920, the squad appeared for the first time in the yearbook, listed as the "Informal Varsity Hockey Team." Although their photo was no bigger than that of the "Senior Engineer Hockey Team, All-Campus Class Champions," which had to beat over a dozen other intramural teams for the title, it was a start.

Michigan's "Informal Varsity Hockey Team" was led by a man the papers referred to only as Coach Lemieux—though he apparently taught in the School of Engineering, his first name is lost to history—who started writing letters "to most of the schools within a reasonable radius," for a game the *Michigan Daily* reported, "and is every day expecting word from them." The idea of a college coach writing letters to opposing teams to schedule games and then waiting weeks, even months, to hear back from them seems as anachronistic today as sending a message in a bottle, but Coach Lemieux didn't have many options in a time when hitching posts still lined Main Street and the town was so quiet a visiting poet named Robert Frost saw fit to extol its virtues as a peaceful place to live.

We don't know how many games Lemieux's team played, or whom it played against, or even the first names of most of the players, but we *do* know that the team's success was due almost entirely to a highly skilled young man named Richard Barkell.

According to the papers, Barkell scored all but two of the team's goals that season.

The papers also reported that student interest in the hockey team grew with each victory. "The crowd," one paper wrote, "which was the largest of the season, was treated to some excellent hockey." Although the Coliseum didn't have protective fencing, heaters, seats or even four walls that year, hundreds of students packed the building to see their newest team play.

At the end of the season the paper concluded, "The first year of hockey at Michigan has been successful beyond the fondest hopes of its advocates." A year or two later, the same paper noted that in a "comparatively short time hockey's popularity has increased rapidly."

The 1922 Michigan yearbook reported that the "ice sextette" played 10 games that year, winning 6 while losing only to Notre Dame and the Michigan School of Mines (now called Michigan Tech). A caption claimed, "Hockey was the popular sport staged daily at the Coliseum or on the Huron."

The innate appeal of the fast, easy-to-understand game has drawn fans to hockey from the sport's inception, but you have to wonder where Michigan hockey would be if this mystery man named Barkell hadn't "caged" so many goals. Would enough students have come around to create a stir on campus without him? Although almost every cold-weather school had some kind of "informal team," they didn't have a Barkell, and consequently they usually didn't generate enough interest to start varsity programs until years later, if ever.

In weighing whether to make hockey a full-fledged varsity program, the board members noted the team's success and the students' obvious enthusiasm for the game, but they also took into account a few things that had nothing to do with their suddenly discovered love of the sport. Because Ann Arbor's survival as a city has always depended on its reputation as a safe, inviting place for parents to send their children to school, Ann Arborites have been intensely image conscious from the day they lured the state's first university from Detroit in 1837.

John Allen and Elisha Rumsey founded Ann Arbor in 1824, 13 years before the university came to town. To lure settlers from the East they produced fancy brochures in which they claimed Ann Arbor's climate "is as pleasant as 'tis possible to be." Even those who love Ann Arbor dearly have to admit that line is a whopper. Each winter the snowfall buries Ann Arbor's streets, the temperature dips below zero an average of six times a year, and the gray blanket that covers the town from December to mid-March is enough to drive people to drink. And that was the problem.

As early as 1863, university president Henry Tappan urged residents to "root out the evil influences" of alcohol. A few years after that President Erastus Otis Haven said Ann Arbor was "disgraced all over the country" as a "place of revelry and intoxication." (Former Ann Arbor mayor Jerry Jernigan would say almost the exact same things a century later about the city's infamous Hash Bash and $5 pot fine.) To stem the so-called drinking epidemic, city leaders illegalized the sale of alcohol on the campus side of Division Street in 1902, but it didn't prevent a record number of arrests for public drunkenness in 1916. Feeling desperate, city voters decided that year to make Ann Arbor "dry" (years before the nation adopted prohibition), while university leaders sought to keep students busy with wholesome activities during the winter doldrums.

"The University has recognized the necessity of encouraging winter sports," the *Michigan Daily* reported. "The healthful and fascinating ice sports should receive their full measure of attention from the student body." To those ends, university leaders created an "Ice Carnival," replete with seasonal celebrations, snow sculptures, demonstrations of "fancy skating," and a hockey game, "the main event of the evening."

Following the team's second season as an "informal varsity" program, the Board in Control could no longer ignore the growing evidence of ice hockey's value to the university. And so, in December of 1922, after more than a decade of rejecting the game and its players, the board voted to add the sport of men's ice hockey to its roster of full-fledged varsity teams. Hockey might have been the next-to-last of the university's 11 current men's sports to be sanctioned, with gymnastics joining the others in 1930, but the hockey team was finally on board.

Once the team got the long-awaited stamp of approval, things started moving fast. On January 7, 1923, the head of the university's "Minor Sports Division," George Little, introduced the 35 students trying out for Michigan's first hockey team to their first coach, Joseph Barss, just minutes before the team's first practice.

Five days later, against the University of Wisconsin, the Michigan Wolverines' varsity hockey team took the ice for the first time, starting something that would become far bigger than anything the determined founders could have imagined at the time.

The Good Doctor

While other programs suffered from poor neonatal care through rapid coaching turnover, inept coaching, or no coaching at all, Michigan's team was in good hands from the day Joseph Barss took over, and that might have made all the difference.

Barss was born in India in 1892, the only child of Baptist missionary parents. When his mother became ill the family returned to their original home, Wolfville, Nova Scotia, just 10 miles down the road from the birthplace of hockey, where his father ran a small grocery store and ministered to Wolfville's Baptist congregation. The young Barss took advantage of the area's fertile sports culture, becoming a semipro baseball player and a world-class hockey player before turning 20.

"He was only about five foot eight," recalls his son, Dr. Joseph Andrew Barss, now 77. "He was sort of a stocky fella, big thighs, who carried himself very straight. A tough guy. His ankles were so strong, he didn't have to lace up his skates." In photos of the early Michigan teams, the dashing young Barss wore a three-piece suit, a bow tie, and his hair slickened with tonic, exuding the same stoic confidence that Robert Redford brought to the role of Jay Gatsby in the early 1970s.

After graduating in 1912 from Acadia University in Wolfville, Barss played two seasons of professional hockey with the Montreal Wanderers. Despite their nickname, the Wanderers were "probably the most famous hockey aggregation in the world" at the time, according to the local paper's profile of Barss. The Wanderers played only 15 seasons in the National Hockey Association, the NHL's predecessor, before a fire destroyed their rink in 1918. But in that short span they won four Stanley Cups and produced 16 future NHL Hall of Famers, including Lester Patrick and Art Ross, both of whom have NHL trophies named after them. Although we have no record of Barss's scoring statistics with the Wanderers—they predate the *Hockey Encyclopedia,* which starts with the birth of the NHL itself—the fact that he could play for a team that regularly thumped Les Montreal Canadiens clearly made him overqualified for the coaching job at Michigan. But he would take a long, torturous road to get there.

Soldier, Doctor, Coach
Joseph Barss played against the Montreal Canadiens and survived gas warfare in World War I and the Halifax explosion before moving to Ann Arbor to attend medical school. The pin on his lapel represents his infantry unit, a symbol he had inscribed on his gravestone.
(Courtesy Bentley Historical Library, University of Michigan.)

Barss left the Wanderers in 1914 to fight in World War I, still considered by military experts to be the grisliest of all wars. The 1916 Battle of the Somme, for example, consumed four months and 1,265,000 Allied and German lives for the Allies to advance just 8 miles—an average of one fatality for every 3 yards gained. The fighting was so chaotic that at war's end, after the British Empire and France had lost 2.7 million sons between them, only half could be found and identified for proper interment. The rest had either been left on the fields or blown to pieces too small to recognize.

The descriptions of Barss's experiences in World War I and during his return to Halifax might initially seem irrelevant to the Michigan hockey program, but both events made dramatic and lasting impacts on Barss's personality, and as a result, the program he started, too. Further, it's clear that without the winds of fate pushing him to the killing fields of France and the disaster in Nova Scotia, Barss never would have made the journey to Ann Arbor in the first place. Without a man of Barss's stature at the helm, there might not have been a Michigan hockey program until decades later.

Barss trained to become a machine gun sergeant in the Princess Patricia's unit of the Canadian Light Infantry, whose insignia Barss would have engraved decades later on his tombstone. In April 1915, Barss's unit found itself in the second of three infamous battles in the ancient walled city of Ypres, France. The area, which inspired the poem "Flanders Fields" ("In Flanders fields the poppies blow / Between the crosses, row on row / That mark our place"), is one of the dreariest landscapes in western Europe, a vast, sodden, gray pasture with almost no signs of life. The water table is so high that a hole dug there just a few feet down will quickly fill with water, making the already ghastly business of trench warfare that much more miserable.

The First Battle of Ypres, in the fall of 1914, cost thousands of Allied lives in exchange for 500 yards of soggy land. The Second Battle of Ypres, in the spring of 1915, was worse—and Joseph Barss saw it firsthand.

April 22, 1915, was a sunny day with a light breeze from east to west—perfect conditions for the Germans to test their recently developed lethal gas. They selected Barss's unit to be their first guinea pigs, opening fire on the Canadians at five o'clock, and following that up with a grayish-green cloud of chlorine drifting from the German trenches toward the Allies. The experiment was, to the Germans, a great success. When the Canadian boys inhaled the gas, they felt their chests sear, then began choking and coughing up their froth-corrupted lungs. They would finally stumble to the ground while their eyes writhed in their heads, drowning in their own boiled organs.

"The scene must have been as near to hell as this earth can show," writes John Keegan in his acclaimed best-seller, *The First World War*. The use of lethal gas in the Second Battle of Ypres so outraged Winston Churchill, then Britain's secretary of defense, that he countered by authorizing British troops to start producing gas shells, too. When the Red Cross protested that the strategy was inhumane, Churchill cooly replied, "So is the rest of war."

Although Barss did suffer permanent lung damage from the lethal gas, unlike thousands of his countrymen, however, Barss was lucky enough to avoid dying from it. But when a conventional shell exploded a few feet from him, a piece of shrapnel ripped through his belly and butted up against his spine but, miraculously, did not sever it. The thick abdominal muscles he had developed playing hockey might well have prevented the shrapnel from making faster progress through his torso and paralyzing Barss for life.

The medics sent Barss to a French hospital, where he recuperated for a year before he was well enough by November 1917 to be shipped to a new Halifax facility, Camp Hill Hospital, which had been built for the war casualties they knew would be coming. He was supposed to mend there, then go home to Wolfville to decide what he wanted to do with the rest of his life. But Barss's brief stay in Halifax seemed timed to bring him in contact with as much tragedy as possible, tragedy designed to bring him to a quick and clear decision about his future—one that would dramatically affect the future of Michigan hockey.

Upon his return to Halifax, Barss immediately recognized that the cozy town he remembered as a boy had become one of the world's busiest ports, the funnel for all of Canada's supplies and personnel heading to the Great War. In the preceding decade the town had tripled to 50,000 people, and had lost some of its innocence in the process.

When the *Titanic* sank in the North Atlantic in 1912, the survivors were sent to New York City instead of the closest major port, Halifax, because ice blocked the route there and the survivors had already seen enough ice to last a lifetime. But the *Titanic*'s search and recovery missions were conducted out of Halifax. The three ships dispatched from Halifax picked up 327 of the 335 victims still floating in the frigid water: 59 were returned to their families, 118 were buried at sea, and the remaining 150 interred in Halifax cemeteries.

Barss's return to his home province coincided with the arrival of some 240 survivors of the Third Battle of Ypres, fought in the summer of 1917. If the first two battles of Ypres were hellish, the third and final battle was hell itself. In John Keegan's words, the three-month battle was "the most notorious land campaign of the war," featuring more dispiriting trench warfare, more gory hand-to-hand combat, and more lethal gas attacks than had ever been seen before. In the first 15 days alone, the two sides detonated over 4 million shells. The Canadian survivors, including seven shell-shock victims, were admitted to Camp Hill Hospital alongside Barss.

On the morning of December 6, 1917, a few days after Joseph Barss had returned to Halifax, a French ship called the *Mont Blanc* entered Halifax harbor to join a convoy headed for Bordeaux. The *Mont Blanc* was loaded down with 10 tons of gun powder, 35 tons of airplane fuel, 200 tons of TNT, and 2,300 tons of picric acid, a poisonous chemical used to make explosives. The ship's cargo was so volatile the crew lined the steel cargo hold with wood, attaching it to the inside of the hull with copper nails because copper is one of the few metals that does not spark when hammered. The captain informed the port authorities of her contents but, for security reasons, told no one else on land or sea.

‑At 7:30 that morning the *Mont Blanc* eased her way into the harbor. At the same time, a Norwegian ship called the *Imo* was heading out to sea, bound for New York to pick up relief supplies for Belgium. When trying to pass each other, both ships ignored nautical conventions and soon found themselves trying to avoid each other, like two people passing on the street who repeatedly move to the same side, inadvertently increasing the chances of colliding.

The awkward dance ended when the *Imo* struck the *Mont Blanc*'s bow. The impact was not forceful, but it was enough to ignite the airplane fuel on board. The 40 French crewmen, fully expecting the ship to blow up at any second, jumped in their lifeboats, rowed across the river to Dartmouth and ran deep into the woods, not stopping to warn anyone of the impending danger. They, at least, would be safe.

The unmanned ship burned for 20 minutes, drifting around the harbor until it settled against a wooden pier at the north end of Halifax, an area dense with factories and homes. Crewmen from other ships, unaware of her cargo, hurried to secure the *Mont Blanc* to the pier and tried in vain to douse the fire. The burning ship was visible for miles and tempted passersby to come closer. Businessmen and housewives stopped what they were doing to get a better look, children paused on their way to school, and some 240 Canadian casualties at Camp Hill Hospital used their crutches and wheelchairs to move up to the big picture windows facing the harbor.

When a rifle is fired, one ounce of explosive powder in the shell burns rapidly, fomenting hot gases that quickly expand and force the bullet out of the shell. *Mont Blanc* held the equivalent of 83 million ounces of explosives, which did collectively what one rifle shell does with 83 million times more force. The instant the *Mont Blanc* finally exploded, at 9:04:45 A.M., December 6, 1917, the stylus on the seismograph at Dalhousie University 1½ miles away flew to one edge of the paper and jammed there.

The *Mont Blanc* itself shattered into thousands of pieces of shrapnel like a monstrous hand grenade, literally vaporizing the sailors from other ships trying to tie her down and knifing those farther away with metal shards. The explosion shot the shaft of the *Mont Blanc*'s anchor, which weighed half a ton, two miles to the east; a cannon on deck flew an equal distance to the north.

The explosion's shock wave rushed toward shore, driven by a bubble of burning gases that traveled at 2,100 miles per hour—seven times faster than the most powerful tornado, about three times the speed of sound. The shock wave needed less than a second to flatten every building on the near slope of Halifax, obliterating 2½ square miles of the city's North End in a whoosh. The explosion's force crushed the concrete floors in factories, threw railroad tracks into knots, reduced wooden houses to kindling, and ripped open brick schools and churches. One-third of the city's buildings were blown off the face of the earth; 6,000 of the town's inhabitants were made homeless in a second; and hundreds more buildings and people burned in the aftermath. The explosion's shock wave traveled downward, too, creating a tidal wave that flooded buildings 60 feet above sea level and drowned pedestrians in its path.

Almost every window in Halifax was shattered, including those where the inhabitants had stood watching. The last thing hundreds of people saw was an incredible burst of light. An instant later they were blind, or dead. Hundreds of people died instantly, some blasted out of all their clothing except their shoes.

All told, over 1,700 were killed in the explosion and subsequent fire, about 200 more than died on *Titanic*. More than 150 victims could not be identified, and dozens more were never found, their lives erased forever in an instant. The *Mont Blanc*'s 40-man crew, however, had watched the spectacle from the safety of the Dartmouth woods. None suffered any discomfort.

The Halifax catastrophe would remain the biggest man-made explosion in human history until the United States dropped the atomic bomb on Hiroshima in 1945. Robert J. Oppenheimer, the mastermind behind the atomic bomb, carefully studied the Halifax explosion to estimate the potential damage of his atom bomb.

Fortunately, because Halifax was mobilized for war and had so many sailors and soldiers in town—including Joseph Barss—

the city was better prepared for a massive recovery effort than most. By noontime the townspeople had already organized crews to put out the fires, to pick up the dead—tagging their names, when they knew them, to the victims' wrists, then piling them onto motortrucks—and to tend to the 4,000 casualties who occupied every flat surface available in the hospitals, the city buildings, and even the doctors' homes.

Barss was somehow lucky enough to survive the explosion unharmed. Unlike the carnage Barss faced in France, however, which gave him only two options—attack or be attacked—he could do something about this tragedy. He could help the people who needed all the help they could get.

Although Barss had no medical training, the city was grateful for anyone who could still walk and see, so Barss was called on to perform tasks normally reserved for trained professionals. He threw himself into the frightful work for days upon days, with little or no sleep during most of them—but in the process he discovered the profound satisfaction that comes from healing others.

After the victims had been tended to or transported elsewhere, Barss returned to Wolfville a changed man. Before the explosion Barss might have taken over his father's grocery store or even his ministry, but after witnessing two of the worst disasters in human history, he decided he would make a career out of helping those who needed it most by becoming a doctor. His dream would have died, however, were it not for his uncle, Andy Barss, who had left him just enough money to enroll in the University of Michigan medical school when it cost just $100 a year, including lab fees, to attend.

"Darned if I know why he went to Michigan," his son says today, "but it's always been a first class school."

We may not know why Barss came to Michigan, but we do know why he decided to become a doctor. If it weren't for the Battle of Ypres, Barss would not have been wounded. If he hadn't been sent to Halifax's Camp Hill Hospital just days before the worst man-made explosion up to that time, Barss would not have discovered his natural affinity for healing others. And if the former professional hockey player hadn't chosen Michigan's medical school, for reasons we'll never know, it's very likely Michigan would never have started a varsity hockey program, just like every other college west of the Alleghenies in 1922.

Despite his obvious love for the game, however, Barss arrived in Ann Arbor in 1921 to study medicine, not coach hockey. Before he graduated from the Michigan medical school in 1924 and started his internship at University Hospital, he met a young coed from Battle Creek named Helen Kolb. The hospital had a strict rule against interns marrying—one of Barss's classmates got married secretly and had to live in the intern quarters while his wife roomed with four women in town to keep their secret—but the administrators made an exception for Barss due to his unusual maturity. The couple wed in 1922 and had a son, Joseph Andrew, in 1923 and a daughter, Elizabeth, in 1927.

Even while Barss was busy starting a family and finishing his medical education in quiet, peaceful Ann Arbor, he was still occasionally haunted by the Great War. Like most of his countrymen, Barss was a stoic man who rarely talked of the epic battles in which he fought, but he couldn't help getting choked up whenever he heard bagpipes, because it was bagpipers who had led his unit into the trenches, and it was bagpipers who had led his unit out, with the soldiers carrying the writhing gas victims and corpses out with them.

Early in her marriage to Joseph Barss, Helen was startled to discover this otherwise self-possessed man would drop to the ground whenever he heard a whistle or a loud bang, a survival instinct he learned in the awful days when enemy shells were dropping all around him. Through the steady support of his family, his friends, and his own strong spirit, however, Barss was gradually able to let his memories of war recede and the simple pleasures of civilian life take their place.

According to the box scores of Michigan's "informal team," Barss officiated many of the Michigan club's games in 1922. Perhaps it was his desire to return to a normal lifestyle and have some fun again that motivated him to find time in his already overburdened schedule for such a trivial pursuit. It's easy to imagine the lightheartedness Barss must have felt when he became reacquainted with the happiness skating on a sheet of ice could bring. And having gotten a taste, he wanted more.

Barss saw firsthand that Michigan's program needed someone with experience to get it going, so he paid a visit to Fielding Yost to ask if he could start a varsity hockey team. Yost might not have known much about hockey, but he knew a natural coach when he met one. Yost wisely accepted Barss's offer.

The Barss family lived in a comfortable home on Granger Street. Joseph attached a thermometer outside their bedroom window, which Helen Barss checked every morning. If it was too warm to skate on the Coliseum's outdoor practice rink, she simply rolled over and let her young husband sleep until he had to go to class. But if it was cold enough for the team to practice, Helen had to stir her bone-tired husband out of bed to make sure he got to the rink on time. After everything he'd seen in France and Halifax, however, Barss was not likely to complain about a little fatigue.

4

The Game Is On

In the days leading up to Michigan's first varsity hockey game, no one knew if this esoteric event was going to flop or fly. The *Michigan Daily* writers, aware of hockey's shaky status with the administration, all but begged their fellow students to support the team.

"Hockey is a game that nine-tenths of the students have never seen, and could not be persuaded to attend," one student wrote, in a piece that is almost as accurate today as it was when the anonymous student wrote it eight decades ago. "There are many others, however, who will turn out for the first game. This last class will be the one that will furnish the hockey following, for few people who have ever seen a game have failed to become confirmed enthusiasts. It is a sport that combines the science of football, the combination demands of basketball and the individual skill of baseball, with a speed that belongs to hockey alone.

"Above all other attributes of the game itself, the greatest reason why the Coliseum should be packed to the doors tomorrow night and Saturday night is Michigan spirit, the quality for which the Maize and Blue is known throughout the country.

"It is up to you. The players cannot do it alone.

"Be there."

A warm spell that week made the ice so soft the game was in doubt until Friday afternoon, just hours before the scheduled face-off. The athletic department didn't sell tickets until one o'clock that day. But by seven o'clock on the night of January

12, 1923, a few hundred students huddled in the newly installed bleachers around the newly installed dasher boards and watched the puck drop for the first official college hockey game west of the Alleghenies.

Thus, before the university built East Quad, West Quad, or the Law Quad; before Ernest Hemingway published his first novel or Charles Lindbergh flew across the ocean; before New York, Boston, Chicago, or Detroit had NHL teams; before hockey games were broadcast on the radio or movies had sound—before all that, the Wolverines were playing varsity hockey.

No, they didn't play in front of a polished pep band and 7,000 savvy fans. They didn't have machines to freeze the ice or even resurface it. The quality of the sheet depended not on coils or Zambonis but on an evening of cold wind and a bucket of hot water. They didn't wear helmets, fancy jerseys, or even numbers

Bare-bones hockey
They didn't have machines to freeze the ice or even resurface it. They didn't wear helmets, fancy jerseys, or numbers on their backs. They rarely checked each other, lifted the puck, or left the ice—but they played a game a modern fan would have no problem recognizing or appreciating.
(Courtesy Bentley Historical Library, University of Michigan.)

on their backs. They rarely checked each other, lifted the puck, or left the ice, making just five substitutions the entire night.

But they played. And a modern fan would have no difficulty recognizing, or appreciating, the game played in Ann Arbor that evening. Reporters described the first game as clean and clever, fast and furious—the same drawing cards that fill Yost Field House today.

Although Coach Barss had only five days to select and prepare his team before the inaugural contest, "the individual play was sensational," wrote a nameless reporter who, it must be said, knew so little about the game that he called the puck a ball. "Michigan counted the first point," he wrote, "when [Eddie] Kahn, by clever work, rushed the ball through the Badger defense for a goal."

But in the second period Wisconsin evened the score at 1-1. The Badgers made it stick throughout the third period and the first five-minute overtime. In the second overtime, the reporter wrote, "the Wolverines seemed held off when Robert Anderson, in a hard shot from the side, slipped the puck through the goal for the winning point."

Final score: Michigan 2, Wisconsin 1. The Wolverines' record: 1-0.

Word spread quickly about the exciting new game in town, attracting a spirited crowd of 800-some fans the next night, but the play suffered due to awful ice. The soft, rutted surface was so bad, one reporter wrote, that "when the offense of either team would carry the puck to within a few feet of the opponent's goal, the attack would be spoiled by an unavoidable spill. This did not detract from the thrills afforded the crowd but, on the contrary, added to the general excitement of the game." It also didn't stop Michigan center Carleton "Shorty" Lindstrom from scoring off a face-off in the second period to put his team ahead, 1-0, a lead the Wolverines protected to win their second game.

How important were those first two narrow victories to the future of the Michigan hockey program? They might seem trivial now, but consider this: after dropping their opening weekend in

Ann Arbor, the Badgers managed to win only one game in their first 10 tries against Michigan, and only 9 of their first 42 games against all comers. The Badgers also developed the bad habit of losing at home, which prevented them from attracting more fans, recruiting the better players already on campus, and generating enough administrative support to build an artificially cooled rink. Put it all together and you have a school that was forced to drop its varsity hockey program by 1933, not to be revived until the mid-sixties. Although Wisconsin now has an excellent program, during the Badgers' hibernation Michigan fans were treated to three decades of exciting hockey and seven NCAA titles.

The Badgers' demise was the rule, not the exception. Michigan Agricultural College (now called Michigan State) lost 12 of its first 14 games against Michigan, and in so doing failed to solicit enough interest or support to warrant playing more than 7 games a year. The Spartans were forced to kill the program when an unusually warm winter, combined with a lack of artificial ice, canceled all their games in 1930. The Spartans wouldn't play varsity hockey again until 1950, when they piggybacked on the excitement created in their absence by Michigan and Minnesota.

Four current Division I programs—Brown, Providence, Maine, and Notre Dame—disbanded before the Depression, due principally to a lack of consistent coaching leadership. Seven more schools, including modern powers such as Boston College, Rensselaer, Minnesota-Duluth, North Dakota, and MSU, were forced to drop hockey during the Depression because they hadn't developed the foresight or the following needed to get artificial ice, an absolute necessity to survive the warm winters and lean years to come.

The lesson is simple: when you're trying to win over uneducated fans and skeptical administrators, it's crucial to get a few big victories early on to gain their support. It might not have been sufficient to ensure success, but it was definitely necessary. After those first two rousing victories, the Michigan hockey team had secured a foothold in campus life—and with it, administrative backing—for years to come. Only four Division I schools have been playing hockey longer than Michigan: Yale, Dartmouth, Clarkson, and Army. And Michigan has more wins, 1,253, than all of them. Of the top 66 active hockey programs, only the University of Minnesota has more victories (1,367) than the Wolverines.

Michigan started building its tall tower of victories with a couple of timely goals scored on a January weekend eight decades ago, goals that captured the Michigan crowd's imagination and put hockey on the map in Ann Arbor for good. Over the years Michigan's program has waxed and waned, but the sport's central place in campus life has always been secure.

Tradition is not something that can be created retroactively. Michigan has it, and you can see it during alumni weekends, when the players come back from the 1940s and 1950s to have a beer with the players from the 1990s and share stories about the common experience of playing hockey for the Wolverines. When the weekend's over, it's invariably the younger alums who talk about how much more it means to have played for Michigan after meeting those who came before.

Mao Tse Tung said the longest journey begins with a single step. Michigan hockey took that first step—a step that would lead to 15 conference championships, 5 Big Ten banners, 11 Great Lake Invitational crowns, and 9 NCAA titles—in front of 800 fans in a three-sided unheated bandbox on soft ice, on January 12, 1923.

The Barss Era

Michigan lost seven games that first season but kept the home fires burning by winning three of five in the Coliseum. The team's 4-7 finish didn't dampen the enthusiasm of the students, who were rewarded the next two years with a 6-4 team in 1923–24 and a 4-1-1 finish in 1924–25. The latter record was good enough to earn Michigan its first league title, although it wasn't much of a league.

When Michigan and Ohio State dominated Big Ten football in the 1970s, pundits called the conference the Big Two and the Little Eight. Those same critics would have had a field day with the Michigan hockey team's original circuit. Although the league gave itself a vaunted title, the Western Intercollegiate Hockey League (WIHL), they could have called it the Little Three and the Nonexistent Seven, since the conference consisted only of Michigan, Minnesota, and Wisconsin. (The circuit changed its name to the Big Ten in its second year, 1925–26. Although the Big Ten has gone by the titles Western Conference and Big Nine, it is always referred to as the Big Ten here for clarity.) The Badgers won the hockey league title only once in their first 12 seasons, and lost their varsity status in 1933. They finished last twice more with an "informal varsity" before quitting hockey altogether, but by that time Michigan Tech had joined the regular rotation (though not the Big Ten). This allowed Michigan to justify its annual trip to Minnesota by adding a stop in Houghton, instead of Madison.

Coach Barss avoided Wisconsin's fate by cobbling together a

credible team out of the limited local talent available and a few ringers from the Upper Peninsula. In Barss's first four seasons the Wolverines amassed a respectable 17-17-4 record, but Minnesota was still the standard Michigan couldn't reach. In the Wolverines' first 13 games against the Gophers, they could manage only 3 victories—all by one-goal margins.

The Wolverines started Barss's fifth and final season, the 1927 campaign, by dropping half of their first eight games, including a split with Michigan Tech and a sweep by Minnesota. Although Minnesota coach Emil Iverson declared, "That is the best team Michigan has ever had," the Wolverines' opening stretch gave the good doctor Barss little reason to hope his last

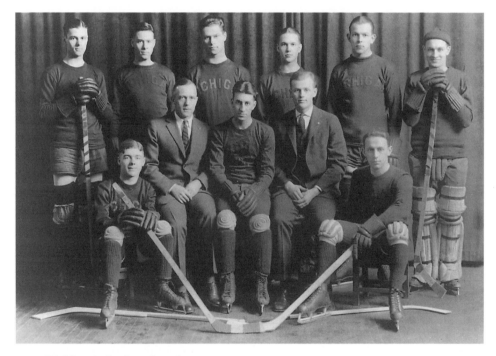

Michigan's hockey founders
Coached by Barss, *seated left,* and captained by Eddie Kahn, *front row center,* who became a leading neurosurgeon. Also pictured: Waldeck Levi, the team's first Ann Arbor native, *top row third from left,* and *to his left,* Pep Reynolds, the team's first U.P. star.
(Courtesy Bentley Historical Library, University of Michigan.)

team could reach .500, let alone challenge the Gophers for "Western supremacy." Later in the season, with a 2-3 league record and only five league games remaining, the Wolverines knew they would have to run the table to win a second league title before their coach departed.

To pull in more fans, all five games were played in Windsor's 8,000-seat Border Cities Arena, which also served as the Detroit Cougars' home before the Cougars became the Red Wings and moved to the Olympia. The 75-piece Michigan marching band decided to make a rare off-campus appearance to generate more fan interest, and it worked. According to newspaper accounts, the 3,000 fans who attended each game—by far the largest crowds to watch Michigan hockey until the Coliseum was expanded after World War II—were as eager to see the famous band perform as they were to see the team play.

But if the band brought them in, the hockey team kept them coming back. The Badgers used only seven skaters the entire week, which limited their offense, but their excellent defense permitted only four Wolverine goals in their three-game series. Incredibly, those four goals were enough for Michigan to sweep the series by the scores of 2-1, 1-0, and 1-0. Suddenly Michigan had a 5-3 league mark and sole possession of second place heading into its two-game series against heavily favored Minnesota. But beating the inexperienced and undermanned Badgers was one thing. Beating the deep and daunting Gophers would be quite another.

The Gophers filled their roster with 15 homegrown players, who hadn't lost to the Wolverines in their last six contests. And they had the aura of invincibility that comes with nationally acclaimed excellence. Before the season's final series against the Wolverines, Minnesota's student paper calmly stated the team's case: "The Gopher sextet ranks as the leading collegiate hockey team in the United States. It was so recognized in the official ratings in 1926 and looms up as perhaps the most powerful contender for that honor this year."

To counter the Gopher juggernaut, the Wolverines had goalie Steve Jones, the team captain, who had thrilled the Windsor crowds with his daring play against Wisconsin; All-Conference defenseman Cornelius Gabler; and a skilled forward line of Bill Hooper, Bob Larson, and future captain Bill Maney, with young George "Nick" Sibilsky serving as Barss's "sixth man."

The first game was everything the Windsor crowd had hoped for, a fast-paced affair in which both goalies stubbornly refused to let the puck past them during regulation. Seven minutes into overtime, however, Nick Sibilsky—an Upper Peninsula boy from Calumet—came off the bench to convert a pass from Bill Hooper for the winning goal. Michigan's improbable dream of a conference title was not only alive, it was within one more victory of becoming a reality.

The final contest was "marked by the best hockey exhibited this season," the *Daily* said. Minnesota took a 1-0 lead in the middle of the second period, but Michigan's All-Conference defenseman Cornelius Gabler, who had been knocked unconscious twice during the game, returned to fire a "brilliant, unassisted long shot from near the center of the rink," past the Gopher goaltender, to tie the game at 1-1.

Once again, the goalies prevented either team from scoring through the first overtime, but Michigan's Steve Jones had to work a lot harder than his Minnesota counterpart. Minnesota coach Emil Iverson would say afterward that Jones was "without question the best goaltender in the Big Ten." Jones proved it by knocking back 27 shots, an unusually high number for the low-shooting era. Jones kept his team in the game through the middle of the second overtime, long enough for Michigan center Bill Hooper to beat the Minnesota goalie on an unassisted long shot, "which equaled Gabler's in excellence."

Michigan 2, Minnesota 1. The conference title had been won, the dragon had been slain.

Barss retired after the 1927 season, his fifth, with a 26-21-4 overall record (.553), two league titles, and a degree from the University of Michigan School of Medicine. Dr. Barss moved his young family to Riverside, Illinois, where he eventually became chief of surgery at the Hines Veteran Hospital in Chicago, then set up a private practice in Oak Park, Illinois, Ernest Hemingway's first home.

"His colleagues said he had a great bedside manner," says Joseph Andrew Barss, his son, who also became a doctor. "He was well read, really interested in many, many things, and he could talk to anyone. He was a two-handicap golfer and a great watercolor painter, too. Just good with his hands. His drawings from anatomy class were just beautiful. You could put 'em in a textbook."

But even as his medical career blossomed, hockey was never far away. Joseph Andrew Barss recalls his father making a backyard rink for his two children every winter by spraying a fine mist on the lawn, late into the cold Chicago nights. "He never flooded it," his son says. "I think he was something of an expert on ice."

In 1957, at the age of 65, Barss had to undergo what was then a fairly risky operation for an aortic aneurysm. He told his family, " 'Regardless of the outcome, I feel I've lived a very full life,' " his son recalls. "I'm sure we all would like to be able to feel that way when our time comes."

Barss survived the operation and retired to Florida in 1962. The same year a 22-year-old center named Red Berenson carried Michigan to the NCAA Final Four, Barss's son took his 70-year-old father to Nova Scotia. It was Coach Barss's first trip back to his home province since the Halifax explosion of 1918, when his life's calling first took him by the hand. While he visited the home where he was raised, the fields where he played, and the hospital where he had discovered the rewards of healing others, Dr. Barss could see clearly the arc of his life, and he savored it.

Joseph Barss came to Ann Arbor to become a doctor, but before he stepped down as coach in 1927 he had completed another mission: he had built the Michigan hockey team into one of the most popular attractions on campus and one of the most respected programs in the nation, one strong enough to pass on to his successor in the full confidence that it would continue to thrive for years to come.

"The games were always exciting, sure!" Nate Weinberg says. "Oh, yes. They always had a pretty good team." The team's success on and off the ice gave Fielding Yost the confidence to buy the Weinberg Coliseum outright in 1925 and install artificial ice there in 1928, the year after Barss left.

The Michigan hockey program has been shaped by several larger-than-life figures, but the best of them secured permanent gains before they left the scene. Barss was the first to do so, spearheading the efforts to attain varsity status, to join a league, to purchase a rink, to stay out of debt, and to win two league titles—a list of lasting accomplishments long enough for any coach.

Barss left his mark on Michigan hockey in more subtle ways, too. He created the expectation that the Michigan head coaching job was not to be regarded as a stepping-stone to something else, but as a final destination. Since Joseph Barss left his post behind the Michigan bench in the spring of 1927, the number of Michigan coaches who have left Ann Arbor to coach for another Division I or professional team is exactly zero. Michigan is the only Division I program in the nation that can make that claim.

Barss's tenure also established the precedent that the Michigan hockey program need settle for nothing less than highly educated, highly qualified, and highly respected gentlemen to coach the team—a description that applies to Red Berenson and the coaches in between, not a ruffian among them. Barss knew the value of a good education, and had seen enough real tragedy in France and Halifax to keep hockey in perspective—values he passed down to his charges. And the lessons didn't stop there.

"He sure gave me a good upbringing, in terms of character and honesty," his son says. "He was absolutely true blue. He was very aware of what was right and what was wrong. It was very black and white to him."

Sadly, after the father-son journey back to Halifax in 1962, the former coach's memories of Michigan, and everything else, began to erode with the onset of Alzheimer's disease, from which Barss died in 1971 at the age of 79. But the memory of what he started at the University of Michigan is alive in the hundreds of players and thousands of fans who have been touched by the team since its inception. The torch Dr. Joseph Barss first lit on January 12, 1923, is still burning brightly today.

The Empire Builder

He couldn't skate, he'd never seen hockey played before he moved to Ann Arbor, and he had no idea how the rules worked. But Fielding Yost has to be listed among the most important men in the history of Michigan hockey.

Yost agreed to sponsor a varsity hockey team, he hired Joseph Barss, he bought the Coliseum, he renovated it, he stuck with the hockey program when other athletic directors were dropping theirs, and he did it all with the unflinching conviction of a Texas judge. More important than any building, however, Yost gave the Michigan hockey team the confidence to be the best in the land and the feeling that they already were—attitudes that sank into the program early on, and are still evident in the speeches at the annual senior banquets today.

The minute Yost's train pulled into Ann Arbor's station (which is now the Gandy Dancer restaurant) he grabbed his bags and actually *ran* up State Street to the campus. The press didn't call him "Hurry Up" for nothing.

When he met a reporter at the top of the hill, the new football coach arrogantly predicted, "Michigan isn't going to lose a game." Then he backed it up for 56 consecutive contests. From 1901 through 1905, the Wolverines racked up 55 wins against just 1 loss and 1 tie, outscoring opponents by a total of 2,821 to 42 points. Those famous "Point-a-Minute" teams launched Yost's 24-season Michigan coaching career, which ended with a record of 165-29-10 and 10 Big Ten titles in just 15 seasons of conference play.

Yost's standing as one of the all-time great football men was already secure when he stopped coaching in the 1920s, but he went on to double his stature with an incredible run as Michigan's athletic director from 1921 to 1941. "We have the first field house ever built on a campus," former athletic director Don Canham says. "We have the first intramural building. We have the largest stadium in the country. That was no accident. That was Fielding Yost."

Yost had a larger-than-life personality—for better and for worse. "He'd talk to anyone, and probably talk too much," Canham says. "It's why he made great copy. The reporters loved him."

Fielding Yost
Fielding Yost, with Yost Field House in the background. "We have the first field house ever built on a campus," former athletic director Don Canham says. "We have the first intramural building. We have the largest stadium in the country. That was no accident. That was Fielding Yost."
(Courtesy of the U-M Athletic Department.)

Someone once asked Ring Lardner, the legendary sports reporter, if he ever talked to Fielding Yost. "No," Lardner replied. "My father taught me never to interrupt." But Lardner, who made his living interviewing the likes of Babe Ruth, Bill Tilden, and Knute Rockne, felt compelled to add, "Yost had more personality than any man I have ever met."

For all his boasting, Yost's ego tended to attract, not repel, like Muhammad Ali's. Journalist Edwin Pope wrote that Yost was "an unashamed ham—that rare person who can boast and be liked for it."

If Yost thought highly of himself, he generally thought highly of those around him, too—perhaps concluding that they had greatness by association. Yost promoted the University of Michigan almost as feverishly as he promoted himself. He liked to ask, with his cocksure grin, "Who are they that they should beat a Meeshegan team?" He asked the rhetorical question so often, it became the refrain for a popular tune.

Yost was also fond of "The Victors," naturally enough. "I reckon it's a good thing Louis Elbel was a Meeshegan student when he wrote that song," Yost once said. "If he'd been at any other Big Ten school, they wouldn't have had much chance to use it, y'know." Michigan's innate confidence—some would call it arrogance—started with Yost, and spread to all its teams.

Yost had some glaring faults, but he looked pretty good compared to the uneducated, uncouth coaches found elsewhere. In his best-selling 1905 book *Football, for Player and Spectator,* Yost wrote that before college students started playing sports, they had only two role models to choose from: the bookworm, who was productive, or the card shark, who was admired. Yost argued that varsity sports resolved this dichotomy by taking the title of "Big Man on Campus" from the hard-living card shark and giving it to the healthy, hardworking student-athlete. Yost sincerely believed sports developed the whole person.

Yost's best counter to the many critics of college sports might be his greatest legacy: In an era when sports were considered social ills run by renegade coaches, Yost argued that, when properly coached, sports developed valuable qualities in students that the classroom could not. The belief that sports build character is now a cliché, but when Yost first espoused it, it was a fresh idea.

"This is the Yost quote that we used the most often," football coach Bo Schembechler says, then recites Yost's speech from memory. " 'I ask *no man* to make a *sacrifice.* On the contrary! We ask him to do the *opposite.* To live clean, come clean, think clean. That he stop doing all the things that destroy him physically, mentally, and morally, and begin doing all the things that make him *keener, finer,* and *more competent.*'

"We used this a thousand times," Schembechler adds. "It says it all. You don't *sacrifice* to play sports. We're just asking you to do what you should be doing *anyway.*"

When Yost became Michigan's athletic director, he hired coaches who had the same attributes that he had brought to the job: a thorough knowledge of their sport, intelligence that transcended their games, and the integrity to play the right way. That description certainly applies to the two hockey coaches Yost hired, Joseph Barss and Eddie Lowrey, and those who followed.

The Vision Thing

In an era when most college presidents thought it unseemly for university teams to draw off-campus spectators, let alone charge them admission, Yost was the biggest proponent of college sports as a public enjoyment, one deserving of excellent facilities. The minute President Marion Leroy Burton named Yost Michigan's new athletic director in 1921, Yost was on a mission to construct an athletic complex built to last well into the next millennium.

"From 1901 to 1921 Yost did not innovate anywhere but on the field," says Canham. "But for the next 20 years as athletic director, he was unbelievable."

Yost took over the athletic department at the perfect time to launch his grand plans. After suffering through decades of a sluggish economy, a number of deadly flu epidemics, and the horrors of the Great War, Americans wanted to bust loose in the

1920s, and they did, indulging themselves with scandalous new swing music, dresses so short they revealed women's calves, and plenty of illegally obtained alcohol.

Ann Arbor was particularly flush with newfound wealth and soaring optimism. The university embarked on an unprecedented building spree that included virtually every structure on campus made of brown brick or white stone, while townspeople enjoyed the nation's highest per capita rates of phone and automobile ownership. College students, especially, were enjoying the high life, buying up so many cars—for as little as 20 bucks a pop—that the university felt compelled to ban them in 1927; and consuming so much alcohol that many fraternities found it necessary to install elaborate electronic warning systems to signal those in the houses' cleverly hidden drinking quarters that university or police officials were knocking at the front door.

The public's thirst for entertainment also fueled a boom in spectator sports. People had the time, money, and desire to follow the exploits of Babe Ruth, Red Grange, Bobby Jones, Bill Tilden, and a University of Michigan graduate named Johnny Weissmuller, an Olympic swimming champion better known for playing Tarzan on the silver screen. The public's immense interest in sports justified the birth of a new league, the NFL; the construction of new coliseums like Yankee Stadium, Ohio Stadium, and Illinois's Memorial Stadium; and the expansion of the NHL into Boston, Chicago, and Detroit. Yost noticed all this, and was eager to catch up with his competition around the country.

Despite the fertile atmosphere for the growth of college sports, however, Yost knew if his ambitious proposals were subject to university politics, he wouldn't win too many battles. And if he had served under a hard-nosed, meddlesome president like James B. Angell—or James Duderstadt—Michigan's athletic campus might look very different today. Fortunately for Yost, he served most of his tenure under president Alexander Ruthven. So long as the teams played clean, Ruthven was happy to give Yost the political autonomy he needed, from which Yost created the financial autonomy that fueled his unequaled building program.

"He fought to keep the money made in the athletic department

in the athletic department, so he had the money to get it done,"
says former football player Kip Taylor, now 91, who scored the
first touchdown in Michigan Stadium in 1927. "*That's* how he
did it. Otherwise, if the administration had a choice between
spending money on a nurse's dorm on the Hill or a stadium,
where do you think it's going?" And that's how Yost bought the
Coliseum and built the Field House, facilities other programs
never had.

In 1921 the Michigan athletic complex was no complex at all,
just a loose collection of open-air, temporary structures, with no
golf course, no basketball arena, and no hockey rink. Michigan
people didn't have much, but they didn't know they needed more
until Yost came along.

Yost coined the term "field house" to describe his first building and naturally wanted it named after himself. Problem was,
the university had a policy against naming buildings after living
people, so Yost did what he always did when he faced administrative resistance: he rounded up the students, the alumni, and
sympathetic reporters to make his case for him. As usual, the
administration buckled.

When Yost Field House was christened in 1923, few would've
predicted that the fledgling hockey team playing its first season
in the small, open-ended structure down the street might some-
day occupy the biggest, most impressive building on campus at
the time—let alone sell it out, night after night, year after year.

The adaptation of the old Field House into a first-class hockey
facility probably would have thrilled Yost. He'd be even more
excited to hear that Michigan's hockey players won two NCAA
championships since moving there, and that Brendan Morrison,
the 1996 team's star from western Canada, was moved to say, "I
think Yost is the best rink in college hockey." For all its modern
amenities, Crisler Arena doesn't have half the soul of Yost's
buildings.

Yost fervently believed that Michigan's rightful place in all
endeavors was high above that of other schools. The son of a

confederate soldier, born in West Virginia in 1871, Yost knew nothing about ice hockey, but he reckoned that if the players were good enough to put the block "M" on their sweaters, they must be good enough to be the very best. So, while Yost was busy finishing the Field House and starting Michigan Stadium in 1925, he quietly purchased the Weinberg Coliseum.

The Coliseum wasn't pretty then or now, but according to a 1923 athletic department brochure, the Weinberg Coliseum was "the finest hockey rink in this part of the country." The Coliseum would serve as Michigan's hockey home for half a century. Buying it was probably the single most important decision anyone made in the hockey team's eight-decade history—the program would have died without it—and Yost made it with confidence that it would pay dividends far into the future.

When Yost passed away on October 20, 1946, at age 75, he left behind one of the greatest legacies in the history of collegiate athletics. Due to his incredible foresight, the buildings Yost created in the 1920s—including the baseball stadium, the golf course, the intramural building, the football stadium, and, of course, the current hockey arena—are still the best around, eight decades later. After his retirement, Yost's admirers gave him a spectacular banquet in the eponymous Field House, broadcast on national radio. At the program's close, Yost walked up to the podium to respond to their tributes.

"My heart is so full at this moment, and I am so overcome by the rush of memories," Yost said, "that I fear I could say little more. But do let me reiterate the spirit of Michigan. It is based upon a deathless loyalty to Michigan and all her ways; an enthusiasm that makes it second nature for Michigan men to spread the gospel of their university to the world's distant outposts; a conviction that nowhere is there a better university, in any way, than this Michigan of ours."

For all Yost's faults, his love for Michigan had no limits. When you hear a Michigan hockey player at his senior banquet talk about what it means to be a Michigan man, often with tears in his eyes, remember that it all started with Fielding H. Yost.

7

Renaissance Resident

In the Michigan hockey program's long history, more than 600 players have scored more than 10,000 total goals, but the man who scored the team's first goal might still be the most impressive one of the bunch.

Eddie Kahn was, first, an exceptional player. On the eve of the program's opening night in January 1923, the *Michigan Daily* wrote, "Kahn is probably the fastest man on the team and is a hard fighter." The student writers later gushed that Kahn "again carried off playing honors," that he "covered himself with glory," and that he "played a furiously aggressive game from start to finish. He was knocked out twice but stayed in the lineup and performed sensationally."

To fully appreciate Kahn's contribution to the embryonic program, it's important to understand how differently the game was played in the 1920s than today. Most teams, including Michigan's, carried only two forward lines, two defensemen, a goalie, and a "spare"—in other words, about half the current roster—and gave all but a few minutes of the playing time to the five starters. The best players had to skate the full 60 minutes. They had to be tough, too, because they were protected only by flimsy shin pads, pants and gloves, and the sharp-edged pucks they used easily cut them. Forward passing was allowed only in the very slim neutral zone until 1927, and most teams had no machines to freeze or resurface the ice, making passing difficult in any case. All of these factors favored individual skill over team play, so much so that a single skilled, fiesty player like

Eddie Kahn could dominate a game the way a basketball star can today.

And so he did. According to game stories during the team's first two seasons, Kahn scored or assisted on at least half of his team's goals, often by skating the entire length of the ice with the puck or scoring from center ice. The diminutive forward's teammates named him Michigan's second captain in 1924, coinciding with his last year as a student in the medical school.

There have been many talented, tough, and hardworking hockey players in Michigan's history, but only one was the son of an internationally acclaimed architect, and only one went on to become an internationally acclaimed neurosurgeon—and his name was Eddie Kahn.

More than half a century after the death of Eddie Kahn's father, Albert Kahn, he remains on the short list of great American architects. He designed over 2,000 buildings, a staggering collection that still comprises the heart of Detroit's downtown, Henry Ford's empire, and Michigan's campus. Kahn's achievements were founded on a sharp intellect, a lot of hard work, and a little bit of luck.

Albert Kahn, the son of a German rabbi, came to America in 1880 as an 11-year-old boy. With only a seventh-grade German education, the teenaged Kahn found work as a draftsman at a Detroit architectural firm. He almost lost the lucky break when an older employee suspected, correctly, that the young man was color blind, a fatal flaw for an aspiring architect. Kahn was hauled into the boss's office, where two men tested his eyesight by asking him to identify the colors in a nearby rug. Most shades are fairly easy for the color blind to pick out, but distinguishing red and green is not. Kahn guessed green. "If I had guessed red," Kahn said later, "I might be a butcher today."

When he was just 18 Kahn received his first commission: to design the porch of Mackinac Island's Grand Hotel, still the world's longest porch. Young Albert Kahn was on his way.

Kahn soon hung out his own shingle, Albert Kahn Associates, and started pumping out the blueprints that would spawn almost every architecturally significant building in downtown Detroit, including General Motors' world headquarters, the Fisher Building, the Belle Isle Casino, Detroit Police headquarters, and the homes of the *Detroit News* and the *Detroit Free Press.* Kahn also designed the Detroit Golf Club, the Detroit Athletic Club, and the Grosse Pointe Country Club—all of which effectively excluded Jews, including him. (Although the DAC offered Kahn a token membership, he quietly turned it down.)

Likewise, the University of Michigan campus has been shaped more by Albert Kahn than any other architect. Kahn's campus icons include Burton Tower, Angell Hall, West Engineering, the Natural Science Building, the graduate library and the hospital (Old Main)—not to mention the *Ann Arbor News* building, the Delta Gamma sorority, and the Psi Upsilon fraternity—plus his personal favorites, the Clements Library and Hill Auditorium. So farsighted was his vision that every one of those buildings except the old hospital, which was replaced just a few years ago, is still fulfilling its original purpose.

Kahn is best remembered in architectural circles, however, for revolutionizing the modern factory. At the turn of the century factory assignments were still given to architectural apprentices, who created "dark, cramped mills with creaking, oil-soaked wooden floors," in the words of journalist Richard Bak. After Kahn won several commissions from the Packard Motor Car Company, he shattered the old notions of factory design by replacing the creaky floors with reinforced concrete, creating a wider floor space, adding plenty of ventilation, and flooding the space with natural light. More important than any single innovation, however, was Kahn's insistence that the factory be taken seriously as architecture, and not treated simply as a glorified warehouse to be thrown together by an uninspired draftsman.

Kahn's already flexible mind was stretched in 1908 by Henry Ford's request to house an entire assembly line under a single roof, something that had never been attempted before. "I thought he was crazy," Kahn later admitted, but the resulting Model T plant in Highland Park that opened just a year later introduced mass production to the world.

To crank out more than 1,000 buildings for Ford alone, Kahn regularly put in 12-hour days, often taking catnaps on drafting tables. His body of work includes the renowned River Rouge plant and Willow Run, the world's largest assembly plant at the time. Built to produce B-24 bombers during World War II, Willow Run could crank out one per hour, and is considered by modern historians to be the centerpiece of the "Arsenal of Democracy" that conquered Hitler. Kahn's factories also produced 25,000 Sherman and Pershing tanks. For all his wartime work for the military, including countless factories and naval bases on Guam, Midway, and Pearl Harbor, Kahn insisted that his fee be cut in half. (Congress readily obliged.) Kahn fought the Nazis on the eastern front, too, by building 521 factories for the Soviets, including the Stalingrad tank plant that was so solidly built it served as the fulcrum of the Soviets' heroic defense of that city, marking the turning point of the war in eastern Europe.

Today Albert Kahn is considered one of the fathers of architectural modernism—a school of thought that maintains surroundings affect our behavior—and still ranks among the greatest architects America has ever produced.

His son, however, was an entirely different matter.

When Eddie Kahn was 11, he went on a camping trip to the shores of St. Ignace, almost a half century before the Mackinac Bridge connected the state from that point in the Upper Peninsula. That night he could see the twinkling lights of the Grand Hotel's famous porch, his father's first important design. "It was such a beautiful sight," he wrote late in his life, "that I scarcely slept. My pride in the porch was unbounded."

Through his teens, however, Eddie Kahn showed no signs of following in his famous father's footsteps. As Eddie writes in his autobiography, *Journal of a Neurosurgeon,* when he was still in high school his father thought his son should take a job in his architectural office as a summer intern. On Eddie's first day a draftsman gave him a tracing cloth—which the draftsman had spent 18 hours preparing—and asked Eddie to erase an errant line from it. "I erased it all right," Kahn admits in his book, but he also erased most of the draftsman's precious work, too. "I put on my hat, left the office, and never returned again."

That evening, Kahn's father told his son that his obvious ineptitude at architecture might be a blessing in disguise, because now Eddie could avoid the burden of being compared to his famous father. But they still had to find something the younger Kahn *could* do. After Kahn graduated from high school with "a most undistinguished record scholastically and otherwise," he writes, "it was decided that a post-graduate year in a preparatory school before I went to college couldn't make things worse."

Kahn immediately took to Phillips Andover Academy in Massachusetts—but Andover didn't take to him. After eight weeks there Kahn was failing 15 of his 22 credits. The headmaster called Kahn into his office to warn him that he was dangerously close to being expelled. When he asked Kahn if he was studying late, Kahn assured him that he was studying every night until one in the morning. Instead of being encouraged by this news, however, the headmaster frowned and instructed the wayward student to put his books away at ten every night and go to bed.

"This was probably the single greatest lesson I ever learned," Kahn writes. "Going to bed at ten meant concentrating in order to finish assignments. Never again was I graded unsatisfactory in any subject." The lesson is an enduring one, known to any serious athlete who also wants to succeed in the classroom: your grades actually *improve* during the season if you master the ability to manage your time and concentrate fully.

Kahn learned another crucial lesson, this one from the athletic fields: confidence makes all the difference no matter the endeavor. Before Andover's final game of the baseball season against arch-rival Exeter, one of Kahn's teachers warned him he would have a busy afternoon patrolling left field against the hard-hitting Exeter batters. "The first inning or two," Kahn writes, "I was as tense as could be. An easy fly came to me, and I was shaking as I caught it. It was the same with the next one. But from then on, I had complete confidence and everything seemed easy. That afternoon, I pulled in seven flies, including some rather difficult chances.

"I cannot overstress how much confidence simplifies the task of the conscientious, competent surgeon. On the other hand, overconfidence is very dangerous for any surgeon." Brain surgery may be woefully complex, but some of the qualities needed to do it well can be learned on a field of grass or a sheet of ice.

Kahn took these lessons with him when he enrolled at Michigan in 1918, living in a beautiful brick home his father designed across Washtenaw Avenue from "the Rock," which students have been painting for decades. Kahn performed so well in the classroom he had no problem getting through both his undergraduate and medical training in six years, toiling in the very hospital his father had designed. Eddie spent his limited free time playing on the informal hockey team, and then on the varsity squad after Coach Barss launched the program. The team's second season, 1924, was undoubtedly the first and only year in college hockey history when a team's captain and coach were classmates in medical school.

"My dad talked about Eddie Kahn quite a bit," Barss's son says. "I know they were good friends who respected each other a great deal."

Kahn also earned the respect of his father. Although the senior Kahn stood only 5'4" and relaxed by attending the opera, visiting museums, and playing competitive bridge, he was also an avid baseball fan who greatly admired his son's ability on the ice and in the hospital.

Despite Eddie Kahn's demanding career and intense work ethic, he was able to mix in some adventure, too. After he graduated from medical school in 1924, he practiced in Vienna and Russia, where he had a meeting with Ivan Pavlov, the scientist who won the 1904 Nobel Prize for his famous discovery that ringing a bell before each meal eventually caused dogs to salivate at the sound of the bell alone, a phenomenon now known worldwide as the "Pavlovian response."

In the early 1930s, a Near Eastern art expert invited Kahn to join him on his trip to Persia, now Iran, after which Kahn traveled to Chamonix, France, home of the second Winter Olympics in 1924. While skiing on the Olympic mountain, Kahn sliced his right shin severely. The injury prevented him from hitting the slopes but not from going to the rink, where Kahn met "two beautiful and intelligent French girls, who had never been on ice skates before," he writes. "Because I had played hockey in college, I was soon in demand for support." It turned out the women were models from Lucien Lelong's, a prominent Paris salon. The two volunteered to be Kahn's personal tour guides for the week, including a memorable New Year's Eve celebration—the details of which he leaves to the imagination.

Kahn volunteered for the U.S. Army medical corps from 1940 to 1945, for $1 a year, the only years of his life he did not attend at least one Michigan hockey game. Kahn entered France via Normandy's Utah Beach just a few weeks after D-Day consecrated the land forever. He mended soldiers at the Battle of the Bulge, and was among the first to arrive in Paris when the Allies liberated the City of Light. "Kahn knew Europe well," says Rudy Reichert, who played for Michigan in the early 1940s and went on to become chief of staff at St. Joseph Mercy Hospital in Ann Arbor. "He knew Gertrude Stein and Hemingway personally. When the Americans entered Paris, it was Eddie who brought the U.S. generals into the city, because he knew his way around and knew about a million languages, so he could show them where to go."

On Kahn's triumphant return to Paris, he remembered the two women he had met a decade earlier: the models from the skating rink in Chamonix. He arranged a reunion with them, and, he writes, "we had a wonderful time"—once again leaving the details to the reader's imagination.

The biggest thrill of Kahn's life, however, was not scoring the University of Michigan's first goal, becoming its second captain or its top neurosurgeon, or serving heroically in World War II. Shortly after he returned to Ann Arbor after the war Kahn ran into Harry Bennett, Henry Ford's infamous union buster, at a cocktail party. Bennett asked Kahn if he wanted to fly in Bennett's personal plane at two o'clock the next day at Willow Run airport. With Charles Lindbergh.

After Bennett convinced Kahn he wasn't joking, Kahn eagerly accepted. The next day Kahn stood on the tarmac at Willow Run. At exactly two o'clock, a small monoplane came down for a landing and taxied right up to him. When the engine stopped, Charles Lindbergh stepped out of the plane. "He was one of the handsomest men I have ever seen," Kahn writes. "He had steel-blue eyes, and spoke in a most beautiful, refined voice. He asked if I would like to fly from the left or right side. All I could do was stammer that the right side was where I wanted to sit, and I meant *sit*."

The famous trio took off in Bennett's plane with Lindbergh at the controls. Lindbergh maneuvered the aircraft with an ease that Kahn, who was a licensed pilot himself, could only admire. "I have never seen a man so relaxed or so much part of an airplane," Kahn writes. As they flew over Ann Arbor, Lindbergh asked Kahn to take over, which he did reluctantly and not very skillfully due to his rattled nerves, before returning command of the airplane to Lindbergh.

While Lindbergh buzzed Kahn's cabin on the Huron River, Bennett leaned forward to shout in Lindbergh's ear, after which the infamous pilot pointed his thumb at Bennett and confided to Kahn: "This man always gets me in trouble." Kahn soon figured out that Bennett had dared Lindbergh to buzz the Huron River, the birthplace of the Michigan hockey team. Although Lindbergh knew it was a little crazy, he took the plane within 30 feet of the river's surface, following the meandering, narrow stream with the steep bluffs on its south side, and kept it there for half a minute before pulling up. Bennett's plane, however, didn't have nearly enough power to clear the riverbank in front of them. "I could only think that at least I was going to go down in good company," Kahn writes. As they flew closer to the side of the bluff, Lindbergh suddenly veered the plane to the right, gracefully avoiding disaster with a grin.

Lindbergh had already won Bennett's bet, but he couldn't resist buzzing the river twice more, nearly touching the wings to the power lines on the bank and the wheels to the water below, just for fun. When Lindbergh gazed over his shoulder at the wide-eyed, pale-faced Mr. Bennett behind him, it was clear Lindbergh's friend would be making no more dares that day.

In between his world travels, Kahn found a mentor at the University Hospital named Dr. Max Peet, a hard-driving, wisecracking man and a charter member of a small band of surgeons who organized the first neurological society in the world, literally inventing the discipline as they went along. The big, beefy Dr. Peet was so impressed by the small, wiry Kahn's intelligence and energy, he groomed the young doctor to join him among the leaders in the field.

Their friendship flourished until one morning in 1949, when word rapidly spread throughout the hospital that Dr. Peet, "a man who was closer to me in some ways than my own father," Kahn writes, had dropped dead of a heart attack while working at his desk. The hospital asked Kahn to replace his mentor as the head of the Neurosurgery Section, a position he held for 22 years until he retired in 1971. Along the way Kahn completed two editions of *Correlative Neurosurgery,* an essential textbook for generations of doctors that remained relevant for so long, Kahn's protégés published a third edition in 1982, 13 years after Kahn retired from University Hospital to go into private practice at age 69. *Correlative Neurosurgery,* does not, however, make for light summer reading. Some of Kahn's chapters include "Papillomas of the Choroid Plexus of the Fourth Ventricle," "Section of the Ninth Nerve for Glossopharyngeal Neuralgia," and the always popular "Lipomas of the Conus Medullaris and Cauda Equina."

You get the idea. This really *is* brain surgery.

Near the end of his career, Kahn completed a second book, his autobiographical *Journal of a Neurosurgeon.* "Dr. Kahn's book would never be written today," says Joseph Andrew Barss, the coach's son, who also became a doctor. "He mentions several mistakes and errors in judgment. Can you imagine such a book in this day of so much malpractice litigation? Today there is too much risk to such confessions. It's too bad."

Unlike most world-class physicians, Dr. Kahn had a surprisingly good bedside manner with his patients and was considerate of his underlings. When Kahn became chief of neurosurgery, Dave Dickinson had just started as an assistant resident at the hospital. Although Dr. Kahn was already among the handful of big name physicians in the building, Dickinson remembers him as being unusually approachable.

"We had many full professors who were ostentatious, supremely self-confident, just very good at blowing their own horns," says Dr. Dickinson, who became a professor of pediatrics and the chief of clinical affairs, an elected position that oversaw all medical decisions at University Hospital. "Suffice it to say, their egos were more than adequate for the job. But Dr. Kahn *never* bragged, he was never egotistical, he never talked down to people. I think we all felt quite comfortable banging on his office door and asking him questions."

One of his protégés, current U-M neurologist Dr. John Segall, recalls working with Dr. Kahn late in his mentor's career. "The other surgeons, maybe they would let you hold a retractor for a few minutes while they worked," Segall says, "but Dr. Kahn would shoo aside even senior residents to let lowly med students like me help him on serious operations like a craniotomy. He always wanted the students to get right in there. I'm sure it all stemmed from the fact that he really got a kick out of teaching, and seeing young students learn.

"He was a bit of a period piece," Segall continues, "and often used outdated expressions like 'Makes you want to get up and slap your thigh!' and 'Boy, they're looking shiny as a bright new silver dollar.' Groovy, he was not—and this was the sixties. But we all admired him so much, he was the kind of guy all of us would imitate. He always wore bow ties, for example, so we'd all wear bow ties, too."

Kahn's former colleague, Dr. Richard C. Schneider, described Kahn this way: "Great empathy for his patients, honesty, humility, and a fine sense of humor were his hallmarks, in addition to his skillful hands. No physician was more deeply admired and loved by his patients."

Joseph Andrew Barss practiced in Port Huron, where he once faced a patient with a serious head injury. He immediately thought to call Eddie Kahn. "I was amazed that he and an associate made the two-hour drive from Ann Arbor to consult on my patient," Barss says today. "I remember Dr. Kahn as a very positive guy, very intense, almost nervous, and always in a hurry. But he knew what he was talking about. Then again, he was chief of the department. After he'd taken care of the patient, we had a good chat about Michigan hockey and my dad."

Rudy Reichert remembers the time Bob Gray, the goalie for Michigan's 1964 NCAA championship team, took a shot in the head in practice, fell backward and struck his head on the ice, where he lay unconscious. They rushed him to Michigan's emergency room and were preparing to operate when the intern confessed he didn't know what to do. He called Eddie Kahn, who correctly identified the problem and snapped Gray out of it in 10 minutes, saving the young goalie from undergoing potentially fatal brain surgery.

Dr. Kahn took his work very seriously, but himself much less so. Al Cain, former chair of Michigan's department of psychology, remembers a meeting led by Dr. William Hubbard, former dean of the medical school, in the early seventies. Dr. Hubbard was concerned that too many of his physicians had become consumed by the demands of specialization, had lost touch with the rest of the field of medicine, and as a result had also neglected teaching the youngest medical school students what they knew. So Dr. Hubbard proposed that the specialists get more involved in teaching new students general medical theory and practice.

After some debate between the determined dean and his reluctant charges, Dr. Kahn stood up to give his support to Dr. Hubbard's plan—with one caveat. "We have been so involved in our specialties for so long," he cautioned, "we're no longer experts at basic care. Speaking for myself, I wouldn't even know which end of the stethoscope to put in my mouth."

"That sudden twist blew up everyone into gales of laughter," Cain recalls, "and also released a lot of the tension in that room. That was Eddie Kahn."

Kahn was an original. He hated mundane tasks like lab work; he resisted playing all the holes of Barton Hills Country Club in numerical order; and because he was already independently wealthy from his father's fortune, he insisted on working for a salary of $1 a year, donating the balance to medical research. "But he never had any money on him!" Reichert recalls. "You'd go down to the cafeteria, where it was 35¢ for a meal, and he'd say, 'Geez, do you have 35¢ for me?' The guy was just oblivious to money.

"People would surround him at the cafeteria just to hear his stories of all these famous people, and he knew 'em all. But he was also an extremely modest guy. Didn't like drawing attention to himself. He wouldn't even go down to pick up his plaque when he was voted into the University of Michigan's Deker Hall of Fame. I picked it up for him."

It is difficult to find much information on Kahn's playing days, because he almost never spoke or wrote of them. "I do recall talking with him about his hockey career," says Segall, who himself had walked on to Michigan's junior varsity program as an undergraduate, "but he was very modest, and depicted himself, at best, as a journeyman in the sport. I suspect he was better than that." And he certainly was.

But Kahn never distanced himself from Michigan hockey. Although he was heard to remark that the game just wasn't the same "since all the boys started playing inside," with the exception of the war years he attended at least one game every season. His passion for the game, and the team, never waned.

During his 22 years as chief of neurosurgery, Kahn trained 44 residents, 16 of whom became the heads or assistant heads of their own neurosurgery departments. If Albert Kahn is still on the short list of great American architects, his son is still on the short list of great American neurosurgeons. Although surgical advances aren't as obvious a legacy as architectural landmarks, Kahn invented enough surgical tools and innovations to be named president of the Society of Neurological Surgery, the field's first and foremost organization.

"Eddie Kahn was a pioneer in the field of neurological surgery, and one of the great teachers at the University of Michigan Medical School,' says Dr. Segall, who can still list some of his mentor's greatest accomplishments, including Kahn's research on the radionuclide brain scan, the precursor to the CAT scan, which was vital to formulating diagnoses well into the late 1970s; and his work on craniopharyngiomas, a type of brain tumor typically seen in adolescents and young adults. Kahn's surgical approach is still used today to treat this condition.

"When he was just starting, so many of the tools were crude," Segall says. "Anesthesia wasn't as good, much riskier—and he did some really gutsy things. I think he is even more admirable to have pursued such a demanding career in spite of having the advantage of the silver spoon."

"He wanted to be known as Eddie Kahn," Dr. Dickinson says, "and not as Albert's son."

It's fair to say, when he died in 1985 at the age of 85, that Dr. Kahn's lifelong quest to make a name for himself was an unqualified success.

Thinking back on his old friend and mentor, Rudy Reichert sums him up simply: "He was just a remarkable guy."

Part II

Surviving the Great Depression
1927–40

8

The Iceman Cometh

If Joseph Barss could have played Jay Gatsby, Ed Lowrey could have filled in for Mr. Chips. With his wire-rimmed spectacles and a stern expression in team photos, Coach Lowrey looks more like the dean of discipline at a parochial school than the hockey coach he was. Although Lowrey was born in 1890, just a year before his predecessor Joseph Barss, players who skated for both coaches were convinced that Lowrey was much, much older than was Barss.

Lowrey's practice attire included an overcoat, a fedora, a necktie, and a pair of small, round glasses that often slipped down his substantial proboscis. In short, he looked like an economics professor who had taken a wrong turn and ended up at the rink.

"He looked like a smart guy, and he was," asserts Reichert, who played for Lowrey during World War II. "But he was a tough guy, too. He ran the rink as part of his salary, and he'd personally throw out any rowdies during public skating."

Despite his dowdy appearance, Lowrey's playing credentials were as solid as his arms. The 5-6, 160-pound center played eight seasons in the National Hockey Association and the NHL, including five seasons for the Ottawa Senators and one for the Montreal Canadiens. His two brothers also played in the league. Lowrey could still stickhandle through the entire Michigan team, well into his fifties. But to guide the program through both the Great Depression and World War II, Lowrey needed more than stickhandling skills. He needed the patience of Mr. Chips—if not of Job himself.

Making the Ice Last

Fielding Yost, Joseph Barss, and Ed Lowrey all realized it would be impossible to get good horses to play for Michigan if they could not offer them a decent stable. The rink Lowrey inherited may have been better than most when the team went varsity in 1923, but it would not have been sufficient to survive the Great Depression.

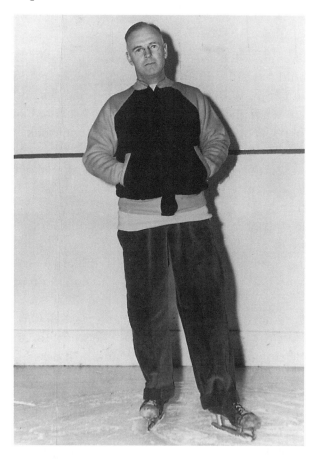

Eddie Lowrey
Coach Lowrey didn't look like a former NHL player. "He was a smart guy," says Rudy Reichert. "But he was a tough guy, too. He'd personally throw out any rowdies during public skating." Lowrey's program survived the Depression and World War II— barely.
(Courtesy Bentley Historical Library, University of Michigan.)

Like many rinks of the era, the Coliseum was a fire trap. Michigan Tech's rink burned to the ground in 1922, consuming all of the team's equipment too. The school and townspeople had to make a concerted effort to restore the program—an effort that probably would have fallen short 10 years later during the Depression.

Michigan's Coliseum was just as vulnerable, and Michigan's program was just as precarious because of it. Before the hockey team became a varsity sport in 1923, Weinberg's older son, Julius, installed an auto paint shop in the back of the building. In 1925, a fire that started there quickly burned through the wooden roof and partitions, but Fred Weinberg's hand-formed concrete walls survived and have survived to this day. Still, the damage almost canceled the season—and possibly the program—but at Yost's command, laborers worked overtime to salvage the building, the six-game season, and with it, the program.

Emergencies aside, the daily difficulties of making and maintaining ice alone were often too much to overcome in the 1920s. Today, with thousands of indoor rinks scattered across the country and NHL teams playing in Miami, Dallas, and Phoenix, it's hard to appreciate how challenging it was to create and keep good ice.

The Winter Olympics held in 1924, 1928, and 1932 all had to cancel large numbers of hockey games when the players found themselves running on slush instead of gliding on ice. The playing surface was so bad at the 1928 games in St. Moritz, Switzerland, that the officials gave the Canadian team, and *only* the Canadian team, a free pass to the final round just to reduce the amount of wear and tear the early-round drubbings would have inflicted on the already soft ice.

Trying to keep natural ice indoors was especially difficult in Ann Arbor's unpredictable climate, and even harder with hundreds of fans huddled around the sheet generating heat. The quality of the ice was so inconsistent in the twenties that almost every writer of the era mentioned the condition of the playing surface in the first two paragraphs of each game story, the way golf writers today mention the intensity of the wind or the thickness of the rough. Thawed ice canceled more than a few week-end series and might have killed Michigan's program altogether if Coach Lowrey and Fielding Yost hadn't recognized the potential of Michigan's program and worked to give the hockey team the finest facilities available at the time.

However, because the athletic department was already sinking unheard of amounts of money and labor to build the world's greatest athletic empire in just a decade—a decade that witnessed the construction of Yost Field House, the Intramural Building, the golf course, the tennis courts, the indoor swimming pool, the women's athletic building, Palmer Field, and Michigan Stadium, all of them state of the art—a hockey rink was hardly a top priority. John Behee's excellent biography of Fielding Yost devotes 24 pages to the football stadium and 8 pages to the Field House, but just two paragraphs to the Coliseum—ratios that accurately reflected the amount of attention each received from the athletic department. With limited resources, Yost and Lowrey had to come up with an expedient solution. The two decided the quickest way to bring the team up to speed was to renovate Weinberg Coliseum for the third time in a decade.

In spite of the building's exalted name, the early Romans would not likely have confused their Coliseum with Michigan's. Even from its earliest years, Michigan's Coliseum was an odd amalgam of additions and changes, none of them very carefully considered or terribly attractive. The rink was 30 feet short of regulation, one end of the building was open, and the whole place was cramped and dusty. But it was, nonetheless, better than most other teams' homes, including the Spartans' open-air rink that refused to remain frozen.

Impressed by the success of Barss's overachievers, Yost bought the building in 1925, but he still didn't have the machinery to make artificial ice. Granted, Michigan had lots of company: As late as 1920 there were only *four* artificial ice rinks in all of Canada. But lacking a reliable freezing system as far south as Ann Arbor left each day's schedule at the mercy of Mother Nature. The weather not only had to be cold enough during the day to keep the ice from melting, it had to be cold enough when the sun went down to absorb the Coliseum's crew's nightly flooding of the rink, which was the only way to resurface the sheet in the old days.

"Making the ice in them days was quite a struggle," Nate Weinberg remembers. "Sometimes it'd get pretty rough."

The late Dr. Eddie Kahn, captain of the 1924 team, recalled finishing some games in a pool of water. If it was too warm the games would be called off altogether, leaving the visiting team to travel hundreds of miles back home with nothing to show for its efforts and expenses.

Yost decided to improve the team's new home by adding stands and boards in 1923, 30 feet of ice in 1927, a fourth wall and artificial ice in 1928, and a $15,000 "modern whirlwind ice planer" in 1929. Yost completed the job right in the nick of time. A year later the stock market crashed, effectively ending Yost's building program. The football stadium debt wasn't paid off until 1947, a year after Yost died. Michigan's athletic campus would not undergo another serious building program until Don Canham converted the department's newfound revenues into a handful of construction projects a half century later, and most of those were renovations of the houses that Yost built.

Yost's timing was also fortunate because, a year after the Depression hit, the unseasonably warm winter of 1930 prevented ice from forming naturally at other schools, forcing Michigan State and others to drop hockey. Thanks to the vision of Yost, Barss, and Lowrey, instead of dropping hockey that year, Michigan won its third league title.

Getting the Horses

Having an attractive stable isn't much good if you don't have any horses to put in it. Unlike Minneapolis, Houghton, and Boston, the Detroit area didn't have enough local players to support a nationally competitive college hockey team. (At the turn of the previous century, Boston's population was almost 600,000, more than twice that of Detroit's.) Lowrey compensated with an influx of Upper Peninsula players who could really play the game; his Canadian connections helped attract skilled skaters from Ontario; and his knowledge of the game helped transform the rest of the kids from Ann Arbor and Detroit into players who could keep up with the hotshots.

Lowrey was also blessed with a lot of students from across North America who simply wanted to attend the University of Michigan because it already had the kind of national reputation that Wisconsin, Marquette, and Michigan State could only envy. It just so happened that some of those students could also play a little hockey, and they landed on Lowrey's doorstep through little effort of his own.

Among Lowrey's stars were captain Art Schlanderer, '31, from Ann Arbor; John Sherf and goalie John Jewell from Calumet, co-captains of the 1935 team; the brother duo of Gib and Spike James, class of '39 and '40, respectively, from Lowrey's hometown of Ottawa; and a guy named Vic Heyliger from Concord, Massachusetts, who picked Michigan for its academics and broke virtually every Michigan scoring record in his three years on the Michigan varsity.

"We had a few first-class skaters," says Les Hillberg, Michigan's captain in 1938–39, "but we didn't have as many as they had later, or now. It was so low key back then, much less was expected of the coaches. Lowrey really didn't have to do much recruiting."

The players had to buy all their own equipment, and it wasn't pretty. Their sticks were thick slabs of wood, with no fiberglass and no flexibility, and they had to use them for so many games they wore the heels flat. The players wouldn't start wearing shoulder pads, elbow pads, knee pads, or helmets until the late thirties. And when they did, the leather helmets were the kind you could fold up and stick in your back pocket. The thin, baggy pants they wore look as anachronistic as their shiny, slicked-back hair. No surprise, then, that game stories from that era often mention players suffering ugly cuts and serious concussions, but the skaters always seemed to come back for more.

A modern fan can also taste the game's primitive flavor in the arcane terms hockey writers used to describe the game's early action. They referred to hockey teams as "puck chasers," "hockeyists," "combinations," and "sextettes," the last term coined because the teams originally used only six players for the entire game. These "aggregations" played "hockey matches" and "ice games," which started at "the opening gun" and consisted of three "quarters"—never mind the math—during which they "caged" or "counted points" past the "goal guards," sometimes from "the middle of the floor." If the players cheated they were charged with "fouls." Scorekeepers didn't start giving out assists or including players' first names in the box scores until the mid-thirties—and that's a shame, because many Michigan players of the era could boast colorful first names like Kynle and Cornelius, Morley and Sherwood, names you just can't find on modern rosters.

The box scores listed positions that we can no longer identify, such as P, CP, and RE. Likewise, many of Michigan's biggest rivals would be hard to recognize by their original nicknames. The Michigan College of Mines Miners are now known as the Michigan Tech Huskies. The Michigan Agricultural College Farmers are called the Michigan State Spartans. The American Osteopathy Institute Osteopaths are probably still called the American Osteopathy Institute Osteopaths, but they no longer play Division I college hockey.

Teams like the Osteopaths appeared on Michigan's schedule because Lowrey had a hell of a time finding other schools that had indoor ice and enough good players to skate on it. To fill the Wolverine's dance card in the thirties, Michigan often had to play teams sponsored by "athletic clubs" in Michigan and Ontario.

But then, the Depression limited every Michigan team's travel budget. The Big Ten canceled the conference cross-country meets from 1933 to 1945 to save money, while the hockey team could afford only one road trip per year to Houghton and Minneapolis, and none out East, the only other region where serious college hockey was played at the time. Of course, the Depression affected everything.

The U.S. economy imploded after a record 16.4 million shares were dumped on the New York Stock Exchange trading floor on October 29, 1929, opening the floodgates for $50 billion in stock losses over the next two years and sparking the Great Depression. When workers finished the Empire State Building a few months later, the world's tallest structure remained almost completely empty until after World War II because so few companies could afford the rent.

Predictably, fewer people were willing, or able, to spend their increasingly sparse dollars on entertainment in the thirties. True, the thirties treated Detroit teams well. The Lions moved to Detroit in 1934 and won their first league title a year later; the Tigers won their first World Series the same year; and the Red Wings took their first Stanley Cup in 1936 and claimed it again in 1937, all of which earned Detroit the nickname "City of Champions." For their part, the Wolverines won eight national titles in swimming during the 1930s and one in football in 1932, led by a center named Jerry Ford.

But hockey elsewhere took a hit. NHL franchises in Pittsburgh, Philadelphia, and St. Louis all folded, and more surprisingly in New York City, Ottawa, and even Montreal, where the English-speaking Maroons gave up in 1938. By the end of World War II the NHL would be reduced to what we refer to today as "the Original Six."

While the unemployment rate of nearby Toledo, "Glass City," soared to 80 percent when the factories slowed down, Ann Arbor's usually hovered no higher than 10 percent. But the city, and the university that depended on it, didn't escape unscathed. Local retail sales were cut in half from 1930 to 1933, while construction plummetted from $7.2 million in 1929 to a little over half a million in 1932. Unemployed men were so common in Ann Arbor that many local families set up picnic tables in the backyard to serve the men knocking on their doors, asking for a meal.

On Michigan's campus, enrollment declined for four consecutive years, 65 teaching positions were eliminated, and faculty salaries were trimmed. A few of Roosevelt's "alphabet agencies" helped construct the Health Services Building and West Quad, and gave 14 percent of the 13,000 students federal money for school-related jobs, but work was still hard to come by. Since most hockey players came from lower-middle class families, they depended on the athletic department to get them campus jobs to help cover room, board, and the $55 tuition each semester.

"When I was a senior I was on the ice 4½ hours a day," recalls Les Hillberg, the captain of Michigan's 1938–39 team. "I policed the ice for public skating for 55¢ an hour. Every day after my shift, Coach Lowrey would buy me a bowl of soup, then we'd practice."

Hillberg and his buddies often worked at the Union serving meals, shooting the bull in their spare time with co-workers like football great Tom Harmon and Bill Watson, the school's first African-American track captain, whom the papers referred to as Michigan's "one-man track team." The guys occasionally snuck meals out the back door to their hungry teammates.

"Usually we'd get a Western Sandwich," Hillberg says, "which was a big square of bread with pork and beans on top of it, for 27 cents."

The athlete-workers swept the football stadium on Sundays for $5 each, and, as often as they were allowed, they gave blood for $25 per pint. "Then you went and bought yourself a steak, which you didn't have any other time," Hillberg remembers fondly. "It wasn't easy. Anyone'll tell ya that. But we were all in the same boat."

Thanks to Michigan's enclosed rink, a few ringers from the U.P., Canada, and the East Coast, and the vital contributions of a few local boys, the Michigan hockey team not only stayed afloat, it thrived. The 1927–28 team, Lowrey's first, went 2-10-1, including five losses to weak sisters like Wisconsin, Marquette, and Michigan State. But in Lowrey's third season, 1929–30, Michigan finished with a 12-7-2 record, good enough to earn Lowrey his first Big Ten title. During the Depression decade, Lowrey's teams won 102 games, lost 60, and tied 13, for a .630 winning percentage. They won five Big Ten titles, never finished lower than second place, and were rewarded with consistently enthusiastic crowds.

The news on other campuses wasn't so rosy. Due to a lack of indoor ice and talented players, several schools located in places at least as cold as Ann Arbor—including Maine, Boston College,

Syracuse, Notre Dame, Marquette University, and North Dakota, among others—either couldn't start or couldn't maintain serious hockey programs.

In fact, only five schools have played competitive hockey from the 1920s to the present without interruption, and just two of them are west of New York City: Michigan and Minnesota. That the Gophers could do so makes perfect sense. They have a natural skating climate and a rich supply of native talent. That Michigan has kept pace makes no sense whatsoever, as it has neither, while other schools with more God-given resources have failed outright. In this light, the Michigan hockey team's enduring excellence has to be considered a rather heroic triumph of wisdom and willpower over daunting natural obstacles.

9

The Calumet Connection

The Michigan hockey team has always drawn players from metropolitan Detroit and Toronto, as you'd expect, but in the course of its rich history, the program has been fortified at three crucial junctures by three surprising sources of talent: the Upper Peninsula's Copper Country, northern Minnesota's Iron Range, and Saskatchewan's frozen farmland. But the most exotic, by far, was the U.P. in its prime.

In 1837, President Andrew Jackson offered the Michigan Territory settlers a deal: he would grant them statehood, if they conceded the coveted "Toledo Strip" to Ohio. As a consolation prize, Jackson offered the settlers a chunk of land now known as the Upper Peninsula. The settlers were thrilled to become a state, but they still felt suckered by the trade. "I wonder why they didn't give us a slice of the moon?" one Michigan congressman complained at the time. "It would have been more valuable."

The annexation of the Upper Peninsula was considered as foolhardy as Secretary of State William Seward's purchase of Alaska in 1867. But in the second half of the nineteenth century Michiganders' opinion of the Upper Peninsula improved considerably. The first U.S. mining boom occurred not in California during the gold rush of 1849 but in the Upper Peninsula during the copper rush of 1844. From the Civil War to the turn of the century the U.P. alone produced more copper, iron, and lumber than any state in the union.

The U.P.'s record-breaking production pace included fully 70 percent of the nation's copper, with the town of Calumet, right in

73

the middle of the Keweenaw Peninsula, single-handedly producing more than one-third of the nation's total. If you bought 100 shares of stock in the Calumet & Hecla mining company in 1866 for $100, you could sit back and collect the 700 percent annual dividend, then sell it for $100,000 in 1916—the equivalent of $1.5 million in 1990 dollars. Hundreds of investors made their fortunes that way, but the new copper millionaires were the financiers living in Boston, not the workers living in the U.P. Still, the workers benefited too—for a time.

It's hard to imagine today, but in the early 1900s 10 trains a day pulled into Copper Country from Chicago and Detroit, Minneapolis and Milwaukee. Locals could hop on streetcars running every 15 minutes, choose from among 20 newspapers in four languages, and attend seven theaters and two opera houses that attracted such luminaries as bandleader John Phillip Sousa and actress Sarah Bernhardt. The area could also boast 30 churches, 30 schools, and 60 bars—ratios that seemed to suit the local lifestyle perfectly.

In the midst of all this newfound prosperity the copper miners started a strike in 1913, which lasted nine months and culminated in disaster. On Christmas Eve of 1913, the strikers and their families packed a local hall to try to generate at least a little holiday cheer during their annual party, but their revelry was interrupted when somebody yelled "Fire!" The alarm was false, but the ensuing panic was real.

"Hundreds of people ran to escape," says local historian William John Foster, 91, "but there were only two doors and they opened inward. The folks at the front were getting crushed and couldn't get the doors open. That's when the people started to pile up and suffocate. Fifty-three children, 11 women, and 9 men died—73 total. They had to use the Calumet town hall as a morgue. "The union blamed the company for yelling 'Fire!' and vice versa, but to this day no one knows for sure," Foster adds.

No matter who was to blame, the area's decline hurt everyone. After Houghton County's population reached a high of 90,000 in 1910, it averaged a drop of 10,000 every decade until it leveled off at about 33,000 in 1970—a third of its former self.

"I saw it go up," Foster says, "and I saw it go down."

The center of all this activity was the Keweenaw Peninsula, a spur of land that juts out into Lake Superior and is home to Houghton and Hancock, Calumet and Laurium. This little spit of rocky terrain also happened to produce a disproportionate number of world-class athletes, including hockey players.

Contrary to popular belief, the home of the world's first professional hockey league was not Nova Scotia, Ontario, or even Minnesota, but Michigan's Upper Peninsula, when a dentist–cum–hockey manager named J. L. Gibson convinced enough mining millionaires to start the International Hockey League in 1904. Based in Calumet, the IHL consisted of the Calumet-Laurium Miners, the Houghton Portage Lakers, the American Soo Indians, and unnamed teams in Sault Ste. Marie, Ontario, and Pittsburgh, which had one of the country's biggest indoor rinks until it burned down. The league attracted top players, such as future NHL Hall of Famer Cyclone Taylor, but collapsed in 1907.

Nonetheless, years after the IHL folded the Upper Peninsula was still producing some of the best hockey players in the world, including the NHL's first American star, Taffy Abel, who hailed from Sault Ste. Marie, Michigan. Abel, a 6-1, 225-pound Chippewa, captained the 1924 U.S. Olympic team, scoring 15 goals in five games to lead the United States to a silver medal, then played eight seasons for the Rangers and Blackhawks, winning two Stanley Cups. His competitive fires burned so intensely that when a team manager had the nerve to say, after a loss, "There's always next game," Abel dropped him with a single punch.

Abel's temper might have been worse than most, but his toughness was characteristic of virtually all U.P. players, most of whom had to seek their fortunes elsewhere after the mining boom ended. The most famous of the Copper Country expats was the legendary George Gipp, better known as "the Gipper."

The revisionists who've written about Gipp's freewheeling lifestyle as a Notre Dame football star generally assume he was corrupted by the city slickers of South Bend—when actually, it was Gipp who corrupted *them.* When Gipp left Houghton County for South Bend in 1916, he left a bustling area of almost 90,000 people—up from 9,000 just 50 years earlier—for a quiet hamlet of 53,000, then proceeded to take the locals' money at South Bends' pool tables and poker games. He brought with him four of his Keweenaw cronies, including Fred Larson, the starting center, and Hunk Anderson, who went on to play for the Chicago Bears and coach for the Irish, the Wolverines, and the Detroit Lions. By 1920, 3 of Knute Rockne's 11 starters, who played offense *and* defense in those days, came from Calumet, Michigan.

Copper Country sent its best football players to South Bend and its best hockey players to Ann Arbor. From the Michigan hockey program's inception in 1923 through World War II, the Wolverines had almost as many players from the U.P. as from Canada—an unthinkable equation today.

Barss and Lowrey both loved the U.P. players because they were as tough and taciturn as the Canadians themselves. The U.P.'s Superior coast gets over 30 feet of snow each year; mining is difficult and often deadly; and working in the woods isn't any easier. To survive up there people have to know how to stick together and not wilt when times are hard. "These are rugged, rugged people," asserts U.P. native Les Hillberg, Michigan's captain in 1938–39, and no one who's been to the U.P. would argue with that.

"Yoopers" don't waste their words on boasting—or anything else. The story goes that a Finnish woman in Negaunee once walked down to the local paper to submit her husband Toivo's obituary. "Toivo died," was all she wrote. When the ad rep told her she could print five words for the same price as two, she thought for a moment, then revised the obituary as follows: "Toivo died. Pickup for sale."

In all, the Upper Peninsula gave the Michigan hockey program about a dozen players from 1923 to 1940, including at least six bona fide stars, four captains, and one of the best players ever to play college hockey anywhere. These ringers could have gone to the Michigan College of Mines right there on the Keweenaw, and some did, but the Miners only had 12 sweaters to pass out, and after the miners' strike of 1913, the appeal of becoming a professional geologist just wasn't what it used to be.

"We all knew Michigan was a good school, with a lot of prestige," Hillberg says. "And you could study whatever you liked there." Further, thanks to President Jackson's compromise, no matter how far away the Upper Peninsula players lived from the University of Michigan, they paid the same low in-state tuition as the Ann Arbor boys, about 50 bucks per semester.

Irving "Pep" Reynolds was the first "yooper" hockey player to take the bait, leaving Gipp's hometown of Laurium, right next to Calumet, for Ann Arbor in 1922. Because the Gipper was also an excellent hockey player, and about the same age as Reynolds, the two probably played together many times over the years. And Reynolds was at least as good a hockey player as the Gipper himself. In his first year at Michigan Reynolds played on the freshman team, where he "raised havoc with the varsity in scrimmages," the *Daily* reported.

As a sophomore, Reynolds started his first game for the varsity squad at center and held the position every game thereafter. By the end of the season, the paper said, "Reynolds is one of the best centers in the conference."

Sure, there were only three teams *in* the conference, but just to play center in that league meant you were one of the three best college players in the Midwest. And in that era of limited substitution, scarce passing, and wildly disparate skill levels, one good player could single-handedly change his team's fortunes.

And that's exactly what Reynolds did for three straight years. Although his junior season was shortened by the Coliseum's fire and soft ice, Michigan went 4-1-1, with Reynolds scoring at least half of the team's 12 goals. Reynolds scored Michigan's only goal in the team's 1-1 game with the more numerous and talented Gophers. "Reynolds was the star for the Michigan team, and the outstanding performer of the entire contest," a reporter wrote. "He was brilliant on offense and indefatigable in checking the Gopher attack, his poke-checking proving especially embarrassing to the Minnesota team."

In the rematch both teams were unable to score for the first 55 minutes, until "Reynolds broke loose, carried the puck the entire length of the rink, and sent it hurling into the Gopher goal," the *Daily* said. "Reynolds was the conspicuous player in every game on the schedule."

Prior to Reynolds's senior year, 1925–26, his teammates unanimously voted him the captain. By season's end, the coaches and reporters around the league picked Reynolds for the All-Conference team, an honor the *Daily* claimed he deserved because "Reynolds has proven himself to be the hardest man to outguess in the Conference and he has also displayed remarkable back checking ability in all games."

If you were trying to build a hockey program in the face of considerable obstacles, an exciting game breaker like Reynolds would be invaluable in attracting students and winning over the athletic department. Pep Reynolds deserves a healthy helping of the credit for Coach Barss's success in getting a better rink and a bigger budget.

Pep Reynolds also induced a few of his old Calumet-area comrades to come down to Ann Arbor, including George "Nick" Sibilsky, a left winger who played on the team from 1924–25 to 1926–27. Whatever goals Reynolds didn't get, Sibilsky did.

In a game against Michigan State in 1925–26, Sibilsky "opened the scoring soon after the start of hostilities," as the paper put it, skating through the entire Spartan team "by some clever work." Sibilsky scored Michigan's second goal on a pass from Reynolds; another Wolverine named Bernard Roach scored the third goal on a pass from Sibilsky; then Sibilsky and Reynolds went end to end "by a clever exhibition of passwork," before Sibilsky buried the fourth and final tally. In all, the two "yoopers" set up or scored all six goals that day. A balanced attack, it was not.

The season after Reynolds left, 1926–27, Sibilsky picked up the slack. In the first game of the famous two-game sweep over Minnesota, Sibilsky broke the 0-0 deadlock in overtime that gave Coach Barss the league title in his final season. Such feats earned Sibilsky a spot in the Deker Hall of Fame, but his smarts and tenacity alone were to credit for his degree from Michigan's School of Dentistry in 1928.

If the U.P. economy started sliding downhill after the miners' strike of 1913, the Depression sent it burrowing south at warp speed. In 1929 the U.P. still had six copper mining companies left, selling copper at 18¢ a pound. Four years later there were only two companies still standing, and they were happy to sell their copper for 6¢ a pound, whenever they could. From 1929 to 1933, 6,000 miners lost their jobs; almost half the residents of Copper Country had to go on FDR's new welfare program, and the other half left the area altogether. The impulse to forgo a mining education and leave the area was never stronger.

That meant more U.P. football players migrated to Notre Dame, including the captain of the 1934 team, Dom Vairo of Calumet, and more U.P. hockey players moved to Ann Arbor. Foremost among the second wave were Laurium goalie John Jewell and Calumet left winger Johnny Sherf, who was such an outstanding player at Calumet High that he was named captain of his team and the recipient of the George Gipp Trophy three years in a row. Even in the talent-rich rinks of the Keweenaw, "He was the fastest skater up there," said his high school coach, "and with no real competition."

Both players held their starting jobs at Michigan for every game from 1932–33 to 1934–35 and served as co-captains their senior year. In the duo's second varsity game, a 6-2 victory over the Chatham (Ontario) Athletic Club, "it was assured that Michigan has a real goalie in the person of Jack Jewell," the local paper wrote. "He performed numerous acrobatics in front of the cords and made several stops which might well have tried the skill of a professional."

Coach Lowrey initially played Sherf at defense, where he averaged almost a point a game his sophomore year, before Lowrey realized the young man's true talents were on offense. Relying almost exclusively on solo rushes and the rare ability in the days before curved sticks to shoot the puck high, Sherf scored 23 goals—over half the team's total of 42—plus 14 assists for 41 points in just 16 games his junior year, 1933–34. His dominance inspired a nickname, "The Calumet Flash."

The duo was virtually unbeatable. In their junior year, Jewell faced the Kitchener Dutchmen's "five man offensive rally that virtually swamped him," the paper said, "but the plucky goal-minder threw himself in front of those drives in a display of saves that overshadowed the best performance Jack Tompkins, former all-conference goalie, ever made." The Dutchmen fired 60 shots on Jewell, and he stopped 59 of them. Jewell kept his team in the game long enough for Sherf to tie the game and go ahead on a patented Johnny Sherf end-to-end rush late in the third period, which he finished with an upper-shelf goal. The rush got the 1,200 students in the Coliseum on their feet and gave the Wolverines a thrilling 2-1 victory.

By their senior year, 1934–35, Co-captains Jewell and Sherf had pushed their team to the brink of its first league title in four years. But just days before a crucial late February series with Minnesota in Ann Arbor, Jewell had to be rushed to the hospital to have his appendix removed. He was out for the series, but the nurses were nice enough to hook up a phone to his room so a rink-side friend of his could deliver play-by-play accounts of the two games. From his hospital bed, Jewell heard the Wolverines tie Minnesota in the first game, 1-1, then beat them in the second, 3-1, on two of Sherf's trademark solo dashes.

That season Sherf finally got some offensive aid when a young prep school star named Vic Heyliger arrived from the East Coast. Coach Lowrey wisely paired the high-flying center with Sherf, which gave Sherf someone to pass to and reduced the need for Sherf's effective but exhausting end-to-end rushes. With Heyliger providing 19 goals and 11 assists for 30 points, Sherf was able to break loose for 33 goals and 10 assists in just 17 games, typically playing all 60 minutes each night.

During Sherf's senior year he not only outscored the rest of his teammates combined, 33 goals to 27, he even outscored Michigan's opponents, who could only bag 30 goals all season thanks to Jewell's brilliant goaltending. In Jewell's three years on the varsity he recorded 28 wins against 13 losses with 4 ties.

In 18 of those 45 games he allowed the opponent only one goal, and in seven he permitted none, finishing with an incredible goals-against average of 1.84. On paper, at least, the Calumet duo could beat every Michigan opponent by themselves.

Before they graduated the two set every recorded league scoring and goaltending record. Sherf played professional hockey for seven seasons, winning two Stanley Cups for the Detroit Red Wings in 1936 and 1937—an exceedingly difficult feat in the days when American players weren't welcome by NHL coaches. As of this writing, 49 Michigan men have made it to the big league, but Johnny Sherf will always be the first.

Thanks to the success of Reynolds and Sibilsky, Jewell and Sherf, U.P. hockey had made a name for itself by the mid-1930s. That tradition changed the life of Les Hillberg, who is today the oldest living Michigan hockey alum.

Hillberg was born in Marquette in 1913, right in the middle of the disastrous miners' strike. His father was a bridge worker for the Lake Superior & Ishpeming Railroad, a lucrative little outfit that hauled iron ore 16 miles from the mines to the Marquette docks. In 1926 Hillberg's sister enrolled in Michigan's nursing school, only to die in her freshman year of a throat infection, a malady that can now be cured in a few days with simple antibiotics. Five months later his father was building a scaffolding for the company electricians when his finger touched a live wire, throwing him off the platform 40 feet to his death.

"We had a tough time," Hillberg admits, "but there was family here, and that's what pulled us through. We all survived."

After Hillberg graduated from Marquette high school in 1930, he went to work nights for the *Marquette Mining Journal*, proofreading copy and covering high school sports. In 1934 Hillberg added a day job, working for the Department of Natural Resources as a forest fire warden. Although Hillberg's day job paid only $97.50 a month and his night job just an additional $60 a month, Hillberg was happy to have work. "On the way to the *Mining Journal*," he recalls, "I'd walk past a lot of fellas on their front porches, wishing they had a job. I knew what I had."

Because the forest work was seasonal, Hillberg was able to enroll in the Northern State Teachers College (now Northern Michigan University) in the fall of 1934. With what little free time he had left, he played amateur hockey for the Marquette Millionaires, a facetiously named team if ever there was one.

Hillberg's life changed forever one afternoon when a man named T. Hawley Tapping, the former field secretary for the University of Michigan alumni clubs worldwide, stopped in Marquette for a day. "Because of the reputation of U.P. hockey players in Ann Arbor, I suppose, somebody had told him to call me, so he invited me out to lunch at the Northlands Hotel." The beautiful hotel is now called the Landmark Inn, where such

Les Hillberg with Bubba Berenzweig
In 1999, captain Bubba Berenzweig met Les Hillberg, the last of Michigan's great U.P. players, who captained the Wolverines six decades earlier. Hillberg enrolled at U-M thanks to a lucky lunch meeting. "You go to the University of Michigan," he says, "it changes your life. Absolutely."
(Courtesy of the U-M Athletic Department.)

international celebrities as Amelia Earhart and Abbott and Costello once stayed. "Mr. Tapping asked me if I wanted to go down to Ann Arbor and play hockey, and I said, Of course I did. I told him I didn't have much money, but he said, 'We'll get you a job.' And they did."

Hillberg worked in the Union serving meals while going to school and playing left wing, center, and defense for the hockey team in 1937–38 and 1938–39, serving as captain his senior year. It was a fine finish to an odyssey that started with an innocent invitation to lunch.

"You know, I never did find out who told Mr. Tapping to call me," Hillberg admits. "But that changed my life. You go to the University of Michigan, it changes your life. Absolutely."

Michigan has dressed only a handful of U.P. players since Hillberg graduated, most of them walk-ons. But the Copper Country kids carried far more than their fair share of the load in Michigan hockey's first two decades, lending the team a style and stature it could only have dreamed of without their help. Bubba Berenzweig honored the contribution of Hillberg and his U.P. brethren when he came out of the visitors' locker room before a game against Northern Michigan in 1999 to pose for a picture with Hillberg—the youngest and oldest living Michigan captains, 60 years apart.

For Hillberg's mother, her son's success on the ice and in the classroom were the first pieces of good news she had received in years. Hillberg put his degree in forestry to work as a lumber procurer and land manager for paper mills in Michigan, Wisconsin, and northern California, before retiring to Escanaba in 1976. When his mother died in 1963, Les says, "I know she was proud. But people were different then. Affection was felt, but it wasn't shown."

Now it is. While Hillberg's youngest daughter was pursuing her degree in computer science at Michigan in the early 1980s, she came upon an old photo of her father on the wall of Yost's corridor. Until that moment, she hadn't even known her dad had played hockey, let alone captained the Michigan team, because the unassuming man had never mentioned it. But there he was, a fresh-faced young man proudly wearing his Michigan practice jersey, gazing back at his granddaughter from a past she never knew. She managed to get a copy of the photo and send it to her brother at Eastman-Kodak, who had the portrait blown up and distributed to all of Hillberg's children and grandchildren. The siblings added a simple caption at the bottom of the frame:

"Les Hillberg. Captain. University of Michigan, 1938–39."

It said more than enough about the man to all who received it.

Part III

Staying Alive
1940–44

The Neighborhood Kid

The severe limitations of the Great Depression didn't prevent Coach Lowrey from raising the program's profile, both locally and nationally. During the thirties the Michigan hockey team bolstered its status as one of the biggest attractions on campus and seemed to be settling in for the long haul. But keeping the hockey program alive during the Depression proved to be nothing compared to getting it through World War II.

In October 1940, American men between the ages of 20 and 36 were required to register for the draft. Gas rationing went into effect two years later, the Detroit area was transformed seemingly overnight into the "Arsenal of Democracy." In 1942 alone, southeastern Michigan produced 20,000 anti-aircraft guns, 45,000 tanks, and 60,000 planes—over $100 billion worth of military vehicles, which allowed the Allies to pound the Axis powers from Okinawa to Omaha Beach. A healthy portion of those workers caused the population of Washtenaw County to balloon from 80,000 people in 1940 to 106,000 in 1944.

From 1942 to 1945, Ann Arbor was invaded by over 12,000 military personnel—equal to the number of Michigan students at the time—who took over the Law Quad and West Quad for training. The mass migration went the other way, too, with some 32,000 Michigan alums fighting the war overseas. Ruth Buchanan, an art museum employee, tried to brighten their tours of duty by sending them over 17,000 letters and 57,000 copies of the *Michigan Daily* during the war years.

One of the recipients was Richard "Burt" Stodden, who grew up in Ann Arbor and won three 'M' letters in ice hockey before graduating in 1941. As a bomber pilot, it was his job to fly the dangerous but crucial air raids over Ploesti, Romania, an area that supplied Hitler with the oil needed for his eastern campaign. Stodden's unit destroyed it, which helped shorten the war dramatically, but cost the United States many good men. Stodden was among them. In all, 583 Michigan alums died in the Second World War.

One of them, although not a hockey player, deserves special mention. Raoul Wallenberg, the son of an illustrious Swedish family of bankers, diplomats, and businessmen, eschewed the Ivy Leagues as too snobbish, deciding instead to attend the University of Michigan, from 1931 to 1935. He admired Michigan's excellent school of architecture and its reputation as a public university where talented students who could not afford the more prestigious eastern schools flourished. Described by a classmate as "full of energy, good humor and generally a good guy," Wallenberg spent his vacations hitchhiking throughout North America, but he was still able to graduate number one in his class.

In 1944 he moved to Budapest, Hungary, at the request of the American War Refugee Board to help save the Jewish community there from Adolf Eichmann. Although Wallenberg was not poor, Hungarian, or Jewish, the multilingual genius risked his life saving those who were all three. He devised clever counterfeit Swedish passports that saved some 20,000 lives, and subtly threatened a Nazi commander with hanging during the inevitable war trials to come, thus sparing another 70,000 from the commander's planned last minute massacre. When the Soviets arrived in 1945, the paranoid Soviet leaders took Wallenberg into their custody, transferred him to a Moscow prison, and finally, it is believed, tortured and killed him in 1947.

Wallenberg's fate is still the subject of articles in national magazines today. His name graces the street off the Washington, D.C. mall where the U.S. Holocaust Museum resides, called Raoul Wallenberg Place. Each year an internationally renowned speaker, such as Elie Wiesel or the Dalai Lama, delivers the Raoul Wallenberg Lecture in Ann Arbor. And in 1981 President

Reagan made Wallenberg an honorary citizen of the United States, an honor previously extended only to Winston Churchill. But there is still no trace of Wallenberg himself, one of the most selfless and courageous men in world history.

Needless to say, the fortunes of a college hockey team didn't amount to a hill of beans in that crazy world, and it showed. During World War II, just about everything went downhill for Michigan's team—and fast.

Because fewer able-bodied males could attend college, the team's roster shrank. Because the government restricted travel, the schedule did, too. During the war years the team had to make do with a shorter bench and watch its schedule atrophy from a healthy 20-game season in 1939–40 to just 8 games in 1943–44, Lowrey's last year. And the team was no longer playing the likes of Colorado College and Illinois, Michigan Tech and Minnesota, but a bunch of hockey clubs from places like Sarnia and Woodstock, London and Paris—and no, not the ones in Europe, but Ontario.

It's one thing to schedule the weaker club teams; it's quite another to get pounded by them, game after game. Like Napoleon's demise, Lowrey's started with Waterloo—which in Lowrey's case was an Ontario club team that beat the Wolverines, 5-3. The 1939 loss marked the beginning of the end for the old coach.

Of course, one man's denouement is another man's golden opportunity. The team's downturn opened the door for some players who could probably not have made the team a decade earlier, including a young man from Ann Arbor named Rudy Reichert.

Reichert was a decent skater, big for his era at 5-11 and 175 pounds, and tough. Ted Heusel, an Ann Arbor radio host who grew up with Reichert in Ann Arbor's Burns Park, remembers a third boy who terrorized the old neighborhood. "Oh, this guy was a big kid, a bully, and we were all scared of him," Heusel says. "Eddie wasn't looking for a fight, but he wasn't backing down either. And I'm tellin' ya, Eddie just beat the *crap* out of this guy. Never bothered us again."

Although he had never played organized hockey before enrolling in college—"Never had a hockey uniform in my life," he says—Reichert went out for the freshman team in the fall of 1939, "and for some strange reason, I didn't get cut." But when Reichert came out for the varsity his sophomore year, Reichert

Rudy Reichert
Edward "Rudy" Reichert grew up playing in Burns Park and put on his first jersey as a junior at Michigan. All he had was a passion for hockey and the university, but during the war years, that was enough. Reichert's teammates were better off the ice than on it.
(Courtesy Bentley Historical Library, University of Michigan.)

says Lowrey told him, "You're really not too good at this game." All Reichert had was a passion for hockey and the University of Michigan. But during the war years, that was enough.

Lowrey told Reichert that if he wanted to play on the varsity some day, he'd have to get in all the extra skating he could. So he had Reichert join the varsity practice from 4:30 to 6 P.M. each day, then stay out for freshman practice from 7 to 8:30. "Well, that didn't fit too well into a premed schedule," Reichert says. "But I did it."

And it paid off. The following fall, Rudy Reichert pulled a hockey sweater over his head for the first time—a moment fixed in his memory. "I'm 20 years old, a junior, I've been in the program for two years, and I'm overwhelmed. Nervous. 'Fraid I'd screw up. First time I played with refs and boards and shin pads and cups was for Michigan.

"I played my first game very defensively, something Lowrey stressed. Back then defensemen weren't supposed to bring it up and shoot it. And the slap shot didn't exist, either, but that was okay, because the coach didn't want you breaking sticks. We couldn't afford them. You had to get at least two weeks out of each one."

The team lost Reichert's first game against the London hockey club, 6-1, and many more thereafter, but the young premed student had justified his place on the squad.

"I wasn't a bad skater, and I was a good passer and a good poke-checker, but that was about it," he recalls. "Now that there are no witnesses left, you can upgrade your skills a little—but our team manager, Sammy Schlecht, can tell you just how bad we were."

Fortunately for those involved, few people on campus were paying much attention. "Everyone was distracted with the war," Reichert says. "Guys were here today and gone tomorrow. But the war helped me, because we had a marginal team."

In the first seven games of the 1941–42 season, the Wolverines tied one and lost the other six by a combined score of 45-11— and they hadn't played perennial league leader Minnesota yet.

Michigan would finish the season with a dismal 2-14-2 record, just one tie better than the miserable record the year before.

The Gophers, on the other hand, had run the table just two years before, going 18-0-0. They won the AAU title, the only national title to win before the NCAA sponsored its own tournament. Coming into their 1942 contest against Michigan they hadn't lost to the Wolverines in 12 straight matches, dating back to 1938. Minnesota was said to have so much homegrown talent they could have fielded 10 varsity teams. The lucky 20 they picked could change lines at will throughout the game without missing a beat—very rare for a team in the 10-player, few-subs era.

All the Wolverines had to counter the Gopher juggernaut were 11 supporting actors without any stars to support. If Michigan's starting forwards wanted to rest, they had to move back on defense for a minute or two. The 1,100 fans on hand in Minnesota's old rink had no reason to expect anything but another Gopher steamrolling of the winless Wolverines.

To upgrade his team's chances from none to slim, Lowrey went to the recipe almost every underdog must use: lots of tight defense, low scoring, and a pinch of luck on the few offensive opportunities they were likely to get. Reichert, defenseman John Gillis, and a forward or two clogged the Michigan slot the entire night, forcing the Gophers "to work hopelessly with long shots from beyond Michigan's defensive concentration," the paper said.

Michigan was rewarded with two lucky breaks in the Minnesota zone. Seven minutes into the game, right wing Bob Collins picked up the puck against the boards from just inside the goal line and quickly fired it at the Gopher net, catching goalie Burt Joseph off guard. Eight minutes later, a reserve player named Max Bahrych came off the bench to score one of his five goals that season to build a 2-0 lead.

After a scoreless second period, Michigan's Paul Goldsmith, who went on to become a successful journalist, scored midway through the final period to give Michigan an improbable 3-0 lead, but the shocked Minnesotans quickly countered with two goals within the next 54 seconds, setting the score at 3-2 with half a period to play. For the remaining 10 minutes Minnesota stormed the Wolverine net, but Reichert and goalie Hank Loud survived the shower of shots to hold on for the shocking victory.

"A huge upset," Reichert says, with a satisfied smile. "I remember it well."

It's a good thing he does, because that memory had to last a while. Michigan wouldn't beat Minnesota again for 10 more contests, starting with a 6-0 payback pasting the next night. Reichert was able to stick around for 7 of those drubbings because the military wanted Reichert to stay home, enter med school, and help out in the woefully understaffed domestic hospitals. In 1942–43, Reichert's senior year, Michigan compiled its worst record in school history: 1-10-2. For Reichert and his teammates, however, the value of their college hockey experience wasn't measured by wins and losses.

In February 1942, before travel restrictions eliminated such extravagance, Reichert and his teammates traveled to Illinois, Minnesota, and Michigan Tech and went on an unforgettable trip to play Colorado College. Since the players had grown up during the Depression, most of them had never eaten in a restaurant before, let alone ridden on a fancy train or stayed in a world-class hotel. Although Reichert's family could afford a restaurant meal twice a year, Rudy had never been on a train.

"And here we were, riding in a dining car on a train, the ultimate in sophistication," Reichert said. "Oh, man! This was the most elegant atmosphere possible."

Planes may go faster, but most of the older athletes will tell you traveling by train was better. Unlike the plane, few storms can stop a train, delay one from taking off, or even disturb it en route. The train offered passengers first-class service from people who felt lucky to have such glamorous jobs, a dining cabin that served fresh meals on linen tablecloths, and sleeper cars that allowed the travelers to enjoy a full night's rest. And when you arrived you were not siphoned off into a modern airport that has all the old-world charm of a chintzy game show set, but an old stone train station with impossibly high ceilings and an aura of understated class.

For the Michigan hockey players going to play Colorado College, it didn't stop there. They stayed at the legendarily luxurious Broadmoor Hotel in Colorado Springs, which attracted celebrities then the way Aspen does today.

The normally reserved Reichert can't help but gush. "The Broadmoor—wow! It was all very fancy for a bunch of country boys." Michigan lost the weekend series, 6-2 and 10-2, but the scenery took the sting out of it. On the train ride home, the players wore their Sunday best, "and the other people on the train made a big fuss over us," Reichert says. "Luckily, they didn't ask us about our record, and we didn't mention it."

(Six years later the Michigan hockey players would return to the splendor of the Broadmoor, but they would have no reason to conceal their record on the way back home, for they would be the first NCAA champions.)

Most of Reichert's favorite memories, however, are of the simpler pleasures. "It was all pretty informal in those days," he says. "If our goalie got knocked out, we'd use the other team's back up. Both teams used the same shower, and we'd all go out together after the game. The varsity hockey team then was probably like a club team today.

"I've always thought, compared to the other sports, that hockey is more of a family thing. I've had my theory that the Canadians, with their British background, are more polite, more respectful, maybe a little more naive but not as jaded as some of the football and basketball players are today, who are coddled from early ages. Hockey's a different game.

"Two things you need in life: one, personal discipline, and two, the ability to get along with others. Almost always, people who get in trouble don't have one of those two attributes. I think you learn those things on a team. And people care about each other. I remember every one of those guys from my team. What you had was a little family in a big place. All the athletes knew each other. Without that, in a big university, I don't know what you'd do."

If Lowrey's last teams collected few wins, no titles, and no profits, it's also true they brought no embarrassment, scandal, or damage to the program's reputation. "Lowrey was a good guy, an honorable guy, a straight shooter type," Reichert says.

The players seemed to fit the same mold. They might not have achieved much on the ice, but off the ice they were as exemplary a group of players as any school could hope for. The character and accomplishments of these players helped keep the team alive when an off-ice misstep or two might have been enough to kill the stagnant program.

Fifty-eight years after he graduated, Reichert can still easily tick off his teammates' names, positions, and careers. Of the 17 members of the two teams Reichert played on, two skaters also played on the tennis team; two played on the football team; and one each won spots on the varsity baseball, track, swimming, and wrestling teams. After college one went on to become a journalist, three entered law (one of whom became a federal judge), six pursued engineering, and three became doctors, including Reichert. Although Michigan hockey's "war teams" set virtually every school record for goals against and losses, you would be hard pressed to find a more impressive group of young men.

"We were better off the ice than on it," Reichert says. "They've had teams that have been the reverse of it."

Reichert should have added his own name to the list of distinguished alums from that team. In 1943, Reichert entered U-M's medical school, thereby following in the footsteps of former Michigan hockey players–turned doctors Eddie Kahn and Mark Coventry, a 1933 letter winner who eventually became chairman of orthopedic surgery at Minnesota's renowned Mayo Clinic, where he developed the first two-part knee replacement in 1969. Reichert and his classmates not only had to endure the normal cutthroat competition and Herculean workload that medical school always presents, they had to perform endless extra tasks because the people who normally did them were off to war. "There were a lot of good guys getting killed, so we worked very hard," he says. "It was an endurance contest."

Thanks partly to the discipline he learned as a hockey player, skating in two practices each night while completing his premed course work, Reichert had what it took to survive the endurance contest. After graduating from medical school in 1946, the young doctor became the director of cardiology at St. Joseph Mercy Hospital in 1955, a post he held until 1989. Along the way, he served as chief of staff during the hospital's difficult transition from the building on Ingalls Street to its new site in Ypsilanti in 1977.

"This decision engendered much controversy from a wide range of individuals, including the medical staff of the hospital," says Sister Yvonne Gelese, the hospital's director then and now. "The integrity, the commitment, the common sense, and the hard work of Rudy were a tremendous asset in the deliberations and decisions that ultimately relocated the hospital at its current location.

"I do not know Rudy Reichert as a hockey player," she adds. "But I do know Rudy Reichert as a competent and caring cardiologist. His reputation in the healing profession is held in high regard by his physician colleagues as well as by his patients."

Reichert's work was so good for so long, and his personality so magnetic, that the hospital named a large wing "the Rudy Reichert Building" in 1984, an honor that usually goes to the hospital's biggest donors not its doctors. "I value my years of association with this medical statesman," Sister Yvonne concludes but then asks, "Maybe you can tell me how a philosophical, skillful, and compassionate physician found his way to the hockey rink?"

"I just got lucky and fell into it," Reichert answers. "The best experience I had at the university was playing on the hockey team."

11

Changing of the Guard

Perhaps the most overlooked contribution of Michigan's first two coaches was the stability they gave the program, a stability that other schools could not match. Wisconsin went through 6 coaches in 14 years before dropping hockey; Michigan Tech had 11 coaches in 24 years before they cut their program; and even Minnesota had 4 coaches before World War II. Michigan needed only 2 coaches to go its first 21 seasons.

But as Lowrey's tenure wore on, the losses started piling up. Lowrey's teams had character, stability, and a plausible excuse for dropping so many games during World War II, but not all of the team's problems could be attributed solely to the war effort. In 1943–44, Lowrey's last season, eight of Michigan's nine varsity teams won Big Ten titles in their sports, a conference record that still stands. The hockey team was the only exception—and it only had two teams to beat, Minnesota and Illinois.

After averaging over 10 victories a season the previous decade, the hockey team won only five games in 1939–40, then five more over the next three seasons *combined*. Lowrey's teams won five league titles and achieved a .630 winning percentage in the 1930s but could manage only one second-place finish, three last-place finishes, and a .214 winning percentage in the first four seasons of the next decade.

Illinois had to endure the same Depression and World War II the Wolverines did, after all, and the Illini also had to surmount a warmer climate and a complete lack of local talent, yet they brought their program up from the outhouse to the penthouse just as quickly as Michigan's program went in the other direction.

Illinois started playing Michigan in 1937–38 with a roster consisting primarily of football players. The first time Michigan traveled to Champaign for a hockey game, the Wolverines jumped ahead, 8-1, so quickly, Lowrey told his players that anyone who scored again would sit on the bench. No one risked it. During the series' first three years, Michigan rattled off six straight victories against Illinois. But the margin of victory shrank with each one until the Illini finally beat the Wolverines, 3-0, in the last game of the 1939–40 season. Michigan proceeded to lose the next 12 contests against its former punching bag, getting outscored 22-0 in the last four contests against each other. Michigan was only spared further embarrassment because Illinois cut the sport altogether in 1943.

If there was any consolation for the Wolverines, it was the fact that Illinois's coach was a certain Michigan alum: Vic Heyliger.

According to Reichert, athletic director Fritz Crisler felt that "if we're gonna have a team, we're gonna have a winning team." Having gone 15-55-6 in their last five seasons, Lowrey's teams were clearly not winning much anymore. Reichert believes Lowrey no longer had the necessary contacts to recruit top players and seemed happy to leave the sport to go into construction full-time after the 1943–44 season.

But by the time Lowrey stepped down, the program itself was in peril. In the spring of 1944, a local headline warned, "Michigan May Remove Hockey from Athletic Program." Before Crisler searched for candidates to replace Lowrey, he first had to decide if he wanted to field a hockey team at all. Crisler believed the program's biggest problem was its truncated, eight-game schedule played exclusively against hockey clubs, not other college teams.

"Hockey has never caught on very well in the Mid-West as an intercollegiate sport," the article said, citing the growing number of major midwestern universities that had dropped the sport, "and transportation difficulties make it impractical for Michigan to play Eastern schools. The chief reason for the lack of hockey teams in this part of the country is that most schools do not have indoor ice rinks, a necessary piece of equipment."

The foresight of Joseph Barss and Fielding Yost had paid off in Ann Arbor, but it would be squandered if Crisler couldn't find a new coach to carry the torch or other regional college teams to play. Fortunately, thanks to the Illini's demise, the one man who save Michigan's program was suddenly available.

Part IV

Heyliger's Heyday
1944–57

12

A Michigan Man

"Heyliger was not a big man," says Les Hillberg, his former teammate. "But he was so enthusiastic about everything. He was just full of fire! And people around him caught it, too."

Heyliger was born in Boston in 1919 and raised in Concord, Massachusetts. After spending a postgraduate year at Lawrence Academy in Massachusetts, Heyliger surprised his friends and family in 1934 by turning down Brown and Dartmouth to attend Michigan—when he was only 15 years old.

His parents warned him that he wouldn't be able to come home for the weekends, but he didn't mind. He was too busy playing baseball for Ray Fisher and centering the great Johnny Sherf's line. In his 51-game collegiate career, Heyliger scored a mind-boggling 116 goals, including 43 his senior year—a school record since equaled by Red Berenson, Dave Debol, and Brendan Morrison, but never topped. Heyliger's admirers voted him onto the All-Conference team all three years of his college career and named him All-American and team captain his senior year.

After leaving Michigan Heyliger signed on with the Chicago Blackhawks, and, although he played in only seven games, just making an NHL team in that era was a remarkable accomplishment for a U.S.-born collegian, especially before World War II made it easier for lesser players to find spots on the rosters. Even those yankees good enough to play in the prewar NHL found the going difficult. Anti-American sentiment ran hot—the Canadian players would occasionally advise their American counterparts to "Go home and play baseball!" after dumping them to the ice—and anticollegiate sentiment ran hotter still. Minnesota's great John Mariucci found it necessary to fight almost every week after he joined the Blackhawks. As late as the mid-'90s, New Jersey Devils coach Jacques Lemaire was known to discriminate against both American and collegiate players.

Recognizing his NHL future was dim, Heyliger accepted the head coaching job at the University of Illinois in the fall of 1939,

Vic Heyliger
"[Vic] Heyliger was not a big man," says former teammate Les Hillberg. "But he was just full of fire! And people around him caught it, too." Heyliger set the school scoring record, started the NCAA tournament, and led his team to six national titles. *(Courtesy Wally Grant.)*

only the school's third season of ice hockey. His considerable experience and energy drew top talent to the cornfields of central Illinois, and his teaching ability turned them into winners. In Heyliger's four years at Illinois the team won three Big Ten titles, two of his players graduated to the NHL, and a third player, a man named Amo Bessone, played in the highly competitive American Hockey League before becoming a famous college coach himself at Michigan State.

When Illinois canceled hockey in 1943, Heyliger returned to the Blackhawks for the 1943–44 season, scoring two goals and three assists in 26 games. Knowing his time in the show would likely end when the boys came back from the war, when Crisler called looking to replace the departed Coach Lowrey, Heyliger listened.

Like Yost, Crisler didn't know much about hockey, but he didn't have to understand the game to understand what good coaching looked like. Crisler won a national football championship in 1947; he changed the game forever by inventing the platoon system in the late 1940s; and he shaped college football by serving on the NCAA rules committee for over two decades before he retired as Michigan's athletic director in 1968. But Crisler might be best remembered for designing Michigan's distinctive "winged helmet," the most recognizable headgear in college football.

Of course, it didn't take a genius to figure out that a man who could transform Champaign's perennial chumps into perennial champs in just four years could do wonders at an established program like Michigan's. If Crisler was going to spend the time, effort, and money to resuscitate the hockey program, he wanted Heyliger on board, and wouldn't take no for an answer.

Crisler got his man. Heyliger started reviving the dying program before he even coached his first game in Ann Arbor. The transition from Lowrey's staid bearing to Heyliger's charismatic personality generated the same enthusiasm on campus as did the transition from Eisenhower to Kennedy nationwide.

"Vic Heyliger is a great guy and a great motivator," says Al Renfrew, who was not only Heyliger's sixth captain and his successor behind the bench, he's also Heyliger's brother-in-law, having married Heyliger's sister-in-law, Marge. "He gave you the idea that you were playing for the most important school in the world. At 20, you might think it's crap, but at 23, you realized it was true."

Heyliger's informal manner was also particularly well suited to the postwar players on his roster, at least a half dozen of whom had served in the military. They often had more life experience than the 25-year-old wunder-coach, and he generously conceded that. After training for war and watching friends die in combat, the odds of them being intimidated by the threat of a few extra laps after practice weren't very great—and to Heyliger's credit, he didn't try.

Connie Hill, for example, was fresh from a three-year stint as a tank warfare instructor in the Canadian army when he came to Ann Arbor to resume his studies. With his professorial glasses, thinning hair, and wizened expression, Hill looked much older than his teammates—and he was, already well into his mid-twenties as a sophomore. ("There has always been some controversy about my age," he says now. "And my instinct is not to fuel the debate by telling you now.") Recognizing Hill's hard-won maturity, the team elected him captain for three consecutive seasons, a length of service that would not be matched for almost five decades. His leadership style was easygoing but certain. After one teammate asked Hill why he referred to another player as "a seagull," Hill replied, "because he's always squawking or shitting."

Coach Heyliger's laid-back approach appealed to the grizzled veterans like Hill, whom he treated like adults, not subordinates. "Vic was never a stern taskmaster," says Renfrew, who had served two years as a fleet air arm in the Royal Canadian Air Force before coming to Ann Arbor. "An important thing to remember is that a lot of guys had been in the service already, so we were older, more mature, hard to scare. So he made it fun to go to practice. And he had to convince Canadians that coming to school wasn't all bad. It was a tough thing to sell at the time, but he did it."

The infusion of Canadian blue-chippers included Deker Hall of Famers Al Renfrew, John MacInnes, and Wally Gacek, but Michigan still could not attract enough top-notch, college-bound Canadians to fill its roster. If Heyliger planned to beat the nation's best teams—and the confident coach certainly did—he knew he'd have to find another source of talent to do it.

13

The Eveleth Express

Heyliger was desperate for some top-shelf players to turn Michigan's program around, and he found a rich vein of them in northern Minnesota—or rather, they found him.

They came from a forbidding stretch of land called the Mesabi Iron Range. This 110-mile strip runs along the Laurentian Divide, the latitudinal version of the Continental Divide. When rain hits the Laurentian Divide it runs either south to the Gulf of Mexico or north to the Arctic Ocean.

The Iron Range boys were tough, plain-talking, and hardworking men, just like the Calumet kids who came before them. That should come as no surprise, because the two regions have more in common with each other than either has with Ann Arbor or even Minneapolis. If you live in the U.P. or on the Iron Range, you leave your keys in your car, your door unlocked, and plenty of beer in the cooler for friends dropping by.

Bob Dylan, born and raised in Hibbing, Minnesota, once told a magazine interviewer: "I'm from someplace called the Iron Range. My brains and my feelings come from there." Dylan's sincere, spare songs reflect the spirit of the Iron Range.

Like the U.P., the Iron Range is pocked with small, self-sufficient old mining towns, with so many perilous miles between them that people feel obligated to help out strangers they find in roadside ditches. It's not an easy place to live, but it's a great place to develop the kind of hockey players coaches love.

Then again, a state with 15,291 lakes frozen from Thanksgiving to St. Patrick's Day *should* produce a few hockey players.

During World War II, a broadcaster trying to describe how cold it was along the Russian front said simply, "Minnesotans would understand," and left it at that. It gets so cold on the range, pond pucks can shatter like porcelain.

With such fertile growing conditions, hockey sprouted in Minnesota just a few years after it first spawned in Canada. The University of Minnesota started playing hockey informally in 1895, with the local high schools following suit the next year. By 1930, the Twin Cities had some 600 teams crowding every available lake, pond, and river. By 1980, over 4,000 teams played organized games in the state, including 160 high school varsity squads.

What high school basketball is to Indiana, high school hockey is to Minnesota. Over 100,000 people attend the three-day state finals each year in St. Paul. As the *Boston Globe*'s John Powers writes in *One Goal*, his excellent book on the 1980 U.S. Olympic team, the annual event is the only time of the year "miners rubbed shoulders with millers, Minneapolis executives with Duluth longshoremen." When the state started the hockey version of March Madness in 1945, you might think the big city teams would have dominated the small-town competition, but in the tournament's first 18 years every title went to a team from International Falls or, more often, the Iron Range.

In the middle of the Iron Range sits the crown jewel: Eveleth. This small city built its first indoor rink in 1903, added three more by 1914—equalizing the number of indoor rinks across Canada—and completed a 3,000-seat rink, one of the biggest in the country, in 1922. That same year Eveleth high school organized its first varsity team, a few months ahead of the University of Michigan's. The tiny town's uncommon passion for the game was bound to produce a handful of great players, but Eveleth surpassed all expectations by producing hundreds.

During the Great Depression alone an incredible 147 Eveleth graduates went on to play college hockey. In 1942, when the NHL still had only six goalies, three of them were Eveleth boys. The coach and the top three players of the 1956 U.S. Olympic team all came from Eveleth, and they returned home from

Cortina, Italy, with silver medals. Of the 57 members of the U.S. Hockey Hall of Fame, 11 once called Eveleth home, and the hall itself is located in—you guessed it—Eveleth, Minnesota.

"Eveleth's ability to produce elite-level players in the first half of the 20th century is one of the most astounding stories in hockey history," according to the game's bible, *Total Hockey.* "No city has meant more to U.S. hockey."

While the Eveleth Golden Bears were busy dominating the state high school tournament, winning the first four titles, the University of Minnesota easily eclipsed all other in-state college teams. For the past century in Minnesota, there's been "the U," and everything else. "We're the main U," said former Minnesota and Olympic coach Herb Brooks. "The others are just small colleges."

Didn't matter if you played for one of the top Range teams like Grand Rapids or Hibbing, Virginia or Eveleth, or even if you suited up for one of the "cake-eater" schools in the city, if you grew up playing hockey in Minnesota, you grew up dreaming of playing for the U. The school encouraged this loyalty for decades by ignoring skaters from Canada and New England in favor of the born-and-bred Minnesota player.

The University of Michigan might not have held any natural appeal for the Range kids, but two factors gave Heyliger an outside chance at some of the better Eveleth players. The old legends proved true: Minnesota really *did* produce far too many talented players to squeeze onto the U's 20-man varsity roster, so the rest had to go somewhere else.

"The Minnesota boys were better hockey players than the kids we could get coming out of Canada," Heyliger maintains. "At least, I thought they were. And we didn't have to go out and recruit those kids. They all came to Ann Arbor anyway."

The second factor was a seemingly innocent encounter in the spring of 1945 between Eveleth star Wally Grant and Gopher coach Larry Armstrong, a smug-looking man who was nearing the end of a 12-year run behind the Minnesota bench, in which he would compile a sterling 125-54-11 record. Despite the fact that Grant quarterbacked the Eveleth high school football team, starred on its track team, and scored the winning goal in the first Minnesota high school state tournament for a team that hadn't lost a single game in three seasons, for some reason Armstrong hadn't lifted a finger to recruit him. So, when Grant and a few of his Golden Bear track teammates saw Armstrong that spring at the state high school meet held on the "U" campus, they decided to introduce themselves to the famous coach.

The coach quickly dashed their hopes. "Armstrong wouldn't give us the time of day," Grant recalls. "A few months later he bent over backwards trying to get me and a couple other Eveleth kids to play for him, but I didn't want to have anything to do with him. Vic Heyliger was already getting a lot of our guys down there to Illinois, before Illinois disbanded its program. And those guys all said, 'Go see Vic Heyliger at Michigan; he's a great guy.'"

Grant and his buddies might have been determined to snub the U, but they made no attempt to contact Heyliger—and in the days before nationwide recruiting, Heyliger didn't know about them, either. So, the day after they graduated from high school, Grant and Clem Cossalter traveled 60 miles due south to the Duluth docks to see if Clem's brother, named Onore but called "Coke," could get them work. Coke said they didn't have any jobs for them on the docks but suggested they go to Michigan, where the former Illinois coach worked. Grant and Clem looked at each other, shrugged, and said, Sure, why not? They had nothing better to do. Coke lent the boys $20 each, just enough money for one-way train tickets to Ann Arbor and a sandwich along the way. It would be Grant's first train trip, but not his last.

When the two boys arrived in Ann Arbor they had no place to go, no money to speak of, and no belongings, not even toothbrushes. No one knew they were coming to town—or who they were. With no other options, Cossalter finally decided to go to a pay phone and call Fritz Crisler at his home. Unlike Coach Armstrong, Crisler was not offended by the boys' interest and told

The "Three G" line
Ted Greer, Wally Gacek, and Wally Grant. Grant hopped on a train from
Duluth to Ann Arbor in 1945 because he had nothing better to do, then called
Fritz Crisler to get the hockey coach's number. He went on to become Michigan's first three-time All-American.
(Courtesy of the U-M Athletic Department.)

them how to contact Heyliger, who happily set them up with a room in the basement of the Sigma Chi fraternity house and a job mowing Fielding Yost's lawn. When the boys called their surprised parents a few days later, the families sent some money for room, board, tuition, and clothes, and the boys didn't return home until Christmas.

And that's how the Michigan hockey team got its luckiest break since Joseph Barss showed up.

Wally Grant would become Michigan's first three-time All-American. Like Pep Reynolds before him and Red Berenson after him, Grant also persuaded a wave of star players from his hometown to follow him to Ann Arbor. A quarter of Michigan's 1945–46 team—Wally Grant, Clem Cossalter, Neil Celley, and Karl Sulentich, the only player to return from the previous year's squad—came from tiny Eveleth High. In the following 10 years, six more Minnesota schoolboy stars, all but two from Eveleth, would turn down the U for Michigan.

The list included Ted Greer, '48, who joined Grant on the infamous "Three G" line (with Wally Gacek) that dominated the first NCAA tournament in 1948; goalie Jack "Black Jack" McDonald, '50; Neil Celley, '51; John Matchefts and Ron Martinson, '53; and Willard Ikola, '54. All but Greer and McDonald grew up in Eveleth.

More than their quantity, it was the quality of the Minnesota defectors that was so stunning. Of the 10 native Minnesotans who played for Michigan from 1946 to 1954, 6 have been voted into Michigan's Deker Hall of Fame; 5 were named to All-American teams; and 3—Grant, Matchefts, and Ikola—were inducted into the U.S. Hockey Hall of Fame. Every one of the 10 players earned at least one NCAA championship ring, with that first wave of Minnesotans winning a combined 15 among them.

The Iron Range ran dry for Michigan soon after it had been tapped. In 1954–55, 10 years after Grant arrived, Michigan had not one player from Minnesota on its roster. But the Iron Range boys had done their part every bit as well as had the Calumet kids before them, first saving the program from extinction and then lifting it to new heights.

Simply put, it is inconceivable that Michigan could have won any NCAA titles in the tournament's early years, let alone six in a decade, without the infusion of the Iron Range stars. But probably none of them would have come to Ann Arbor were it not for an arrogant old coach from Minnesota named Larry Armstrong and a gutsy young kid named Wally Grant.

14

The Skating Soldiers

Amazingly, the story of Grant's "recruitment" was closer to the norm than not during the postwar years. Al Renfrew and his Toronto De LaSalle high school buddies, John MacInnes and Ross Smith, for example, had never seen Michigan's campus—and Coach Heyliger had never seen them—until they started classes in the fall of 1945.

For all the changes Ann Arbor underwent during the war, the changes that took place after V-J Day were more dramatic. From 1945 to 1948, Michigan's enrollment doubled to 20,000 students, 12,000 of whom were veterans going to school on the G.I. Bill. The fact that 11,000 of the postwar students were married made space even more scarce. Housing was so tight students were forced to live out in Pittsfield Village, in temporary Quonset huts set up in the Coliseum parking lot, and as far away as Willow Run in the apartments Henry Ford had built for his B-24 factory workers.

Al Renfrew, Connie Hill, Wally Gacek, Gordon MacMillan, and Jack McDonald solved their personal housing problem by sleeping above the locker rooms in the old Coliseum. "I got them jobs at the rink," Heyliger recalls, "and they slept on a cot up there. Those damn trains that came in at night were loud as can be. It must've been terrible!"

"Hardest bed I ever had," Renfrew recalls. "Couldn't figure out why until I lifted the cot and found the guys had slipped their sticks underneath it for a prank.

"Connie's job was to keep the fire going in the lobby so we wouldn't be freezing when we got home at night," Renfrew adds.

"Before you went to a party you'd take a wooden post from Fingerle Lumber across the street and put it in the fire to keep it going."

In lieu of scholarships, athletes received jobs and cheap places to sleep. Nine players lived in the basement of Zeta Beta Tau, a predominantly Jewish fraternity, and washed dishes right up to game time on Friday nights. It was not uncommon to see a half dozen hockey players running down Hill Street to get to the rink before the puck dropped. So many athletes worked in frat kitchens or the Union that if you played on a team and needed a meal, you could count on a fellow jock slipping you a tray out the back door to fill your belly.

"It was a lot different than it is now," Renfrew says, and you get the feeling he misses some of the old ways. "We all struggled," Grant says, "but we had such good guys, so much camaraderie."

Of course, the camaraderie of any team is greatly improved by winning. And under Heyliger, Michigan won a lot—but not initially. His first season at Michigan, 1944–45, opened with a loss to a club team called the Detroit Vickers, 6-12, followed by a drubbing at the hands of arch-rival (really, Michigan's last remaining rival) Minnesota, 10-0. A few weeks later, Minnesota whipped Michigan again, 15-2, just to let Heyliger know what he'd gotten himself into.

But if you were looking for some positive signs in Heyliger's first year, and Crisler undoubtedly was, you would've noticed Heyliger's men redeem themselves later that season in a double-overtime loss to the Vickers, 4-3, and a victory over Waterloo in a 5-4 thriller at home. After spending a half decade on the critical list, Michigan hockey was at last showing some signs of life. The team's 3-6 record that year would be Heyliger's first and only losing season.

Heyliger rode the first wave of Eveleth athletes who arrived in the fall of 1946 back to national prominence. The revamped Wolverines played a beefed-up 25-game schedule and won 17 of them, including weekend sweeps over Minnesota and Michigan Tech, whose program had been revived after the war.

"Vic got the program back on the right foot," Renfrew says, "and he kept it going."

In 1946–47, with travel restrictions just a memory and Crisler now squarely in the new coach's corner, Heyliger put together a schedule of considerable ambition, including away games at Minnesota, Colorado College, and even Cal-Berkeley, which actually had a decent team for a few years after the war. Although the Wolverines lost six games to college competition en route to a 13-7-1 record, they went 2-1-1 against Minnesota, they split with Colorado College, and they lost a respectable 6-3 game to Dartmouth, widely considered the best hockey team from the nation's best hockey region.

Heyliger's timing when he took the coaching job at Illinois right before the war was as bad as it was good when he accepted the job at Michigan in 1944. He returned to Ann Arbor right before the campus became flush with new students, new buildings, and a new sense of confidence.

Ann Arborites rewarded Heyliger's efforts by filling the Coliseum in record numbers. The 1947–48 Michigan hockey team's eight-page "media guide," hammered out by sports information director Les Etter on a heavy, manual typewriter and mimeographed for the few reporters who covered the team, admitted the Coliseum was "aged and relatively small" but added that "Because of an unprecedented demand for student tickets, enthusiastic townspeople have of necessity been excluded from all but vacation-time games. With the success attained by last year's squad and increased interest, it is anticipated that the attendance will break all existing records."

It did. The team had no trouble selling out all 1,100 seats and 200 "standing room only" passes for all 14 home games. At $2.00 for a reserved seat and just 60¢ for a student ducat, it was the best deal in town.

"The thing that really got you about playing in the Coliseum was the game was right *there*, in front of the fans," Renfrew says. Because Frederick Weinberg had not originally designed the building to house spectators, the seats were closer to the rink and much steeper than in sanitized modern arenas, where the crowd's energy is often dissipated in the spacious surroundings.

"Ann Arbor was really more of a hockey town than a basketball town," Renfrew adds, "and it still is, I think. In the old days they'd start the basketball games at seven and the hockey games at nine, so people would leave the Field House to come see the last two periods at the Coliseum. That was just a great place to play hockey."

The fans came back to see a better team, of course, but also to enjoy a better game. Throughout the Depression and World War II, hockey's caretakers created a rack of new rules that replaced the endless individual rushes and dump-and-run tactics of the game's early years with faster play, better playmaking, and higher scoring. Between 1930 and 1943 the rule makers introduced the goal line, the red line, offsides, icing, and forward passing in all zones, and added such fan-friendly features as penalty shots, visible game clocks, and intermissions to clean the ice for faster play. With the advent of shoulder pads, elbow pads, and knee pads, the game as we know it had finally taken shape by the end of the war.

The confluence of the veterans' renewed appetite for entertainment and a new hockey coach, new rules, and new equipment pulled a program teetering on the brink of oblivion back to center stage. Crisler had flirted with the idea of killing the hockey program near the end of the war, but he quickly dismissed that notion after he saw Heyliger strengthen the schedule, boost the team's record, and pack the enlarged rink in just a couple of years.

But Heyliger knew the program had to be part of something bigger, something more permanent, if it was to survive another storm. Heyliger sought to build a house of not straw or wood but brick.

15

A Tournament Is Born

"The thing that made college hockey what it is today was the NCAA tournament," Renfrew says, "and Vic was the driving force behind it."

At the conclusion of the 1946–47 season, Heyliger, only 28 years old at the time, wrote a bold letter to 20 other college coaches around the country, in which he posed a simple question: "How does the idea of a national college hockey tournament sound to you?"

Apparently it sounded pretty good. "They said, 'What the hell?'" Renfrew relates. "'If basketball has a playoff, why can't we?'" Nineteen of the nation's top 21 coaches met at the Lincoln Hotel in New York City and quickly confirmed their desire to be part of it. All they needed was a place to play.

Surprisingly, that turned out to be the hard part. It didn't matter that the vast majority of those 19 teams were located in the Northeast, home to the nation's biggest cities and largest indoor hockey rinks. No school or city in New England wanted to touch it.

Heyliger's dream looked as if it was going to die on the vine until it was rescued by an unlikely angel: a short, portly, unathletic man whose name sounded like a speech impediment. Thayer Tutt was a Harvard graduate, an avid hockey fan and, most important, the president of the glamorous Broadmoor Hotel in Colorado Springs. He not only strong-armed the hotel directors to host such a tournament over their vociferous objections, he even persuaded them to pick up the tab for the teams' transportation and lodging.

Having set up the first NCAA hockey tournament, Heyliger then had to make sure his team got invited to it. The tournament's founding fathers made one oversight that would come back to haunt Michigan decades later: they never established clear criteria for selecting teams for the tournament. But no matter what secret formula the first committee used, the 1947–48 Michigan squad was absolutely impossible to overlook. The Wolverines blasted through their rigorous 21-game schedule, filled with highly regarded schools like Yale, North Dakota, Minnesota, and Michigan Tech, with an 18-2-1 mark and a .900 winning percentage, still a school record. Michigan was a lock.

In the winter of 1948 the committee decreed that the champion of the Quadrangular League—consisting of Harvard, Yale, Princeton, and conference champion Dartmouth—would get an automatic bid, as would the winner of the loosely organized New England League, which turned out to be Boston College. Although Michigan was no longer a member of any conference after Illinois dropped out, the committee wisely picked the Wolverines anyway. The committee awarded the fourth and final spot to Colorado College, partly due to its respectable 19-7 record, partly due to its sweep over Cal-Berkeley, one of the few Western schools then playing hockey, and partly due to its location in Colorado Springs, which increased the fan base while reducing lodging costs for the Broadmoor. The tournament was born.

In the NCAA's first semifinal game in March 1948, the Riley brothers of Dartmouth easily eliminated Colorado College, 8-4, on the strength of Joe Riley's four goals. The results only confirmed long-held suspicions about the superiority of Eastern hockey.

Michigan took on Boston College the following night in the tournament's second East-West battle, which was broadcast on radio back in Boston. "There have been many other hockey broadcasts since then," former BC coach Snooks Kelley recalled a few years ago, "but that was the first one that had them pasted to their radios."

The Eagles gave their listeners something to shout about when they took a 3-2 lead into the third period, until Michigan's ageless captain and two-time All-American, Connie Hill, took a shot from 40 feet out and scored on "my famous break-an-egg slap-shot," he says. "The goalie fell asleep watching the puck come towards him."

The tally completed Hill's unlikely hat trick and tied the game at 3-3. With a little less than six minutes left in the game, Al Renfrew found himself with the puck in front of the Boston College goalie, Bernie Burke, and wasted no time burying the biscuit for a 4-3 lead.

At the two-minute mark, Coach Kelley shocked the crowd by pulling his goalie. The strategy was so rare at the time the P.A. announcer saw fit to draw the attention of the 2,700 capacity crowd to the Eagles' empty net. The revolutionary tactic paid off when the Eagles tied it up with just 50 seconds left, forcing a 10-minute overtime period. In 1948, overtime was settled not by sudden death but total goals, similar to basketball's overtime format today.

Just 18 seconds into the extra period, Wally Grant, the pioneer from the Iron Range, fed Wally Gacek, who whipped it into the twine for a 5-4 lead. Seconds later, Connie Hill risked falling from hero to goat when he was penalized for a minor transgression, and was penalized *again* two minutes later for leaving the penalty box too soon. But Michigan goalie Black Jack McDonald, another Eveleth man, saved Hill's hide by keeping the puck out of the net during both penalties. As the seconds ticked away, Coach Kelley pulled Burke again, but this time the tactic backfired when Michigan tapped in an empty net goal to seal the victory. Heyliger's crew had made it to the first NCAA final.

The stage was set for the showdown everybody wanted: the Beast from the East against the Best of the West. Back when Dartmouth's mascot was still the Indians, the "glass" was fence, and the boards were *boards*, eastern teams rarely played western teams, so the NCAA finals provided a rare test of regional strength—similar to the early Super-Bowl battles between the NFL and the AFL, with Michigan clearly representing the lowly regarded, upstart AFL.

Dartmouth entered the final contest with a 21-2 record. Michigan came in at 19-2-1. But Dartmouth was the heavy favorite, and it wasn't solely due to eastern bias. Under Coach Eddie Jeremiah, Dartmouth rattled off a 45-0-1 run from 1941 to 1946, an unbeaten streak that lasted longer than World War II itself. Many believed Dartmouth's 1947–48 team was even better than Jeremiah's unbeaten squads, due to the addition of goalie Dick Desmond, considered the nation's best collegiate goalie, and the renowned Riley brothers, who had been unstoppable against the top schools on the East Coast. The year before, Dartmouth had come to Ann Arbor and beaten the Wolverines soundly, 6-3, with virtually the same personnel on both sides.

Well, *almost* the same personnel, that is. One man, Wally Grant, sat out that season while completing an 18-month stint in the U.S. army. When he returned Heyliger wisely put him with Wally Gacek and fellow Minnesotan Ted Greer to form the famed "Three G" line. Any hope the Wolverines had against Dartmouth's dominant Riley brothers rested squarely on their shoulders.

Due to the stakes—the first national title and bragging rights for regional hegemony—the players' passions ran hotter than usual. The rugged play resulted in 16 penalties, very high for the era, and created an intensely competitive atmosphere for the spectators.

Early on the Indians looked to be too much for the Michigan boys. Bill Riley struck first, and Dartmouth's Whitey Campbell followed to give the Indians a 2-0 lead, which many knowledgeable observers thought would be insurmountable. Michigan showed some life with two Wally Gacek goals, but fell behind again, 4-2, by midgame.

But that's when the 20 bucks Coke Cossalter gave Wally Grant three years earlier paid handsome dividends. The kid who came in on the train from Eveleth with a few borrowed bucks, no one to call, and no change of clothes scored two goals to tie the game and spark his teammates. The Three G line scored two more, Gordie McMillan scored two more, and Michigan buried a stunned Dartmouth squad, 8-4.

"The best memory I've got was winning the national championship as a player," Renfrew says. "It was the first one they had, and we'd been together for three years already. Back then 10 guys came in at once and stayed for four years. We were really close."

The icers' title added to a stellar year for the entire Michigan athletic program, which won Big Ten titles in basketball, swimming, and football, plus a Rose Bowl and national championship in football. The first NCAA hockey tournament also put college hockey on the national map for good. In other sports, leagues like the Big Ten and Pac Ten regulated the games long before the

1948 NCAA championship
In the NCAA's first tournament Michigan upset Dartmouth, 8–4, with five future All-Americans, including the bespectacled Connie Hill. The Broadmoor, in Colorado Springs, hosted the event in grand style. "We were treated like kings," Ed Switzer recalled.
(Courtesy Bentley Historical Library, University of Michigan.)

NCAA was willing to sponsor championships in their sports. But years before the birth of the ECAC and the WCHA, and decades before the CCHA was even a glint in athletic directors' eyes, the NCAA sponsored a hockey tournament. It was the NCAA tournament that begat the hockey leagues, not the other way around.

No single weekend had a bigger impact on the future of the Michigan program since Eddie Kahn and his buddies beat Wisconsin in the program's first weekend. Michigan's first NCAA title was a high-water mark the program would not surpass for more than four decades.

16

Title Town

From 1947–48 through 1956–57, when Heyliger retired, the Michigan hockey team won 195 games, lost only 41, and tied 11. The Wolverines' record got them 10 consecutive invitations to the Final Four, whence they came home with the national crown six times—records that have never been in danger of being broken by any college team a half century later. The run also ensured the team its place on campus for years to come, filling a hole created by the football and basketball teams' mediocrity during the fifties.

The 10 Final Fours provided the players their best memories of college hockey, thanks partly to Thayer Tutt and the Broadmoor Hotel. After the Broadmoor hosted the first tournament, Tutt, the son of hotel cofounder Charles Tutt, persuaded his company to host the tournament every year thereafter for the next 10, and they did far more than just organize a few games. They spoiled the players with free plane tickets—the first flight for most of the players—elegant meals and the unmatched elegance of the Broadmoor Hotel itself. Even now, 50 years later, the players often remember more about the tremendous hospitality they received in Colorado Springs than the games they played there.

Spencer "Speck" Penrose was born a few months after the Civil War. The black sheep of a wealthy Philadelphia family, Penrose traveled to the Rockies to make a name for himself, but failure followed him there, too. When he joined forces with his old childhood friend Charles Tutt, however, the two unearthed their potential, building fortunes in gold, iron, and real estate.

In 1916, at the age of 51, Penrose sought to start a second career by purchasing the Antlers Hotel in Colorado Springs and making it the centerpiece for a lavish resort, but the Antlers refused to sell. Instead of giving up on the idea, Penrose gathered over $1 million to build a new resort in front of a crystal-clear lake at the base of the Cheyenne Mountains, which he decided to call the Broadmoor.

Penrose hired the same architect who drew up the Greenbriar spa in West Virginia, President Eisenhower's favorite destination. Penrose then made plans for a state-of-the-art casino and a golf course designed by architect Donald Ross, who created Inverness, Pinehurst, Oakland Hills, and Ann Arbor's Barton Hills, among other distinguished tracks.

Penrose's attention to detail bordered on the manic. His insistence on using only the very best of everything available—or, if it wasn't yet available, inventing it himself—was absolute. Penrose's guests were treated to grandiose chandeliers in the dining room, beautiful frescoes on the ceilings, scientifically advanced seeds to grow lush putting greens in the thin mountain air, and dazzling bone china trimmed in the hotel's signature colors, blue and gold.

Penrose knew such extravagances enraged the Broadmoor's board of directors, but he ignored their protests while burning through the group's $1 million start-up fund. He kept spending until he had to put up a million of his own—and then another. He undoubtedly appeared mad to outsiders, but he was certain his unrelenting commitment to excellence would thrill his guests and ensure that the Broadmoor would fulfill his vision of building, in his words, "the finest hotel in the United States."

By June 1918, less than a year after breaking ground, Penrose had accomplished his seemingly impossible dream.

"Didn't matter if you were from a big city like Toronto," Renfrew proclaims, "it was a helluva place."

So fabulous was the new resort that everybody who was anybody quickly found their way to the Broadmoor. Just a sampling of the list of frequent guests included actors Will Rogers, Jimmy Stewart, Henry Fonda, Marlene Dietrich, Joan Crawford, and Shirley Temple. World-class musicians such as Igor Stravinsky, Vladimir Horowitz, Sergey Rachmaninoff, and Arthur Fiedler all performed there. Pierre Trudeau, Margaret Thatcher, and every U.S. president from Eisenhower to George Bush have stayed there while in office. Gerald Ford has been a regular for years.

As Penrose started succumbing to old age in the late 1930s, he was surely satisfied to see the value of his fortune and his resort increase many times over. This former black sheep had become the runaway success of his high society family.

The year before he passed away, Penrose made his last major decision regarding his resort: he would convert the Broadmoor Riding Academy into a rink. In typical fashion, he burned through $200,000 to complete the project in 24 days, but he did it right, seeing to such details as embedded heaters in all 2,700 seats. When Penrose died in 1939 at the age of 74, his faith had been vindicated by a public triumph only he could have envisioned, but even the ambitious Penrose could never have foreseen his final accomplishment would create lifelong memories for hundreds of college hockey players and thousands of fans. Since Penrose's death, his rink has sponsored numerous national and international championships that have drawn the likes of Sonja Henie and Dick Button, Peggy Fleming and Dorothy Hamill—and, for 10 straight years, the Michigan hockey team.

"The tournament wasn't run for the money involved," Heyliger points out. "It was more a social event, an experience for the players." And what an experience it was. The Broadmoor staff picked up the teams in enormous Cadillacs and put on a parade, a banquet, a ball, and a beauty contest just for the players' enjoyment.

"They even had cowboy hats with each guy's name on it waiting for us in our closets," recalls Ed Switzer, who played on Heyliger's last Michigan team. "I'm telling you, it was just fantastic. We were treated like kings."

Even when things went wrong, the Broadmoor made them right. The off-ice activities always included a ritualistic "branding" of all the players and coaches. A souvenir slab of wood was roped to the seat of their pants while a brander burned their initials into the wood. But when Harry Cleverly, the Boston University coach, bent over for his branding, the piece of wood slipped, and the brander burned Cleverly's pants instead. To make sure there were no bad feelings, Tutt not only apologized and replaced the pants, he bought Cleverly an entire wardrobe of first-rate clothes to take home with him.

"They'd set us up with fantastic pregame meals, even steak," Renfrew says. "All the meals were special to us, because we normally didn't eat like that. Back home we didn't even *have* a pregame meal."

"They showed a bunch of kids what western hospitality was all about," said Boston College coach Snooks Kelley, 30 years after the first tournament. "Thayer Tutt did everything possible to see that the hockey players enjoyed their visits. I don't think any member of the team will forget that week. It was just—well, heaven on earth. That's what we called it—heaven."

The NCAA was so grateful for Spencer Penrose's contribution to the development of college hockey that it named the NCAA Coach of the Year trophy the Spencer Penrose Award. Few recipients recognize the name on the trophy anymore, but those who were there can never forget it.

17

Decade of Champions

The players who stayed at the Broadmoor say the food was consistently good, but it always tasted just a little better after a Michigan victory. By that measure, most of the meals the Wolverines were served there were delicious, but a few had to be choked down. In the 20 NCAA Final Four games Michigan played at the Ice Palace—10 semifinal games, 7 finals, and 3 consolation contests—Heyliger's Wolverines won 16, lost just 4, and never lost both games of the weekend.

Wally Grant's teams made it to the first three Final Fours, in 1948, '49, and '50, and won four of their six games—but it's not the four wins, nor that first title, that Grant recalls most clearly. "The ones I remember most," Grant says, "are the ones we lost that hurt so bad."

If the 1947–48 NCAA championship team was good, the 1948–49 team looked great. The 1948 team had three All-Americans: Connie Hill, Wally Gacek, and Wally Grant. All three were named to the All-American team again in 1949 and were joined by Dick Starrak and two-time All-American Ross Smith. The nation's first returning NCAA champions returned to the Broadmoor to defend their title with a 19-1-3 record, a 90-27 goal differential, and a 10-game winning streak. They had all the momentum of a runaway freight train.

"We had some great players in '48," says Renfrew, who captained the '49 squad. "But we had a much better team in '49."

The NCAA selection committee's task became tougher when

the loose eastern leagues rescrambled, while the western teams still hadn't organized a league at all. But the previous year's Final Four teams rescued the committee by demonstrating their superiority over their peers throughout the season, which justified the return of all four schools.

This time, however, the NCAA scheduled Michigan to play Dartmouth first, but it acutally looked like a lucky break for the Wolverines because Boston College had a 19-1 record, far more intimidating than the Indians' 17-5.

Early in the St. Patrick's Day game, Michigan had little trouble with the Indians but plenty of problems with the officials. Just 18 ticks into the contest Michigan's Gil Burford hammered home a goal, but the officials erased it. They proceeded to give the Wolverines 24 penalties, against only 3 for Dartmouth. Although Michigan defenseman Dick Starrak had received just 2 penalties during the previous 23 games, the officials saw fit to charge him with 5 in the Dartmouth game alone, including a penalty for a mysterious violation called an "attempted trip." A couple dozen power plays were all the Riley brothers needed to score three goals en route to a 4-2 victory.

"They were a good team," Renfrew says of Dartmouth, "but if we'd'a played 'em 10 times, we'd'a won 9 of 'em."

In the other semifinal the Boston College Eagles mopped up Colorado College to create the first All-Eastern final, in which they trimmed Dartmouth, 4-3, for their first title. Western hockey's inaugural triumph the year before suddenly looked like a fluke to the eastern hockey establishment.

The Terrier Curse

If Michigan's 1948–49 machine was powerful, its 1949–50 model was phenomenal. Wally Grant captained a squad that had seven solid seniors on it, a team that had been to the NCAA Final Four twice and won it once. True, the team's 23-4-0 record included two more losses than Renfrew's 1948–49 team, but they also won three more games and suffered only one loss to another U.S. college team, a 3-2 defeat up at Michigan Tech. The '50 squad beat every team it played at least once, including five teams from Canada, three from the Ivy League, and four from the West. There didn't seem to be any college team out there they couldn't take.

Michigan, Colorado College, and Boston College all returned for their third Final Four, but Dartmouth was dropped from the invitation list in favor of Boston University, which brought an 18-4 record to the dance. A good record, certainly, but everyone agreed Boston College would present the biggest obstacle between the Wolverines and their second title.

For the second year in a row Michigan had to play its first game on St. Patrick's Day. Unfazed by superstition, the Wolverines jumped out to a 2-0 lead against BU on goals by Paul Pelow and Wally Grant. At the other end the Terriers could manufacture only 14 shots on net the entire game—yet somehow, BU scored four unanswered goals in the second period alone, leaving Grant's crew stunned in the locker room between the second and third periods, down 4-2.

Determined not to lose to the upstart Terriers, the Wolverines redoubled their efforts, firing 36 shots on Terrier goalie Ralph Bevins. But Bevins didn't give Grant's guys anything, shutting them down cold that period and killing the Wolverines' hopes of a second title.

"This was the best team I played on," Grant states flatly. His claim is supported by an anonymous reporter who wrote that the players from the other three teams all believed Michigan had the best squad at the tournament. "I was so disappointed," Grant says, "I didn't even want to play the consolation game."

But he did. Michigan easily defeated Boston College, 10-6, in a game with no penalties, a statistic that suggests the lack of intensity the teams felt. Adding salt to the wound, BU's Bevins, the same goalie who stopped almost everything Michigan could throw at him on St. Patrick's Day, suddenly couldn't stop a beach ball in the finals, losing 13-4 to Colorado College—the same team Michigan had beaten 5-1 and 11-1 in February. But Bevins was so good against Michigan that he won the tournament MVP award anyway.

"To this day," Grant says, "I still wonder how the hell we lost to BU."

The players could not have known it then, but Boston University seemed to have put a curse on Michigan—call it the Terrier Curse—that dictates that whenever the Wolverines are favored to win the title, they will fail.

On a Roll

The following year the Wolverines enjoyed the flip side of the Terrier Curse: when they're the underdogs, they win it. Although the players maintain their 1950–51 team (22-4-1) was not the equal of the 1949–50 bunch, the '51 squad had no trouble buzzing through Boston University, 8-2, in the semifinals and Brown University in the finals, 7-1. The *Michigan Daily* called that game the team's "greatest performance of the season." Michigan had All-American goalie Hal Downes in the net, but they could have replaced him with a second-string high schooler because Brown couldn't manage a single shot on net in the game's first 15 minutes, and few thereafter.

Having led the change to bring the NCAA tournament to life and gotten his team in it during the tournament's first four seasons, Heyliger next turned his attention to organizing a formal league on the other side of the Alleghenies. The persuasive coach succeeded in forming the Midwest Intercollegiate Hockey League in the fall of 1951. The newborn circuit changed its name the next year to the Western Intercollegiate Hockey League (WIHL) and, later, to the now familiar Western Collegiate Hockey Association (WCHA), but by any name Heyliger's league has been at the forefront of college hockey since its inception.

The NCAA encouraged the nascent league's growth in the hopes that it would make picking the Final Four easier for the tournament selection committee. But the new league only muddied matters when Colorado College won the WIHL's first crown in 1951–52 and Michigan and Denver tied for second. The NCAA bypassed Denver for Michigan, and Michigan—perhaps because it wasn't expected to— justified the decision by breezing past St.

Lawrence, 9-3, to face league champion Colorado College in the finals. The Wolverines quickly turned the tables on the favored Tigers to gain a 3-0 lead in the first period, which allowed the Wolverines to cruise to a 4-1 victory and their second consecutive NCAA title.

Despite winning three of the NCAA's first five hockey titles, Michigan was unable to win its own tiny league for the second consecutive year. The following season, 1952–53, Minnesota took three out of four against the Wolverines to win the second WIHL title, but the NCAA invited both teams to the Broadmoor Ice Palace for the Final Four.

In 1953, Michigan promptly blew out Boston University, 14-2, to gain a measure of revenge for the Terrier's upset in 1950. This set up a meeting with Minnesota in the second consecutive All-Western final, but no one in their right mind would have picked Michigan to beat the Gophers that year. Although the Wolverines could boast two-time All-American defenseman George Chin and two future Olympians from Eveleth, goalie Willard Ikola and two-time All-American center John Matchefts, they arrived in Colorado Springs with a 15-7 record, their worst mark since the war.

Minnesota, on the other hand, had one of the finest Gopher teams in its long, glorious history, and proved it by rolling over their league opponents and everyone else en route to a 21-4 record. Minnesota had six future U.S. Olympians on that squad, including John Mayasich, one of the greatest collegians ever to play the game. He would go on to play on a record three U.S. Olympic hockey teams, from 1956 to 1968.

Didn't matter. "Even though we were considered underdogs, we didn't play like underdogs," recalls Ikola, Michigan's goalie. "We took the pace right from the drop of the puck. We were simply the better team that night."

After the Wolverines fought back to tie the game at two in the second period, they buried the Gophers with five unanswered goals. The onrush so stunned the Gophers that their coach, the great John Mariucci, pulled his goalie, Jim Mattson, with a full seven minutes left in the game and sporadically thereafter. The bold stratagem worked to a point, insofar as Minnesota generated more shots on Michigan's net, but Ikola was more than up to the task. When the game ended, Michigan had a 7-3 victory and its third consecutive NCAA title.

"Coach Heyliger's charges," the *Ann Arbor News* reported, "who little more than two weeks ago were not even conceded a

Willard Ikola, goalie
Willard Ikola was one of 10 Minnesota schoolboy stars to migrate to Ann Arbor between 1945 and 1955, half of them All-Americans. Ikola won a silver medal at the 1956 Olympic games in Italy, then turned Minnesota's Edina High School into the state's dynasty.
(Courtesy Bentley Historical Library, University of Michigan.)

good chance to gain a tournament berth, completely outclassed Minnesota in one of the most dramatic triumphs in history."

"We always came on in January and February," Ikola remembers. "Because of the tradition of the program, and the number of NCAA titles we'd won, it seemed like when the puck dropped in the NCAAs we were always playing the best we could play. There was a lot of pride there."

The Circus Is in Town

No one under the age of 30 had ever seen a period of peace and prosperity like the 1950s. The respite allowed Americans and especially college students to be as carefree as they had been in the twenties. Having survived the Depression and World War II, they had a lot more pent-up desire to satiate themselves, too.

It was an era of renewed confidence—and consumption. Chuck Yeager flew a record 1,600 miles per hour, more than twice the speed of sound; Francis Crick and James Watson unlocked the secret of DNA; and Dr. Jonas Salk's polio vaccine was declared to be "safe, effective and potent" at an international conference held at Ann Arbor's Rackham Auditorium. A seemingly endless stream of home appliances—dishwashers, clothes dryers, and refrigerators—flew out of stores faster than manufacturers could make them. Gas rationing was out. The new superhighway system was in.

Sparked by the GI Bill but fanned by good times, Michigan's enrollment exploded from 20,000 in 1951 to 41,000 in 1968. To accommodate the new wave of students, South Quad, the Undergraduate Library, the Business Administration Building, and the Literature, Science and the Arts Building, among others, all popped up in the years immediately following the war. (Their resemblance to military structures was probably unintentional.)

Americans' long-dormant desire to indulge themselves after almost two decades of self-denial also fueled a renaissance in sports. A new magazine, *Sports Illustrated,* debuted in 1954, and there was plenty to write about. The NBA grew up in the fifties, led by Bob Cousy's Celtics. New York became the capital of base-

ball, home of the game's three best teams with the three best center fielders: the Dodgers' Duke Snider, the Giants' Willie Mays,
and the Yankees' Mickey Mantle. Thanks to advances in air travel
the Boston Braves were able to move to Milwaukee, where they
averaged over 2 million fans their first five seasons, enticing the
Dodgers and Giants to migrate even farther west in 1958. And
thanks to advances in television, Americans could watch their
favorite teams without leaving home. Up north, both frozen TV
dinners and Hockey Night in Canada became weekly habits.

While the Detroit Tigers were mired in the second division that
decade, the Lions won three NFL titles on the strength of Bobby
Layne's arm, and the Red Wings took four Stanley Cups on the
strength of Gordie Howe's elbow. "You're working a game, and
you see a player down," referee Vern Buffey once explained. "You
know that Howe did it, but how can you prove it?"

Michigan's Ed Switzer experienced Buffey's dilemma firsthand
during one of the 12 exhibition games the Red Wings and the
Wolverines played at the Coliseum between 1947 and 1959.
Although the Wolverines were in top form—coincidentally, the
thirties, the fifties, and the nineties have been the most successful decades for the Red Wings *and* the Wolverines—they were
still a bunch of college kids with no realistic hopes of playing in
the NHL. When they chose to, the Wings could easily bury the
Wolverines by scores of 10-1, 13-2, and 14-5, but they usually
took it easy on their understudies by making midgame trades
and replacing Hall of Fame goalie Terry Sawchuk early in the
contests with equipment manager Lefty Wilson, who also served
as the team's backup goalie in those informal days. Wilson made
the most of his appearances by taking to the ice wearing a 10-
gallon hat, puffing on a big cigar, and chatting up the crowd the
entire night.

"Those games were just a lot of fun," Switzer recalls. "We were
a bunch of college kids playing against Sawchuk, Howe, and Ted
Lindsay—and those guys weren't getting a dime for it."

The Wings did have their limits, however. In one game the Red
Wings let a comfortable 7-2 lead slip to 7-5. Detroit coach Jimmy
Skinner warned his players, "If you guys lose this game, there'll

be a two-hour practice on this ice." The Wolverines didn't get a shot on the Wings' net the rest of the night.

Red Wing Hall of Famer Ted Lindsay recalls another Michigan exhibition game Detroit barely pulled out at the end, which left general manager Jack Adams fuming. Adams stormed into the visitors' locker room and bellowed, "'*nobody* will ever wear a Red Wing uniform and embarrass it,'" Lindsay recalls. "He singled out a defenseman named Al Dewsbury, and told him, 'You'll never wear it again,' and he never did. I don't know why he picked Al—he was a good guy, could shoot and skate the puck—because it was all of us that night."

Still, Lindsay remembers those exhibitions fondly. "It was always a fun time, a relaxed time," he says. "That rink was so cold. When you got on that ice after playing in those hot NHL rinks, you could skate forever, but we tried to avoid getting off-sides to keep playing. The guys on the bench were always yelling and hollering because they were freezing their butts off on the bench. I always looked at it as a chance for us to sell our game to the people at Michigan who supported our profession. Plus, Vic Heyliger was such a tremendous coach. I knew what he was like as a person. Those are very important things to people like me."

Which brings us back to Switzer's run-in with Howe. During another exhibition Switzer lined up for a face-off against him, and when the puck went into the corner, he and Howe went in after it. "I tried to push him into the boards," Switzer recalls, "but it was like pushing a cement wall. You just couldn't do it. On the same shift, the puck goes into the corner again, but I'm in there first this time—reluctantly. He about throws me onto Hill Street. I'm on my back, and he stops to look over me and says, 'That's how it's done, sonny.' Obviously, I never forgot."

In the 1950s, Michigan won NCAA titles in baseball, tennis, swimming, and wrestling, but with the Wolverine football and basketball teams going nowhere, there was still a void to fill in spectator sports, and the hockey team filled it. With or without the Red Wings in town, the students and townspeople packed the Coliseum every night to cheer on the nation's most successful college hockey team playing the country's fastest game—but one still loose enough that the goalies wore not masks but long, knit hats hanging down their backs, with the puffy yellow tip whipping around their heads with each dramatic save.

It was a great time to be a University of Michigan hockey player.

Second Wave

While the Wolverines weren't favored to win any more NCAA titles the next three seasons, they weren't expected to lose to lightly regarded Rensselaer Polytechnic Institute in the semifinals of the 1954 NCAA tournament, either. But RPI upended the Wolverines, 6-4, then pulled off a bigger upset by beating top-ranked WIHL champion Minnesota in overtime, 5-4. It was the second consecutive year the Gophers lost the NCAA final game against a team they were fully expected to beat. Perhaps they, too, had a touch of the BU flu.

Michigan was up to its old tricks in the 1955 tournament. Although the Wolverines failed to win their own league for the fourth consecutive year, they qualified for the Final Four by finishing a solid second in the WIHL with a 16-5-1 record. Still, they looked to have little chance against Colorado College in the finals. The Tigers had finished first in the WIHL with a 22-6 record; they had beaten Michigan along the way, 4-0 and 5-4; and they would be playing in front of their home crowd in the finals once again.

But the Wolverines knew better than anyone there how to craft an upset: play tight defense, get great goaltending, and don't waste whatever chances you get on offense. Heyliger used only two lines the entire night, relying largely on two-time All-American goalie Lorne Howes to keep them in the game long enough for Michigan's snipers to get a few at the other end.

The swamis were right: the Tigers had a much better team than Michigan's, outshooting the Wolverines 47-21. But through 2½ periods, the hardworking Howes allowed only two goals, while his forwards squeezed four goals out of their few chances at the other end to forge a 4-2 lead. With 2:37 left in the game, Colorado's swarming offense finally pulled within a goal and looked to be on the verge of tying the game when Michigan took a penalty with a minute left. But Howes proved to be every bit the equal of his predecessor, Eveleth's Willard Ikola, turning back shot after shot from the Tigers until Michigan captain and two-time All-American Bill MacFarland settled matters by clearing the puck down the ice into the empty CC net.

As the *Ann Arbor News* put it, "Michigan's Cinderella hockey team, skating as if its collective life depended on winning, throttled Colorado College, 5-3." The 1955 tournament marked the third time the unpredictable Wolverines had beaten their own league champion in the NCAA finals.

The next season, 1955–56, Heyliger's players tried doing it the hard way—for them—by winning the WIHL title for the first time and coming into the NCAA tournament the heavy favorites. Led by yet three more two-time All-Americans, Howes, Bill McFarland, and Bob Schiller, Michigan blitzed through its schedule with an 18-2-1 record, demonstrating a dominance over all other teams that made them the team to beat in Colorado—and that was the scary part.

Michigan's semifinal opponent, St. Lawrence, was considered far weaker than the Wolverines, and even more so when it lost four players to an eligibility ruling right before the tournament. In other words, the conditions were perfect for the Wolverines to succumb to the Terrier Curse yet again. Sure enough, Michigan could score only one goal against St. Lawrence in regulation and had to go into overtime before Michigan's Tom Rendall could dispel the ghosts 1:24 into the extra period.

In the other semifinal bracket Michigan Tech trounced Boston College, 10-4, to earn a rematch with its old rival. Michigan had closed out the regular season with four consecutive victories over the Huskies by a combined score of 21-7—a fact that should've given knowledgeable Wolverine boosters the willies.

Michigan Tech, with the crowd and its brass band urging them on, ground its way to a 5-4 lead by the second period of the

finals. But youthful spunk ultimately proved no match for seasoned confidence, and Michigan had way too much of both. No
sooner had the Huskies gone ahead than the Wolverines' Ed
Switzer scored his second and third goals of the game to zip past
the Huskies, 7-5, and give Michigan its sixth title in nine years.

1956 remains the only year that a top-seeded Michigan team
has won the tournament.

The 1956–57 team made it back to Broadmoor's Ice Palace but
got swamped in the finals by Colorado College, 13-6—Michigan's
first loss in the tournament's final game. It felt like the end of an
era, and it was. It would be the last Michigan team coached by
Heyliger, the last to go to the Final Four at the Broadmoor, and
the last one to make it to the NCAA finals for seven years.

Not only was it the closing of Michigan's incredible 10-year
run—unequaled to this day—it was the end of the fabulous Final
Four weekends at the Broadmoor.

"The NCAA didn't make a dollar out of it, and after 10 years
they wanted a piece," Renfrew explains. "And for their centennial
the University of Minnesota wanted to host the tournament, so
it went up there. Then it started to move around the country.
But after a while, we realized what a special thing we had going
in Colorado and asked the Broadmoor to buy it back, but you
had to reserve those kind of rooms years in advance. We'd lost
our place."

The NCAA tournament now hosts 12 teams in three cities
each year, including such unlikely locales as Cincinnati, St.
Louis, and Anaheim. The change has generated a lot more exposure and profits, but it's hard not to feel that something has
been lost. That magical era—the era of train travel, work-study
jobs, and Final Four weekends at the Broadmoor—ended forever
in 1957.

Part V

The Renfrew Era

1957–73

Mister Roberts

It would be difficult to imagine a more successful run than Heyliger's. His Michigan teams made it to the Final Four 10 straight years, won six NCAA titles, and helped shift the locus of power from the East to the West when it was previously thought to be the other way around. Led by Michigan, the West won 18 of the first 20 NCAA championships, settling the question rather emphatically.

Of Michigan's 42 players who have earned All-American status over the past 54 seasons, more than half (24) played for Heyliger between 1948 and 1957. During that stretch he never had fewer than 2 players on the All-American team. Four times he had 5 players so honored, and in 1956 he had a record 6 players on the squad. In Michigan history, twelve Wolverines have won it twice or more. Heyliger coached 9 of them and recruited the tenth, Bob White. No other school has ever amassed and developed such a mother lode of talent in the history of college hockey.

For all this Heyliger was given the NCAA's Spencer Penrose Award for Coach of the Year, he was inducted into the U.S. Hockey Hall of Fame, and he was selected in 1996 by the American Hockey Coaches Association as one of the five best college coaches of the century, and the very best of the first half. In 1980 he became the first hockey player or coach to be inducted into the University of Michigan's Hall of Honor.

"Michigan built its reputation," Coach Red Berenson says today, "from the strength of its national championships in the fifties."

Heyliger's severe asthma forced him to leave the team and Ann Arbor in the summer of 1957. He moved to Colorado Springs, home of the NCAA tournament, where he'd already noticed he could breathe much better in the dry western air. Shortly after settling there he couldn't resist starting a new Division II program at the Air Force Academy.

Through Heyliger's tenure athletic director Fritz Crisler had seen the virtue of having a Michigan man head the hockey program. When it came time for Crisler to conduct his second search for a hockey coach, therefore, he sought out Al Renfrew, an affable man who had captained the 1948–49 Wolverine squad and had already been coaching college hockey for six years.

After he graduated from Michigan in 1949, Renfrew worked for two years as a salesman in town for Cushing-Malloy, a printing company. It was a decent job but still a vocation, not an avocation. The opportunity to get back into hockey popped up when Amo Bessone, who had played for Heyliger at Illinois, ended a three-year run as Michigan Tech's coach in 1951 to accept the job at Michigan State, which had finally built an indoor rink the previous year. When the folks up at Michigan Tech asked Heyliger for a candidate, he told them to hire Renfrew, and they did.

Renfrew took over a program that had revived hockey just six years earlier—and played like it, finishing 5-14-2 in Bessone's last season. In 1951–52, Renfrew's first team played even worse, going 0-18 in the newly formed WIHL and 2-2 outside it. But Renfrew's knowledge of the game, his recruiting connections in Toronto, and his likable manner gradually turned the team around. Renfrew's guys bumped their annual win totals up to 6, 7, and then 12 in 1954–55, including a stunning 4-1 victory over the eventual NCAA champion Michigan Wolverines.

By Renfrew's fifth season, 1955–56, he had built a team good enough to stand atop of the WIHL standings with a surprising 14-2 league record, with just four league games remaining. The Wolverines lurked in second place, at 11-2-1. The catch: all four of those remaining games would be played between the two schools. If the Huskies could win just one of the four, they would earn their first-ever league title.

No luck. The master showed the student how it was done, taking the first two games up in Houghton, 5-2, 6-3, and the last two in Ann Arbor, 5-1 and 5-1, to win Heyliger's first league title.

The Huskies had a chance for redemption the next week when the two teams met again in the NCAA finals, in the Huskies' first Final Four appearance. Although Michigan Tech held a 5-4 lead in the second period, the young coach still couldn't beat his mentor, whose team pulled out a 7-5 victory.

The Huskies' heartbreaking losses to the Wolverines notwithstanding, the college hockey world took notice of the upstart team and its young coach. North Dakota offered Renfrew the head coaching job there in 1956–57, and he took it.

On his way out of Houghton Renfrew recommended his old high school and college buddy, former Michigan goalie John MacInnes, for the Husky head coaching job. MacInnes had stayed in Ann Arbor after graduating to start up the Ann Arbor Amateur Hockey Association, among other endeavors. He accepted Tech's offer, which effectively turned the WIHL into the Heyliger Club. Four of the league's seven head coaching positions were filled by Heyliger or his former players. In addition to Heyliger's 13 years behind the Michigan bench, Renfrew coached 22 years in the league (16 at Michigan, 6 at two other league schools); MacInnes put in 26 years at Michigan Tech; Bessone served 31 seasons for Michigan Tech and Michigan State; and Neil Celley, a 1951 Michigan captain and graduate, coached the Denver Pioneers to a 82-43-6 record from 1951 to 1956.

In all, Heyliger and Sons coached 96 years in the league, now called the WCHA. They exercised more influence over the new circuit than all other coaches combined and were the prime movers in the WCHA becoming the most successful, respected college hockey conference in the country. Heyliger's impact on the Michigan program, the NCAA tournament, the WCHA, and college hockey would be hard to overstate.

It was Heyliger and his disciples who set the tone for the young league too. The idea of playing dirty or running up the score against your former players, teammates, or coaches was completely foreign to them, but the idea of getting together after the games for a nice meal and a few beers, with the refs along for the ride, seemed completely natural. This collegial spirit trickled down to the players, who thought nothing of battling each other during the game then breaking bread at the home team's party afterward, a tradition that continued until Michigan and three other teams left the WCHA for the CCHA in the early eighties. The family feeling that enveloped the circuit for decades suited the easygoing Renfrew perfectly.

When Renfrew agreed to leave Michigan Tech for North Dakota in 1956, he replaced the oddly named Fido Purpur, who had just finished two consecutive losing seasons in the WIHL. Renfrew once again turned his new team around, leading the Fighting Sioux to an 18-11 overall record in 1956–57 and third-place in the WCHA, and very nearly beating the defending NCAA champion Wolverines in Ann Arbor, taking them to overtime before falling, 3-2.

At the end of Renfrew's first season in Grand Forks, Heyliger stepped down from the Michigan job and told Renfrew to put his name in for it. Renfrew wrote Fritz Crisler a letter in March indicating his interest, but Crisler didn't respond for over a month. Renfrew had already concluded he was out of the running when Crisler called to offer him the job.

Renfrew's decision should have been harder than it was. "I had recruited a helluva team at North Dakota," he says, "and they won the national title two years after I left with the players I had recruited, but I was too excited to be back in Ann Arbor to worry about it."

Michigan also overlooked a few things on paper to make this marriage happen. Renfrew was only 32 years old and had an anemic record of 1-18 against his old coach, Vic Heyliger. But Crisler and Heyliger were both confident Renfrew could do the job because of his demonstrated ability to turn programs around in Houghton and Grand Forks. And, incredibly enough, Renfrew's 32 years made him the second oldest of Michigan's first four head hockey coaches. Only Lowrey, at 37, had been older when he took the job.

If Barss had the dash of Gatsby, Lowrey the stoicism of Dwight Eisenhower, and Heyliger the New England charm of John F. Kennedy, Renfrew had the innate likeability of Mister Roberts, whom Henry Fonda played in a Broadway hit and movie by the same name. Renfrew earned the respect of his players not through severe discipline but sincere devotion.

Gordon Wilkie, one of Renfrew's first recruits and the captain of the 1964 NCAA championship team, remembers Renfrew as "a players' coach. We had 20 guys, and he played 'em all—and that's what it's all about. He'd give you the shirt off his back. 'Course, a lot of his shirts weren't worth much. He wasn't exactly the world's greatest dresser."

"He didn't have much, but he'd do whatever he could for us," adds Dave Butts, '63, citing Thanksgiving dinners at the Renfrew home as one example. The players' affection for their unassuming coach was obvious when the team played Colorado College at the Broadmoor in December 1960, a few days before Renfrew's birthday, and the dirt-poor players chipped in to buy him an overcoat. The appreciative coach wore that simple coat for the next 12 years, long after the buttons had fallen off. "That was a great coat," Renfrew says today. "I tell ya, we haven't had too many bad guys playing hockey at Michigan."

As nice as he was, Renfrew knew that goodwill alone wouldn't be enough to keep his job. He inherited a team that had gone 18-5-2 and finished one victory short of its third consecutive NCAA title in 1956–57—and then Renfrew promptly suffered Michigan's first losing season since World War II. Renfrew's skaters finished 8-13 in 1957–58, his first year, and 8-13-1 his second.

But Renfrew wasn't worried—he knew he had a secret weapon coming in.

19

The Red Baron and
the Regina Regiment

If you get in a car, or a train, or even a plane and cruise across the vast prairies of western Canada, sooner or later you'll come upon a little oasis of humanity sticking out of the endless acres of grain.

You have reached Regina.

Regina, the capital of Saskatchewan, is a tight circle of a city with no sprawl to speak of, which 180,000 farmers, politicians, and businesspeople call home. For over a century, Regina's main businesses have been grain and government, neither of which is terribly thrilling to watch.

You don't move to Regina for the scenery. Saskatchewan has few trees, fewer lakes, and no hills. It's so flat, kids who want to sled have to use off-ramp embankments, and you can see three provincial capitals just by standing on a park bench. You don't move there for the weather, either. It's horribly humid in the summer and bitterly cold in the winter. And you can forget about culture or night life. "If you've seen the movie *Fargo*," says the daughter of one former Michigan player, "you've seen Regina."

But if you're a hockey fan—or better yet, a hockey player—Regina's the place to be. The list of Saskatchewan natives who've played in the NHL runs 12 pages long, a remarkable feat for the only province west of the Maritimes that's never had an NHL franchise. The list includes Eddie Shore, Sid Abel, Ace Bailey, Johnny Bower, Glenn Hall, Bryan Trottier, Theo Fleury, and a guy from a place called Floral—a town so tiny it's not even listed in the Rand-McNally index—named Gordie Howe.

In Russia, the cream of the hockey crop inevitably flows

toward Moscow; in Sweden, to Stockholm; and in Saskatche-wan, to Regina. A hugely disproportionate chunk of Saskatche-wan's hockey talent was born in Regina, but even those who started playing in places like Big River, Yellow Grass, and Good-soil; Moose Jaw, Oxbow, and Cudworth; Saskatoon, Swift Cur-rent, and Sandy Lake Reserve—from which a man named Fred Saskamoose once left to play 11 games for the Chicago Black Hawks—even they invariably made their way to the provincial capital, if they were good enough. And the very best of the best played for the Regina Pats, a Montreal Canadiens' farm team and one of the greatest junior teams in hockey history.

Gordon "Red" Berenson, the oldest of fireman Otto Berenson's three children, grew up in Regina. The young Red Berenson and his friends would skate outdoors on the natural rinks and ponds all day, then go home for dinner with their skates on so they could rush back out to play some more as soon as they were excused from the table. When the snow drifted up to the top of the boards they shoveled it off, and when the 40-mile-per-hour winds rushed across the plains from Alaska, they leaned hard into them and kept skating. "Some days," Berenson recalls, "skating into that wind felt like you were going up hill."

While still in high school Berenson had already become a highly touted major junior player, one good enough to join the Montreal Canadiens' system straight out of high school, but he had other ideas. A serious student, Berenson became aware of the world of American college hockey when the Pats' high-profile coach, Murray Armstrong, migrated south of the border for his next coaching job.

From 1936 to 1946, Murray Armstrong scored 188 points in 270 NHL games playing for Toronto, New York, and Detroit. He then turned his considerable talent and energy to coaching the Regina Pats for the next 10 years. Armstrong loved coaching the Pats and was remarkably good at it, but the growth of the NCAA tournament and the WIHL caught his attention. In 1956, he accepted the head coaching job at the University of Denver.

"No question," Berenson says, "Armstrong influenced a lot of us to think about college."

Armstrong brought a bunch of ex-Pats with him to Denver,

but not enough at first. Armstrong's first Denver team finished 12-14-2, including a 4-1 exhibition loss to the Pats themselves. The next year, 1957–58, he loaded up with still more ex-Pats to win Denver's first WIHL title and zipped through the NCAA Final Four, 6-2, 6-2, to claim the school's first NCAA crown. A dynasty was born.

Armstrong coached Denver for 21 seasons. He won eight league titles, made it to 11 NCAA Final Fours and won 5 of them, relying on the best players from Saskatchewan, including future Chicago Blackhawk star Keith Magnuson. But not everyone admired his approach.

Minnesota's legendary player and coach John Mariucci, who filled his roster almost exclusively with Minnesotans, resented the fact that Armstrong filled his roster almost exclusively with Canadians, particularly 22-year-old freshmen from Saskatchewan. Several eastern schools, including perennial power Boston College, shared Mariucci's views, partly because they also built their teams on local talent.

Herb Brooks, who played for Mariucci from 1957 to 1959, is quick to clarify the record. "John wasn't anti-Canadian," he says. "He was pro-American."

Although Michigan's roster had become dominated by Canadians—for a couple seasons in the mid-fifties the team was composed entirely of Michigan's neighbors to the north—Michigan joined Minnesota, Michigan Tech, and Michigan State in protesting the use of "overaged" Canadians, who consistently thrashed those schools. The practice of recruiting Canadians, even 22-year-old ones, was legal at the time, but the six protesting schools felt it violated the spirit of the league, especially after the loophole was stretched to absurd lengths by Colorado College head coach Tony Frasca. Just 30 years old, Frasca had several players on his roster older than he was, including a 36-year-old skater named Jack Smith, who lettered from 1957 to 1960. The four protesting schools had had enough, and withdrew en masse from the WIHL shortly after Armstrong won his first NCAA title in 1958. Ironically, they were soon joined by North Dakota and, oddly enough, Colorado College, the biggest offender. The ruckus grew loud enough to attract the attention of both *Sports Illustrated* and *Fortune* magazine, which normally didn't cover college hockey too closely.

Michigan had some additional problems with the league. In early 1956 the WIHL had declared Michigan's Mike Buchanan and Wally Maxwell ineligible for one year because a minor league team had paid their expenses during a brief tryout while they were still in high school. The league reinstated them for the second half of the 1956–57 season, but just before the team departed for the Final Four in Colorado Springs, the NCAA declared them ineligible for more serious offenses. It turns out Buchanan played one game for the Chicago Blackhawks in 1952 and Maxwell two games for the Toronto Maple Leafs in 1953— but why the league discovered this just days before the Final Four is unclear.

Michigan's coaches and players were outraged, but their beef was with the NCAA, not the WIHL—until they learned that the head of the NCAA Eligibility Committee was a representative of Colorado College. The timing of his decision, just days before the Final Four, seemed odd at best. To add insult to injury, CC swamped the Wolverines in the final that year, 13-7. The dustup provided additional incentive for Michigan to leave the league, and for the NCAA to move the tournament to another site so no single school could oversee it each year.

Although some of the animus against Denver and the older Canadian players can probably be attributed to sour grapes, some of the other teams' concerns over Armstrong's practices seem justified. One of Armstrong's Final Four appearances was later revoked due to NCAA, not WCHA, violations; and his last year behind the bench, 1976–77, ended with the NCAA imposing a one-year probation on the program for a variety of serious offenses. Thus, even taking into account the often unearned resentment of other coaches, it's probably fair to say Armstrong's competitive spirit sometimes got the best of him.

In any case, the damage to the WIHL was done. With no league to play in for the first time in almost a decade, all seven former WIHL teams had to face the difficulties common to all independent schools, including scheduling, maintaining fan interest without league standings, and attracting the attention of the NCAA tournament selection committee, whose picks necessarily became more subjective.

The demise of the WIHL raised the possibility of a Big Ten hockey league. Fielding Yost himself first posited the notion at the annual Big Ten meeting in 1937, two years after Wisconsin had dropped its "informal varsity" team and a year before the Illini started theirs, but the motion didn't get very far. By 1957, Illinois hadn't had a varsity program since 1943, but the Illini and the Ohio State Buckeyes both fielded competitive club teams. Michigan State had jumped into the Big Ten with both feet—and a varsity hockey team, too. But the motion failed again because the club schools had no intention of going varsity. It would not be the last time, however, that the specter of a Big Ten hockey league would surface.

After muddling through the 1958–59 season, all seven former WIHL teams came to their senses and agreed to form a looser association, called the WCHA, which kept standings and crowned a champion but allowed teams to schedule whichever league teams they wished. And that's how Minnesota was able to boycott Denver for more than a decade of regular-season play.

While the hockey powers waged their epic battle on the big stage, far simpler negotiations were taking place in the malt shops of Regina. About the same time Mariucci and company had become aware of Armstrong's transgressions, a high school student named Gordon "Red" Berenson had become aware of women—and one in particular.

"We used to go to a high school hangout, the Dutch Mill, for french fries, Cokes, and hamburgers," the former Joy Cameron remembers, describing a scene that could have been lifted right out of *Happy Days* or *Back to the Future*. "He was with a boy I knew, and they both had motorcycles. They asked me and a friend to go for a ride."

"I remember exactly what I was thinking," Berenson confesses. "There was something about her that caught my eye then—and still does. She didn't see herself the way I do—

and still doesn't. I wanted to say, 'You're comin' with me,' but I couldn't muster the nerve."

Instead, Joy recalls, her friend hopped on one bike, "then Red turned back to me and says, 'You gettin' on?' I got on. My mom said, 'I knew there would be trouble the minute I saw the motorcycle pull up.' I suppose she was right."

"I'd never had a girlfriend," Berenson says, "but I knew the second I saw her, I was going to marry her." Although he was young, Berenson was smart enough to recognize a good thing when he saw it.

He was also smart enough to realize the job market offered by the six-team NHL wasn't anything you could count on, especially in an industry where a broken ankle could force a guy to retire at age 20 without any compensation, pension, or prospects for other work. Until the World Hockey Association created a bidding war for players in the 1970s, pro hockey contracts were the worst among the four major sports. Once you signed a contract as an 18 year old, you were the property of that team for life. Even as late as the 1960s, an average player could expect to make about $10,000 to $15,000—about the same as a school principal or a small-town police chief, only with more danger and less job security.

When most ex-Pats started considering colleges, naturally the first place they looked was Denver. By 1958 the Pioneers had their old coach, many of their former teammates, a WIHL title, and an NCAA crown. But Berenson was less concerned about peer pressure than he was about the quality of education Denver offered. "Some of the guys playing for Armstrong weren't very academic, and they were telling us the classes were fine," Berenson recalls. "So I wondered."

The staunchly independent Berenson decided to conduct a thorough investigation of U.S. colleges. In the spring of twelfth grade, he and his hockey buddies trotted down to the only library in town to search for the school that had the best combination of academics and hockey. Drawing on the same conviction he used to pick his future wife, Berenson knew the college for him when he saw it.

"It was pretty clear Michigan stood at the top," he says.

Berenson and his buddies wrote letters to a handful of schools, which resulted in Berenson visiting North Dakota in 1958 as the pilot fish for his friends. Berenson was favorably impressed by North Dakota and the caliber of players the former coach, a man named Al Renfrew, had lured to Grand Forks before Renfrew returned to Michigan the year before. But soon after Berenson's visit to North Dakota, Dale MacDonald, a Saskatoon native playing for Renfrew at Michigan, told his coach that Berenson was the rare player worth going out of his way to get.

"Al called me and said, 'North Dakota's great, but you gotta come see Michigan,'" Berenson remembers. Renfrew scraped together enough money to fly the young phenom to Michigan, thereby making Berenson the first hockey player ever to receive a free recruiting trip to Ann Arbor. It also marked Berenson's first trip on an airplane.

The extra effort was worth it, for both parties. "Once he was on campus," Renfrew says, "we didn't have to sell him on it."

"After I came down on a visit," Berenson confirms, "I came back and told the other guys, 'This is where we're going.'" And just like that, a pipeline of hockey talent was created between Regina and Ann Arbor.

If you spend over two years conducting research for a history book, you quickly learn any story with two sources will have two different versions—and sometimes more. People's memories of the same event rarely jibe completely. So it's amazing how consistently one phrase pops up throughout the testimony of the ex-Pats who migrated to Michigan. They all remember their decision to come to Michigan the same way, and even use the exact same words: "Red told us, 'Michigan's the place to be,'" they say, and that was it. The players didn't need to know anything else. "I just came here because Red told me to come here," Dave Butts says.

"Most of us were going to Denver," Alex Hood explains, "until Red got on the phone and said, 'This is the place to be.' So five or six of us came down, and that was it. But don't overlook the fact that we already knew this was a great school."

"A lot of us were considering Denver and Colorado College," Wayne Kartusch remembers, "but everything we heard said, Michigan's the place to be. The whole hockey program, the academics—it all just sounded a lot better."

It has to be said, however, that some of the ex-Pats based their decisions on less sublime criteria. "I looked in a book at the Saskatoon library," Joe Lunghammer admits. "It said Ann Arbor's 38 miles from Detroit. I'd never heard of the University of Michigan, but I'd heard of Gordie Howe, and I figured, if it's that close, we can go see him play. And that's how I picked it."

In the same way Pep Reynolds convinced the Upper Peninsula stars to become Wolverines, and Wally Grant led a group of high school state champs from Eveleth to Ann Arbor, Red Berenson singlehandedly delivered a rich lode of ex-Pats to Michigan. Without tapping into those three far-flung sources of talent, the Michigan hockey team would never have achieved half of what it has over the past eight decades.

From 1958 to 1964, some 14 players made the trek from Saskatchewan to Ann Arbor, and the process was always the same: Berenson would tell them to come down; they'd drive 28 hours in one stretch in an old car with no radio, no air conditioning, and no cruise control; they would go through Chicago instead of the U.P., even though it took a couple hours longer, just to avoid the $3.75 toll at the Mackinac Bridge ("None of us had any money," Lunghammer explains, with a smile and a shrug); they would sleep on cots on the second floor of the golf course clubhouse; they would meet Coach Renfrew, see the rink, take the SAT, and go home, secure in the knowledge that Berenson was right: Michigan was the place to be.

And for the ex-Pats, it was. Most of them were realistic enough to know they didn't have much chance of breaking into the six-team NHL, and they felt lucky to get a free college education just for playing hockey. The vast majority of Michigan's ex-Pats were the first members of their families to go to college.

"We all pretty much came from nothing," Lunghammer says. "We led simple lives. For us, it was big money when *Playboy* did a thing on campus fashions and paid us $50 to model clothes.

Berenson as player
On his first shift Red Berenson went end to end to score and bagged a record
43 in his senior year but lost in the 1962 NCAA semifinals. "At the time it
doesn't seem so important," he says, "but 20 years later, you ask yourself: 'Why
the hell didn't we do that?'"
(Courtesy of the U-M Athletic Department.)

They had me holding a flute. Man, I didn't even know which end of the damn thing was up. But that was a nice break. Without Michigan, I might have been a bricklayer."

"My dad ran a meat market in Regina," says Gordon Wilkie. "He simply couldn't afford to send me here. Michigan hockey *was* my chance at an education. I spent a lot of Saturday nights in the library." But it paid off when Wilkie earned a 3.5 grade-point average from the business school, plus an award for being the top student-athlete on campus. "I owe Red and Coach Renfrew for the opportunity to be a part of this great tradition."

Berenson's decision, at least, came with a price. Frank Selke, the Montreal GM who had drafted Berenson, warned him, "If you go to an American college, you'll never become a pro."

Fully aware he might be sacrificing the dream of every Canadian boy to play in the NHL—and for the Montreal Canadiens, no less—Berenson didn't flinch. After sitting out his freshman year, which the NCAA required of all freshmen at the time, and playing one semester for the Canadian national team, Berenson suited up for his first game on February 5, 1960, against Minnesota.

"Ninety seconds into his first game he takes it all the way down the ice and scores," Renfrew says. "Mariucci turns to me and yells, 'Man, at this rate we're going to lose, 60-0!'" Berenson assisted on another goal five minutes later and scored a third later in the game. Everyone in the building that night had just seen the future of Michigan hockey, and it looked bright indeed.

Berenson finished his abbreviated sophomore season with 11 goals and six assists in 16 games, but what people remember is *how* he did it. Rudy Reichert, who has attended a game in every season since he graduated in 1943, recalls Berenson's playing days well. "When he first got here he couldn't get the puck from his teammates, because he was going too fast," Reichert says. "They were always passing behind him. And when he'd get the puck, he'd go off and leave 'em. They couldn't keep up. I tell ya, he was in the wrong league."

"Some guys say there are naturals," Renfrew says. "But from what I've seen, the 'naturals' are the guys who work the hardest. Red was a special player in a lot of ways, but the biggest thing about Red is he always worked hard to get better."

Back to the Brink

Until the late sixties all college athletes had to sit out two semesters before joining the varsity squad. Because it was not uncommon for hockey players to start college in the winter semester, many played their first game in January of their sophomore year and their last in December of their senior year.

Berenson was one of those late starters. His debut on the varsity in 1960 thrilled the Coliseum crowd, but Michigan still lost 10 of its last 13 games—including a couple drubbings by Armstrong's Denver squad—and failed to make the NCAA playoffs for the third consecutive season.

With Berenson and seven other ex-Pats on board from the start of the 1960–61 season, however, the team improved to 16-10-2 and earned a spot in the WCHA playoffs. Michigan drew Minnesota, a team it had beaten three out of four times during the regular season, but the Gophers knocked them out in the total goal format, 3-1 and 2-2.

Renfrew notched his first winning season and first league playoff berth since taking the job four years earlier, but his Wolverines still lagged well behind Denver, which finished the regular season at 26-1-1, far atop the WCHA. In the NCAA playoffs the Pioneers blew past Minnesota 6-1, and St. Lawrence 12-2, to take their third title in four years. The 1960–61 Pioneers can still make a strong claim for being the greatest college hockey team of all time.

But the Wolverines were full of hope the following fall, and for good reason. The squad's first class of ex-Pats would be seniors, and super sophomores Gordon Wilkie and Wayne Kartusch were eligible to join the varsity. The Berenson-captained squad didn't lose a game through New Year's, and finished the regular season with a Denveresque 20-3 mark. The Wolverines had beaten Denver three out of five games, including their WCHA semifinal match. Although Michigan lost the WCHA final against Michigan Tech, 6-4, the Regina regiment had beaten the Huskies three times in the regular season, so they were not overly worried about the possibility of facing them again in the Final Four.

As expected, the Wolverines received their first NCAA bid under Renfrew that spring, while Denver had to sit the dance out. Michigan was the slight favorite entering the Final Four in Utica, New York, but Wally Grant could have warned them about the Terrier Curse: when the Wolverines are expected to win it, they usually don't.

When the original brain trust schemed up the NCAA tournament, conventional wisdom held that the eastern teams would mop up on their weaker western sisters, but the West had dominated the East for years. Since RPI upset Michigan in 1954, western teams had gone a perfect 12-0 against the eastern squads in the Final Four. In fact, so great was western dominance that in 1961 the NCAA committee put the two western teams in the same bracket as the only way of ensuring an East-West final for the first time in seven years. Denver spoiled the plan that year by embarrassing eastern representative St. Lawrence so badly in the final game, 12-2, that even the eastern boosters voted to go back to the old format. If there had been any doubt before, by 1962 everyone had conceded the West ruled the college hockey world.

In 1962 Michigan would not face Michigan Tech until the finals. The Wolverines assumed, reasonably enough, that the only thing separating them from their seventh NCAA title was Michigan Tech. By their own admission, they gave little thought to their semifinal opponent, Clarkson.

But when the Golden Knights jumped out to a 2-1 lead before the first intermission, and doubled it to 4-2 after two, the Wolverines were forced to think about them plenty. "We had a bad first period," Wayne Kartusch deadpans. "We were looking ahead to Michigan Tech. That was the big thing. Guess we were a little cocky." Michigan climbed back into the game with a couple goals by the Red Baron, closing the gap to 5-4 with 2:45 left.

Renfrew can still recount the last seconds of that game as if it had been played yesterday. "Thirty seconds to go, Berenson passes to Ross Morrison, right in front of the net. Morrison shoots, the puck hits the goalie's skate, then one pipe, then the other pipe, and pops out. You see a shot like that, you know you're not supposed to win. It's just not in the cards. That was all there was to that."

"That was a game we had no business losing and they had no business winning," Berenson says today, with uncharacteristic remorse. "I don't remember much about that game, except what a lousy feeling that was to lose it."

"We were thrown by a hot goalie," Wilkie recalls. "The next night, the same guy couldn't stop a balloon." In the finals the Golden Knights got mauled by the Huskies, 7-1. Michigan beat St. Lawrence, 5-1, in the consolation game, but despite its name, the game was little consolation.

In a life with few regrets, the game against Clarkson ranks near the top for Berenson. "We should've won it," he says flatly. "We were destined to meet Michigan Tech in the finals, but got knocked off by an underdog—Clarkson—back when eastern teams weren't that good. You don't get too many chances to win it all as a player. At the time it doesn't seem so important, but 10 years, 20 years later, you ask yourself: 'Why the hell didn't we do that?'"

Just minutes after scoring his school record-tying 43rd goal against St. Lawrence—a team captained by future MSU head coach Ron Mason—Berenson caught a ride to Boston, where he played for the Canadiens the next night, making him the first player to jump directly from college to the NHL. Montreal GM Frank Selke's warning—that if Berenson went to college he'd never become an NHL player—had proved false.

21

Getting It Right

At first blush it looked as if getting beaten in the NCAA semifinals by an underdog might be a blow from which Michigan could not recover, especially without Berenson. Michigan's media guide published the following fall said of him, almost mournfully, "The big gun was the finest player ever to put on skates for Michigan."

But, as Renfrew had learned from watching the '49 and '50 teams lose the NCAA tournament and seeing the underwhelming '51 team somehow win it, college hockey was not played on paper. "You never know what's going to happen," Renfrew explains. "Here's one: in 1965 Michigan Tech beat us up at their place 10-2. That night the puck was fitting in holes on its edge. The next night we beat 'em, 6-1. You figure, the same teams the same weekend, how does this happen?"

Who knows? But that's hockey—and college hockey especially. The year after Berenson left, the team seemed to be fine without him, winning 5 of its first 7 games, before the Baron-less Wolverines went on an 11-game winless streak. The team finished out of the NCAA playoffs, out of the WCHA playoffs, and under .500 (7-14-3) for the first time since 1958–59, the year before Berenson arrived.

The following team looked like it might be a little better than the last, but only a little. The 1964 squad returned its two leading scorers from the previous season, Gary Butler and Gordon Wilkie, both ex-Pats, who had combined for 79 points in 24 games the previous season. They also had two newcomers, Wilf

Martin and Marty Read, both ex-Pats, who looked promising. But a squad that wound up in the WCHA cellar the previous year would also have to replace captain Larry Babcock's 23 points.

No matter. Where everything went wrong the year before, everything went right in '64. Butler and Wilkie played better than expected, combining for a remarkable 135 points in just 29 games—*both* players finished just shy of Berenson's single-season record of 70 points—while rookie Wilf Martin added an unexpected 58 points. And he wasn't even the team's biggest surprise.

Mel Wakabayashi, all 5'5" of him, joined the varsity in January 1964, centering Rob Coristine and Bob Ferguson on the third line. The trio added 107 points—manna from heaven—which would have made them the top-scoring line the previous season.

Add it all up and you've got the first Michigan team to score more than 200 goals in a season (217), averaging a prolific 7.5 goals per game. In 7 of their 24 victories they lit up their opponents for more than 10 goals. Thanks largely to the unprecedented scoring streak, this unheralded but determined bunch beat every opponent at least once en route to a 24-2-1 record, winning more games than any team in Michigan history.

In one memorable weekend against Ohio State, a glorified club team at the time, Michigan scored 21 goals in the first two periods, including two by goalie Bob Gray, who played out that game. "Rennie's gettin' kind of nervous," Wilkie remembers. "He says, 'Anyone who scores this period is benched.' The backup goalie, Bill Bieber, tried and tried to score anyway, but he couldn't." The game ended at 21-0, still a Michigan record.

It had been a great season, especially in light of the previous year's depressing downturn, but the 1963–64 Wolverines still weren't expected to win either the WCHA or NCAA playoffs. Denver was the odds-on favorite for both titles, and for good reasons: the Pioneers had beaten the U.S. Olympic team, tied the Canadian Olympic team, and built an 8-2-2 record against WCHA opponents.

Michigan, meanwhile, struggled to shake Michigan Tech in

the WCHA semifinals, held in Ann Arbor, winning the first game just 4-3. The two-game total goal series dictated that Michigan merely had to hold on for a tie in the second game. "Tech hit 19 pipes that night," Dave Butts says. "But we knew we *had* to win that series," or Michigan would have been excluded from NCAA playoff consideration. But this resilient bunch held on for a 5-5 tie to earn a date with Denver in the WCHA finals.

Denver showed Michigan who was boss in a 6-2 rout on Michigan's home ice. "It was obvious they had a better team," Wakabayashi admits. If the Wolverines couldn't beat the Pioneers in their own barn, the thinking went, it was a foregone conclusion they couldn't finish the job in Denver, site of the 1964 Final Four.

But if the '64 Wolverines lacked power, they had a few intangibles on their side, not least of which was the corollary to the Terrier Curse: when the Wolverines aren't supposed to win it, they usually do.

"We had 20 guys who fit together as a team," Wilkie says. "Any night any line could take it, not just a few guys. And we had six good defensemen. We got along as well on the ice as off it, and that's big in college hockey. The Regina guys used to joke with the Toronto guys who produced the best players, but we had good harmony, even with the American kids."

At the 1964 Final Four, Denver took care of Rensselaer, 4-1, while Michigan survived a close brush with Providence, 3-2. For the final game 7,000 Pioneer fans packed the Denver arena to watch their team battle for its fourth NCAA title in seven years. They wanted to see their team vanquish the opposition, of course, but also to strike a blow for Coach Armstrong's methods, which had caused the WIHL to disband in 1958.

But Michigan's uncommonly balanced offense chipped out a 3-0 lead early in the game, quieting the hometown crowd. The talented Pioneers closed the gap to 4-3 early in the third period, but the Wolverines continually sacrificed offensive opportunities to back-check and ensure their eighth NCAA title.

"We put it to Denver's goalie pretty good," Wilkie attests. Michigan goalie Bob Gray, Wilkie adds, "was hot and everyone gelled. Winning the NCAA, with 7,000 fans packing their home rink—man, that was the greatest."

"You know, there's something about this team," Wilkie said at the group's thirty-fifth reunion. "You call a meeting, and somehow they all show up. Maybe it's just the winning, but I think it's more than that."

The 1964 NCAA Title Team
The underdog Wolverines beat Denver, 6–3, in the Bulldogs' backyard. It was the last hurrah for the Regina regiment, a group of some 14 players who came to Ann Arbor between 1958 and 1964. "This is the place," Berenson told them, and they followed.
(Courtesy Bentley Historical Library, University of Michigan.)

22

Little Mel

Mel Wakabayashi, Michigan's leading scorer and MVP in 1965 and 1966, is perhaps the most unlikely star in Michigan's long history, and surely one of the most inspirational.

Wakabayashi's story begins during World War II. Shortly after the United States forced over 100,000 Japanese Americans from their homes into squalid internment camps, the Canadian government followed suit. Relocation administrators removed Wakabayashi's Japanese-born parents, Hatsuye and Tokuzo, and their three children from their modest Vancouver home in 1942, taking their few possessions in the process. A year later, Hatsuye gave birth to her fourth child, Mel, in the dusty camp.

The government held the Wakabayashis and the other Japanese Canadians in the camps until the war ended. In spite of the obviously unwarranted cruelty of the move, Wakabayashi's parents rarely talked about it.

"And when they did," Wakabayashi recalls, "they gave it to us as a positive thing, not a negative. They'd say, If we were in Japan, your father would probably have to go to war and we probably wouldn't be able to eat, and we would have no shelter." Wakabayashi inherited his parents' remarkable ability to turn injustice into opportunity without bitterness, a strength he would draw on many times throughout his life.

After the war the Wakabayashi family, now with eight children, moved to Chatham, a small town of 30,000 surrounded by Ontario farmland. To support his family Wakabayashi's father worked long hours in a local cosmetic factory. "It was very loud

and smelly, as I recall it," Mel says. "I didn't go there very often."
Although the Wakabayashis had to contend with a tight budget
and a "few little [racial] incidents, it was a good life," he insists.

When Renfrew first came into contact with the family, he was
immediately struck by the depth of their community spirit. "The
Wakabayashis had eight kids and not a lot of money, I don't
think," he says, "but they had a big New Year's party every year.
Seemed like the whole town of Chatham was there."

Mel and his younger brother Herb spent whatever free time
they had playing baseball, street hockey, and pond hockey with
a black guy down the street named Eddie Wright. The trio eventually formed what their white teammates on the Chatham
Junior Maroons called the "international line." Wilf Martin, who
played for the Regina Pats before coming to Michigan, remembers a diminutive Japanese player from Chatham "making a fool
of our All-Star team in Regina." Word spread.

"Of course I dreamed of playing in the NHL one day," Wakabayashi says, "but knowing my size, I didn't think it would ever
be a reality. I really didn't expect to sign any contracts, or even
go to the U of M."

But other Chatham natives like Larry Babcock, Al Hinnigan,
and Ron Coristine had gone to Michigan and done very well, with
Babcock captaining the 1962–63 team. Wakabayashi suspects
one of them—he's still not sure who—tipped off Renfrew that
there was another player back home he might want to gamble
on.

In the fall of 1963, when Wakabayashi entered Canada's
grade 13 to take "all these courses I didn't want to take," Renfrew came up to see one of his games. Wakabayashi had no idea
the coach was in the stands—or even who he was—but he performed well enough for Renfrew to approach the young center
after the game and initiate a conversation Wakabayashi recalls
well.

"He asked me if I had any interest in going to Michigan. I said,
'I can't afford to go, no way, and if it is difficult to get in, that
could be another problem,'" Wakabayashi recounts, echoing the

response Marquette's Les Hillberg had three decades earlier to a similar question posed by T. Hawley Tapping of the Michigan alumni association. "My grades were only so-so, because I concentrated on sports in high school. Well, he brought me down to Ann Arbor to see the campus and take the SAT, and I did okay."

Wakabayashi with Renfrew
Two of the most popular figures in Michigan hockey history. The 5′5″ Wakabayashi was born in a Japanese internment camp and rose to become an All-American. Renfrew would give you the shirt off his back—even if it wasn't worth much.
(Courtesy Bentley Historical Library, University of Michigan.)

In January 1963 Wakabayashi settled in Ann Arbor as a college student. "It was not a dream come true, because I didn't even let myself dream of it," he says. "It was just unbelievable! Obviously, it changed my whole life."

Due to freshman ineligibility, Wakabayashi could not join the team until January 1964. "The year off was really good for me because I was worried that I couldn't make the team," he says. "But seeing the players from Chatham do so well gave me a little confidence. I was able to work out with the team, and we had a very good team. I was a little surprised to make it, actually. But with the [wide-open] style of college hockey in those days, I could get a lot of breakaways and take advantage of my speed."

"The college game was made for him," asserts former teammate Dean Lucier. "He's the best player I've ever stepped on the ice with, for or against, and that includes Tony Esposito and Keith Magnuson. He had tremendous game sense."

Magnuson himself, who starred for Denver and the Chicago Blackhawks, puts Wakabayashi on the short list of great college players he faced. "We only played him two times, but Wakabayashi you didn't forget," he says. "He was very quick and could find a way to beat you if you didn't have your senses about where he was on the ice. He was the guy you watched."

"Ron Coristine told us about him," Wilkie recalls. "Once I saw him in practice, I knew he could help us. He was just a very astute hockey player—and a gentleman, on and off the ice."

One telling measure of the man is what he remembers, and what he doesn't. Although Wakabayashi scored two goals in the thrilling upset over Denver in the 1964 championship game, he can't recall which ones he scored or how he scored them. He can, however, recount in photographic detail the single penalty he received in his three years of college hockey—one less than the great Hobey Baker himself.

"We were playing Loyola University out of Montreal at the Coliseum during my sophomore year," he says. "Another guy and I got tangled up together; he fell, and I got a tripping call. Since I started playing hockey in pee wees, my coaches really banged it into my head that I was supposed to score the goals, not try to knock the big guys around and end up getting hurt or getting a penalty. I remember very clearly the feeling of sitting in that penalty box—and how much I realized I didn't like sitting in that box!"

While at Michigan, Wakabayashi never again suffered the sensation of sitting in that box, although another man would probably have been sorely tempted to retaliate against the kind of cheap shots the darting center had to put up with weekly. "I know a lot of guys took runs at me," he says philosophically, "but it really helped me in the long run, because it forced me to be aware of everyone on the ice at all times." The same uncanny game sense that helped him avoid oncoming thugs helped him become one of Michigan's craftiest scorers, too. Wakabayashi had obviously inherited his parents' ability to adapt to hostile surroundings, and without bitterness.

Every Michigan man who skated with Wakabayashi remembers one story above all others. In February 1965, 11 months after Michigan won its seventh NCAA title and 1 month before Michigan State would win its first, the Spartans came to the Coliseum for a regular-season game—although there is nothing "regular" about a Michigan–Michigan State game, then or now. Things had gotten a lot hotter between the two schools after the Big Ten (then the Big Nine) voted to admit Michigan State College to the conference in 1949, over Fritz Crisler's vehement objections. The Spartans have never forgotten the slight. MSU won national football titles in 1952 and 1965 and relished every victory over their big brothers in every sport—including, of course, ice hockey.

"Even in the 1960s Michigan State was already our biggest rival," Dave Butts says. "At home the place would be packed, and we'd get the football players to sit behind their goalie and ride him all night long. Man, it was war. Absolute, freakin' war. Those games were just blood and guts hockey."

In one UM-MSU game, Michigan's Bill Lord took advantage of the Coliseum's glassless and fenceless side boards by knocking a Spartan clear out of the rink, head over heels. The Michigan students, surprisingly, helped him back on the ice—but they kept their feet on his stick.

Just like real wars, though, these intrastate battles still had rules, some written, some not. Among the unwritten codes of conduct: "You weren't supposed to touch Mel, plain and simple," Butts says. "But this guy McAndrew gets him good."

"Brian McAndrew ran me into the boards quite hard," Wakabayashi calmly recalls. "It wasn't the worst injury of my career, but it hurt the most. I was on my back, and my stick was in the air. Back then we didn't have any glass or fence on the side boards, so one of our fans—Dale Richards, who was using my season tickets for that game—grabbed my stick and clubbed McAndrew over the head with it."

Richards ran out of the building and turned himself into the Ann Arbor police the next day. Crisler barred him from returning to the Coliseum, but no Ann Arbor jury was going to convict him for that crime. He walked.

Wakabayashi remembers, "Hockey was not as popular as football and basketball, but it got good coverage." "But most students didn't know us individually. For me it was great, because I didn't like being recognized. I liked being low key, behind the scenes. Besides, whenever I tried to tell someone I was a hockey player, they wouldn't believe me anyway."

Wakabayashi avoided the spotlight as readily as he savored the camaraderie of his teammates, with whom he lived all four years of college, and took advantage of the extra academic assistance afforded him as an athlete. "I was never a good student," he says. "I needed a lot of help, in psychology, physiology. You needed a 2.0 to be eligible, so I tried to keep up. A lot of people were willing to help you out."

Renfrew's teams never equaled the success they enjoyed during Wakabayashi's sophomore season, when they won the NCAA title. But that didn't stop the tiny center from becoming the team's leading scorer and MVP as a junior and, as a senior, the team captain, the WCHA's leading scorer, the league's MVP, and an All-American. The little kid from Chatham, who didn't dare dream of playing for Michigan, had proven beyond any doubt that he not only belonged, he was one of the very best.

Trying to prove himself outside Ann Arbor proved tougher. In the spring Wakabayashi played baseball for fun, and was good enough to be named to the All–Big Ten team as a second baseman. At former coach Don Lund's urging, the Tigers invited him down to Lakeland for spring training but didn't sign him. Whether Wakabayashi's size or his race was a factor is impossible to know now, but if they were, the scouts missed out.

Wakabayashi characteristically didn't give it a second thought and signed with the Red Wings instead. The NHL still only had six teams in 1967, so Wakabayashi found work in the spring of 1967 with the Memphis Red Wings in the Central Hockey League and, later, with the Johnstown Jets in the Eastern Hockey League. In both cities he demonstrated once again that, despite his size, he could play with the big boys, so they invited him to join the Detroit Red Wings camp in the fall of 1967.

About the same time, Wakabayashi received an intriguing offer from the Japan Hockey League, then in its second year, to become the first foreigner to play there. When he accepted, Wakabayashi once again became the outsider, trying to show that he belonged.

"I spoke no Japanese," he says. "It was not as easy to adapt then as it is now for the foreign players. It was especially tough for me, because I had a Japanese face but not a Japanese mouth. And I didn't have an interpreter, either, so I had to learn fast."

He also had to learn how to handle the new culture, including playing away games on an outdoor rink in Furukawa, where the natives would throw their sake bottles at the players if they were happy—or unhappy. But that was nothing compared to the culture shock Wakabayashi encountered on the ice. In North America, you want to advance the best players and bring the other players up to that level. "When you're brought up in Japan, you're taught not to stick out," he says. "The coaches pound the best players down to the level of the ordinary guys."

One of the most important pillars of Japanese civilization is the relationship between older mentors and their younger protégés, called "sempai-kohai," with the "kohai" always deferring to his "sempai." The protocol governs all work relationships, including those on the rink.

"On a hockey team," Wakabayashi explains, "sempai-kohai means the younger players have to go in the corner and get the puck. In my first year over there, when I passed the puck, very seldom would it come back to me. There are advantages to the sempai-kohai system, but I don't know if the Japanese approach is always good for sport."

Regardless, Wakabayashi was good for Japan. He played 12 years in the six-team Japan Hockey League, mostly for a team called the Kokudo Bunnies, whose logo is so pathetically cute that any 5-year-old boy with an ounce of testosterone would be embarrassed to have it displayed on his Carter pajamas. Killer rabbits, they're not.

They are, however, owned by Yoshiaki Tsutsumi, whom *Forbes* magazine once calculated was the richest man in the world. Tsutsumi owns the Seibu department store chain, the Seibu railroads, hundreds of supermarkets, and thousands of real estate ventures, making him the largest landowner in Japan. He also owns 39 ski resorts, 37 golf courses, and all 82 Prince Hotels, whose excruciatingly consistent quality no American chain can approach. Tsutsumi wields so much weight, the emperor has to make appointments to see *him.*

Tsutsumi also owns Japan's best baseball team and its two best hockey teams. These days he only watches 3 baseball games each season, while attending 30 hockey games a year. On a beautiful fall day in 1982, even as Tsutsumi's revamped Seibu Lions were winning the first of their 11 Japan Series titles, Tsutsumi instead watched his beloved Bunnies play an *exhibition* game.

"Baseball games are decided more in terms of individual skills, not like hockey," he said in a rare interview. "Hockey has more speed, and it depends more on teamwork and passing. I love watching five men working toward one goal."

Wakabayashi's playing style fit in beautifully with the Japanese ideal—he was always among the league leaders in scoring while playing for seven consecutive seasons without taking a single penalty—and his advanced skills forced the other players to improve. He was named the Bunnies' player–assistant coach in 1972, player–head coach in 1978, and head coach of the Japanese Olympic team in 1980. His younger brother Herb, who had been a two-time All-American at Boston University before joining Mel in Japan, was selected by his peers to carry Japan's flag into the opening ceremonies in Lake Placid. "Walking into the Olympic Stadium in Lake Placid, with my parents in the stands," Wakabayashi says, "*that* was my biggest thrill."

Four years later, in 1984, Berenson—in his first season behind the Michigan bench—invited Wakabayashi to bring his Japanese national team to play in Ann Arbor. Although Wakabayashi's team lost 6-4, they had played well and gained a measure of respect. Afterward many of Wakabayashi's younger players discovered the big black-and-white photo of Wakabayashi in his prime in the Deker Hall of Fame and had their pictures taken next to it. Remembering this, Wakabayashi's voice becomes soft. "That surprised me," he says, obviously touched by the gesture.

When he reflects on the serpentine course of his life, which started in a decrepit internment camp and wound through Chatham, Tokyo, and Lake Placid before turning to Toronto in 1994, where he now works as president of Seibu Canada directly under the most powerful man in Japan, Wakabayashi's thoughts return to his days in Ann Arbor and a bunch of guys who were neither rich nor famous but changed his life forever.

"If not for Al Renfrew and the Michigan hockey team, I would probably be working with my dad in the factory in Chatham," he says. "I don't even want to think about that one."

Renfrew Retires

As the University of Michigan's campus heated up throughout the sixties, athletics cooled. By the end of the decade the athletic complex was crumbling; the financial books were bleeding; and the football, basketball, and hockey teams were once again mired in mediocrity. Michigan's athletic problems started at the top.

When Crisler stepped down in July 1968, the athletic department was $250,000 in debt, the football stadium frequently had 40,000 empty seats, and every facility seemed to be falling apart. "Crisler started losing his grip in the last five years," says his successor, Don Canham. "He had cancer—although people didn't know it—and he just wasn't Fritz Crisler."

The man picked to rescue Michigan from the doldrums was Don Canham, hardly a household name at the time. "I was not a popular choice to succeed Crisler," Canham confesses in his refreshingly candid autobiography, *From the Inside.* "I think the average Michigan alumnus was saying something to the effect of, 'Who the hell is this track coach to take Fritz Crisler's place?'"

Canham's doubters grossly underestimated the man. As Michigan's track coach, he took a temporarily moribund program and returned it to the top of the Big Ten, winning 11 conference titles; he turned the NCAA indoor track meet into a nationally televised moneymaker; he wrote a large feature story for *Sports Illustrated* on the eve of the 1956 Olympics, boldly predicting a sweeping Soviet triumph when few others saw it coming; and unlike Crisler, Canham was a superb businessman. He started his own instructional video company, School-Tech, and turned it into a multimillion-dollar conglomerate—all on the side, the same way Yost did it.

Canham's first act as athletic director did not involve football coaching, stadium seating, or direct marketing. No, the first thing he did was paint the block "M" on the south side of Yost Field House, on what is now the Zamboni door. "I did it just to change things, and it's still there," he says, pleasantly surprised that his successors have seen fit to repaint it every few years. Canham then knocked down the crumbling stands at Ferry Field and put up new scoreboards for the football stadium.

But Canham knew that mere window dressing wasn't going to save the ship. If he didn't fill those football seats, and fast, he wouldn't be able to afford any other improvements, no matter how urgently they were needed. Under Canham, Michigan became the first college program to produce and mail color brochures to potential customers, to market souvenirs, and to promote tailgating, a practice Canham is credited with popularizing. He was also one of the first men to recognize that wives, not their husbands, determine the family's weekend plans, so he made his pitch to them. Canham's marketing methods drew gasps in stuffier academic circles, but they worked. In just 18 months, Canham erased the Michigan athletic department's $250,000 deficit.

"In some ways I was lucky I stepped into a tremendous void," Canham says, "so I could do a lot right away."

That void included lots of vacant coaching positions. Canham's first two hires were basketball coach Johnny Orr and football coach Bo Schembechler, who shared the lion's share of the pressure to turn two feckless programs around and get the athletic department back on its feet. After both coaches were well on their way to accomplishing their missions by the early seventies, Canham turned his attention to the hockey program. It's hard to imagine he liked what he saw.

For starters, the old barn called the Coliseum, which wasn't designed for hockey in the first place, was 60 years old. "That was the coldest, meanest, dirtiest place that anyone could conceive," recalls Kip Taylor, 92, who grew up skating at the rink and later ran the building from 1964 to 1973. "It could get to six degrees below zero *inside*, colder than a stepmother's hug. Everyone in there was stomping their feet, trying to stay warm."

Canham agreed. "The arena was horrible," he says today. "It had a sand floor, so the pipes and everything down there froze when it got cold. In my second year as AD the old rink flooded, so I was going to build another rink. But former Brooklyn Dodger and U-M baseball coach Don Lund said, 'You should build a rink at Yost.' When we sat down to think about it, we concluded we had two options: build a brand new rink where the track and tennis building is now and build an indoor track where Revelli Hall is today, or renovate Yost. I was worried about sight lines, but I'd seen the plans to renovate Yost and it looked good."

Canham converted the former Field House into an ice rink in the summer of 1973 for a paltry $400,000, and encouraged the WCHA to become a more formal organization by playing an orthodox round-robin format. But he knew the program needed more to improve.

Since returning to the top of the college hockey heap in 1964, Renfrew's boys had placed no higher than fourth place in the WCHA, hadn't returned to the NCAA playoffs, and they hadn't had a winning record in four seasons. They finished the 1972–73 campaign with a demoralizing 6-27-1 record (including a forfeit), the worst season since World War II.

There were many reasons for the program's demise. So much had changed on and off the ice between 1958, Renfrew's first season coaching the Wolverines, and 1973 that it would be impossible to catalog it all here. In that span goalies traded in their comically long wool hats for sophisticated protective masks; players started using curved, fiberglass sticks to shoot slap shots, both innovations; the sweaters that had been *sweaters* for four decades were replaced with nylon then mesh; the old Coliseum's cyclone-fenced end zones were replaced by Yost's full-circle, space-age Plexiglas; freshmen became eligible; the World Hockey Association opened for business; the NHL doubled then tripled in size; and the entry draft opened.

The competition for top talent ended the quaint days when future All-Americans would hop on trains to come to Michigan sight unseen, or decide "Michigan's the place" while doing research in a local library. Between 1966 and 1971, Minnesota-Duluth, Wisconsin, and Notre Dame joined the WCHA, while smaller schools started their own programs, including virtually all of the other current CCHA members. Where Heyliger had been able to recruit 26 All-Americans in 13 years, Renfrew had recruited just 6 over 16 seasons.

Renfrew not only had to compete against the growing number of college coaches for the available talent, he had to do battle against the pros, too, because the NHL had expanded from 6 to 18 teams from 1967 to 1974, thus tripling the number of players they needed to fill their rosters and their minor league systems. The introduction of the draft in 1969 gave the top junior players even more incentive to eschew college teams for the pros.

WCHA schools, which had won 18 of the first 20 NCAA titles, also saw their dominance diluted. Under the tutelage of Ned Harkness, Cornell claimed the NCAA crown in 1967 behind the goaltending of a man named Ken Dryden, then completed the NCAA's only perfect season in 1970. Boston University followed up with its own titles in 1971 and 1972.

This brave new era required aggressive, year-round recruiting, which didn't match the style of the old-school coaches. Between 1966 and 1979, venerable coaches like Mariucci, Armstrong, and Bessone were replaced by a new breed, led by Wisconsin's Bob Johnson, Minnesota's Herb Brooks—who went on to lead the United States to the 1980 Miracle on Ice in Lake Placid—and Michigan State's Ron Mason. The young Turks were so good and so original they not only returned the West to the top of college hockey and changed the college game, they transformed hockey the world over by combining the best of North American hockey with the best of the innovative European teams. It was a costly time for Michigan to fall behind. Proof positive that the times were a-changin' was the success of Johnson's Badgers, who, less than a decade after resurrecting a dead program, won the NCAA crown in 1973.

In such an environment, Michigan's rundown rink was a tremendous liability in recruitment, and Renfrew's relaxed approach—which had worked so well with the more self-disciplined generation Renfrew coached in his first decade—was no longer enough to keep the new wave of players focused on team goals. Renfrew treated his players like adults, and so long as there weren't any major problems, he let them go about their business. That laissez-faire style worked better with Berenson's bunch than with the seventies set.

Almost everything that had been taken for granted when Berenson graduated in 1962 was openly questioned in the decade that followed. The assassinations of President John F. Kennedy, Martin Luther King, Jr., and Robert F. Kennedy cost the country three of its greatest leaders, while Viet Nam and the growing specter of Watergate cost the country much of its citizens' faith in government.

During the same span, Michigan's campus was in the midst of another building boom in which it erected the graduate library addition, the physics building, and North Campus. The annual Hash Bash was complemented by student sit-ins and strikes, which prompted the fearful architects of Michigan's new administration building to design a riot-proof structure.

Sports do not exist in a vacuum. Athletics were dramatically altered by the changes sweeping the nation. The flagship leagues in football, basketball, and hockey all faced competition from the WFL, the ABA, and the WHA, respectively; free agency changed the sports forever; and the understated Johnny Unitas handed over the mantle of the most popular football player to the brash Joe Namath. That style shift was mirrored in the Michigan hockey team's hairstyles, from Berenson's tight brush cut to the unruly mane of every would-be Paul McCartney on the squad a decade later.

You could make the argument that the sixties, as we know them, did not start on January 1, 1960, but on November 22, 1963, with the faith-shattering shots in Dallas. The 1964 NCAA championship team, therefore, had much more in common with

Heyliger's teams than it did with Renfrew's just a few years later. It was a different crowd, inspired by different things.

By his own admission, Renfrew wasn't a strict taskmaster on the ice or an aggressive salesman off it, and the new era required coaches to be both. To his credit, Renfrew recognized the changing landscape of the game and called Canham for a meeting in the spring of 1973.

"I went in and talked to Canham," Renfrew recalls, "and told him the way the recruiting was at that time, it was not to my liking. We didn't have any full-time assistants, so I was always leaving practice and going somewhere to see a game and not coming home until two in the morning. It gets old after a while. I kind of got sick of it.

"And other schools were telling kids things like, 'You gotta make a decision before you leave the campus.' That's what turned me off. I didn't want to be involved in that anymore. But I really enjoyed the kids; they were great. I knew I was going to miss them."

The easygoing Mister Roberts did not leave with his head down, however, having gained the respect and admiration of hundreds of players and colleagues during his 15 seasons as Michigan's coach.

"Renfrew couldn't tell a lie if his life depended on it," Canham says. "He wasn't phony at all. Just not interested in impressing people. He's one of the people I've respected the most over the years. He probably wasn't tough enough, but the players loved him. And Al went on to become a sensational ticket manager."

Thus, in the spring of 1973, Michigan went looking for its fifth coach in 50 years.

Part VI

The Rise and Fall
1973–84

24

A Different Kind of Coach

One of Don Canham's greatest skills, though arguably his most overlooked, was his ability to recognize, recruit, and develop young coaching talent. That ability came in handy when he had to replace the coach for every varsity sport, plus all the inaugural women's coaches, during his two decades at the helm. Among dozens of savvy hires were Bo Schembechler, Johnny Orr, tennis coach Brian Eisner, and swimming coach Jon Urbanchek.

Canham was not afraid to take a chance on a young, relatively inexperienced outsider, even for important posts. In 1973 Dan Farrell was just 35 years old, with only 5 years experience as an assistant coach to Michigan Tech's John MacInnes, but Canham didn't hesitate to call him about the Michigan vacancy.

Renfrew and Farrell are both honest, decent men, but put a whistle around their necks and Farrell was virtually Renfrew's antimatter. Where Renfrew was relaxed and content, Farrell was intense and driven. Renfrew relied on instincts, Farrell on intellect. Renfrew had spent his entire adult life playing or coaching hockey, while Farrell had spent three years teaching math and science in a Thunder Bay high school and three more in Africa, but only five years coaching hockey. And coaching pursued Farrell, not the other way around.

Farrell may not have been a Michigan man, a team scoring leader, or a former captain, as both Heyliger and Renfrew had been, but he was brainy, hardworking, and innovative—three qualities Michigan would surely need if it was going to return to the top of the league standings. It helped that Farrell knew what it was like to march to a different drummer, an essential ingredient for anyone guiding Michigan athletes in the 1970s.

In just one decade, Ann Arbor had changed from a surprisingly conservative city to a largely liberal one. In spite of its reputation as a bastion of left-wing politics, Ann Arbor voted for FDR's opponents in all four elections and did not vote for a Democratic presidential candidate until 1964. (No, Ann Arbor did not vote for JFK.) The change occurred after President Johnson introduced his "Great Society" antipoverty program during his 1964 commencement address in Michigan Stadium, just months before his election.

Ann Arbor would never be the same. When it came to sixties' student protests, sit-ins and strikes, Ann Arbor was in an exclusive league with Berkeley and Columbia. Michigan alum Lawrence Kasden defined an entire generation when he wrote and directed his famous film *The Big Chill*—a movie in which the adventurous, idealistic Farrell himself could have played a part.

Dan Farrell was born and raised in Barrie, Ontario, the only son of Red Farrell, one of the top amateur hockey players in Canada. Dan attended St. Mike's prep school, a hockey hotbed that has sent over a dozen players to Michigan, from Bob Watt in 1956 to David Harlock in 1989, and a dozen more to Michigan Tech.

As a player, Farrell's one sterling attribute was his superb skating ability. "At my size," he jokes, "I couldn't play any other way."

Great skater or no, college coaches didn't recruit very aggressively in the 1950s, least of all small, light players. Because some of Farrell's classmates had succeeded at Michigan Tech, including the Huskies' two-time captain Pete Buchman, Farrell thought he might be able to play at that level. He wrote letters to several Division I schools, hoping for a nibble. No college coaches had ever seen him play, but apparently one of his high school buddies told Al Renfrew, who was coaching at Michigan Tech at the time, "that at least I could put on my skates," Farrell jokes.

That recommendation was enough to get a response from an eccentric Michigan Tech mineralogy professor–cum–hockey recruiter named Kiril Spiroff. Dubbed "The Mad Russian," Spiroff was famous for hosting parties for Renfrew and company after Saturday night games in Houghton. "Christ, he was a character," Farrell says. "But he was a very, very good teacher and the guy you dealt with if [the coaches] were interested in you. He was a legend."

The summer before Farrell arrived on campus, however, Renfrew left Houghton to coach at North Dakota. John MacInnes, Michigan's former All-American goalie and Renfrew's best friend from high school days, took his place at Tech that fall.

To get to Houghton from Toronto, Farrell had to take a train that stopped in Chicago. "I was too nervous to explore," he admits, "so I just hung out in the train station all day." The scenery was dramatically different when he reached the U.P. "When the train passed a little town called Champion, about the only thing I saw was Derry's Bar, a little dive standing there by itself. Looked like the end of the world. And I had to ask myself, 'What the hell have I gotten myself into?'"

The relationship between Farrell and Michigan Tech may have started on a blind date, but it would grow into a very happy marriage for both parties. Farrell's timing was good, too. He joined the Huskies in 1956–57, the same year John MacInnes took over the once-proud program that had managed only two winning seasons (one each by Amo Bessone and Al Renfrew) since being resurrected in 1945. MacInnes took those pieces and turned them into a dynasty.

During MacInnes's 26-year reign, the Huskies posted 23 winning seasons (555 wins against 295 losses), seven WCHA titles, and three NCAA titles. MacInnes won the WCHA Coach of the Year trophy six times and the Spencer Penrose NCAA Coach of the Year crown twice. Ninety-four percent of his players earned college degrees, which is especially impressive at a school that doesn't have any easy majors.

Although MacInnes had never coached anywhere else, he made an immediate impact with his personable recruiting style, his hands-on teaching, and his uncommon ability to find the individual buttons that motivated each player. By 1959–60,

MacInnes's fourth year in Houghton and Farrell's last, the Huskies made it to the NCAA finals.

Farrell might have been the smallest guy on the team, but his wheels afforded him plenty of ice time killing penalties and filling in where needed. In Farrell's senior year MacInnes put him on a line with Jerry Sullivan, one of the 18 All-Americans MacInnes coached from 1959 to 1967, who scored 142 points in his three years at Tech. That season Sullivan's wingman, the little number seven from St. Mike's, scored more points than he had in his previous three years combined, and finished his career with 30. In the 1960 NCAA finals the Huskies faced Denver. Although they had beaten the Pioneers three out of four times during the season, they lost the title game, 5-3. (Two years later, during Berenson's senior year at Michigan, Michigan Tech's Lou Angotti and his teammates would finish the job by winning MacInnes's first WCHA and NCAA titles.)

When Farrell graduated from Michigan Tech in 1960 with a degree in geology, he figured that was the last he would see of serious hockey. He taught math and science at Thunder Bay high school for three years, then signed up for a three-year hitch with the Canadian International Development Agency (CIDA) to teach in Africa.

"It just seemed like a neat thing to do," he says. "My wife and I were very adventurous—some people would say unstable—and we just felt it was a great opportunity to see the world." The Farrells worked in Ghana and the eastern highlands of Rhodesia, which Farrell remembers as "one of the most beautiful places on earth, I have to tell ya, a Shangri-la."

But apartheid was alive and well at the time, and Shangri-la was threatened by civil war. Black people were not allowed to live in the cities, and they were getting impatient with the glacial pace of progress. Farrell felt the undercurrent of revolution in the beer halls at night, occasionally drowned out by the white-run government's jet fighters buzzing the black townships to intimidate the residents.

In the summer of 1967, after the Farrells' second year in Africa, Dan, Jolayne, and their two boys spent the summer in

Europe to avoid the heat, the malaria, and the growing political tensions. John MacInnes somehow tracked Farrell down in London and offered him the recently opened assistant coaching job. Farrell informed his old mentor that he still had a year left on his teaching contract but said if the position was still open in a year, he'd love to come back. Taking Farrell at his word, MacInnes arranged to let a graduate assistant keep the position warm for a season until Farrell returned the following year.

"I loved teaching in Africa," Farrell says, "but three years was enough." Right before the uprising that successfully toppled the white-run government in Rhodesia and changed the country's name to Zimbabwe, the Farrells returned to Houghton in 1968. "I had a tough time integrating back into our society," Farrell admits. "I couldn't go into department stores because the crowds freaked me out. I couldn't ride in an elevator for I don't know how long. And I hadn't seen snow for three years."

The Farrell family saw plenty of it back in Houghton. As MacInnes's new right-hand man, Farrell earned his keep by recruiting and coaching some of the best college players in the nation, while learning from a master coach up close.

"John stressed fundamentals," Farrell says. "Tech played the game pretty simply over all those years, in a very disciplined manner. But his success was also due to the fact that he changed as the times changed. Some old coaches can't change, but he could. When the students went on strike around the country after the Kent State shootings, the administration called in MacInnes to get the kids back. He spent one night talking to them. He was a very compassionate man, but tough when he had to be. He treated the players like adults. He gave 'em enough leeway that they could enjoy life, but step over that line, and he'd come down on them pretty hard. One night when two future NHL defensemen stole a couple pillows from a Lake Superior State hotel room, MacInnes called them in and told 'em you're going to send them back, and sit out Friday night."

During Farrell's five years as Tech's assistant, the Huskies finished first in the league twice and in second twice, and made it to the NCAA Final Four twice. Farrell also helped MacInnes win the NCAA's Spencer Penrose Coach of the Year Award in 1970 and the WCHA's trophy for best coach in 1971. The Huskies were on a roll.

Farrell was making a name for himself, too. He started Michigan Tech's summer hockey camps—still among the best in the nation. He coached Tech's junior varsity team and he rightly received much of the credit for Tech's success. He attended every clinic he could and integrated the European emphasis on constant movement and puck possession into the Husky system. Farrell quickly earned a reputation as a top recruiter and one of the best young minds in college hockey.

Put it together and you've got a strong candidate for the Michigan job. "He was my first choice—and a good one," Canham says. "Farrell was a good coach for Michigan."

When he got the job, Farrell was understandably gratified that he'd have a new rink to work with, something Renfrew could have used. "It couldn't have been easy to recruit players before," Farrell says of the Coliseum. "It was one of the poorer facilities in college hockey. When the kids visited that first spring, I never took anybody to the old place.

"You have to give Canham credit for the vision to go from that old building to refurbishing Yost. You got a huge building at a fraction of the cost of a new one. It made an immediate impact on the program and certainly made recruiting the class of '77 a lot easier."

The Class of '77

Farrell took the Michigan job right before Michigan Tech entered the 1973 playoffs, which put him behind the eight ball in the annual recruiting race. But if the competition for players had grown more intense by the early 1970s, it was also true that Farrell was among the more intense competitors.

Another advantage: by the early seventies the top prospects had seen others before them get drafted by NHL teams and wash out in the minors with nothing to fall back on. At the same time, the improved quality of college hockey was making it a more viable path to the pros than it was in Berenson's day. Although the latest crop of candidates figured they had a better chance at the NHL if they played Junior A hockey in Canada, the Junior A teams couldn't offer college educations, and most of Farrell's early recruits were determined to get one.

Farrell had to play catch up, but he played it well. "Doug Lindskog was coming because his brother, Tom, was already here," Farrell remembers. "But the other guys I had to work my buns off for."

Rob Palmer and Dave Shand played together on the Junior B Toronto Nationals, but, because they were only 16 in 1973, neither had been recruited by any college coaches. The two figured they would play Junior A and try to squeeze college classes in somewhere along the line. But their plans changed when Farrell came to the Nationals Junior B championship series against the Sarnia Bees to recruit John McCahill, and wound up talking to the young defensive pair, too.

Farrell advised them to play Junior B again the following year instead of Junior A, so they would still be eligible to play college hockey at Michigan. Palmer and Shand surprised the coach when they informed him that they were already in grade 12, so Farrell recruited them on the spot. Ironically, McCahill came to Ann Arbor the next year, after finishing grade 13.

"I always figured I was just part of the package to get Shand," Palmer says, "but I can never get Farrell to admit this."

"Ah, Palmer's been after me for 25 years on that," Farrell responds, exasperated. "And the answer is no. I knew I wanted him—absolutely—and I was right."

Farrell's first recruiting class consisted of Greg Natale, a small but highly skilled defenseman who could contribute immediately; Russ Blanzy, a dedicated role player; and John Saunders, who left Ann Arbor after a year for Western Michigan and eventually rose to be a star broadcaster on the ESPN and ABC networks; plus Pat Hughes, Gary Morrison, Kris Manery, Rob Palmer, and Dave Shand, all five of whom would make it to the NHL, playing a combined 32 seasons.

"That was a phenomenal class," Farrell says, "especially recruiting that late in the season."

The young players still had a lot to learn, but teaching was Farrell's second big strength. "John MacInnes was a great teacher, great at skill development, and that's why Tech was so successful," Farrell says. "The Tech guys were so coachable, so easy to work with, so disciplined. When you have a program that's successful, that's winning, new players just kind of move in and get into the mold. Guys came in here and fell in behind the upperclassmen, doing whatever they did."

When Farrell left the land of the clean-cut engineers for Ann Arbor's long-haired hippies, he was in for a culture shock. The media guides of the era are filled with guys with uncombed coifs, lamb chops, and shirt collars pointy enough to poke your eye out. When the Farrells moved to Ann Arbor in 1973, the city had already gained national notoriety as the home for the Hash Bash and the $5 pot law. A magazine called *High Times* declared Ann Arbor to have the highest per capita pot use, securing Ann

Arbor's reputation as one of the most liberal towns around. As always, the hockey players were influenced by the atmosphere around them, be it the Depression, World War II, or the seventies counterculture.

"I tried to bring some of MacInnes's ideas to Michigan," Farrell says, "but some of those guys were right out of control! I was in a state of shock. It was a revelation to me."

A defenseman from Canada we'll call Paul Richards served as the catalyst for the crazier upperclassmen. The stories his former teammates tell about him could fill a chapter by themselves. Dave Shand recalls the time Richards drove him to practice in Richards's old, beat-up boat of a car, when Shand was still a wide-eyed, 17-year-old freshman. On the way Richards asked Shand to grab a phone book off the car's rusty floor, after which Richards proceeded to tear off a corner of one of the Yellow Pages and roll a joint with one hand while steering the car with the other. Seeing the surprised look on his young passenger's face, Richards explained, "Gotta have a joint before practice. Gets ya in the mood."

"My favorite Paul Richards story," Manery says, with his index finger in the air in the manner of a Greek philosopher. "My first weekend of dryland training, Dan pairs us up for stretching, and he puts me with Paul. I'm on my back with one leg in the air, which Paul's pushing back toward my shoulder, when he says, 'Kid, if I puke on you, don't take it personally.' I was too stunned to say anything. I just covered my head.

When Dan first got here he said the same thing Red Berenson did a decade later: Don't follow the seniors."

Farrell admits, "That was really tough, I'll tell you, going through that learning curve. It was a challenging start, for sure. You think you have all the answers until you have to make all the decisions."

In fairness, there were a few upperclassmen who had their eye on the ball. Randy Trudeau, who captained both the 1973–74 and 1974–75 teams, "was a super guy," Farrell asserts. "He came to work every day. And Frank Werner, one of the older guys on the team, was just the best. He was hard nosed but understood discipline and what it took to win—but they weren't all Frank Werners."

Faced with a recalcitrant group of upperclassmen, Farrell decided to bet on the future. In his first meeting with the team, he told them, "We're gonna win, and this is how we're gonna win: We're gonna be better conditioned than our opponents, we're gonna be stronger, we're gonna be systems oriented, we're gonna work hard and practice hard. Discipline on and off the ice, that's the bottom line. That's what it takes to win."

Farrell's no-nonsense approach is evident in the old media guides. Whereas the player profiles the previous season were so unfailingly flattering they could have been composed by the players' mothers, Farrell's descriptions of each player were written as open letters daring the players to do better, such as Angie Moretto's: "Powerful center who must have good season. . . . Tough to move in front of net, but must score more."

"When I first got there, the challenge was to raise them up to another level of intensity," Farrell says. "They thought the whole thing was a gas. It took a lot of ratcheting up, fighting it out every day with the upperclassmen. And the freshmen were torn between the coaches and the seniors. But if you've got guys like Manery and Palmer, Angie, Foxie, and Tom Lindskog, you're not going to have too much trouble down the road."

When Palmer was growing up, his father told him repeatedly to concern himself with only two things: work hard and support your teammates. "Really, everything you should be doing on a team boils down to those two things," Palmer says. "That's what I always focused on."

That attitude eventually spread to the other players. And Coach Renfrew hadn't left the cupboard bare.

"Angie Moretto, Greg Fox, Robbie Moore, and Tom Lindskog—man, that's a great class," Manery says of Renfrew's last recruits. "Angie and those guys just needed another class to help them out."

"The sophomore class was going to be excellent," Farrell agrees. "That really was a great class, and [Assistant Coach] Jimmy Keough deserves a lot of credit for recruiting them. Angie

Moretto had great talent and was a great competitor. And if Greg Fox wasn't the best defenseman in college hockey by the time he graduated, he was damn close to it."

The loudest buzz, however, was generated by Michigan's brash young goalie, Robbie Moore, one of the first netminders in college or pro hockey to play the puck like a defenseman. "It was all the news in town," recalls Roger Bourne, a local little league player at the time, who later starred for Pioneer High School and the Wolverines. "'They got a goalie who comes out of the net and handles the puck, and he can shoot it as well as the forwards!'"

Farrell needed all the horses he could get, because he'd be going head-to-head against the best college coaches in the country—maybe the best hockey minds anywhere. In the mid-seventies the NHL was still a brain-dead league offering little more than dump-and-run offenses and bench-clearing brawls brought to you by Philadelphia's Broad Street Bullies. The unconventional Soviets might have opened a lot of eyes when they took the NHL All-Stars to the eighth game of the 1972 Summit Series, but it wasn't the NHL coaches who got the point. It was U.S. college coaches like Herb Brooks, Bob Johnson, and Dan Farrell who first figured out how to mix the European training methods and offensive systems with the North American emphasis on physical play.

"Our preparation and training was in the forefront," Brooks says today. "We had a group of real outstanding coaches—Murray Armstrong, John MacInnes, Bob Johnson—and Dan Farrell was right up there. It was just a real tough league."

"I just loved playing against Michigan Tech, Minnesota, and Wisconsin," Farrell says. "They were so well coached, I just enjoyed dueling with them."

Like his peers, Farrell was highly educated, well traveled, and open to new ideas, helpful traits in an era that introduced the American Football League's pass-happy offenses, the American Basketball Association's slam dunks, and the American League's designated hitter. Everything was being revised, even in athletics, and the smartest coaches made the most of it.

"I loved the way the European guys emphasized puck control,"

Farrell says. "In soccer, football, and basketball, you hang onto the ball. Made a lot of sense to me. And I think the Michigan guys liked the more sophisticated practices, with more variety. After four years, they were much better players."

"When we played, Farrell was at the forefront of hockey," Palmer says. "We learned things on his team I didn't see from any NHL coach until my seventh or eighth year in the league."

The Turnaround Teams

The underclassmen took to Farrell's innovative methods like ducks to water, and he rewarded them with important roles from the day they arrived. The injection of freshman talent combined with a rejuvenated sophomore class got the team off to an opening weekend sweep over Waterloo—the same team that initiated Coach Lowrey's demise years earlier. Palmer scored one goal and one assist in the opening 6-2 victory, which provided the inspiration for a *Daily* subheadline proclaiming "Palmer Sparkles in Debut." From that clip, a nickname was born: "Sparky."

"'Sparky' may be bad," Palmer concedes, "but 'Sparkles' would've been a lot worse."

The freshman trio of Manery, Hughes, and Doug Lindskog alone accounted for 75 points that first year. All three were among the top eight scorers on the team, while freshman defensemen Palmer, Shand, and Natale added 30 points from the blue line. Michigan finished the season at 18-17-1, its first winning record in five seasons.

Whatever Michigan would become under Farrell, it was clear the doormat days were over. As a testament to their newfound competitiveness and grit, the young Wolverines beat 7 of 9 conference foes at least once, and won 7 of their 10 one-goal games—games they would have likely given up the previous season, when they finished 6-27-1.

"The first year was the transition year," Farrell says, "but we clearly made a lot of progress."

That spring Bo Schembechler stopped Farrell in the hallway of the athletic department and asked him, "How long do you think it's gonna take to turn this thing around?"

"Bo," Farrell said, "we're gonna do it by the fourth year."

"You think you can do it that fast?"

"Yeah, I really do," he replied. Looking back, Farrell says, "I felt really confident at that time. I knew the class we had."

With the Wolverines warming up, their old rivalries heated up, too. Nonetheless, the players had plenty of friends on most of the WCHA teams, so it was customary for the home team to invite the visitors to the postgame party on Saturday nights. The exceptions were North Dakota and Minnesota. In North Dakota, 10 below was nothing unusual *inside* the arena, which was actually a Quonset hut. It was so cold the Sioux coach often told his fourth-line players he wouldn't hold it against them if they didn't dress, and many didn't. "North Dakota, we just hoped to get out of there," Manery says.

Minnesota remained the only team in the WCHA that could fill its roster almost completely with homegrown talent. As a result the Gophers tended to be more insular, even arrogant, toward their opponents. "We didn't get along with them, because they were all Minnesota guys," Manery says. "No one knew them, and they didn't seem to want to get to know us. They thought they ruled the hockey world."

The Wolverines also had ferocious ongoing battles with Michigan State, Denver, and especially Michigan Tech, Farrell's alma mater. "Man, those were the best games, by far," Manery says. "We knew Farrell would be *out of his mind* all week, but he was good for a pep talk. 'They're bigger than us, they're faster than us, they're better than us.' By our senior year one guy whispered, 'Who're we playing, the freakin' Montreal Canadiens?'"

There was method to Farrell's madness. "I tell ya what, I had to crank these guys up another notch to get them to compete at those levels," he says. "In the early going, Tech had superior talent. That's a fact."

The Huskies made it to the NCAA Final Four in 1974, 1975,

and 1976, winning it all in 1975, but they couldn't get the upper hand on Farrell's upstart Wolverines. Michigan won 11 of 23 games against Tech during Farrell's first four seasons, in a clear case of overachievement. The contests were so fierce, so well played and so appreciated by the fans that to this day Michigan Tech's attendence totals against Farrell's Michigan teams are still the highwater mark, more than two decades later.

"The guy knew the game inside and out," Manery says, explaining Farrell's success. "Dan knew all the best drills, the

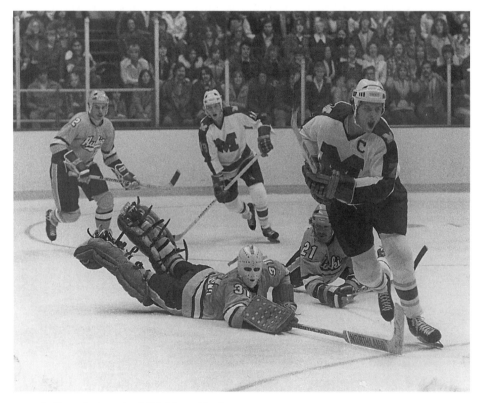

Action shot against Michigan Tech
Yost offered a new pep band and ferocious battles with Michigan Tech, Farrell's alma mater. "Man, those were the best games, by far," Manery says. "Farrell was good for a pep talk. 'They're bigger than us, they're faster than us, they're better than us.'"
(Courtesy Bob Kalmbach.)

latest power plays. He had all the opponents scouted so thoroughly that we knew exactly what the other team was going to do, and they'd do it, so we never had any surprises. The guy was right every time. It was amazing. A *huge* advantage."

If the intellectual, intense Farrell had a weakness, it was handling game pressure. Farrell's second team, the 1974–75 squad, finished the regular season with an overall record of 20-15-1 and a 17-15-0 mark in the WCHA, making it the team's first winning record in the league since 1968–69, and its first 20-win season since the 1964 title team. In the WCHA playoff series against Colorado College, Farrell actually passed out on the bench—but then you might too, if your career depended on the performance of a bunch of 20-year-olds who barely beat the Tigers 4-3 on Friday and 9-8 on Saturday. They narrowly lost the next series to defending NCAA champion Minnesota, 3-3 and 5-2, but the year marked another clear step back to the top of college hockey.

The 1975–76 team looked ready to take the program to the next level with its 10-4 start, including a five-game winning streak through the Great Lakes Invitational (GLI) holiday tournament. The triumph was only the school's second GLI title and its first since 1966, the tournament's second year. Michigan beat every opponent on its schedule at least once that year, including the defending NCAA champion Huskies twice and the 1976 U.S. Olympic team, in overtime.

Angie Moretto played the same low-finesse, high-scoring style of Boston's Phil Esposito to a "tee"—and even resembled the Bruin great. He led the team in points the previous two years and was on pace to become Michigan's all-time leading scorer until one day when he was scraping out the contents of a coconut his roommate had brought back from Florida and sent the serrated knife through the tendons in his left palm. The freak accident forced him out of the lineup for a couple months. (It also forced him to stand up Donna Bucci on their first date. To make amends, Tom Lindskog took her to Moretto's hospital room that night to prove Moretto was a man of honor. It must have worked, because Ms. Bucci is now Moretto's wife.)

Shortly after Moretto returned to the lineup weeks later, he suffered a groin pull so severe it left his body black and blue from the middle of his right thigh to the middle of his ribs, an injury the university doctors found so fascinating they studied it for medical journals. The team's potent chemistry was shaken, not stirred, when Moretto had to sit out 15 games to mend from his two injuries.

Moretto came back just in time for the team's playoff run, but was far from 100 percent. Michigan Tech easily swept the hampered Wolverines in the WCHA finals to bring the promising season to an abrupt end.

"Moretto's injuries might be the difference of us not playing for the title in '76," Farrell says. "Minnesota, Michigan Tech, and Michigan were the three best teams in the nation that year by a country mile. But that year was a defining year for the program. We were back."

26

Come Together, Right Now

By the fall of 1976, Farrell's program was going nowhere but up, having finished in seventh, sixth, and fourth place in the league, and had strung together the first back-to-back 20-win seasons since 1952. The 1976–77 team still had a solid core of seniors in Manery, Palmer, and Natale and a potent junior class of Dave Debol, Kip Maurer, and Bill Thayer, plus a couple surprising underclass snipers, Dan Lerg and Mark Miller.

But there was no guarantee the team could continue its ascent because the '77 team had lost a bushel of talented players from the '76 squad.

Angie Moretto, Tom Lindskog, and All-American goalie Robbie Moore had graduated, though not before Moore set the still-standing school record for most saves, with 4,434, which no one has topped. His replacement, Frank Zimmerman, alienated his teammates by blow-drying his hair between periods to look his best while working the bench door, and turned off the coaches with his unfulfilled promise. He eventually lost his job to Rick Palmer (no relation to Rob), a walk-on from Grosse Pointe Woods. The 1975–76 team's rookie of the year Dan Cormier left campus, and Doug Lindskog and Pat Hughes left early for the pros.

"We had more talent our junior year than our senior year," Manery says, "but we didn't have a lot of discipline that year. It was just a different group of individuals. Our junior year we would generally win easily on Friday night and then struggle on Saturday night." Michigan split 10 of its 16 weekend series in 1975–76, a testament to the team's inconsistency.

"I look at those teams," Palmer reflects, "and I think our most talented team was '76, not '77. But the '76 team might have had *too* many leaders, guys like Foxie, Moore, Tommy Lindskog, Angie Moretto, plus all the guys in our class. The next year, we just had Kris, me, and Natale. So much has to do with chemistry and leadership. That's true in every sport, but especially hockey, I think."

Farrell maintains that the two least heralded players from his first star-studded recruiting class made the greatest impact: Manery and Palmer.

"Well, yeah," Palmer shrugs. "After Hughsie, Shand, and Dougie Lindskog left early for the pros, we were the only guys left!"

Because the class of '76 was so tightly bonded with the class of '77, the upperclassmen had little connection with the underclassmen. When the class of '76 moved on, however, the division between upper and lower classes eroded, and the team became one. "We really had two teams in '76," Palmer says, "and in 1977 we didn't. There was no fractionalization along class lines."

Like all good teams, the 1976–77 group bonded on and off the ice. Unlike their predecessors, however, whose off-ice partying and hazing occasionally damaged team unity, the mischief Manery's class made usually had a good-humored warmth to it. "These guys would find our house in the middle of the night and jump in our pool just for kicks," Farrell remembers with a grin, shaking his head. "My wife and I knew better than to look too closely to see if they were properly attired." Farrell tried to do his best to strike a balance between accountability and fun, and for the most part, he seemed to succeed. "Natale played a guitar in a local bar on Wednesday nights," Farrell recalls, "so I knew where the guys were one night a week, anyway."

"If Farrell were smarter," Manery counters, "he'd know where we were Thursday night, too, because that was fraternity-sorority night at the Pretzel Bell (now Champion House, a Japanese restaurant on Washington) and we wanted to meet the sorority girls."

However they did it, Manery's crew became the closest hockey team in Ann Arbor since Gordon Wilkie led the '64 gang to the

NCAA title. "That senior class was just exceptional people," Farrell says. "Kris Manery was such a tremendous leader. On the ice, he ran those guys. I've really never seen a leader like that guy."

A Hot Time in the Old Town Tonight

Despite the exodus of all-stars the previous year, the players knew they had something special after the first two weekends of the 1976–77 season, when they earned tough splits on the road at Wisconsin and Michigan Tech. The team's 5-3 victory in Houghton was Michigan's first victory over the Huskies in six tries, and only the second Wolverine triumph in Houghton in a decade. Michigan looked like a team to be reckoned with.

Manery and company were 13-6 when the Huskies came to town in January. Michigan beat them in an overtime thriller on Friday night, 9-8, but lost the next night, 3-2—a defeat that triggered a seven-game losing skid. The team actually wasn't playing that badly—three of those losses were by one goal—but rubberized objects with sharp edges are bound to bounce funny, and the WCHA was a remarkably balanced and competitive league. If you didn't give your best effort on a given night, you'd probably lose, no matter who you were playing.

Unlike losing streaks in previous seasons, however, the men stayed calm, stayed focused, and rebounded by rattling off eight straight wins to end the season in second place with a 22-14 mark, not far from the 1964 team's record of 24 victories. "We just got on a roll from February on," Manery says. "Pretty amazing, really, because when Hughsie and Lindskog left early, no one would've guessed we'd get that far. The last two months of that season are my best college memories. I was in a slump until Denver came to town in February, then I got five or six that weekend and broke the scoring record. It all meshed that year."

Manery's output was complemented by Dave Debol, who enjoyed a break-out season. "Dave Debol was clearly the best offensive player in the country that year," Farrell says. "He could go end to end with the puck and turn the game around single-handedly. An incredible talent."

"My senior year we had a real strong offensive team, with two outstanding offensive lines," Palmer says. "Even on the fourth line, we had Billy Wheeler, who could fly, and guys who could score. We loved to get into those wide-open games."

Boy, did they. To give you some idea of how potent offenses were in the seventies, Farrell's seven Michigan teams went into overtime 34 times, and all but five of those games were settled within the 10-minute overtime period. Employing the free-flowing European offensive systems, Michigan shattered the 1964 squad's previous high mark of 217 goals with 260, a record that still stands, averaging 5.8 goals per game. Hell, Rick Palmer, the *goalie*, had six assists—which is also still a record.

Like Michigan's 1964 team, its 1977 model could score goals but, again like the '64 squad, they had a harder time keeping it out of their own net. While the team re-wrote almost every Michigan scoring record, it was also the first to give up more than 200 goals in a season, letting in 211.

In 41 of 45 games that season, even the losing team scored at least two goals. It was the kind of year where Michigan could lose to Wisconsin 11-8 one game and beat Denver 11-4 the next. In contrast to today's tight-checking, low-scoring contests, in those days you could be down 5-2, and you'd still know you were in it. It was great hockey for the fans—and the guy who supplied the coaches with Rolaids.

With their wide-open offense, long-haired Canadians, and funky pep band that wore bright yellow overalls and delighted in surprising the crowd by popping up all over the building, Michigan hockey games offered fans a cheerily off-beat evening, perfectly pitched for a crowd looking for something different. The spirit of the era was manifest in one minor incident when play stopped because no one could find the puck. It turned out it had lodged in the cuff of Ben Kawa's glove. When he discovered it there, he had the presence of mind to pull it out with a two-fingered flourish—ta da!—like a magician, busting up the fans. You got the feeling the players were having as much fun as the guys in the yellow overalls.

In hindsight the 1976–77 season might have been the WCHA's

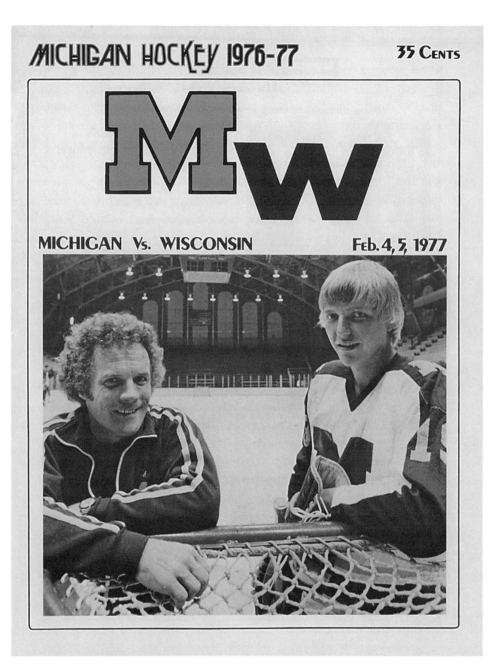

MICHIGAN HOCKEY 1976-77   35 CENTS

Mw

MICHIGAN Vs. WISCONSIN   Feb. 4, 5, 1977

Coach Dan Farrell and Kris Manery
Dan Farrell's first recruits included Pat Hughes, Gary Morrison, Kris Manery, Rob Palmer, and Dave Shand, who would play a combined 32 seasons in the NHL. "That was a phenomenal class," Farrell says, "especially recruiting that late in the season. I never realized until after they left what an impact Rob Palmer and Kris Manery made on those guys."
(Courtesy of the U-M Athletic Department.)

finest hour. From 1973 to 1983, the WCHA produced 10 of the NCAA's 11 champions, and also supplied the runner-up eight times. The league also had balance—six of the league's nine teams made it to the NCAA's final game during that stretch— plus the most innovative coaches, the highest-scoring games, and the wildest arenas.

A few highlights: Minnesota's mascot, Goldy the Gopher, once tackled Wisconsin's Bucky the Badger on the ice before a game. It was not staged. When Minnesota visited North Dakota one weekend the Sioux fans welcomed them by throwing a dead gopher onto the ice.

The Wolverines, for their part, once snared a Kermit the Frog doll hanging over the glass in North Dakota during warmups and took the felt figure back to the locker room. The Sioux fans went ballistic in the stands above the visitors' locker room, chanting, "We want Ker-mit! We want Ker-mit!" and grew louder still when the Wolverines returned to the ice with the unfortu-nate Muppet hanging in effigy from goalie Rudy Varvari's stick.

Perhaps because the players' faces and expressions were not concealed by masks in those days, the fans felt a closer connec-tion to them. And with the face unprotected, any unresolved hos-tilities could be quickly redressed through old-fashioned fisticuffs. Michigan's Dave Richter initiated one memorable melee during warmups at Minnesota, when he saw a Gopher skating innocently on the other side of the center line—and punched him right in the face, inciting a huge fight with no refs on the ice. Problem was, Richter's parents had driven down from Manitoba to see him play college hockey for the first time that night, and he had to spend the weekend in the stands with them.

It is undeniable that college hockey today has more skilled players, but it has never been more fun to watch than it was in the seventies. Michigan's crowds, which often failed to break 3,000 in the old Coliseum, steadily grew during Farrell's reign to an average of 5,003 in 1977–78. The team broke 100,000 for the season in 1975–76 and again in 1979–80, Farrell's final year, a mark the old Field House wouldn't break for a decade.

Bad Breaks and Guilty Consciences

Going into the last regular-season game against Michigan State, the Wolverines felt they were ready for all comers—and justifiably so. They had swept Denver, Minnesota, and Minnesota-Duluth and were about to do the same to Michigan State. Farrell and the boys would have been forgiven if their thoughts wandered to their upcoming WCHA playoff series against Michigan Tech. Even with the loss of freshman defenseman Dave Brennan to a neck injury they still had five solid defensemen, including Greg Natale, the quarterback of their potent power play. Palmer believes Natale might have been the most talented of the bunch, and would have gone to the NHL if he was taller than 5-8.

The Wolverines had beaten the Spartans 6-3 in the final weekend's first game and were ahead 5-2 in the second with just 17 seconds remaining when the puck went behind the Michigan net and Natale chased it down. Before he could look up for a passing option, Michigan State's Russ Welch charged in from the blue line and gave him a full-blast check from behind. Natale hadn't missed a game all season, but when he crumpled to the ice with a broken collarbone, his college hockey career was finished.

"It was a flagrant foul," Farrell told a reporter that day. "It was just brutal. I'd say Natale was one of the best defensemen in the league in the second half of the season. But we're just going to have to play over it."

"With those two guys out," Farrell says today, "we had to mask a lot on defense during the playoffs."

Palmer remembers a meeting with Farrell a few days later. "He pulled McCahill and me aside and says, 'I need you guys to *lead.*' We used only four defensemen from then on. Dean Turner and John Waymann, playing with a broken foot, took the other shifts. On the positive side, there wasn't time to think about the mistake you just made during a game, because all you were thinking about was getting your next breath."

The team was as short on defensemen as it was long on forwards. "We had three top lines," Palmer says, "but our fourth line was just as important, because it was the first time the fourth line understood its role." The team respectfully referred to the line of Gary Morrison, Bill Wheeler, and Russ Blanzy as the Detroit Demolition Squad. "These guys didn't always get a regular shift—and Morrison played in the NHL, fer crissakes—and they accepted that. It was pretty easy for Manery and me to show leadership because we were on the ice, but Morrison and Blanzy, geez! Those guys were working as hard as anyone in practice, which made it pretty hard for anyone else to complain about *their* role."

With Farrell and the seniors doing their best to cover up the team's weaknesses with putty and paint, the team swept archrival Michigan Tech in the first round of the WCHA playoffs. Michigan's next series, against Murray Armstrong's Denver squad, was only a WCHA semifinal series but it took on much greater weight because the NCAA had already decreed that the WCHA's first- and second-place teams would get automatic bids. Win the WCHA semifinal, therefore, and you win an NCAA berth.

On the night before the team's do-or-die series, Farrell was returning from a recruiting trip. Along the way on I-94, he was surprised to see Dave Debol's Camaro blow past him in the left lane. When Farrell got back to town he decided to check on Debol to make sure he was obeying the curfew the night before the team's most important series of the year.

"Dan knew where everyone lived and what they drove, too," Manery says. "Remember, Farrell was a detail guy. So he goes to Debol's house, and he's not there. Then he goes to Deebs's girlfriend's house—Farrell knew where all our girlfriends lived, too— and sees his car, on a curfew night. That's one problem. Then Farrell decides to check on the rest of the guys—just to make sure Deebs is the exception, I'm sure."

Farrell discovered a half dozen players' cars parked outside homes that weren't theirs. He even found one guy's car parked in front of another player's girlfriend's house, then, an hour later, he discovered the first player's car gone, replaced by the original boyfriend's car.

Farrell shook his head and went home.

"When it was all said and done," Manery sums up, "during Dan's tour of Ann Arbor he found about six guys breaking curfew before the biggest game of his life—and ours too, for that matter. The next day he asks us, 'How many guys broke curfew last night?' Now at this point we figure, correctly, that he probably spent the night checking on us, so we're not messing around. Five hands go up. One doesn't. Dean Turner's. Dan was probably madder at Turner than anyone else."

(It might be worth noting that Turner has since found himself on the wrong side of the law numerous times, including one financial felony that resulted in a front-page lawsuit filed by his famous mom, former WXYZ-TV personality Marilyn Turner.)

Despite the players' sins the night before—or perhaps because of them—Michigan blew out Denver that weekend, 6-4 and 11-4. "I admit it," Palmer says. "We swept that weekend playing on *guilt*. It's a great motivator."

The two wins gave the team a school record 26-14-0 mark and an automatic bid to the NCAA playoffs, which took the heat off the league finals against Wisconsin. Michigan lost the two-game set, played on a temporary rink in Madison with a laughably truncated neutral zone, but they showed they could play with the Badgers in the second game, a hard-fought 5-4 loss.

Michigan returned to the NCAA tournament for the first time since—you guessed it—1964. Anyone who knew the history of the Michigan hockey team might have been encouraged, because when the Wolverines are not supposed to win it, they usually do.

27

Crunch Time

In the first round of the 1977 NCAA playoffs Michigan faced Bowling Green, which had Ron Mason behind the bench, future NHL star Mike Liut in the net, and future Olympians Ken Morrow and Mark Wells on the ice—but the Wolverines blitzed them. Michigan's early onslaught created a 5-1 lead in the first period, compelling Liut to pull himself before intermission and allowing Michigan to play all four lines in a comfortable 7-5 victory.

The Wolverines' next stop was the NCAA Final Four at the Olympia, where they would face Boston University. The Terriers upset the heavily favored Wolverines in 1950, but if they beat Michigan in 1977, it would be no upset. BU was led by three-time All-American Rick Meagher and four future Olympic legends: captain Mike Eruzione, goalie Jim Craig, and forwards Dave Silk and Jack O'Callahan.

"We were huge underdogs," Palmer insists. "*Huge* underdogs."

But if the Wolverines were scared, they didn't show it. The teams were tied at 2-2 when Michigan's Doug Todd and Ben Kawa scored 22 seconds apart. With walk-on goalie Rick Palmer playing superbly and Rob Palmer and John McCahill taking more than half the shifts on defense, the Terriers couldn't catch the Wolverines. They wasted Silk's hat trick and ultimately fell, 6-4. Michigan had its twenty-eighth victory, a record that would hold for 14 years.

To win their eighth NCAA title the Wolverines needed to win only one more game, and they needed to beat only one more team. But there was a catch: the game they had to win was the

NCAA finals, in front of a standing room only crowd. And the team they had to beat was Wisconsin.

"Mark Johnson, Mike Eaves, Craig Norwich—that's a serious group of players," Palmer says, referring to Wisconsin's trio of two-time All-Americans. "They had some tremendous hockey players there. And they had an amazing power play."

"When Craig Norwich got the puck on the blue line on the power play," Farrell says, "it was money in the bank."

"We were pretty heavy underdogs, no two ways about it," Manery acknowledges. "We just knew we had to play our best

Less Talent, More Success
"We had more talent our junior year than our senior year," Kris Manery says, "but we didn't have a lot of discipline that year." The next year, 1976–77, was far more successful.
(Courtesy Bentley Historical Library, University of Michigan.)

game. But no one expected us to go that far anyway, so we had nothing to lose."

Michigan had already lost 5 of 6 games to Wisconsin that season, but it was in good company. The Badgers were 36-7-1, including a 22-3-1 run in their last 26 games. They had beaten every opponent on their schedule at least once and had never lost as many as 2 games in a row. The Wolverines could take some solace in the fact that they had played the Badgers as well as anyone had that year, with four of their five losses coming by one-goal margins. Further, while Michigan had a day off before the finals, Wisconsin had just beaten New Hampshire in overtime the night before and had to be feeling lead-legged in the finals on Saturday. The Wolverines figured if they could just keep the Badgers close and get a couple breaks, they just might be crowned the new NCAA champions. After all, in a one-game format, anything can happen.

"They had a good team. We knew that," Debol says. "But confidence is the greatest thing, ya know? And we had it."

The vaunted Badger power play was as good as advertised, and produced a 3-0 Wisconsin lead just 15 minutes into the game. Power-play goals by Maurer and Debol pulled Michigan to within one before Wisconsin's Mike Meeker and Mark Johnson stretched the Badgers' lead to 5-2, the fifth goal coming just one minute into the third period.

"When they scored their fifth goal," Debol remembers, "it was, 'Ah, crap. We're in deep.'" So they started digging.

"It seemed like we had the game well in hand," recalls Mike Eaves, Wisconsin's only three-time captain, and still its all-time leading scorer. "But one team was afraid of losing, and the other team had nothing to lose."

Every Wolverine who tells the story of the 1977 NCAA finals invariably starts with the phrase: "We were down 5-2 in the third period . . ." For the Wolverines, that's where the story begins.

"We weren't a bunch of rah-rah guys between periods," Manery says. "That wasn't our style. But no one was panicking. We weren't giving up. And [after Wisconsin's fifth goal] we absolutely *dominated* them. They never got it out of their end."

Michigan outshot the Badgers in the final stanza 15-8. Mark Miller fired a long slap shot past Wisconsin's All-American goalie Julian Baretta 26 seconds after Wisconsin's fifth goal.

Five-three. 18:24 left.

Just seconds after *that* goal, the Wolverines gave the Badgers another chance to put them away when they took a penalty. "We know if we go down 6-3, that's it. We're done," Debol says. "Bill Thayer's killing the penalty with me. We've got a face-off to the right of Baretta. Thayer's a lefty, so I tell him to take the face-off and just tip it ahead to the net. He did it, I got it, I jumped around their defense and put it into the top shelf, right up there with the socks and underwear."

Five-four. 17:46 left.

Michigan battered the Badgers for the rest of the period but struggled to get anything past Baretta, who would win the tournament's Most Outstanding Player Award for his acrobatic performance. With less than six minutes left center Kip Maurer took a face-off in the Wisconsin end and drew the puck back to sophomore defenseman John Waymann, playing with a broken foot, at the right point. Waymann didn't hesitate, and ripped his shot past Baretta.

Five-five. 5:38 left.

The capacity crowd of 14,423—the biggest crowd Olympia had hosted all season, watching what the *Detroit Free Press* called "the best hockey game in Olympia in years," including the Red Wings—went crazy, egged on by Michigan's adrenaline-addled pep band. Having given up three goals in 14 minutes, the Badgers should have heard the wake-up call loud and clear, but they looked paralyzed by Michigan's hell-bent attack. It seemed inevitable that Michigan's unrelenting pressure would break Baretta sooner or later. "If we had another five minutes in the third period," Farrell says, "we would've won it right then."

In the waning minutes of regulation Michigan's tenacity created a number of good chances. Manery got off a clean shot from the slot, which Baretta stopped. Ben Kawa had another high-percentage opportunity on a two-on-one, but Baretta again rose to the occasion.

With 1:10 left, Baretta stopped another Michigan blast from the blue line but kicked the rebound directly to Michigan's Dan Hoene, skating to the left of the net. It arrived on Hoene's backhand, which put him even farther away from the net on the left side, "but my instincts said, Don't wait. Don't look. Just shoot the puck," Hoene recalls. Hoene's instincts were correct. Baretta, a gutsy goaltender, decided he had no choice but to attack Hoene, giving him even less to shoot at. But Hoene got off a good backhand, a quick riser that surprised the charging Baretta. The puck bounced off Baretta's shoulder straight into the air, right as his feet came out from under him. He landed on his backside a few feet in front of the net, while the puck fell behind him.

Some players say the puck rolled along the goal line. Others say it twirled on its side a foot and a half from the red stripe. And still others remember it sitting still, right behind the fallen goalie. But everyone agrees on one thing: there was nothing and no one between the puck and the Wisconsin net. If a Wolverine could get to it first, Michigan would be the new national champions.

After finishing his backhand, Hoene was about to skate behind the net on the left side, but when he saw the puck behind Baretta he cut hard toward the little black biscuit.

The playoff program listed Dan Hoene at 5′10″ 170 pounds, but that was probably a stretch. A fast-skating junior from Duluth, Hoene's value to the team was not his knack around the net—he scored six goals in 44 games that season—but as a rabid forechecker and pugnacious penalty killer. It was on the kill that he scored half of his six goals. The simple fact that Farrell put him on the ice with a minute left in a tied NCAA title game says a lot about how much the coaches trusted him. When the hardworking winger took a Minnesota Gopher's stick in the face that January, he suffered 25 stitches and a broken jaw—and played the next night.

Palmer remembers Hoene as a "thoughtful, introspective guy, very sincere. A real solid citizen." In sum, Dan Hoene was the kind of quiet, unassuming guy everybody on the team would have been happy to see become a hero.

Wisconsin's All-American defenseman John Taft quickly recognized the Badgers' problem and tried to force Hoene wide away from the net, but Hoene managed to sneak around him.

"Hoene was about to go behind the net," Debol narrates, "but he sees the puck just *sittin' there* on the freakin' goal line. He cuts in, full speed, skating right at the side of the net, and bangs at the puck—but the shaft of his stick *hits the pipe*, and the puck just squirts away. If he'd been able to stop in time, he'd've scored."

"Baretta was down, it was a wide open net—" Farrell starts to recount, then stops himself. "Christ, I can still see it," he says, unable to finish.

Hoene can, too. "Of course I wish I had banged it in," he says. "But I knew I didn't miss a tap in. Far from it, I made the right play to take the shot, but the goalie made a daring play, too, being so far out of the net. And their defenseman forced me wide, so I couldn't go straight to the puck. There's a lot of what if, *Field of Dreams* stuff. But there it is. They clear the puck, and the horn blows and we're all tied up."

"I remember thinking, 'Let's just get into the locker room and get regrouped,'" former Wisconsin captain Mike Eaves says today. In the Badger dressing room between the third period and overtime, Baretta vomited. Not from nerves, he said later, but from the sheer exhaustion of facing 39 difficult shots in three periods. When Eaves hopped back onto the ice for overtime, "I remember my legs just hurt," he says. "Everybody was still sore from overtime against New Hampshire the day before."

Thirty-six skaters came out for the extra period knowing that anyone on either team could score at any time by virtually any means. It is the nature of hockey's sudden death, something no other sport has. Still, the stars seemed aligned for Dave Debol to bury the winner. With 43 goals and 99 points, another tally would break Berenson's and Heyliger's old record for scoring and make Debol the first Wolverine to break the 100-point barrier, too. But he wasn't the only one intent on ending things.

"Steve Alley was one of those guys whose will was greater than his skill," Eaves says of his former teammate, which might help to explain why so many Wolverines despised him. "Losing was not an option for Alley. Right off the opening drop, he got the puck in a scrum, got it into Michigan's zone, forechecked like crazy, and got a whistle down there."

All the former Wolverines start the end of this story the same way, too. "We had a face-off in our end," they say, "23 seconds into the overtime."

When the puck hit the ice, Alley again banged it forward, this time into the Michigan corner. There the Badgers' Tom Ulseth picked it up, skated behind the Michigan net and attempted a

Dan Hoene's big chance
Down 5–2 against the nation's top team, Michigan tied it at 5–5 in the third period. With 1:10 left, light-scoring winger Dan Hoene's backhand rolled over Baretta's shoulder and dropped inches from the goal line, but Hoene could not cut in to bang it home.
(Photo by Bob Kalmbach. Courtesy of the U-M Athletic Department.)

wraparound on his backhand. Rick Palmer saw it coming and made the stop, but no one anticipated the rebound popping right out into the slot to Wisconsin's Mike Eaves.

"I had a good chop at the puck," Eaves recalls, "and I couldn't believe [Palmer] stopped it." While Eaves tried to find the puck, Alley simply banged the rebound home, just like that.

"Talk about a euphoric high," Eaves says. "I don't remember *anything* from the time we scored to the time we left the ice. It blows by you."

"Everyone remembers Dan's opportunity, but we had a *lot* of opportunities to score," Palmer says. "And they scored five goals in regulation, so we had a lot of opportunities to keep *them* from scoring, too. We won a lot of games, and we won them together. When we lost, we lost them together, too. No one was ever pointing fingers. On paper, we should've probably lost to Bowling Green and definitely to BU, and Wisconsin had already beaten us five times."

"We played 'em seven times, and only beat 'em once," Palmer rationalizes. "They were all close games, but we couldn't say we were the better team."

No, but the better team doesn't always win, of course—witness the crushing disappointments the Wolverines suffered in 1950 and 1962, when *they* were clearly the better team.

So what if Hoene *had* been able to knock in the loose puck? "Well, we would've been NCAA champions, for one thing," Farrell deadpans. "It would have made a big difference in recruiting, and the recognition for the program would certainly have skyrocketed. It also would've given me a lot more leverage with the athletic department for getting more publicity and getting a second assistant coach. But to get that team, from where we were four years before, *that* close to a national title—well, it was a defining moment. That's what it was. I was extremely proud of those guys, and what they had accomplished."

Shortly after the game ended, Farrell asked the reporters, "Have you ever seen anything like that? Have you ever heard anything like that? It was thrilling, it was exciting. This will bump our program up 50 percent. We don't have to apologize now. We're for real, and we'll be back."

Farrell was right on every point but one. No one would have guessed it then, but Michigan would not come that close to an NCAA title again for almost two decades.

Some of the young men who played in the 1996 NCAA final weren't yet born when Dan Hoene's second shot slipped past the far post. But they would feel the effects of the hex of Wisconsin goalie Julian Baretta: If Michigan misses its chance to win it in regulation, it'll lose in overtime. Between 1977 and 1995, Michigan played in seven NCAA and CCHA playoff games that went into overtime. The Wolverines would lose all but one of those seven overtimes—three of them season-enders, every one of them a heartbreaker.

28

Ups and Downs

The overtime loss against Wisconsin was undeniably disappointing, but with four of the team's top five scorers returning, Farrell and his players had every reason to believe they would get a return invitation to the dance. The hockey team was once again an important part of an athletic department that was arguably the best in the land. In the fall of 1977, the Michigan hockey, football, and basketball teams were all ranked number one in the nation, probably the first and last time any school could claim that.

The hockey team justified its top ranking by jumping out to an 11-3 start, including a humiliating sweep of the defending champion Wisconsin Badgers, 11-3 and 7-3, in early December.

"Our guys just *kicked their ass*," Farrell says. "I watched our team that night, and I thought, We're going to be a great team."

The following weekend up at Houghton provided another litmus test—one the team failed miserably, precipitating a tailspin the team could not pull out of the rest of the season.

"I can tell you the exact shift where the tide turned," says Deker Hall of Famer Kip Maurer. "In the first game we were up early on, maybe 2-0, and we get a five-on-three power play. We had pressure all over them—it was just a shooting gallery—but we couldn't put it in the net. Their guy comes out of the penalty box, goes down the ice and scores, and they score again a few seconds later. And we never recovered. The whole season went down the drain from there."

Michigan got swept, 6-2 and 7-3. "We got beat up," Farrell

acknowledges. "We rolled over, and gave up. When we played Tech a few weeks later in the GLI finals and lost again, 8-3, I knew it was all over for that team."

It was. Michigan lost 17 of the season's remaining 22 games, although 7 of those losses were by two goals or less. "We were going great guns, then right after Christmas, we couldn't win a game," Debol says. "We never got blown out, actually, but the year before everything went in, and that year nothing did. We were picked to finish first—and damn, there it goes."

"That was the low point of my career," Farrell says. "I never realized until after they left what an impact Palmer and Manery made on those guys."

The 1977–78 team finished 15-20-1, just one floor from the WCHA basement.

Farrell knew he needed more firepower the next year, and he went out and got it, recruiting the two best prospects in North America. Murray Eaves, Mike's younger brother, had lightning speed with a supernatural game sense and scoring touch, while Terry Cullen was simply the best junior player in Canada. Cullen's father, Barry, had played five seasons in the old six-team NHL, his uncle Brian had played seven, and Terry looked like a sure-fire bet to join them in the NHL for at least that many.

With Eaves and Cullen on board, the fiery Dan Lerg coming back for his junior year, and Ann Arbor's own Roger Bourne—who had set the Pioneer record for goal-scoring—entering his sophomore season, Michigan probably had the best collection of centers in the country. "If Roger Bourne is your *fourth* center," former hockey sports information director Jim Schneider opines, "that team is *awesome*."

But in Cullen's second weekend as a Wolverine, a Minnesota-Duluth player cross-checked him into the ice. When Cullen woke up the next morning, he was numb, but didn't tell anyone in the hopes that his condition would fade. Though he tried to play that night, he couldn't overcome the mysterious malady. A few days later the doctors discovered Cullen had suffered a serious spinal injury that ended his promising career before it had started.

That same ill-fated weekend Lerg hurt his knee badly enough to miss the next 12 games. The situation became almost laughable when, just three weeks after Lerg returned, Eaves suffered a knee injury in mid-January that knocked *him* out for the rest of the season. To say the '79 team was star crossed is to say the *Titanic* experienced a few bumps in the night. Of the 108 combined games Michigan's top three centers could have played that year, they dressed for a total of 48. That team never had a chance.

But don't blame Mark Miller, the 1978–79 team captain. In a December game against Michigan State, Miller hurt his knee so severely he had to be carried off the ice. "I figured his career was done that night," Schneider says. "But he came back the next night, we won, and he played in all 36 games. Miller was always there, and he gave us a big-time presence even with everyone else out."

After that weekend series with MSU, the team won just *one more game* the rest of the season, a historically bad 1-18-1 run. They dragged an 8-27-1 record across the finish line, good for last place in the league. If there was an opportunistic time for Farrell to quit coaching, that was surely it.

Instead, Farrell redoubled his recruiting efforts to attract players like Bruno Baseotto, Paul Tippett, and Paul Fricker, an unorthodox, acrobatic goalie the NHL already coveted. With both Eaves and Lerg skating at top speed once more, the team redeemed itself in 1979–80 with a 23-13-2 season and a fourth-place finish in the WCHA.

While Eaves's skills were celebrated throughout college hockey, "I don't think Danny Lerg ever got the credit he deserved," Farrell says. "He was truly a great college player. And man, did he come to play. He was a *competitor*."

If Michigan wasn't the best team in the league, it might have been the most fun to watch. The five first-team power-play skaters scored a colossal 338 points, more than many Michigan *teams* totaled just a few years earlier. With Eaves (85 points), Lerg (76) and Baseotto (76) up front, and Tim Manning (51) and John Blum (50) on the blue line, the Farrell Fivesome ranked one through five on the team scoring leader board, lighting the lamp on almost *half* their power-play opportunities, when 20 percent is considered very good. Even taking into account all the great lines Michigan has put together over the years, no other quintet has ever come close, on paper or on the ice, to the five players Farrell put together in 1979–80.

"I don't care how good the power play is now," Schneider argues. "*That* was the best power play Michigan's ever had. They were so much fun to watch because they didn't feel like they had to be the one to score. They would pass up a good shot for the extra pass just to make sure the final shot was a slam dunk in an open net. I am convinced, to this day, that the refs failed to call a lot of penalties against our opponents because they knew that that was giving us a sure goal. Those guys were just that good."

The 1979–80 season restored Michigan hockey's good standing. With future NHL'er Bill Terry recruited to join returning veterans like Richmond, Blum, and Manning and young players like Eaves, Baseotto, and Fricker, "It was the start of a great young team," Farrell says. "That team was going to be a team of destiny, the next great team at Michigan. I felt they were ready to win a national championship."

Farrell had to weigh the temptation of coaching that team with his desire to try something new while he was still young enough to do so. Before the signing date for recruits, Farrell decided to leave Ann Arbor for Toronto to pursue a career in finance. "When I left I really had to think about that team," he says. "But I had already made the commitment to leave."

Hockey's relatively low status at Michigan was reflected in Farrell's salary of $22,000, but Farrell is quick to correct the assumption that he resented the attention the football and basketball teams received on campus. "We got a lot of mileage out of the success of the football and basketball programs," he says. "They gave us a higher profile, and that's where we took our recruits on their visits. I had a great relationship with Johnny Orr, and Bo often came to our games. Those teams were a bonus for us.

"No, the biggest disappointment of coaching the Michigan hockey team, quite frankly, was the relative low level of publicity we got within the athletic department," Farrell says. "They missed a great opportunity. It would've helped our recruiting, our attendance. After coming from Tech, where hockey got lots of attention, that was a huge frustration.

For his part, Canham says, "Farrell was a good coach, but I don't think he was comfortable with me. I had a hard time talking to him."

"But the main reason I got out of hockey," Farrell says, "as much as I loved it—was that I could not see spending my entire working life in coaching. It just wasn't part of the agenda. At times I've regretted that, quite frankly. But something about the idea of doing this the rest of my life didn't seem right."

In the final analysis, Farrell did a lot to bring Michigan hockey back to respectability and into the modern era in a very short period of time. He had taken over a team that had gone 6-27-1 and finished dead last in the conference the year before he arrived and turned it back into a winner in his first season. He brought the team to the brink of a national title in his fourth season, without the aid of full-time assistants, and he brought fans back to the rink through word of mouth.

"The bottom line is we made tremendous strides," Farrell says. "Coaching at Michigan was a great experience for me. I met a lot of great people, I have a lot of fond memories, and I made a lot of lifelong friends. The positives far outweigh the negatives."

"Winning is a habit," as Vince Lombardi said. "Unfortunately, so is losing." After Farrell left, the program quickly squandered all his hard-fought gains, and then some. Thus began the worst era in Michigan hockey history since World War II.

Farrell left a team poised to challenge for NCAA supremacy. But within weeks of Farrell's departure, Murray Eaves decided to jump to the Winnipeg Jets, and incoming recruit Bill Terry opted to go to Michigan Tech instead, where he captained the team for two seasons and scored 180 points in 150 games. He still ranks sixth on the Huskies' all-time scoring list.

Canham wanted to get a Michigan man to coach the team. He settled on Wilf Martin, a member of the original Saskatchewan contingent and captain of the 1964–65 team. When Martin stepped down after his first weekend behind the bench due to health problems, second-year assistant coach John Giordano filled in.

"John had been a great assistant coach for me the previous year," Farrell says. "We had one of the best power plays in college hockey, and he had a lot to do with that."

But Martin had never coached a varsity team, and Giordano had never recruited for one. Perhaps due to the "substitute teacher" syndrome, the players went astray shortly into the new administration. In October 1980, the *Detroit Free Press* published an article about hockey hazing at Michigan, alleging that the upperclassmen had shaved a walk-on freshman's entire body, forced him to drink until he became sick, and left him naked and babbling incoherently on the steps of his dorm for hours. The players responded to the charges with a letter, stating, "We do not condone our actions but feel the facts around the incident have been greatly distorted." Nonetheless, Michigan's Board in Control of Intercollegiate Athletics suspended three players for one game each. That same week Wilf Martin stepped down, and Giordano took over as the interim coach.

In the wake of the unexpected coaching changes, the hazing incident, and the ensuing negative publicity, Bruno Baseotto left the team a few days later. Baseotto, who set the freshman scoring record with 76 points the year before—a record that still dwarfs the next closest by 18 points—thereby became the third star who would not be playing for the Wolverines that year.

The 1980–81 team performed admirably under trying circumstances, winning 23 games against 17 losses, good for a fifth-place finish in the WCHA. The players thought it might be enough to warrant a serious look from the NCAA selection committee, and it was. Former hockey sports information director Jim Schneider got the inside word that the five-man committee initially voted for Michigan, 4-1. But after Wisconsin (24-14) made an unexpectedly early exit from the WCHA playoffs, Coach

Bob Johnson used his week off to lobby the NCAA committee members.

Johnson wasn't afraid to call in some favors, nor was he reluctant about reminding the committee members that he had already announced his retirement effective at the end of that season. They, in turn, weren't above switching their earlier votes for Michigan to the Badgers. When the Badgers, seeded fourth in their region, went on to win the NCAA title, they became the lowest-seeded team in NCAA history to claim the crown. And that's how they came to be called the "Backdoor Badgers."

Giordano didn't get an NCAA bid in 1981, but he did win the *Hockey News*'s Coach of the Year Award. When Canham announced the team would leave the powerful WCHA for the upstart Central Collegiate Hockey Association (CCHA) the following season, the conventional wisdom held that the Wolverines would dominate the new circuit behind their successful young coach.

A League of Their Own

Jumping leagues wasn't Canham's first choice, but he had to do something. Michigan was playing in a league spread across half the continent and dominated by the schools in the far West, schools that valued hockey far more than football or basketball. The extensive travel costs showed up on Michigan's bottom line, and the disparity in athletic priorities showed up in the league rankings. Four conference schools—Denver, North Dakota, Minnesota, and Michigan Tech, where hockey was king—accounted for 25 of the WCHA's first 31 league titles. Michigan had won just 2—and none since 1964.

"The whole structure of the WCHA was breaking down," Canham maintains. Notre Dame athletic director Moose Krause was going to drop hockey altogether, Canham says, "because it was costing him a bundle. It was costing us a bundle, too."

To cut costs, Canham and others proposed splitting the WCHA into eastern and western divisions, with Notre Dame and the four other Big Ten teams—Michigan, Michigan State, Minnesota, and Wisconsin—all in the East. The West would consist of Denver, Colorado College, and North Dakota, logically enough, but also Minnesota-Duluth, which is slightly east of the University of Minnesota, and Michigan Tech, which lies east of both Minnesota and Wisconsin.

The athletic directors passed the proposal at the WCHA meeting in the spring of 1979, but they repealed it two months later by a single vote. According to Canham, the late John MacInnes "fought us tooth and nail on that. He just didn't trust us. I guess he thought he'd get the short end of the stick. Well, Krause and I figured, Notre Dame and Michigan together would make one helluva league in any sport."

When Canham and Krause approached Michigan State athletic director Doug Weaver, he jumped at the idea of leaving the WCHA for the CCHA. With three of its oldest rivals already in the new league, even Michigan Tech decided to switch, upgrading the CCHA into one of the nation's strongest circuits overnight.

But many players and fans viewed the change as a demotion. From then on the team would be taking buses instead of planes. They'd be playing not Minnesota but Miami of Ohio; not Wisconsin but Western Michigan; and not North Dakota but Northern Michigan. Instead of playing in a league of one-name teams that had taken home 27 of the first 34 NCAA titles, Michigan had entered a circuit of schools that needed four names to describe themselves (Lake Superior State University) or hyphenations (Illinois-Chicago). Worse, the CCHA teams could claim not a single NCAA crown among them. The new league might have made business sense, but the glamour was gone.

But the CCHA was not without its charm. In some ways, the CCHA in the eighties felt like the WCHA in the sixties, when the league produced fewer NHL players but more good stories. The youthful CCHA generated plenty.

One night in East Lansing, Ferris State trailed Michigan State 5-2 in the first round of the CCHA playoffs. In the game's waning minutes, former Ferris State coach Bob Mancini sent out his third-line center Tim Christian—a quiet, well-behaved player who would be the last man suspected of pulling a prank—to shadow referee Steve Pietrowski, a Ferris State grad who bent over backward to avoid appearing biased toward his alma mater. Mancini would argue he bent over too far.

Christian took the face-off, then followed Pietrowski all the way down the ice, and all the way back. Finally Pietrowski turned to Christian and screamed, "Tim, whatya doing?!"

"Coach sent me out here to cover the most dangerous man on the ice," Christian replied, "and tonight that's you."

Red-faced, Pietrowski immediately blew the whistle, gave

Christian a two-minute penalty for unsportsmanlike conduct, and threw him out of the game.

But that was nothing compared to the scene that developed during a Ferris State–University of Illinois-Chicago game up at Big Rapids. A bit of background: the CCHA had passed a rule stating that no mascot could be on the ice between the third period and overtime after the buzzer sounded to beckon the players back on the ice.

Now, Ferris State's mascot, the comically angry Bulldog with a tiny baseball hat on its large head, was unquestionably the most aggressive mascot in the league. Sure enough, before the game's first overtime period the Bulldog was still on the ice after the buzzer sounded. The referee could've given Ferris State an automatic two-minute bench minor penalty right then, but gave the oversized dog a warning, asking him to leave and be done with it.

Nothing doing. With the crowd following his every move, the mascot performed an exaggerated swan dive, delighting the fans. By this time Mancini, recognizing the risk at hand, was screaming at the mascot to get off the ice, but he was too late. The ref, less amused than the crowd was by the dog's antics, gave Ferris State a minor penalty to start the overtime period.

The cartoon canine, *still* not getting the message, skated to the referee's circle to protest the call. His antics stirred the crowd into a frenzy, but the ref showed some mercy and didn't tack on any additional penalties. Mancini, however, showed no forgiveness toward the felt-faced dog. When the mascot finally left the ice—to a standing ovation—the coach grabbed the mascot's oversized head, seized its baseball cap, and whipped it down the hallway.

Ferris State managed to kill the penalty and win the game, after which Mancini walked under the stands to the locker room. On the way, he saw a little kid point at him and heard him say to his father, "Look, daddy, that's the man who hit the bulldog."

"Son," his dad replied, "that Bulldog is very, very lucky."

That night, Ted Halm, Ferris State's sports information director, composed the game summary for the wire services and the league office. He could have simply recorded a bench minor given to FSU; but instead, the bottom of the roster sheet read as follows: "Mascot, no games played, no goals, no assists, two-minute bench minor."

To this day, that dog is the first and only mascot in college hockey to make the scoresheet.

If the difference between the WCHA and the CCHA could be reduced to a single place, it would be Ohio State's 1,400-seat arena, which was creatively named "Ice Rink." To get to Ice Rink, visitors had to walk past the classically designed St. John's Arena and the regal Ohio Stadium, only to be met with a broken-down Zamboni with four flat tires, sitting on concrete blocks in a setting so decrepit weeds threatened to camouflage the machine. For reasons clear only to the Buckeyes, they never moved the rusty beast, which came to symbolize the entire Ohio State hockey experience—and even made North Dakota's Quon-set hut look appealing.

The visiting locker room was smaller and more rancid than the ones you typically find in any old-time municipal rink. Goalies had to put on their pads in the hallway and a few others had to dress in the showers. The ceiling of Ice Rink was so low players could easily bounce the puck off it on a clearing pass, and on more than a few occasions refs had to stop play so the crew could sweep up shattered lightbulbs off the ice.

The rudimentary press box sat directly above the team benches. To get there reporters had to go through the Ohio State bench and both penalty boxes, then up a narrow, attic-style lad-der and through a 3-foot opening in the press box floor, which required them to bend at the waist to make it. Once in the press box, they sat directly above the team benches, even overhanging the ice itself, not more than 8 feet above the playing surface. When the puck was along the near boards reporters couldn't see it unless they bent over the railing.

So, during one Michigan visit to Columbus the ref charged a bench minor penalty to Ohio State. Buckeye coach Jerry Welsh was incredulous and demanded to know what motivated the penalty. The ref said, "Coach, one of your guys in the press box questioned my call a bit too loudly."

Welsh replied, "Who ya talkin about? We don't *have* any guys up there!" When the ref pointed to an old, pudgy, bald man, Welsh exploded, "He's not a coach! He's a reporter from the freakin' *Columbus Dispatch!*"

The ref looked at him, then back up at the reporter, then back at Welsh, and said, "I don't care. That's two minutes." Welsh threw up his arms, helpless.

That was the old CCHA.

30

A Slippery Slope

If the CCHA was a step down from the WCHA, it should have made it easier for the Wolverines to manhandle their new opponents, but they didn't come close.

Farrell had left the cupboard amply stocked for the next coach, including one forward and four defenseman who would play in the NHL and a fifth defenseman, Tim Manning, who still holds the school record for most points by a backliner with 142. "He was small," Jim Schneider recalls, "but you couldn't get the puck from him. He could skate in circles with it if he had to."

As Farrell's recruits graduated, however, Giordano failed to replace them with players of equal ability. He turned down Terry Cullen's brother, John, because Giordano felt he didn't skate well enough to play for the Wolverines. But Cullen apparently skated well enough for Boston University, where he became the team's only three-time MVP, and well enough for the NHL, where he played more than a decade.

Instead of searching for the best junior players in North America, as most college coaches do, Giordano filled his roster with U.S. high school players. Given his limited coaching background at Notre Dame high school, it's not surprising that Giordano felt comfortable with those kids. But there weren't enough Michigan high school players who could keep up with the Canadian junior stars, and the best Minnesota high schoolers were picked up first by Minnesota, then Wisconsin, and then Minnesota-Duluth, leaving Giordano to sift over players the other guys didn't want.

In Giordano's second year, 1981–82, the team finished fourth in the CCHA, then ninth, and ninth again. Michigan's new CCHA peers might never have won a national title, but they were burying the tradition-rich Wolverines night after night, month after month.

Giordano's weakness was not laziness, however. "Giordano's answer to everything was more work," says Glen Williams, who has served as Michigan's P.A. announcer since 1968. Giordano often scheduled extra 6 A.M. practices for the defense, before the NCAA outlawed such excess. "If they lost, of course that meant more work," Williams says, describing Giordano's reasoning, "and if they won, that meant more work, too, because then everyone's gunning for you. And he hired an assistant who said he couldn't recruit for Michigan because he couldn't get good players who could meet Michigan's academic standards." Michigan's crumbling foundation required a serious overhaul, but Giordano didn't recognize the need for it.

Giordano's overwhelming need for control created an adversarial relationship with his players. While Farrell had followed the MacInnes model of maintaining a few important rules and otherwise treating the players like adults, Giordano tried to monitor virtually every waking hour of his players' lives—which the players eventually took as a challenge. During Giordano's endless track workouts, the players devised a clever system whereby two players would sneak into one of the nearby doorways of the Intramural Building, concealed by their teammates running by, then they'd switch with two teammates when the group came running by again.

After Farrell's team played a Saturday night game on the road, he would simply tell his players that the bus was leaving at 8 in the morning, and that he recommended they be on it, thereby allowing them to join their friends playing for the home team for a night on the town. Not Giordano, who insisted that his players be back at the hotel before curfew, which was generally long before the bars closed. One night after Michigan completed a stirring sweep of the Huskies in Houghton, however, a group of players stayed out well past the curfew. When they finally returned to the hotel they saw Giordano waiting for them in the lobby—and that's when back-up goalie Rudy Varvari decided to take one for the team. He told the others that he'd go up to Giordano and distract him while the rest snuck back to their rooms.

"But what about you,'" Roger Bourne asked.

"Me?" Varvari replied, "Hell, I haven't seen a game in weeks. What's he gonna do, bench me?!"

But when Varvari approached the coach, Giordano told the likeable netminder that his tardiness wasn't a problem. This caught Varvari flat-footed, so he had to think of something, and fast, to allow his teammates enough time to escape, much the way a baseball player caught in a run-down has to keep the fielders occupied long enough for his teammates to advance.

"Not a problem?" Varvari objected. "Whatya mean, not a problem?!" And with that ingenious response, the back-up goalie was able to engage the head coach long enough for his teammates to slip past, unnoticed.

When Michigan failed to qualify for the eight-team CCHA playoffs in Giordano's third and fourth years, the fans stayed away in droves. Michigan averaged a little over 3,000 fans per game during those years, the leanest crowds in Yost's hockey history.

Adding insult to injury, in 1980 Jeff Lowe, then-treasurer of the Dekers booster club, decided to use some $6,500 of Dekers' money to pay the bills for his failing catering business—an act as dirty as it was dumb. As Lowe's case knocked around the courts, then-president Fred Hatfield and his wife Diane paid the Dekers' bills out of their own pocket just to keep it going. That scandal, coupled with the team's demise, resulted in Deker membership falling to about 60 faithful followers by 1984.

More damaging than the losses were reports of scholarships being pulled from seven players Giordano decided weren't good enough to play for Michigan anymore, including players Giordano himself had recruited.

Doug May, whose father, Ed, and brother Dennis both played for Michigan, scored 23 points in his freshman year, 1981–82, followed by 14 and 15 his next two seasons. Nonetheless, according to a letter May's father submitted to the Board in Control, Giordano told Doug that "no financial aid whatsoever was available" for his senior season. He went so far as to suggest that May "should perhaps consider going to another university for his last year." Bizarrely enough, a few days later Giordano told May he would receive a partial scholarship and would even be the team captain.

By this time May and his teammates had had enough. In the spring of 1984, shortly after the completion of Giordano's fourth season as head coach, a mutiny was afoot. They appealed to Canham to make a coaching change, but didn't get very far until they showed up a second time with a signed letter outlining their grievances, including Giordano's practice of pulling scholarships. The players added that Giordano was "an embarrassment to all of us in front of other coaches and players."

"I never talk to players about their coaches," Canham says. "I coached myself, and I know enough not to do that. But when all 22 players walked into my office the second time with a signed petition to say this situation is intolerable—well, I just had to let him go. He just never could get along with the players."

In reporting the decision, the *Michigan Daily* described Giordano as being "very unpopular with the players, parents, fans and alumni"—which didn't leave many in his corner.

In the spring of 1984, the once-proud Michigan hockey program, which needed only five coaches in its first 57 years, went hunting for its third coach in four seasons. With the bills mounting and no fans around to pay them off, Canham had to pick a winner, and fast.

Part VII

Rescued by the Red Baron
1984–91

31

Back to the Future

The eighties may seem like yesterday to some readers, but consider this: When the decade began Iran hadn't yet freed the U.S. hostages, the U.S. Olympic hockey team hadn't yet beaten the Soviets, and the current crop of Michigan players hadn't yet been born. Personal computers were a luxury and the "Internet" hadn't yet been coined. Cable TV was an oddity, Pac Man was the fanciest video game around, and AT&T was the only long-distance company to speak of.

The Detroit Tigers were great, and the Red Wings were awful—although the Wings would wisely draft a teenager named Steve Yzerman in 1983. Likewise, Japan was riding high, and America had been laid low. The state of Michigan was hit hard by the economic slump, with so many residents leaving for Texas that a Houston billboard asked "Would the last person to leave Michigan please turn out the lights?" The shrinking state budget forced University of Michigan president Harold Shapiro to carve out a "smaller but better" university, axing the School of Geography and slashing the budgets for the schools of Art, Education, and Natural Resources. During the Reagan years campus protests were out and patriotism was in. Drug-soaked house parties, like the kind featured in Michigan alumnus Lawrence Kasden's classic movie *The Big Chill*, were replaced by the kind of beer-soaked frat parties featured in *Animal House*.

Down at Yost Field House, the funky flying circus of the late seventies had left town. In its place was an unimaginative, uninspired team playing before bored fans—and not many fans, at that. Something had to give.

Since Red Berenson had said good-bye to his Wolverine team-mates just minutes after they won their consolation game in the 1962 NCAA Final Four, he'd managed to keep himself fairly busy.

That night he joined the Montreal Canadiens in Boston to become the first player to jump straight from college to the NHL—and he stayed there for 17 years. Berenson was also the first player to wear a helmet who didn't already have a metal plate in his head. When his "old school" teammates asked why he wore a helmet, Berenson replied, " 'So I don't *have* to wear one.'" he recalls. "They didn't get that."

They also wouldn't have understood how he graduated from Michigan in 3½ years, after changing majors from engineering to geology to business, or why he was so pleased to get a modest-paying job offer out of college from U.S. Steel in Gary, Indiana. "Probably not the nicest place in the world," Berenson admits with a smile. "But it made me feel so good to have something else to rely on instead of hockey."

Three years later, in the 1965 Stanley Cup playoffs, Berenson's Canadiens played the Chicago Black Hawks for the Stanley Cup. One day Berenson was holding Bobby Hull's line in check in the seventh game to win the grail, the next day he was sitting in a Michigan business school classroom starting work on his M.B.A. (There is drama in Berenson's final games.)

Although his B-school classmates didn't know who he was, Berenson remembers "very clearly what a good feeling it was to be there. I was preparing for life after hockey." Berenson readily admits he didn't think his NHL career would last 17 years, or that he'd still be in the game today. Berenson played six seasons in the NHL's brutally competitive original six, where 30 was over the hill. Because he scored only 19 goals in 185 games over those six seasons, no one could blame him for making alternative plans for the future.

"I always thought about what I'd do when [hockey] was over, but for one reason or another, it hasn't ended," he says. "I was lucky. With expansion and the WHA, I played until I was 38."

In addition to the Canadiens, with whom he won the Stanley

Cup in 1965 and 1966, Berenson played in New York, Detroit, and St. Louis, where he became one of only two players in the modern era to score six goals in a game. And Berenson scored all six goals without the help of power plays, screens, tips, or rebounds. Berenson was so impressive that night that the Philadelphia fans—not known for exhibiting brotherly love to opponents—started chanting "We want Red! We want Red!" in the game's final minute.

"Red was a strong player who got his chance when the league expanded in 1968," says Scotty Bowman, who coached Berenson in St. Louis. "He was the top player in the West for three years in a row."

Each time the league expanded—in four waves, from 6 teams in 1967 to 18 teams in 1974—Berenson's numbers went up. He scored at least 20 goals in 7 of his last 11 seasons and finished with 658 points. He then accepted a job on the Blues' coaching staff in 1978–79; two years later in 1980–81, as the head coach, he led the Blues to a 45-18-17 record, still the best mark in their 34-year history. Berenson earned Coach of the Year honors that year and a pink slip the next.

Welcome to the NHL coaches' club.

The following year Berenson took an assistant's job in Buffalo with his former coach, Scotty Bowman. "As a coach he was well prepared and a good one-on-one coach," Bowman says. "I think he had a good way of giving the young guys confidence."

Joy Berenson recalls a conversation her husband had when they lived in Buffalo. "One of the coaches there said, 'You've gone to college, why don't you go back and get one of those cushy college jobs?' We both laugh at the memory."

Michigan athletic director Don Canham tried to recruit Berenson for the head coaching position after Renfrew retired, and again after Farrell left for Toronto, but both times Berenson was under contract to NHL teams. When the Berensons brought their oldest son, Gordie Jr., to Ann Arbor in the spring of 1984 on a campus visit, word got to Canham that the Red Baron was on campus, so he rushed a staffer to bring him down to his office, where he offered him the head coaching job once more.

The third time was the charm. Berenson took it.

"Red was brought in to save the program," says Jim Schneider, who speculates that "if he didn't, it was gone." There is no way to test that theory, of course, but the situation was undeniably dire.

"I never saw myself as a college coach—but then I never saw myself as a coach," Berenson says. But there he was, the fourth Michigan captain behind the Wolverine's bench, standing up at his first press conference to tell people how he intended to restore the emaciated program to its former robust health. "My first goal is to change the image of the program," he said at the

The Red Baron to the rescue
Michigan's most celebrated player, here flanked by Assistant Coach Mark Miller and Athletic Director Don Canham, returned to coach in 1984. "I thought we'd turn things around in a couple years," Berenson now admits, "but after three years, we were still under .500. I had no idea what I was getting into."
(Courtesy of the U-M Athletic Department.)

time. "I have a good feel for Michigan, the tradition, the excellence, and what I call a 'Michigan kid.'"

"I had a lot to learn," Berenson says in hindsight, "but I knew what I thought [the program] should be. I wanted the boys to play an exciting, clean style; to take advantage of the academic opportunities here; and to build something we could be proud of."

One of his first acts as head coach was to call the seven players into his office who had lost all or part of their scholarships under Giordano, and reinstate their grants. Word of the gesture spread quickly through the high school and junior ranks. If Berenson's program was to be nothing else, it would at least redeem its reputation as an ethical and fair place to play hockey.

"Red didn't run them off," Schneider says of the players Berenson inherited. "He played the hand he was dealt."

Despite his easy confidence during his first press conference, "I had no idea what I was getting into," Berenson now admits, with a self-effacing chuckle. "I was not the perfect choice. I didn't know about recruiting, about networking, or about the skill level I'd be dealing with." And what of NCAA rules? "Oh, cripes. I don't know if they *had* any rules back when I played."

Of Berenson's many blind spots, his ignorance of NCAA rules, at least, could be quickly corrected. Berenson took the rule books home, studied hard, and got the highest score on Canham's written test given to all Michigan coaches.

Everything else, however, came a lot slower.

32

Miracle on Ice, Michigan Style

"I thought we'd turn things around in a couple years," Berenson says, smirking at his naiveté. "But after three years we were still under .500. I was always convinced we were doing things right, but we had a lot of work to do." Just how much work became apparent in Berenson's first month on the job, when his inherited captain got a five-minute major penalty for spearing one of his own teammates in the blue-white intrasquad scrimmage.

Even the team's broadcasts were lousy. When Berenson took the Michigan job in 1984 Ken Kal was working as a reporter on the Red Wings' beat for WTKA. Station manager Skip Diegel asked Kal to broadcast the Michigan games that year, even though Kal had never called a hockey game before. "After 10 games I wanted to quit because I was so bad," Kal confesses. "So I had a meeting with Skip, and he said, 'Let's be honest. You stink, but the team stinks, too. Keep working at it, and when the team gets better, you'll get better, too.'" Years later, the comment would prove prophetic for both parties.

Until 1987 Berenson tried to handle all the coaching, teaching, and recruiting duties with the help of only one assistant coach, Mark Miller, while the teams they were competing against had two, which greatly hindered Berenson's ability to improve the team's morale, playing style, and personnel. "When he came back here he thought Michigan would sell itself," says current assistant coach Mel Pearson. "I don't think he realized there were a lot of other good programs out there by then. He expected kids to just realize what this program was all about, the way *he* had, and want to come here."

But they didn't. "I was so new," Berenson confesses, "I didn't realize how important it was to have two assistant coaches. But I also had a lot of pride. I hadn't been back here in a long time, but I just didn't feel we should be losing to Ferris State—or Michigan State, for that matter."

But they did. Berenson's first season started well enough, with the team splitting with Miami and sweeping Ferris State. Then things turned ugly. Michigan lost 9 of its next 11 games, including drubbings by Michigan State, Western Michigan, and Illinois-Chicago. *Illinois-Chicago!* When Berenson last skated for Michigan 22 years earlier, Michigan didn't play any hyphenated teams, let alone lose to them.

If the first half of Berenson's inaugural season tested his patience, the beginning of the second half almost broke it. In early January 1985, the Wolverines took on Ferris State, the only team on their schedule they hadn't yet lost to. In the opener, Michigan was comfortably ahead 7-2 in the third period when a Bulldog shot sailing wide of the cage bounced off Michigan defenseman Todd Carlisle into the net. No big deal. It was the kind of fluke goal you can laugh about when you're up, 7-3, in the third period.

But it didn't stop there. Ferris State scored four goals within 2:55. Incredibly, amazingly, incomprehensibly, when the night ended Michigan had lost, 9-7.

"That was the lowest point," Berenson says. "A devastating loss. It was hard for me to accept. The expectations of the players and the coaches were different, and it was slow to change. After that game, I didn't want to be around the players, and they probably didn't want to be around me."

Berenson sent the team bus back to the hotel without him, so he could make the three-mile trudge through the mid-winter wind, slush, and ice with himself and his thoughts. The next night Berenson tried to put the debacle behind them by mixing things up, changing the lines and the goalies. Nothing doing. The Bulldogs sent them packing with a 9-0 spanking, completing the sweep and a 16-0 scoring run.

"It was a long ride home," Berenson says. "It was only three hours, really, but it felt like 33. And then the bus breaks down on the way back."

The weekend was already the worst in Michigan history—but it wasn't over yet. The following night Michigan had scheduled a rare Sunday exhibition game with Spartak, the Soviet Union's second-best program behind the famed Red Army club. The touring team's average age was 27, replete with four players who'd made the national teams for the Olympics and Canada Cup. Not surprisingly, they were undefeated in their six games against the best American college teams, including a 5-2 win over Minnesota and a 7-3 victory against top-ranked Wisconsin, in which Spartak graciously let the Badgers stick around until Spartak decided to flip the switch and blow three goals past the bewildered Badgers in the third period.

"They're the best I've seen come over here the last few years," Wisconsin coach Jeff Sauer told the paper. There was little doubt what they were going to do to a struggling Michigan team, a team that was fresh off a horrendous weekend against a mediocre opponent, after which they got home at 2:30 A.M. The only question was not *if* Spartak would win, but how ugly it might get.

The Spartak players had arrived in town the day before, so they had heard of the reports of Michigan's incredible collapse against Ferris State. "They probably saw our scores and thought that we'd be a team that would have trouble showing up," Berenson said after the Spartak game. And if that wasn't enough pressure, Michigan had its best prospect, Myles O'Connor, class valedictorian of his high school and a third-round pick of the New Jersey Devils, in the building for his official visit.

"He had his choice of schools," Berenson says. "He could've gone anywhere he wanted. Michigan Tech, where Mel Pearson was, and BU were also in the hunt. I was just happy to get him to visit us. But I was so mad at my players, I wouldn't have blamed them if they didn't show up to face my wrath that Sunday."

"That Ferris State series was the lowest point in my career, probably of all our careers," recalls Joe Lockwood, a Milford native who was a freshman on that team. "And then we had to come home to play a team that had just de-pantsed Wisconsin. You had to figure, Here we go again. I was totally intimidated by those guys—I mean *totally*."

Early in the game Spartak was content to pass the puck endlessly before shooting, and they hit the post as often as not. Everybody who played in that game remembers a veritable symphony of pipes, including several "two-post" shots and at least one that hit all three pipes before popping out. They hit so many pipes, in fact, that former hockey SID Jim Schneider is convinced they were *trying* to. "I think they had some pact where they had to hit two pipes before trying to score," he says, and he's serious. Berenson's not so sure, but he stops short of dismissing the theory altogether. "They were clearly just toying with us," he acknowledges. "They were probably trying to help us save face in front of our home crowd and avoid embarrassing us."

Fortunately for Michigan, it was only an exhibition game, and both teams initially played like it. But when Doug May "just went out and *smoked* one of them," Lockwood says, "just blew him out of the water—then you knew it was no longer an exhibition game. It was for real. The fans were just going *bananas*. At that moment the intensity went from this easygoing exhibition atmosphere to an absolute hatred for those guys, a passion to win. That [hit] just set the tone."

The Wolverines might have had no business being in that game, but when they retired to the locker room after the first period with an improbable 2-1 lead, then found themselves tied 3-3 after two periods, they realized they actually had a chance. "I remember the feeling," Lockwood says. "We kind of looked around the room, and it hit us: *we could actually win this game*."

With the score tied 4-4 in the third period with less than a minute left, the puck came up the boards in Michigan's defensive end. The Spartak defenseman pinched just as Doug May got to the puck. May flipped it past the Soviet defender to the red line, and then took out his man for good measure. Young Joe Lockwood was leaving the zone at that same instant and suddenly found himself all alone with the puck at center ice.

"It was like time slowed down," Schneider recalls, "like something out of *The Natural.*"

"For a second or so, everything got so quiet," Lockwood told reporter Neil Koepke immediately after the game. "I could hear the puck moving."

"Every guy on our team knew exactly what I was going to do, because I only had one move," Lockwood says today. "I telegraphed that shot from the red line in." One move or not,

The Russians Are Going
In Berenson's first year Michigan blew a 7–2 lead against Ferris State, then lost 9–0 the next night before upsetting powerful Spartak, 5-4, on Joe Lockwood's breakaway goal—captured here in the only existing copy of this photo. "It was like we'd won the Olympics," Berenson says. "The best thing to happen to us all year."
(Photo by Bob Kalmbach. Courtesy Bentley Historical Library, University of Michigan.)

Spartak goalie Sergei Goloshumov had never seen it before. So when the freshman forward dipped his left shoulder to fake a deke and shot the puck straight to the upper right corner, the Russian goalie was leaning the wrong way, and was therefore unable to stop the shot from punching the twine behind him. "It was like a dream goal," Lockwood says, "exactly the way I imagined it."

The goal gave Michigan a stunning 5-4 lead, but there were still about 30 seconds left, so Lockwood and company weren't at all certain they had sealed the victory.

"If he'd scored with five minutes left, we'd have lost by five," Schneider maintains, "because, man, the last 30 seconds the Soviets played a whole different game."

"The last 30 seconds were a *war*," Lockwood says. "Man, *I* knew we'd won, but the team didn't have that same feeling. There was still this reserve on the bench. But Schneids is right: If there were any more time left, we would've gotten killed."

But they didn't, and the 5-4 upset stood.

"It was like we'd won the Olympics," Berenson says. "The atmosphere, the big crowd, it was just great. It was the best thing to happen to us all year. And Myles sees all this, the only time he saw our team play. Had he seen us the night before, he never would have come."

Road Warriors

Coach Berenson and Mark Miller were convinced that getting Myles O'Connor could be the key to turning Michigan's fortunes around. So convinced, in fact, that when they learned O'Connor was on his way back home to Calgary after visiting Harvard, the two coaches flew to Toronto just to meet his connecting flight at the gate to talk to him before he started the second leg of his trip.

"Dumb luck," Berenson says, "we run into Gordie Howe." Berenson knew Howe from their playing days, and Howe knew of Michigan's program because Howe's youngest son, Murray, made it to the last cut of Berenson's first tryouts. (Don't feel too bad for Murray. His essay on being Gordie Howe's son won him a prestigious Hopwood Award, and he went on to graduate from the Michigan medical school.) Howe had access to the Air Canada VIP lounge, so the ad hoc foursome sat and talked hockey for three hours. Howe chatted up Michigan, the importance of getting an education, and the ever-improving quality of college hockey. "I'm sure it made quite an impression on Myles," Berenson says. "It gave a lot of credibility to Michigan. It added a lot to our case, and we didn't have much of a case at that time."

Berenson's determination to revitalize Michigan's program, Joe Lockwood's unexpected heroics against the Soviets, and Gordie Howe's serendipitous appearance in the Toronto airport combined to persuade O'Connor that Michigan was the place for him. "Myles was the first big name player we recruited," Berenson says. "His coming here sent a statement to other top players, and they all knew each other from the All-Star camps. He was the key guy."

Berenson finally added a second assistant coach, Mel Pearson, in 1988, but the real momentum for any program starts when the players already on the team start recruiting their own kind. A maxim: Coaches recruit the first blue-chipper, and the blue-chippers recruit the next ones. Most prospects pick a school based on the players who are already there, so having a friend on campus is a huge lure.

In the old days a talented player might be able to persuade his teammates to follow him. But in the modern era, in which Triple A teams cover half a continent and All-Star camps bring the nation's best players in constant contact with each other every year, a blue-chipper's peer group can span hundreds of miles. So when a player of O'Connor's stature decides to go to Michigan, the ripples can spread over several time zones. In the same way that Pep Reynolds created the Calumet connection, Wally Grant initiated the Eveleth express, and Red Berenson pioneered the Regina route, O'Connor opened a pipeline of talent from western Canada to pour into Ann Arbor.

Future team captain and scoring leader Todd Brost left Calgary to join O'Connor the same year, followed by fellow Albertans Randy Kwong, Brad Turner, Ryan Pardoski, and goalie Warren Sharples the next. The western Canadian pipeline has since stretched farther west to British Columbia, delivering such world-class players as David Oliver, Brendan Morrison, and Billy Muckalt, among others.

The year after O'Connor opened Western Canada, in 1985 Todd Copeland opened the Eastern U.S., a talent source that became especially productive for Michigan in the mid-nineties. Such stars as Billy Powers, David Roberts, Rick Willis, Matt Herr, Bubba Berenzweig, and Jeff Jillson all arrived from New England prep schools. By Berenson's third year, Michigan started getting many of the best in-state players, too, including Alex Roberts, Denny Felsner, Chris Tamer, Patrick Neaton, and Kevin Hilton, players who would probably have gone to Michigan State if Berenson had not returned to Ann Arbor.

In Berenson's first year, 1984–85, only 3 of the 28 players on his roster were Canadians, while 10 came from U.S. high school programs. By the start of his fourth season, Berenson had tripled the number of Canadian players to 9.

But there was still room on the roster for scrappy local players, often walk-ons, who frequently worked their way into important roles on the team. The short list includes Don and Mike Stone, Mike Knuble, Bobby Hayes, Dale Rominski, Rob Brown, Harold Schock, and Ann Arbor's own Tim and Mike Helber and David Huntzicker. Most of them turned down more scholarship money elsewhere to pursue their dream of playing for Michigan, and became some of the most respected players on their teams.

In many cases the players came to Ann Arbor because Michigan had a better reputation academically than other regional schools, a profile high enough to be seen from both coasts. And, not least, the character of the people already on the team started attracting young men of equal character. This is where the classes of the late 1980s deserve more credit for the triumphs of the 1990s than they commonly receive. Without people of their caliber recruiting the next generation, Michigan would never have gotten the Jason Botterills, the Brendan Morrisons, the Matt Herrs, and the Billy Muckalts. The tremendous talent of the nineties came to Ann Arbor because of the tremendous character of the eighties.

Alas, not every recruiting mission was as charmed as was the pursuit of O'Connor. Berenson, Miller, Pearson, current assistant coach Billy Powers, and former assistant Larry Pedrie each made hundreds of trips and thousands of phone calls to get their man. They earned their frequent flier miles the hard way, traveling to freezing bandboxes across the continent. They've taken single-prop planes over the Rocky Mountains, they've taken ferries to Prince Edward Island in the dead of winter, and they've driven rental cars through treacherous passes to get to Merritt, British Columbia—and once they got there, they were treated to one of the worst places on earth.

Berenson once drove some 16 hours to Amos, Quebec, in 35 below weather, through a route covered in a foot of snow. The road was so barren he had to make the first tracks. When he finally got to the rink, he was not terribly surprised to find he was the only college coach there. Heck, he was the only spectator brave enough to travel by car. "That was one of those trips where my western Canadian culture helped me," he says. But, at least it paid off: Sean Ritchlin and Bubba Berenzweig agreed to come to Michigan.

That sojourn was a proverbial walk in the park compared to the trip Berenson made to Vernon, British Columbia, to see the Centennial Cup, the Junior A Tier II hockey championship. Top prospects Bill Lindsay, Jason Marshall, and a kid named David Oliver were all scheduled to play that weekend, and Berenson would have been elated to get any of the three to come to Michigan.

It seemed simple enough on paper. Berenson planned to take a flight to Seattle and pick up a rental car for the ride to Vernon, which Pearson had assured him would take only three hours. Berenson's flight arrived in Seattle at noon without a hitch, but when he walked up to the rental counter and reached for his wallet, all he found was pocket lint. No license, no car. Bypassing the rental counter, he tried to get a plane ticket to Vernon on a puddle jumper, but again, with no identification, Berenson was out of luck.

"It was like I wasn't a person," he remembers. "I had a little cash, I had a Visa card, but it didn't matter. I felt like I didn't exist."

Berenson went back to the rental counter to see if there was some way, *any* way, around the problem. The clerk told him the only way she could give him a car without a license was if he joined the U.S. Army and quit the military when he came back to the airport a few days later.

"It shows you my state of mind that I even thought about it," he says. "I was that determined to get there."

Berenson came to his senses and called his wife, who found his wallet sitting idle on his dresser, right where he'd left it that morning. She drove down to Metro Airport to put the leather wad on the next flight to Seattle—but that flight had just taken off, so she put it on the next one, for 50 bucks, which got into Seattle around midnight, 12 hours after Berenson had landed.

While the coach cooled his heels in the Seattle airport, he went to the cafeteria to buy a hot lunch with the cash he had in his pocket. After he picked up his food and put his tray down on a table, he realized he'd forgotten to grab a salad. When he went back to the front to get one, a cafeteria worker assumed the customer had left, so the busboy threw out his untouched food. Berenson returned with his salad to find his table bare.

After his wallet landed Berenson finally got his rental car, then drove out into a snowstorm so severe he became disoriented within a few hours. He wisely pulled off the road to get some rest. He woke up at dawn, then drove another five hours, until he saw a sign warning drivers that they'd better use tire chains if they planned to go any farther. Berenson pulled off to open the trunk of his rental car only to discover he had none. He decided to press on anyway, however slowly, and finished the drive to Vernon.

Berenson's luck turned when he pulled into Vernon. He was gratified that all three were clearly worth seeing, and that his friend Gordie Howe would be the banquet speaker after the games. On the downside, Bill Lindsay bypassed college for junior hockey and now plays for the Florida Panthers. Jason Marshall committed to Michigan, but the day before fall classes began he also jumped to junior hockey and eventually made it to the NHL, too.

But David Oliver, of course, did enroll at Michigan, where he finished his career eighth on the all-time career scoring list and pulled the team to the brink of an NCAA title.

"If you look at it that way," Berenson says, "the whole [trip] was worthwhile."

Sometimes, from the players' perspective, the recruiting process is just as problematic. When Steve Shields came for his campus visit in 1990, his weekend host Dave Roberts took him to a frat party where they were supposed to meet senior captain Alex Roberts and some other friends. To get in, Dave Roberts had to make contact with one of the fraternity brothers his cousin Alex knew. But the doorman, a power-tripping 6'5" hammer-head, would have none of it. While the hockey contingent waited for someone to get Alex from inside the party to resolve the matter, Alex's brother Andy, who didn't attend Michigan, started making things interesting outside. Whenever the doorman made an unnecessary threat and looked away, Andy would chirp his protest from the back of the small circle of players. When the doorman looked back, Dave would calmly insist that they weren't looking for any trouble—which everyone but Andy wasn't. (It must be said, however, that Shields was game for almost anything that night.)

Finally the doorman gave them an ultimatum. "I'll give you 10 seconds to leave."

Dave waited until the doorman reached eight, in the hopes that Alex would emerge, then turned to go. But the doorman grabbed Dave Roberts anyway, inciting his cousin Andy to tear the doorman's shirt. The fight was on.

"One guy tries to sucker punch me," Dave Roberts recalls, "but Brad Turner sees it coming and puts the guy's nose on the other side of his face. Brad gave some of the guy's buddies the same treatment. The doorman finally goes after Turner, but Turner takes care of him quite nicely, too. On the way out of their yard I heard one of the frat guys ask another, 'Who the hell was *that*?' And the other guy says, 'One baaad m— f—.'"

The next day Dave Roberts learned that their would-be liaison was actually the doorman himself, who apparently forgot about his promise to Alex Roberts. Needless to say, all this made quite an impression on Shields—a very *positive* impression. He left the scene thrilled, asking incessantly, "Where do I sign up?! Where do I sign up?!"

"Man, we don't do this every weekend," Dave Roberts told the giddy recruit, "and we don't *want* to."

But the damage was done. Shields went back home to tell his buddy Cam Stewart about his exciting weekend in Ann Arbor. When Stewart arrived a few weeks later for his recruiting visit, he did his best to bump into every big guy he saw, in the hopes of inciting a similar melee.

Stewart was having no luck, however, when he noticed two-time All-American football player Greg Skrepenak, who was 6'6" and 320 pounds, across the street. But the moment Stewart's hosts Dave Roberts and Chris Tamer saw the look in Stewart's eyes, and the size of Skrepenak's body, they lifted Stewart off the ground and moved him bodily in the opposite direction.

"Not tonight, Tiger," Roberts told his disappointed guest.

During the same recruiting season, Steve Shields and Brian Wiseman got off on the wrong foot. Shields was an unorthodox but effective goalie playing for a weak Junior B team, the St. Mary's Lincolns, while Wiseman was an undersized but equally effective center skating for the rival Chatham Micmacs, named after the Nova Scotia tribe that manufactured the first modern hockey sticks.

Berenson and company saw Shields have a few excellent outings early in the season, and signed him up right away. When they started looking at Wiseman, too, they asked Shields what they thought of him. "Shieldsie didn't speak too highly of me, that's for sure," Wiseman says. "'You mean that little s— from Chatham.' Something along those lines."

"I just thought he was a little rat out there," Shields remembers thinking, an opinion he shared freely with the Michigan coaches. Shields is quick to add, however, "that was before he started scoring on me every night.

"I pretty much went belly-up after I signed. I can remember being on the wrong end of a few nine- or ten-goal games. I'm single-handedly taking responsibility for Wiseman breaking the all-time Junior B scoring record."

If Shields initially figured Michigan had no business recruiting Wiseman, the feeling was mutual. "After those first two outings," Wiseman recalls, "Shields didn't have too many good games against us. My thinking was, 'I can't believe Michigan's recruiting this sieve.' When I realized he'd be my goalie if I went to Michigan, St. Lawrence suddenly sounded pretty good!"

Of course, both players enrolled at Michigan, along with Cam Stewart, David Oliver, Aaron Ward, and Mike Stone, all but one of whom went on to play in the NHL. They met at orientation in

June 1990, hit it off immediately—after they shared a good laugh over their unofficial scouting reports the previous season—and moved into a house together after their freshman year.

"We had a really tight class, basically from the day we met," Wiseman says. "We found our spot within the group, and got along throughout. Right from the very first day it worked like that."

"I can't remember one time," Shields says of Wiseman, "that we've ever been mad at each other."

The Class of '94 stays in almost daily contact during the hockey season. And in the off-season, "we all seem to find ourselves back in Ann Arbor one way or the other," Wiseman adds, with three of them buying a house together in town.

"That's about the farthest thing I expected from where we started," Wiseman says, reflecting on his decade-long friendship with his former nemesis. "But we were led down the right road by Donnie Stone's class, who were seniors when we got here, guys like Kent Brothers and Mark Sorensen and Jimmy Ballantine. And then hopefully we passed that on to the other classes, too, like Knuble's, Halko's, and Morrison's. All those classes are tight, too. But that's just what Michigan's all about, I think."

34

Determination

No matter how much the Michigan players helped recruit the next generation, however, it was the coaches who had to get things started. Mark Miller carried the load for four years, before leaving hockey altogether for the business world in 1987. "Mark was the savior," Berenson says. "I didn't know the recruiting network, but he knew the teams and the coaches. The poor guy'd come home on a Sunday morning, and I'd want to go up to Toronto to go see some prospect that afternoon. He spent an awful lot of time on the road and in the rinks."

Larry Pedrie succeeded Miller in 1987 and was joined by Mel Pearson the next year. "Seven nights a week, we were watching hockey," Pearson recalls. "We'd practice, get in the car, go see a game somewhere, play our games on the weekend, then get back in the car to see a prospect play on Sunday night."

Rebuild it, and they will come. And they did, year by year, man by man. But the game is played not over the phone or on a sheet of paper, but on a sheet of ice. And on the ice, Michigan's progress was agonizingly slow.

Berenson's first team, the 1984–85 squad, went 13-26-1, and finished in ninth place. Fair enough; he was learning a new job. But his second team finished in eighth place, with one less victory than the year before. And his third team was only slightly better, finishing in seventh place at 14-25-1.

Rob Palmer, the former defensive standout on Farrell's teams who went on to play seven seasons in the NHL, saw the struggle up close when he returned to assist the team from 1986 to 1989 while getting his M.B.A. "It was a great way to wean myself from the game," he says. "Red gave [fellow assistant] Dave Shand and I a lot of leeway to speak our minds—what was he going to do, fire us? If I performed any service for Red, I was someone he could talk to."

After Saturday night games, the Berensons and the Palmers would retire to Berenson's home, where the wives would talk upstairs and the husbands would settle into the downstairs den to wind down, have a few beers, and talk about the game. More often than not, they wouldn't finish until three or four in the morning.

"Red may be very confident, but maybe he wasn't as confident then," Palmer recalls. "They were improving, but not as quickly as he would've liked. Red kind of thought he'd turn it around faster. He was *discouraged.*

"I'd say, 'Red, don't get discouraged, because you're doing the right things. You've got the right philosophy, and they'll feed on that and make it go right.' When the kids screw up, their biggest fear is going to see him.

"What he'd talk about was leadership. Red wanted to recruit his idea of what a Michigan man should be. And that's what's perpetuating Red's success now: The seniors tell the freshmen, 'This is the way we do things here.' Now you come in, and the captain is a Mike Knuble, or a Brendan Morrison, or a Billy Muckalt, guys who are sticking around to teach the younger guys. They're Michigan men."

But in the first years of the Berenson era they suffered loss after loss—some of which bordered on the comical. In Red's third weekend on the job the team traveled to Durham, New Hampshire, to take on the UNH Wildcats. Michigan was 3-1, with a new coach and a new sense of confidence. Michigan built a 3-0 lead in the first game, but it could have easily been 5-0. Future U.S. Olympian Jeff Norton, playing in his fifth game at Michigan, scored his first goal in that contest. But when Brad Jones went to retrieve the puck out of the net to give the freshman a keepsake, long after it went in, the ref called Jones for being in the crease and disallowed the goal. John Bjorkman also had a goal called back, which set up the joke: "How do you get a three-goal lead against New Hampshire? Answer: Score five goals." The refs also helped the Wildcats' cause by throwing a string of Wolverines into the penalty box and not giving Michigan its first power play until after New Hampshire had caught up and gone ahead, but by then it was too late, and Michigan returned to the hotel with a 7-4 defeat.

Some Wolverines went home earlier than others. After team manager Jim Kneidert learned that the myopic official worked as an accountant by day, he said, "I hope you're a better accountant than you are a ref!" The official quickly turned to Berenson and said, "The trainer's got to go."

"Why?" Berenson replied. "Everything he said is true."

With that, the ref whipped around and, using his superhuman powers of sight and judgment, tossed out equipment manager A. J. Duffy, who had been silently watching the debate.

Ironically, Michigan has since been credited with a victory in that game because the University of New Hampshire used an ineligible player. If the player in question had skated in the following night's 9-4 Michigan loss, the Wolverines could have earned a sweep.

In the fall of 1986, Berenson's third season behind the Michigan bench, the team traveled for a weekend set against University of Illinois-Chicago. Michigan had already stumbled out of the gate with a 2-4 record, all against CCHA teams, and dropped the Friday night contest to UIC, 5-2. Shortly after Saturday's pregame meal at the Days Inn, all but a few players contracted severe cases of food poisoning. Some say it was from spoiled salad dressing. Others maintain it was from bad meat in the spaghetti sauce. But Ryan Pardoski asserts, "Don't listen to that salad dressing stuff. It was the meat sauce, man." Like the Grassy Knoll theory or the identity of Deep Throat, this is one mystery that might never be solved. But the upshot, if you will, was impossible to ignore. Six players became so violently ill they couldn't leave the hotel, and the rest spent the night throwing up on the bus going to the game, on the bench in the team's large Gatorade coolers, and on the bus going home—a scene suitable for an *Airplane* movie. By the third period there were so few players still skating that the bench was empty during line changes.

Goalie Warren Sharples got so sick he had to come out, but his backup, Glen Neary, was no healthier. Neary got so few chances to play, however, that he didn't want to tell Berenson just how sick he was. Neary finished the game by making occasional trips to the bench to throw up.

Because the UIC players felt just fine, their coach, Val Belmonte, decided to kick the Wolverines when they were down, keeping his first power play on the ice throughout the game en route to a 13-3 slaughter. "They shoved it right down our throats," recalls Alex Roberts. And that's the story of the Chicago Massacre—a humiliation Berenson never forgot.

"When I first got here, I was struck by Red's intensity, his work ethic," Pearson says. "He was *not* satisfied with the way things were going. He didn't want anyone to be comfortable or happy with the way things were."

A truth about all great athletes and coaches: They love winning far less than they hate losing. Berenson falls squarely in that camp. And that's why the eighties were so difficult for the prodigal son to take.

Berenson was desperate to bring Michigan hockey back to prominence. He didn't take lunch breaks or go for morning workouts, and would often walk back several miles to the hotel after tough losses. And there were many, 77 in his first three years alone. Small wonder that all the pressures and demands didn't leave much room for getting close to his players.

"At the end of some weekend series where we took two losses I remember looking at him and thinking, 'Wow, this devastates him twice as much as it does the team,'" says current assistant coach Billy Powers, who played for Red from 1985 to 1988. During Powers' playing days, Michigan was swept a disillusioning 18 times, 9 in his first year alone. "Red couldn't act with us the way he can with the players now. He had to be on his game every second. He couldn't give us that much freedom, because we couldn't handle it. If he let his guard down, we'd say, Time to party."

Ask Berenson's players from the early years for their impressions of the man, and you're not likely to hear adjectives like "easygoing," "fun loving," or "hilarious." While most of them have come to know the lighter, warmer facets of Berenson's personality, they didn't see much of those in the mid-eighties. Alex Roberts remembers a game during his freshman year, in which Berenson was hit with a puck on the cheek while coaching behind the bench. "We could see him bleed a little," Roberts says. "I was sitting next to Glen Neary, our backup goalie, and he whispers to me, 'At least now we know he's human.'

Berenson behind the bench
"Red was more on a mission than we were," says former player and current assistant Billy Powers. "He tried to push and pull every single thing out of us because he was trying to teach us how to win, but it took us a lot of time to realize what it took."
(Photo by Mark A. Hicks. Courtesy of the U-M Athletic Department.)

"At first I think it was like a business to him, until he realized he was dealing with kids," Roberts reasons. "But each year he got better with the players."

"When I look back on it," Powers adds, "I can see that he was so intense because our record and our standing were obviously much more embarrassing to him than they were to us. He was more on a mission than we were. He tried to push and pull every single thing out of us because he was trying to teach us the Michigan tradition and how to win, but it took us a lot of time to realize what it took. It must have taken a lot out of him, doing everything in his power and only getting marginal returns. That poor bastard."

"During my four years at Michigan [1984–88] I always felt we had a better team than our record was," says Brad McCaughey, who finished among the team's top five scorers each year. "We had a group of guys who'd show up for the important games and maybe not for the other games. My teams often split with Michigan State, but we'd always finish in the bottom four. Very inconsistent. But you could see the quality of the recruits that were coming in."

If Berenson's program was making progress, it was hard to see it on the ice. But you could see improvement in the locker room and in the classroom, the places Berenson most wanted to see fundamental changes take root. Rebuilding from the ground up takes more time than just remodeling the facade, after all, but the changes last. Berenson felt it was just as vital to the long-term success of the program to get blue-chip recruits like O'Connor and Brost as it was to fill the rest of the spots with character players like Billy Powers and Mike Moes, Alex Roberts and Rob Brown, the kind of men whose full value to the program couldn't be expressed on a score sheet.

35

Baby Steps, Broken Hearts, and Heavy Lifting

By 1987–88, Berenson's fourth season, he had recruited 20 of the 23 players on the team, including junior captain Todd Brost and a couple sophomores named Alex Roberts and Rob Brown, both of whom grew up a few miles from Michigan State's Munn Arena and turned down Ron Mason to go to Michigan.

Changing allegiances was especially tough for Roberts, whose parents graduated from Michigan State. His father, Jack, had played hockey for the Spartans, and even lined up against Berenson a few times. Roberts grew up wearing an endless wardrobe of Spartan paraphernalia; attending countless Spartan football, basketball, and hockey games; and hating Bo Schembechler. He had never, not once, been to Ann Arbor until Berenson came calling.

But like Brown, when Roberts was considering colleges, he couldn't ignore the fact that State was loaded with top talent, while Michigan offered him the opportunity to play right away. Further, both were convinced that Michigan offered a better education. And then there was the Red factor.

"The biggest thing for me was Red Berenson," Roberts says. "He had this presence about him. It was hard to say no to him. That pretty much sealed it."

Still, there was an adjustment. "I committed to Michigan on my birthday, January 11, 1986," Roberts recalls. "A week later I'm at the Michigan–Michigan State basketball game when Scott Skiles lit up Michigan and Antoine Joubert. I was still rooting for State, when I realized I had to start cheering for Michigan."

Before the Lansing-defectors played their first home game against Michigan State, on November 14, 1986, the Wolverines huddled at the top of the stairs, as they always do, "and all I could hear was 'Go green! Go white!'" Brown recalls. "I'm just wondering what the hell is going on. How are we playing the biggest game of the year, *at home,* and it sounds like we're playing in East Lansing? Now, down deep I knew going to Michigan was the right move for me, but I had to wonder about it at that moment. Holy smokes. That could have been *me* on the other side."

"The atmosphere in Yost was unbelievable," Roberts concurs. "Six thousand State fans and 2,000 Michigan fans. The goal was simply to try and shut the State fans up. At *home.*"

With Brost spreading the Berenson gospel inside the locker room, the team's internal improvements eventually became visible on the outside too. "Brostie made us set our own goals," says Kent Brothers, a freshman on that team who experienced the seismic shift occurring in the program in the latter half of the eighties. "We went around the locker room, and every guy got up and gave another one. Then Brostie laid down the rules: no weekday parties, no Friday parties, no parties after losses. Only on home Saturday nights after wins. You'd get down on any guy not toeing the line. The new guys tell me they still stick to all that now, but it started with Todd Brost."

The 1987–88 team finished in fifth place with 22 wins and 19 losses—Berenson's first winning record. Berenson also got Michigan's first weekend sweep of Michigan State since 1980, which probably no one appreciated more than Alex Roberts and Rob Brown.

"That's the year when the behavior and the attitude started changing," Brown says. "That's when we felt we finally made the turn. We were upset when we lost. And that attitude is still there."

In the first round of the CCHA playoffs, Michigan beat Western Michigan 5-4, for Berenson's first CCHA playoff victory in seven tries. But the Broncos won the next game, 4-3, and then humiliated Michigan in the rubber match, 10-0. "I'll never forget looking around that locker room," Roberts recalls, "and seeing [seniors] Joe Lockwood and Brad McCaughey, the disappointment in their faces. It was their last game as Michigan Wolverines, and we just got *annihilated*."

Another step forward, another heartbreak. But in 1988, even a heartbreak was progress. The players, at least, finally had something to be heartbroken about.

The 1988–89 team was Michigan's first all-Berenson squad, one captained by Todd Brost and Myles O'Connor, the linchpins of his first recruiting class, who had turned out to be every bit as good as originally advertised. The Wolverines won 7 of their first 10 games that year, before skidding their way into midseason with just one win in the next 10 games. They backed into the Great Lakes Invitational (GLI)—a two-game holiday tournament in which Michigan had won its opening game just once under Berenson and hadn't won both games since 1975—with an 8-9-3 record and a need for a shot in the arm.

The Wolverines opened with a solid 7-5 victory over Michigan Tech, but the next night North Dakota seemed to dash Michigan's hopes of getting the GLI monkey off its back when the defending national champions staked a 5-1 lead after two periods, sending the fans at Joe Louis Arena searching for their cars in the parking structure.

But with 15 minutes left fourth-line skater Kent Brothers scored to make it 5-2. Jeff Urban, another reserve player, "played out of his mind," Brothers recalls, and scored Michigan's third goal. Next, Denny Felsner, who still holds the school record for most career goals, followed that up by firing a big league shot into the upper shelf to pull Michigan within one, 5-4. Then captain Brost himself, standing off the corner of the net, sent one upstairs to tie it, 5-5.

When the third period ended Michigan had already mounted its most impressive comeback in Berenson's first five years—and against the defending national champions, no less. But the night didn't end until the second overtime, when Mike Moes suckered Russ Parent, one of the Fighting Sioux's best defensemen, to bite on a fake shot, then slipped the puck through him and snapped the biscuit into the open corner of the net for the winning tally.

At one in the morning of December 31, 1988, Michigan had won its third GLI in 19 attempts, and its first for Berenson.

"That was probably the biggest accomplishment for our team to that point," Roberts says. "We'd still never won a playoff series, but we realized we could play with a good team in a big game."

While the Wolverines celebrated their rare triumph, the Sioux already dreaded the punishment that was bound to follow their fabulous fall-down. "When we flew home we knew—we *knew*—we'd be skating the next day," says former North Dakota winger Justin Duberman. "We didn't even drink on New Year's Eve, because we knew what we'd be in for, and we still skated until we threw up our food. Such a great collapse."

Three months later the Wolverines lost in the first round of the CCHA playoffs for the fifth consecutive year, but they did manage to take Bowling Green to three overtimes in the third game before dropping.

Another season, another step forward, another heartbreak.

The 1989–90 team would be relying on a senior captain few would have predicted would rise to the role during his freshman year: Alex Roberts. In Roberts's first training camp, in the fall of 1986, Berenson was putting the team through its usual paces up and down the stairs of the football stadium—on one foot, hopping on two feet, hitting every other step, carrying a team-mate, you name it—when Roberts reached the landing far behind the pack, gasping for air and bent over at the waist. "I look down," he remembers, "and all I see is a pair of black Nikes—Berenson's. I look up, slowly, and the only thing he says is, 'So you want to be a hockey player, do you?' At that moment I was about two inches tall."

Roberts struggled throughout his freshman year, 1986–87, on and off the ice. He would set a school record for penalty minutes that year, with 117, while contributing only one goal and seven assists in 37 games. Off the ice he squeaked by with a 2.0 grade-point average and was in no danger of being tabbed as a future team leader. Roberts sums up his freshman year simply: "I was not helping the team."

Things came to a head for the young defenseman during an

early December road trip to Minnesota. The Wolverines got waxed, 11-2 and 5-2, which so infuriated Berenson that he warned his players, "I don't even want to see anyone peek their heads out of their hotel rooms tonight." But Roberts's roommate on the road, junior defenseman Jeff Norton, snuck out to meet some of his former Michigan teammates who had moved back home to Minnesota—then returned to the hotel with his buddies and a woman at one in the morning.

"Man, I'm scared s——less," Roberts says. "I'm already on the edge with Red as it is." Eventually everyone left but Norton and the woman. When someone knocked on the door, Roberts opened it, only to be blasted with a fire extinguisher by former Wolverine Tom Stiles. Just as Stiles finished covering every-thing, including Roberts, with the incriminating white powder, the room's fire alarm went off from the man-made fog. Roberts frantically tore the white plastic device out of the ceiling to squelch it, but the outside of the door was still painted white. Minutes later Berenson entered the room with the help of hotel security, surveyed the scene, looked at Roberts, shook his head, and departed without a word.

After they returned to Ann Arbor the next morning, Berenson summoned Roberts to his office. "He told me I'm on a tryout basis from now on," Roberts recounts. "My career at Michigan is in jeopardy. And if I don't turn the corner, he'll cut me. I'd keep my scholarship, but I would not be a hockey player. That day scared the hell out of me."

With renewed motivation, and the considerable help of Myles O'Connor, then an All-American senior captain, Roberts righted his ship. He made fewer trips to the penalty box, played better defense, and hit the books, hard. Despite his slow start, Roberts would become an obvious pick for captain his senior season and graduate with a 3.0 grade-point average.

"Myles was my mentor," Roberts says. "He'd tell me what classes to take and how much time to put into each one, and he got my head straight on the ice. Myles was awesome."

With a wizened Alex Roberts and steady co-captain Mike Moes leading the team, Berenson's boys took another step forward in

1989–90 when they successfully defended their GLI title against Northern Michigan and Michigan State, and took another when they won their first CCHA playoff series in school history by sweeping Western Michigan, a series in which Roberts scored his first and only hat trick. Although they lost to Michigan State in the CCHA semifinals at Joe Louis, 4-3, they redeemed themselves by winning the consolation game the next night against a good Bowling Green team, 5-4, giving them 24 wins for the season and, they figured, their first NCAA invitation since 1977. "A lot of heartache, a lot of groundwork, a lot of recruiting went into

The Class of 1990
"The class of Alex Roberts doesn't get enough credit," says Dave Shand. "They weren't the most talented bunch Red's had, but I tell you what: those guys could *lead*." Roberts's class went from below .500 as freshmen to the brink of an NCAA berth in their senior year.
(Courtesy Alex Roberts.)

that effort," Berenson says, "and we thought that would be good enough for an NCAA bid."

So did the Bowling Green Falcons. In the postgame hand-shaking line, BG coach Jerry York and his stars Nelson Emerson and Rob Blake all wished Berenson, Roberts, and company good luck in the upcoming NCAA tournament, conceding their own elimination from consideration.

These days the players gather in Yost's plush new meeting room to watch ESPN's NCAA selection show on the Sunday before the tournament to find out whom they will be playing. But in 1990 Michigan didn't have a plush new meeting room, and ESPN didn't cover the selection process in any case. Roberts didn't hear the news until goalie Warren Sharples came up to him at a Michigamua Society meeting and said simply, "We didn't get in. Bowling Green did."

Roberts was apoplectic. "I've never been more disappointed in my entire life," he says. "When we took our jerseys off after beating Bowling Green, we figured we'd be playing again, that it wasn't the last time we'd be taking them off. We earned the odd distinction of being Berenson's only team to win its last game without winning a title." Berenson had finally developed a team good enough to present at hockey's high society ball, only to see his boys turned away at the door by the historically capricious NCAA committee.

The seniors might not have sufficiently impressed the NCAA, but the underclassmen they molded remembered the lessons their elders had taught them, and those lessons would propel the team in the seasons to come. "The class of Alex Roberts doesn't get enough credit," says Dave Shand, who played one year under Farrell and eight in the NHL before returning to Ann Arbor to attend law school and work as an assistant coach from 1989 to 1993. "They weren't the most talented bunch Red's had, but I tell you what: those guys could *lead.*"

In the history of the program, there has probably not been another class that had a bigger gap between their contributions and the recognition they received for them. They had signed up for a program that had finished in eighth place with a 12–26–0 record the year before they arrived, and left it in fourth place with a 24–12–6 record. They had bequeathed a team that was poised to become a national contender, while falling just short of that plateau themselves. The classes that followed were able to reach the top only because they were standing on the shoulders of the Class of 1990.

During the 1990 senior banquet, Berenson called up Rob Brown, the man who turned down his hometown school, Michigan State, to walk on at Michigan and play in every single game for four years, 164 of them, a record that still stands. Unlike his classmates, who had prepared written remarks for their senior speeches, Brown "had a few ideas, but I figured I'd just talk from my heart—and that's what happened," he remembers. "I just got up there, and looked out at all the faces of these guys that I'd gone to war with for four years—and I knew I was never going to have that kind of closeness again no matter what I did—and it was then that it hit me: hockey was over. It was done. And I just lost it. I was all choked up. I couldn't talk."

Brown excused himself, stepped down from the podium, and returned 10 minutes later to say his piece, but the precedent of crying at the senior banquet had been established. "Now it happens all the time," he says, "but I think I was the first one to bawl up there.

"But beyond wanting to do it all again, I didn't have any regrets. I don't think I left anything at Michigan. Whatever I had, I gave."

And so did his fellow seniors, the class that did the heavy lifting.

36

The New Look Wolverines

The Michigan hockey team has gone through almost as many helmet designs as head coaches. The team went hatless in the 1920s, then strapped on leather bowls for the next two decades before switching to plastic boxes, synthetic domes, CCMs, Coopers, and finally Nikes. But the most dramatic change in headgear occurred on an otherwise uneventful day in late February 1989.

Former captain Alex Roberts remembers it like it was yesterday. "Right before the league playoffs, we're coming up the stairs to the locker room" he recounts, "and we start smelling fresh paint. The smell's everywhere.

"We get up to the top of the stairs and see the training room tables in the hallway, with a bunch of helmets on 'em painted dark blue with the yellow wings, just like the football team's—and we literally thought it was a joke. The helmets were totally out of the normal protocol. We're like, 'Where are our real helmets, the white ones? What the hell are *these*?' We were just laughing our asses off. Then Red comes in and says, 'You guys are wearing these.'

"That night we bought Red one of those baseball caps with the football helmet design on it and gave it to him the next day. 'If we're gonna wear these things on our heads,' you are too.' He did."

Paul Gallagher, an Ann Arbor attorney and Michigan hockey fan, gave Berenson the idea to borrow the famed design, which definitely was not an immediate hit with the hockey players.

"Funny thing was," Roberts adds, "we had all gotten buzz cuts that week for team unity before the playoffs. And now we all had to readjust our helmets to fit our smaller heads, which meant the yellow stripes were all out of whack."

But the design got the attention it was supposed to get. When the Wolverines came out for warm-ups against Bowling Green to open their best-of-three playoff series, the Falcons actually stopped what they were doing to gawk at the Michigan team's new look. "We just said, 'Hey man, this is us,'" Roberts recalls, chuckling. " 'We've gotta do what we're told.' All I can say is, we felt pretty corny."

Berenson's hockey players might have been more shocked at their first sighting of the unorthodox design than Fritz Crisler's football players were a half century earlier.

Fritz Crisler won a national championship in 1947, he changed the game forever with the platoon system in the late 1940s, and he shaped college football by serving on the NCAA rules committee for over two decades before he retired in 1968. Yet the former Michigan football coach and athletic director might be best remembered for designing Michigan's distinctive "winged helmet," still the most recognizable headgear in college football.

But here's a dirty little secret: Crisler first designed the winged helmet at Princeton, not Michigan, and brought it with him to Ann Arbor.

Back then football helmets resembled the leather biking helmets favored by the Tour de France riders in the 1980s. They typically consisted of a leather bowl with an extra pad on the front to protect the forehead, from which three strips of padding ran to the back. Teams usually painted the entire contraption or not at all. To help his Princeton quarterback identify his receivers downfield and give his team a little style in the process, Crisler simply painted the reinforced padding Princeton orange, and—voila!—the winged helmet was born.

When Crisler came to Ann Arbor in 1938, he brought the winged helmet with him. The Princeton Tigers dropped the design in 1937, a year before Crisler left, and only started using it again in 1998—no doubt inspired by Michigan's success in popularizing the look during the intervening decades. The University of Delaware Blue Hens also adopted the design when former Michigan fullback Dave Nelson became their head coach. Unlike Princeton, however, the Hens have worn the Crisler design ever since.

No matter the origins, there is no question that the unique helmet has been Michigan's calling card for six decades. Michigan's football coaches can't count how many times they've heard recruits say that it was the first thing they liked about Michigan. Some players have even said their desire to wear the famous winged helmet was their *primary* motive to come to Ann Arbor, including Michigan's long-time rushing leader, Jamie Morris.

"I had three older brothers play for Syracuse [including Joe, who later starred for the New York Giants], but I just loved Michigan's helmets," he says. "That's the reason why I came here—that and the little guy storming up and down the sidelines," he adds, referring to his coach, Bo Schembechler.

Michigan's opponents aren't quite as fond of it. When the Wolverines gather under the tunnel before games, the maize strips on their dark helmets give them the appearance of a bunch of bees from the stands, ready to attack anything in their path—an effect that's amplified when they charge through the "M Go Blue" banner and jump on top of each other at the far end of the field. Any opposing player can tell you that is one of the scariest sights in college football—so much so some visiting coaches won't even let their players watch. Several Michigan opponents, including Notre Dame and Indiana, have taken to taping the design over their helmets during practice to lessen the shock of seeing the maize and blue helmets come flying out of the tunnel and set up across the line.

But that's not the same as the real thing. The design has come to symbolize so much—power, discipline, excellence—that after the Wolverine hockey team adopted it, the swimming and baseball teams did, too. The look seems to help the hockey coaches recruit almost as much as it does the football coaches. Keep in mind, virtually every Michigan hockey recruit sees Michigan's football team on TV before they see the hockey team, and the helmet always makes an impression.

What seemed so foreign at first now seems completely natural. "When I look back at photos of our plain white helmets," Roberts says, "it just doesn't look right. Everybody loves the winged helmets."

Over the past decade, the unique design has become a symbol closely linked with the hockey team's excellence, too. The team has never had a losing record wearing Crisler's design, earning 11 consecutive NCAA bids and two national crowns since switching over. Other hockey teams are learning to loathe the helmets almost as much as Michigan's football foes do.

"Everybody else has got regular helmets," says Bobby Hayes, class of '98. "No one else has helmets like we do. That helmet, that's Michigan."

A Sophomore Captain, Pink Floyd, and Some Tough S.O.B.s

Berenson has always let his players pick their captains by secret ballot. Sometimes they've selected the team's biggest stars, sometimes they've picked lesser-known players with a knack for leadership, but they've always picked the players they respect the most.

Todd Brost and Myles O'Connor passed the torch to Alex Roberts and Mike Moes, who in turn handed it to Don Stone, a former walk-on the coaches initially thought had no chance of being a college player at all. "Shows you how much we know," says Dave Shand, the assistant at the time. "Idiots!"

The players that season, 1990–91, made an even more surprising selection when they tabbed David Harlock to be the team's co-captain, thereby making Harlock the first sophomore to captain the team since the ageless Connie Hill in 1945–46. Not bad for a guy who didn't even expect to come to Ann Arbor.

Michigan, Cornell, and Lake Superior State, among others, all coveted the Toronto native, but Harlock scratched Lake State off the list when Coach Frank Anzalone met with Harlock's parents and described Lake State as "a glorified high school." "My parents are both college educated, so my mom wasn't too impressed with the idea of a glorified high school," Harlock says, grinning at the memory.

In the early stages of the courtship of David Harlock, Berenson didn't do much better. "Red used to infuriate me during recruitment," Harlock admits. "He'd say, 'Look, it's cut and dried. It's an easy decision. You're either a Michigan man or you're not. This is the place.' Well, that was easy for him to say. But I'm 17 years old, and I've got two dozen schools slobbering over me and telling me I'm the greatest."

Harlock's third suitor seemed *juuuust* right. The Cornell coach pushed all the right buttons, and Harlock initially liked him best. But Harlock calmly decided to play another year of Junior B hockey in Toronto, then visit both schools again. The next year his decision boiled down to the same choices, but Harlock, playing a hunch, picked Michigan.

"I promised myself that I'd never ever look back and second-guess the decision I made," he says. "But it's funny how things turn out. The players I knew at Cornell ended up hating the coach at Cornell, and I ended up loving it here—and pretty quickly. In hindsight, Red was right: you're either a Michigan man or you're not. But at the time, geez!"

Harlock didn't campaign to become a sophomore captain, but he didn't muzzle himself, either. Unlike Alex Roberts, who himself wouldn't have predicted he'd be voted a senior captain after his freshman year, it was clear early on that Harlock was to the manner born.

"I didn't make any earth-shattering speeches as a freshman," Harlock says. "For the most part I just kept my mouth shut and listened to what other people had to say. But from Christmas on I wasn't that intimidated. I had respect for the upperclassmen, but I didn't necessarily feel I had to defer to them. I felt I could challenge the older players to be better on the ice and in the weight room. I wasn't afraid to tell 'em it was time to pick up the pace, or give encouragement, or speak my mind, either. But I was certainly surprised to be selected as a captain my sophomore year."

"The guy was a sophomore captain, which means the seniors had to be voting for him—and it wasn't even close," Shand divulges. "Harlock was a better coach than we were. His first season as captain he started the tradition of huddling around the net before each game. That wasn't our idea, that was his. We knew from that point on we had interior leadership."

That leadership was put to the test early in the 1990–91 season against the Soo Lakers, who'd won their first NCAA title in 1988 and would win their second in 1992.

"They were the measuring stick," explains Brian Wiseman, a freshman on that team. "If we couldn't beat them, we knew we couldn't get very far."

"I couldn't agree more with that," Harlock adds. "I remember the first time I saw those guys up at their place. They were bigger and stronger, and it seemed like half the players had full-grown beards. I felt like a boy playing among men. Michigan State was probably a bigger rival, but Lake State was the team we'd have to learn to beat."

Rallying around the net
The team gathers around the net before a game, a tradition started by three-year captain David Harlock. "The guy was a sophomore captain, so the seniors had to be voting for him—and it wasn't even close," Shand says. "He was a better coach than we were."
(Photo by Bob Kalmbach.)

Entering the 1990–91 season, Berenson's Wolverines had won only three times in their last 26 attempts against the Lakers. But with a 7-2-1 record going into their first series against Lake State on November 16, 1990, the Wolverines felt they might be ready to slay the giant.

No chance.

A 10-5 thrashing erased that illusion from the young players' minds. "All I remember from that game was their band playing a *lot*," Wiseman says. "They kicked our butts and good, and we start thinking, maybe we're not as good as we think we are. Seeing Red walk back to the hotel in a blizzard, *that* was a sight. We were freshmen. Red was not unapproachable—but I didn't want to talk to him then."

"It's freakin' minus 25 out there, and Red decides he's walking back to the hotel," Shand recounts. "I'm wearing a pair of expensive Italian loafers, and we're sloggin' along in ankle-high slush. The bus roars past us, and we're there trudging along the side of the road, and I'm thinking, What the hell am I doing?"

When Berenson and company made it back to the hotel, half an hour after the bus had returned, Berenson put the game tape in, and watched it with his coaches four times. "The next day at the hotel," Shand says, "Red tells his team, 'If you are men, you'll play.' That night Patrick Neaton scores in overtime, and we win, 4-3. Berenson was in the locker room smoking a big stogie—a dramatic moodshift from the 'blizzard walk' the night before. On that 10-hour bus ride home, it was like the guys had life again. We had just come through something. The Lake State jinx was over. We started realizing we had a chance to be a pretty good hockey team—and that we had a lot more tough S.O.B.s back there than we thought we had."

Throughout the sixties, only one player born and raised in the United States, Tommy Williams, played a significant role on an NHL team. Seeking to improve the professional prospects for U.S. collegians, a group of four men led by Michigan Tech coach John MacInnes and former Michigan great Jack Tompkins created the Great Lakes Invitational (GLI) tournament in 1965, to be held in Detroit each year between Christmas and New Year's. Michigan became Michigan Tech's co-host of the four-team tournament in 1974, and the duo has invited Michigan State every year since 1979.

For Michigan, the tournament presents a unique opportunity for the players to get to know their teammates better in an otherwise empty college town, when the other students are home with their families. Freshmen leave their dorms to live with the upperclassmen, and everyone gets to spend some quality time with each other for a few days.

But as the team's personnel improved, more and more of Michigan's top players were invited to play for national teams around the globe over the holidays, which required the rest of the players to pick it up a notch for the GLI in the stars' absence. But it also offered third- and fourth-line players a rare chance to prove themselves in a pressure situation.

For the 1990 Great Lakes Invitational, for example, the team's top two defensemen, David Harlock and Pat Neaton—both future NHLers—accepted invitations to play in All-Star tournaments elsewhere.

"We figure we've got no chance in the GLI," Shand admits. "I told our fifth and sixth defensemen, Mark Sorensen and Doug Evans, 'You have to be the best players on the ice this weekend.' And they were."

But that left at least two more defensive spots to fill. "I get to practice," Shand says, "and Red tells me, 'You have to teach Don Stone and Kent Brothers how to play defense—today.' Sure, no problem. I told those two, 'When you're in trouble, just throw it high off the glass. On three-on-twos, all I want you to do is back up, pray, and hope someone gets back to help you. And if you handle the puck for one freakin' second back there, you're benched.' It was an idle threat. I mean, who else was I going to put out there?"

"I flew back from Newfoundland that day," Brothers recalls, "and they tell me I'm going to be a defenseman. Man, when I left for vacation, I was barely a forward!"

The ad hoc defensive pair decided to call themselves Pink Floyd, after a rock group whose best-known album is titled "The Wall"—exactly what the makeshift defensive pair aspired to be. (They confess, however, that they never could decide who was Pink and who was Floyd.)

In Michigan's opening game against Michigan Tech, the defensive duo put it high off the glass whenever they got in trouble. On three-on-twos, they got back, prayed, and waited for a forward to get back and help. And they didn't handle the puck for "one freakin' second" behind the blue line the entire night.

Of course, it didn't hurt that the forwards back-checked like never before, goalie Steve Shields all but stood on his head, and Denny Felsner scored the go-ahead goal with 2:35 left in the game. But they couldn't have done it without Pink Floyd.

Michigan 2, Michigan Tech 1. "Simple game," Brothers says.

Next up: Maine, the defending NCAA champs. Same defensive pairs, same strategy—same result. The game was tied 1-1 late in the third when David Oliver put Michigan ahead for good at the 3:35 mark. Final score: Michigan 3, Maine 1.

"Pink Floyd *was* a wall," Shand says. "When the guys who'd been playing for their national teams heard about Pink Floyd, they came back with their knives out to make sure they got their jobs back."

"When they got back," Brothers recalls, "we'd say, 'You got a gold medal? Big freakin' deal! We won the GLI.' But the next week I was back fighting for my spot on the fourth line."

38

Taking Two Steps

The 1990 GLI title—Michigan's third in a row—launched a 15-game winning streak, still the longest in Michigan history. "The NCAA's decision the previous year motivated us to not even make it close from then on," Berenson says. "We decided we can't be the eleventh or twelfth best team in the country and leave ourselves at the mercy of the committee."

With the pain of the NCAA's snub still fresh, the 1990–91 team was determined to take the decision out of the committee's hands, and it succeeded. The team's 32-7-3 record through the league playoffs shattered the 1976–77 team's record of 26-16-0 and gave the NCAA no choice but to grant Michigan its first bid since 1977.

After so many had given so much over the previous seven years to get the team an invitation to the NCAA's annual ball, March 17, 1991, should have been a coming out party for the rejuvenated Wolverines. Instead, they played Cornell as if their invitation had been some kind of a mistake, losing the first game in the best-of-three series, 5-4, in a lackluster effort.

The 1991 senior class, consisting of Jim Ballantine, Mark Sorenson, captain Don Stone, and Kent Brothers, was reduced to three when Ballantine suffered a lacerated liver in the first game and left the building in an ambulance. After the game Sorenson ripped his equipment off, threw it around the locker room in disgust, showered, and stormed home. "I don't know what kind of message that sent," Sorenson says, "but that's just how I felt."

Two left.

The seniors were supported by a junior class that was small but hungry; a loaded sophomore class of Chris Tamer, Dan Neaton, David Harlock, David Roberts, Dan Stiver, and Mark Ouimet—the first four of whom would play in the NHL; and a legendary freshman class of Steve Shields, Brian Wiseman, Aaron Ward, David Oliver, Cam Stewart, Mike Stone, and Chris Gordon, the first five of whom would make it to the big leagues.

But the team's bottom-heavy roster had a downside for the seniors: "Unlike the new guys," Brothers points out, "we wouldn't be coming back; we didn't have a future in hockey, and we *knew* that. This was it for us. Next loss, we're done."

If Berenson was growing impatient with the program's steady but slow progress, Brothers was downright intolerant—even if he did notch just one assist in 24 games that year, for a career total of 19 points. "I was tired of taking baby steps, baby steps," he explains. He looked around the room that night, and took stock. Ballantine, Brothers's roommate and fourth-line center, was in the hospital, and Sorenson, his housemate, was at home stewing.

"Now there's just two left from my class in the locker room, Stonie and me," Brothers says. "We were not a great class, but we had a lot of role players and great leadership. Jimmy's gone, Sornie's gone, the coaches are out the door. Red gave a short speech, handled 'em with kid gloves, and left. We were expected to win, and we'd lost. I couldn't figure out what had just happened to us. I don't know what came over me, I couldn't hold it in any longer. I just started talking."

Brothers closed the locker room door, walked to the middle of the room, and said, "My hockey career ends when we lose our next game. But I'm not ready to finish. One of the keys to this program is to remember the guys who came before. And this time we've got to do all we can for the guys who never went on. We need to pull it together. Either I'll do it all by myself, or you'll join me."

"By the end of my little speech I was screaming at the top of my lungs," Brothers says. "I don't know if the coaches heard me, but I didn't care. There are times when you have to stand up. I didn't know what I was going to say, but when I sat down, I knew I had said something."

Jim Hunt has covered Michigan hockey since 1993 on WTKA, but he's never seen a show of leadership like that. "The joke in the press box was, even if you counted all Kent's practice goals, he still wouldn't be close to leading the team in scoring," Hunt says. "But somehow, that team became Kent's team, a fourth-line guy with one assist to his name."

"It came from a guy who'd obviously been through a lot of lean years," recalls goalie Steve Shields, a mere freshman at the time. "Obviously it affected us quite a bit. I think it suddenly became very important to everyone to give it everything we had."

Brothers didn't know it, but Berenson was in the next room and could hear him loud and clear. "He just let everything pour out," Berenson remembers. "The next night, I didn't have to say anything."

In the second game Michigan came out flying, and took a 3-0 lead. Despite a Big Red comeback that brought them within a goal at 5-4, Michigan finished them off, 6-4. "After that game, we had a renewed sense of confidence," Brothers says. "We had a new goal now: take two steps this year."

The rubber match on Sunday night was more than a game. For the first time since Farrell left, Michigan filled the house that Yost built without relying on Spartan boosters to do it. The team was going to make a lasting impression that night on the 6,000-some fans, one way or the other. "It was the loudest and most raucous I had ever seen that building," Harlock says.

You might think the only thing left to do would be to play the game, but up in the coaches' room, Berenson and his staff were considering a risky change: replace freshman goalie Steve Shields, who had started 37 of the team's 44 games to that point, winning a school record 26, with freshman backup Chris Gordon.

"Shields had been our goalie throughout the season, but he was fighting the puck," Berenson explains. "Geez, that was a big-time decision. We had to wonder if we were being fair to Gordon, throwing him in like that." But they did.

When the Big Red grabbed a quick 1-0 lead the coaches had reason to second-guess themselves, but they stayed the course. Gordon settled down, while the team—fueled by all the frustrations of the previous six years and a three-man senior class that was determined to make its mark before pulling off their jerseys for the last time—scored seven consecutive goals, erasing all doubt of the game's outcome and igniting the capacity crowd.

"There have been only two times I've cried at Michigan," Brothers says. "When we played Western Ontario and they played 'O, Canada' and the last 30 seconds of the Cornell game, my last period at Yost. I'm on the bench, and I look at [assistant coach] Shandy and say, 'The seniors have got to be out on that ice.'"

Berenson called a time-out with less than a minute left and told the three healthy seniors to take the ice. The fans, many of whom had never seen a Michigan hockey game before, stuck around to give the seniors a standing ovation. The moment the puck dropped in the Michigan zone, Brothers's tears started falling. When the game ended, "I just stood there," Brothers says. "There were 6,000 fans cheering, and I didn't know what to do. I'm crying, and Red's standing at the gate. I never hugged a man before, but I hugged him then."

Broad Ripples

Although Michigan was swept by—who else?—the Boston University Terriers, 5-1 and 8-1, in the NCAA quarterfinals, the aftershocks from that season lasted longer than anyone suspected at the time. "That was our first NCAA series, and we won it in front of our fans, our band, our people," Berenson says. "The win gave us some credibility outside the league, but what it really did was spark interest on campus. We'd had some good crowds before then, but nothing like it was during that series. That was a real turning point."

"I remember walking from West Quad during my freshman year down to Yost for Friday home games around 4:30 or so," Wiseman recalls. "The only time you could tell there even *was* a game back then was when we were playing Michigan State, and everyone you saw was wearing green and white. But after that Cornell game, you could always tell there was a game that night when you walked down to the rink. When I walked home from the final Cornell game that night I felt a buzz on the streets, like something had happened here tonight."

Something had. The next season the athletic department put its full force into promoting the hockey program, effectively pouring gasoline on a tinderbox.

Berenson's first team drew just over 3,000 fans per game. The following six seasons' average attendance never exceeded 5,000. But the year after the Cornell series, the average jumped to 5,513 per game and has been in the 6,000 range ever since. It started on that night back in 1991.

For the players, the triumph meant something more. They realized they no longer had to be content with just one step forward each year. They could take two, even three, steps in one season. With the glittering freshman and sophomore classes coming back, and über-captain David Harlock, the secretary of defense, leading the charge, it was impossible not to dream of NCAA titles. This was the bunch that could do it.

C-C-H-A! C-C-H-A!

Michigan's slow but steady rise from obscurity paralleled that of its new league, the CCHA. Founded in 1971, the new league could boast only four teams: current members Bowling Green and Ohio State and former members Ohio University and St. Louis University—but don't laugh. The St. Louis Billikins won half of the league's first six titles.

The league's survival was very much in doubt when Ohio University dropped varsity hockey, leaving only three teams to compete for the championship in 1973–74 and 1974–75. Instead of collapsing like Michigan's first three-team league did, the CCHA bounced back by adding Western Michigan and Lake Superior in 1975–76, Northern Michigan two years later, Ferris State the year after that, and Miami of Ohio in 1980–81.

Although the league had grown to include seven quality schools, all of which are still in the CCHA, the circuit was little more than a glorified bus league through its first decade. Only one CCHA team, Bowling Green, made the NCAA tournament in the seventies, and the Wolverines made short work of them during the 1977 playoffs.

The league raised its profile overnight when four WCHA defectors—Michigan, Michigan State, Michigan Tech, and Notre Dame—signed on for the 1981–82 season. Bowling Green's George McPhee became the first CCHA player to win the Hobey Baker Award the same season, and his school became the first CCHA team to win the NCAA title in 1984.

Despite garnering some of the trappings of big-time college

hockey, however, the CCHA could still not claim to be on the same plane as the WCHA, the ECAC, or Hockey East. In terms of profits, exposure, and respect, the CCHA was barely on the map. But in 1985 the CCHA gained something that ultimately proved more important than George McPhee's Hobey Baker, Bowling Green's national title, and even the absorption of the WCHA four: it hired Bill Beagan to be its commissioner for a paltry $16,000 a year. In the history of college hockey, never has so little money been spent so wisely.

Bill Beagan grew up in Ontario and played hockey in Parry Sound, home of Bobby Orr. Beagan assesses his ability as a player thusly: "If Berenson was a nine, I was a four." Not content to spend his time knocking around the minors, however, Beagan decided to join the Canadian military, which in turn lent his services to the United Nations Emergency Force. In 1959 Beagan's unit helped resolve the Suez crisis, and in 1964 he was transferred to the Canadian Embassy in Washington.

The Canadian government also loaned him out to military bases in Madison, Wisconsin, and Duluth, Minnesota, where he took up officiating hockey games "after my eyes got too bad to play," he jokes. Although Beagan was earmarked to become an attaché in some glamorous European city or other, when the NHL offered him a contract to officiate games in 1967, he couldn't resist.

While reffing in the NHL, Beagan came under the spell of Clarence Campbell, who served as the league's president from 1946 to 1971. Though few hockey fans know it, Campbell had been a Rhodes scholar at Oxford, the commander of the Fourth Canadian Armed Division headquarters for European operations throughout World War II, and one of the leading lawyers in the war crime trials at Nuremberg.

"He was my mentor," Beagan says. "There was nobody in the world I respected more than him."

Apparently the feeling was mutual. When the International Hockey League was looking for a new commissioner in 1969, Campbell helped Beagan get the job, even though Beagan, at 31, was younger than every one of the IHL's owners, general managers, and coaches. "I got my MBA in the IHL," Beagan says. "I talked with Campbell three, four times a week, about everything. I learned that being a commissioner is simply understanding the people you're dealing with."

After a successful 10-year run, Beagan left the IHL in 1979 to launch the Eastern Hockey League, which he ran for two years. He went on to own and operate the Toledo Goaldiggers for three years and once organized a $30 million bid for the Detroit Red Wings, eventually losing out to current owner Mike Ilitch. At about the same time, then–NHL commissioner John Zeigler suggested Beagan look into the commissioner's job with the CCHA. Because Beagan had never been involved in college hockey or even attended college, he didn't take the idea seriously until Don Canham called him for an interview in 1985.

The 13-Year Temporary Job

Canham chaired the search committee in his typically decisive manner and quickly settled on Beagan. "If you're going to market the sport, you *must* have a strong commissioner," Canham says today. "Beagan was *dynamite*, absolutely instrumental in the success of that league. He was just the master."

Given the league's meager resources, he had to be. In Beagan's first year, he ran the league from his den. Canham eventually convinced him to move the CCHA's headquarters to U of M's Marie Hartwig Women's Athletic Building, right across the parking lot from Yost.

"It was officially a part-time job, but it turned out to be a seven-day-a-week job, a labor of love," Beagan says. "I'd go to 40 games a year, not because I had to but because I wanted to. I fell in love with the college game, the campus culture, and all the rah-rah stuff. It was all pretty invigorating. The kids kept me hopping. When I'd come into a rink with a tie on, they'd say, 'You stylin', Commish?' I loved 'em!

"I only thought I'd be there for a year, but somehow it turned into a 13-year 'temporary' job."

Early on Beagan could see that the success or failure of the league would hinge on how the dichotomy between the Division I and Division II schools was handled. For guidance, Beagan harked back to some lessons Campbell had taught him. "Campbell always said you must treat all people equally, be they general managers, coaches, or players," Beagan says. "Do not create any cabals or conspiracies, and you'll never have any big problems. You have to treat the people like a campfire: you don't want to get too close or you'll get burned, but if you get too far away you'll get frozen out."

The difficulty of Beagan's balancing act between the league's Davids and Goliaths was leavened by the eagerness of the giants to lay low, starting with Canham.

"Canham would insist—*insist*—that everyone's equal," Beagan says. "Even when Michigan was not going that well, he would never miss a meeting. And he'd go out of his way to schedule a meeting up at Lake Superior and be there with everyone else. I never once saw Canham or Ohio State's Rick Bay or MSU's Doug Weaver step out of line or walk on anybody. They were just a bunch of guys who really wanted to help each other. There are some people in the West who would love to see the Big Ten schools in a conference by themselves, but Canham has been one of the strongest voices for the Division II schools.

"I think the Ferris States, the Lake Superiors, the Northern Michigans, they knew they enjoyed equality in this league," Beagan adds. "When it was touch and go for places like Ferris and Miami, especially with Title IX, I'd bring them articles from the *Washington Post*, the *New York Times*, and *USA Today*. 'You see this here? You're mentioned in the same paragraph with Notre Dame, Michigan, Ohio State. That *has* to have some impact on the credibility of Ferris State.'"

All Aboard

After he'd consolidated strong support from the member schools, Beagan raised his sights from merely surviving to thriving, starting with the annual awards banquet.

The league used to hold its modest season-ending awards banquets in the bowels of Joe Louis Arena, with just 20 people from each team in attendance. "It was really a joke, almost embarrassing it was so bad," Beagan admits. But Beagan took some cues from the Academy Awards and decided to dress all the players up in tuxedos. The NCAA said the league couldn't pay for them, so he offered President's Tuxedos free airtime in exchange for the tuxedos. The banquet now draws 800 people, who are entertained by string quartets and brass bands.

Beagan also worked tenaciously to get Notre Dame, which had dropped hockey in 1983, to resurrect the sport and rejoin the league. With Canham's help, he finally prevailed in 1992.

In the interim Beagan put together one of the most impressive TV deals in the country, for any sport. Few CCHA schools had a smattering of games on cable each season, but Beagan knew that, to be successful, the league needed a conference-wide contract with a "game of the week." This would require every team to put aside two dates a year for the league, forgoing the right to sell those dates to anyone else.

To help forge the contract Beagan went to the guru of college TV negotiating—Canham himself—who pledged Beagan his complete cooperation. "He could've said, 'I don't give a damn about the CCHA. PASS [a local sports channel] is already doing seven games a year for us.' But he said, 'You run with the ball. I'll let you know when you screw up.'"

Canham never had to. Beagan was a natural. With Michigan, Michigan State, and Ohio State committing two dates each season as bait, Beagan could force any bidder to take the Lake Superior and Bowling Green games, too, or take a hike. It worked. Having found that alumni groups from Arizona to New England eager to watch college hockey, Beagan got a deal to broadcast CCHA games around the country. The league now reaches 45 million homes each season.

All of this new energy and excitement added up to profits. The league never made a cent before Beagan came on board, but in his first 10 years as commissioner, his office cleared $4 million, which went directly back to the member schools. When Ferris State and Lake Superior started getting five-figure checks each spring, they could hardly believe it. It's no accident that Northern, Lake Superior, and Ohio State have all constructed new arenas in the past few years. They could see investing in hockey made sound business sense.

When Beagan first took over, most of the schools sent one or two low-ranking officials to attend the desultory league meetings. But once he got the ball rolling, league meetings started hosting three or four representatives from each school, including the athletic director and the faculty rep. "They finally realized that this is an income-producing sport," Beagan says. "This is big business, and they wanted to be a part of it."

The enhanced cache of the league was also manifest in the rising entrance fee, from $7,000 when Beagan started in 1985 to $100,000 by 1987. Among others, Notre Dame paid it happily—although secretly, to avoid raising a ruckus in South Bend—to join the fastest-growing hockey league in the country.

At the end of the day, the league's success was still predicated upon the members' on-ice performance. In the CCHA's first 14 seasons, only 12 of the 83 teams that played in the NCAA tournaments were from the CCHA, and never more than 2 per year in the tournament. In Beagan's 13 seasons, 40 of the 164 NCAA bids went to CCHA teams, 25 percent of the total field. Since 1983 the CCHA has never had *fewer* than 2 per year in the tournament. Further, CCHA teams took the national crown in 6 of those past 13 seasons. The next closest league was the venerable WCHA, with 4. When Beagan resigned in 1998, it would be hard for any objective observer to deny that this former "minor league" had become the most prestigious college hockey circuit in the country.

With so many CCHA teams competing in the Final Four, Beagan naturally wanted the NCAA to do a better job promoting that event, too. The NCAA had been holding the event in small towns like Duluth, Grand Forks, Albany, and Lake Placid, too far from the fans and media for Beagan's taste. Beagan urged the

NCAA—which he liked to call the Vatican West—to rent out the big arenas in the big cities, but NCAA officials were afraid they couldn't sell them out.

"I told them, you're never going to raise the profile of college hockey if you don't play in Carnegie Hall," Beagan recalls. "An old jazz musician says, 'It ain't *what* you play, it's *where* you play it.' Christopher Columbus proved the world ain't flat, and we're going to prove we can sell college hockey in L.A." Beagan was vindicated once more when the 1999 Final Four weekend in Anaheim drew almost 40,000 fans.

"College hockey is never going to go back," Beagan says. "Michigan's going to be sold out every year. So is Michigan State, and some others are heading that way, too. The college hockey culture is just going to get better and better and better."

"Bill Beagan revamped the officiating, the TV contracts, the scheduling," Canham says. "Of all the leaders in all the sports in all the administrations in all the leagues that I've been involved in, Bill Beagan was as good as any of them. I have tremendous respect for Bill Beagan. He simply made college hockey what it is today."

Beagan won't go that far, but he's justifiably proud of his accomplishments. "If you've got the only national TV contract in the country, and you've won 7 of the last 16 NCAA titles—well, as Dizzy Dean would say, 'If you did it, you ain't bragging.'"

Beagan knew he would retire after the 1998 season. That spring, Michigan won the NCAA title in Boston, after which Beagan broke for the first time with his own private protocol and entered Michigan's locker room. "I don't know why," he says. "I just walked in, and I gave Red a big hug. Billy Muckalt had his jersey off, all sweaty, and he came up to me and gave me a hug, and then the whole room started chanting 'C-C-H-A! C-C-H-A!' I just lost it. I had to leave."

"Red," Beagan said, "I gotta get out of here." He walked out the door, leaned against the wall, and covered his face with his right hand, sobbing.

Looking back on his 13-year temporary job, he says, "It was a great romance."

Part VIII

Exorcising the Demons
1992–98

40

A Sisyphean Task

Want to make God laugh? Tell him your plans.

Every Michigan team Red Berenson coached his first seven seasons had done better than the team before, from ninth place in
1984–85 all the way up to second place in 1990–91, so it only
seemed logical that if the 1991–92 team followed suit, the
Wolverines should have the NCAA trophy in their sights by
March. The team seemed to have exactly that in mind, tearing off
consecutive winning streaks of eight, seven, five, six, and five
games over the course of the season, casting a wide net that
snared its fourth straight GLI title, its first-ever regular-season
CCHA title, and a first seed in the West Regional of the NCAA
tournament.

Michigan's first opponent, the defending NCAA champion
Northern Michigan Wildcats, had just won its second WCHA
playoff title and was riding an eight-game winning streak—
which they extended with an 8-4 victory over Clarkson the night
before—when they met Michigan at Joe Louis Arena. Predictions
of a tight battle were thrown out the window when the Wildcats
scorched Michigan for a 6-3 lead in the second period.

David Roberts did manage to pop one in the basket with the
clock reading 00:00.5 at the end of the second period to give
Michigan some hope, but between periods, down 6-4, the Michigan players sat in their locker room stalls in wide-eyed disbelief.
The coaching staff, including graduate assistant Kent Brothers,

stood in a circle in the narrow hallway, not handling it much better.

"What do we do, what do we say?" Brothers recalls the coaches discussing. "While we were all standing around, I figured, what the hell, I was one-for-one so far.

"I didn't tell the other coaches what I was going to do. I didn't ask permission, I just went in there. I said, 'One year ago I was in a room like this, and I took off my jersey for the last time, and I felt like I was taking off a layer of my skin. Once it's gone, it's gone forever. And you'll spend the rest of your life wishing you had it back. Go out there. Go out there and give yourself another game. Don't let it go so quickly.'"

They didn't. The players attacked the Wildcats the way they attacked North Dakota in the 1988 GLI when they came back from a 5-1 deficit. Their efforts were rewarded just 3 minutes into the third period, when Patrick Neaton scored Michigan's fifth goal. With 10 minutes left, Denny Felsner's tally tied it up, and, with just 1:38 remaining in regulation, Ann Arbor's own Mike Helber scored his eighth goal of the season to keep the Wolverines from having to settle the matter in overtime. Michigan was headed to the Frozen Four.

It marked Berenson's first trip back to the Final Four since his 1962 team made its ill-fated journey to Utica, where they were upset by Clarkson in the semifinals. Berenson knew all too well that in a single-elimination hockey tournament, any one of the four teams could win it. But this time, he thought, the format's unpredictability might work for him.

With top-seeded Michigan facing sixth-seeded Wisconsin in one bracket, and Michigan State facing Lake Superior in the other, it looked like it was going to be an All-CCHA final. But Wally Grant could have warned them about the Terrier Curse. Getting the top seed was the first tip-off.

"Of the three CCHA teams in the Final Four," Harlock asserts, "we were the best team. We'd done well against Michigan State and Lake State that year, sweeping both of them in our last series against them. We had confidence that if we were to play one of those two teams we'd match up well and have a real good chance of winning. Wisconsin was the great unknown."

Sure enough, Wisconsin derailed Michigan's grand plans with a 4-2 upset. "Honestly," says Harlock, who went on to become the first Canadian Olympic player in Michigan history, "losing that game is the only real regret I have about my college career." The song remained the same: another step forward, another heartbreak.

The Wolverines slipped slightly the next year, notching two fewer victories and finishing second in the CCHA regular season and the league playoffs, but they were still plenty good enough to make a serious run come March Madness. They once again earned a first-round bye but this time took care of Wisconsin in triple overtime, 4-3. One bit of hard-won experience, at least, had paid off.

Michigan had earned a return trip to the Final Four, this time in Milwaukee. The Wolverines wisely didn't bask in their revenge over Wisconsin because their first Final Four opponent would be top-seeded Maine, led by goalie Garth Snow and Paul Kariya, two of the best collegians ever to play the game. But if the Wolverines were scared, they didn't show it, taking only four minutes to pull ahead, 2-0. The Black Bears apparently weren't intimidated either, when they fought right back to tie it up 2-2. Michigan went ahead again on an Aaron Ward goal, to hold a 3-2 lead at the end of second period. Having gone a perfect 24-0 when leading after two periods that season, the Wolverines had every reason to believe they could finish the job. But with just four minutes left in the game, the linesman threw center Brian Wiseman out of the face-off, forcing Cam Stewart to take the drop. He lost both the draw and his man, who walked around him to score the tying goal. Nonetheless, it looked like the Wolverines could still avoid the dreaded overtime if they could just finish one of their many odd-man rushes.

"We outplayed 'em," Wiseman recalls. "We came down three, four times and didn't get a shot on net but once. Eight seconds to go, Dan Stiver, who had the best shot on the team, had an open net on a 3-on-1—he could've *walked* it in—and he hits the side of the net. Any other time that season, we'd've scored three goals off of those chances."

But they didn't. One minute, thirty-six seconds into overtime, a Maine player tripped in front of the Michigan net, screening goalie Steve Shields. At the same time, Maine's Lee Saunders snuck into the slot and slipped the puck past the fallen player and Shields, straight into the left corner. Even on slow-motion video, it's not at all clear exactly how the muddled shot went in, but no one needed an autopsy to know Michigan's dream had died once again.

Their quest was not the Holy Grail or even the Stanley Cup—just a slab of cherry wood, ten inches wide and two feet tall, but it might as well have been made of gold, such was their desire for it. But once again, the wooden board had eluded them.

41

Hope Is a Dangerous Thing

Most recent hockey alums maintain that any Michigan team from the nineties *could* have won the grail, but the 1993–94 squad is one that definitely *should* have. Going into its senior year, the class of Wiseman, Shields, and Oliver—easily Berenson's best to that point—had already won three GLIs, a league title, three NCAA tournament bids, and four NCAA playoff games. And they were joined in the fall of their senior year by an even bigger and better class, the class of '97.

On defense, the freshmen had Harold Schock, Chris Frescoln, Peter Bourke, and Blake Sloan, who would go on to win a Stanley Cup with Dallas; up front they had John Madden, Mike Legg, Warren Luhning, Jason Botterill, and Brendan Morrison—all of whom, after graduation, went on to play professional hockey, four in the NHL. It was, quite possibly, the single best class in the history of college hockey. Between the bookends of those celebrated classes, the sophomore and junior classes provided hardworking role players and respected leaders, with a few stars in the mix like Mike Knuble and Steve Halko.

Wiseman and company swept the first College Hockey Showcase against Minnesota and Wisconsin in the fall. They won the school's sixth consecutive GLI. Through its first 31 games, the 1993–94 team had an unimpeachable record of 28-2-1. Although the squad dropped three of the last four regular-season games when Berenson gave the ringers some rest, they won their second CCHA regular-season title, their first league playoff title, and the NCAA's number one seed. No hockey team at Michigan had ever done it better. It seemed as if there was nothing this team couldn't do. Whatever these guys wanted, they simply took, without asking permission.

They even made their former tormentors look like lambs. From 1984 through 1991, Michigan had beaten the Soo Lakers just 8 times in 42 attempts—an anemic success rate of 19 percent. That ignominious run included three consecutive losses to the Lakers in the CCHA finals. So it was no small thrill for the Wolverines when they beat up their old league bully in all three regular-season meetings, and tacked on one more for good measure in the CCHA tournament finals, a 3-0 whitewashing for Michigan's first ever CCHA playoff title. Michigan's first goal in that game broke Laker goalie Blaine Lacher's streak of 375 minutes without letting in a single goal, a stretch that covered almost a month of games. All signs pointed to Michigan's first NCAA title since 1964. Even the symmetry of the thirtieth anniversary seemed right—provided you ignored Michigan's history with number one seeds.

The players had little reason to fear the Lakers when they drew them a week later as their first opponent in the NCAA tournament. The Lakers, seeded fourth in the Western Regional held in East Lansing, needed overtime to get past their first-round opponent, Northeastern, the fifth seed.

But Lake Superior blindsided Michigan with an early burst of scoring, leaving the Wolverines down 3-1 after the first period. But the men in blue had been there before. They knew what to do: Don't panic. Don't try to get them all back at once. Just stick to the game plan and chip away. Sticking to their comeback plan, the Wolverines took the lead in the second period on goals by Mike Stone, Jason Botterill, and David Oliver. With three seconds left in that period, however, the Lakers tied it up, 4-4. The Wolverines had numerous chances to take the lead for good in the third period, but missed them all.

Like the '77 Wisconsin Badgers, the '94 Lakers attacked Michigan from the moment overtime began. Just 2:31 into the extra period, while Shields prepared himself to stop an outside shot, the puck was tipped in front of him, sending the puck on an end-over-end arc just over his right shoulder and landing right behind him—behind the goal line. The fluky goal never hit the back of the net, it simply splatted on the ice inside the cage like a dead bird, but it was still enough to end Michigan's dreams once more.

"We had a ton of missed prime scoring opportunities, and they win on a deflection," Wiseman spits. "We were the class that missed by inches."

"That's the difference between our class and all the others," Shields adds. "We dominated Lake Superior all year, and then we lose on a tip. What made it hurt more is that the Lakers went on to the NCAA finals and waxed Harvard, 7-1. That should've been *us.*"

Mike Knuble was a junior on that team and therefore knew he'd be back for another shot, but he was too smart not to realize such golden opportunities don't come around every year. "Our junior year was probably our best chance to win it all," he says, "and we didn't even get to the Final Four."

This game, as much as any other played in Michigan's history, sticks in the craw of those involved. The season ended with the most painful gap ever between the team's expectations and its final results—bigger even than the 1949, 1950, or 1962 teams suffered. The '94 squad didn't lose in the finals or even the semis, the kind of setbacks all good teams must occasionally suffer in a one-game elimination format. They lost in the quarterfinals, in East Lansing, in their first game of the playoffs. They didn't feel like they'd lost a photo finish by a nose, they felt like they had been disqualified for a false start. It was more than an upset, it was an obscenity.

(The following week, at the Final Four press conference, a reporter asked Lake Superior coach Jeff Jackson who the best team in the tournament might be. "The best team," he replied, "isn't even here," referring to the vanquished Wolverines turning in their equipment back in Ann Arbor.)

"I sat down for a long time in the locker room after that Lake State game," Wiseman says. "In junior hockey, or pro hockey, you lose and you get over it. You'll have more games. But in college hockey, you might not get another chance. It was hard to take all the equipment off for the last time. After that one I told Red, 'Hey, I'm exhausted.' He said, 'Well, that's all we ask of you.'"

But the coaches and players wanted more—they wanted that ten inch by two foot slab of cherry wood.

Hope is a dangerous thing. It's what motivates us to keep working harder and aiming higher, but each time it goes unfulfilled, it feels like a broken promise, a betrayal. After enough disappointments, most people quit hoping and give up on their dreams.

You'd think the Michigan players would be in that category. Each attempt to capture the title seemed to push them half the remaining distance to their destination. They seemed fated to get closer and closer to their goal without ever reaching it.

"It was just really disappointing to sit through the entire summer, waiting for another chance to show how good we were," says Rick Willis, who would be named captain of the 1994–95 squad that spring. "We always talked about it. 'Do we wanna have another crappy summer?'

"With the exception of Knuble, our class was not the most high-profile class, but we filled a lot of roles," he adds. "The seniors accepted the freshmen, even if they were better than we were. And that's not as easy as it sounds. You work your butt off for three years, then some hotshot freshman comes in and takes your place. But you know this new kid's better than you are, so you accept it and see how you can help. So what if I play on the fourth line? This is my role. The good thing is, if you've got talent like that, the coaches don't have to go around and put the fear of God into everyone. If you're in fast company, you have to perform."

Then-assistant coach Dave Shand, however, thinks Willis is selling his skills short. "Ricky could skate like the wind, and he could close the gap on the forecheck faster than anyone I've ever seen. Great hitter, too. All shoulder, not with his hands or stick. If the guys on the bench were pretty quiet, he'd wake 'em all up with a big hit. 'You see that! Holy Christmas!' I think we had the biggest, toughest team in college hockey in the mid-nineties. That was a fun team to coach, too, boy. Hitting wasn't something you had to talk them into doing—and it started with Ricky.

"He'd hit one defenseman in the beginning of the game, and after that, he had every defenseman looking over his shoulder, looking out for him. He scared the living crap out of guys. Hell, he scared the living crap out of *our* guys! He was one of the few guys Red ever had to tone down in practice. 'Ricky, could you please leave us a couple defensemen to play this weekend?'

"When I scouted him at Northwood Academy in Lake Placid, I came back and told Red, He's the whole package. He's tough, he can hit, he can skate, he can score. It turned out, at Michigan, that he didn't score that much. But he turned into a great leader, a great captain, and that was one thing we didn't antici- pate. He just took over the team his senior year."

Willis's 1994–95 Wolverines won 30 games for the fifth con- secutive season—20 used to be the standard for excellence—and reclaimed almost everything the previous class had won the year before. The class of '95 took home Michigan's seventh consecu- tive GLI, its third CCHA regular-season title, and its third num- ber one seed into the NCAA playoffs. The only thing the Wolver- ines failed to win was the CCHA playoff title, which the Lakers took from them in—you guessed it—overtime. They were not alarmed, however, because they had beaten Lake Superior three times during the season and were 3-1-1 in overtime that year. Michigan's old Achilles' heels seemed to be on the mend. Going into the NCAA playoffs, the players allowed themselves to believe that this might be the year.

In the first round of the NCAA playoffs in Madison, Wisconsin bumped off Michigan State, 5-3. The Badgers had to face a well- rested Wolverine team the next night, but they had momentum and the home crowd on their side. They seemed poised to upset the Wolverines, especially after tying the game 3-3 in the third period, but Mike Knuble squelched any possibility of another nerve-racking overtime period by scoring the kind of ugly goal that had victimized Michigan for years, a sloppy, squirrelly thing off a face-off. No quarterfinal obscenities this year. The Wolverines were heading back to the Final Four for the third time in four seasons.

In Providence, Rhode Island, they had the chance to exorcise some demons. If they could beat their semifinal opponents, the Maine Black Bears, they would become the first Michigan team to get to the NCAA finals since 1977. They would also redeem the class of 1993, which had beaten Wisconsin in overtime, 4-3, before losing to Maine in overtime by the same score. And they could get the bad taste out of their mouths from the previous year's premature departure.

"We knew if we just played one good game we'd get it," Knuble says. "It was *right there.*"

"In those big games we *always* had the best team," Willis says. "*Every* game we lost in the playoffs, I thought we were going to win. The only question was, would we get the breaks to finally win it? I went into that game against Maine not even thinking about losing. I was *excited* to get to the rink that day and *crush* them. Take the weight off the program's back, once and for all. Take the weight off *my* back."

Michigan showed off its scoring balance with early goals by junior Kevin Hilton and freshman Matt Herr, giving it a 2-0 lead just 4 minutes into the game. But Maine had been there before, too, and tied the score early in the second period. With 14 minutes left in regulation the Black Bears went ahead 3-2 on a power-play goal, but Michigan, showing a determination born of a half decade of frustration, evened it up just 49 seconds later on Knuble's fifteenth power-play goal of the season.

Nobody there would have guessed at that moment that the game wasn't even half over. Neither side would score again for more than 53 minutes—almost another game's worth—but not due to any lack of scoring chances. Freshman goalie Marty

Turco made 52 saves that night, many of them gymnastic feats, while Willis, John Madden, and Brendan Morrison all missed golden opportunities to end the game on odd-man rushes.

"Brendan and I were on a two-on-one," Knuble recalls. "I fed him a one-timer at the top of the circle, with a wide-open net. He gets off a hard shot—ping!—off the post."

A few seconds into the NCAA-record third overtime period the two teams lined up for a face-off in Michigan's end. Mike Legg lost the draw against Maine's Dan Shermerhorn, who pulled it back to Reg Cardinal. Cardinal gave it right back to Shermerhorn, suddenly alone in front of the net. Turco lunged toward Shermerhorn to execute a desperate poke check, but Shermerhorn jumped to the right of Turco and tucked the puck neatly behind him into the open net.

Willis still shakes his head at the memory. "See? Look at that guy," he says, referring to Shermerhorn. "He's not in the NHL, he's nothing special. That game was just another example of us losing to guys who were not as talented as we were." But there it was.

The finality of Shermerhorn's goal, and its significance, hit them hard and fast. "If you're down 6-3, you see it coming, you can prepare yourself for it," Knuble says. "But losing like that— it was just brutal. Three years we lost in overtime. And each time was more painful than the last."

"Oooooh," Willis whispers, recalling that moment. "Complete disbelief and disappointment. Complete disbelief and disappointment. When you come in with a team that's more talented, and you're playing a better game, and you lose—that's complete disbelief and disappointment. The seniors, we huddled on the ice together for a few extra minutes, stunned, just stunned. At the press conference, we were [like] deer in the headlights."

The hockey gods had teased the Job-like Wolverines to the point of torture, doling out miserly nibbles of glory to a bunch of starving players, a family that hadn't enjoyed the full feast since 1964.

Thanks to pioneers like Todd Brost, Alex Roberts, Don Stone, and Kent Brothers, the team first developed character. With the arrival of Denny Felsner, David Roberts, and Aaron Ward, the team could boast top-notch talent, too. And when lifelong bonds developed among guys like Steve Shields and Brian Wiseman, Mike Knuble and Rick Willis, the team had togetherness.

What else could they offer? What else would it take appease the hockey gods? A miracle, a break—or both?

42

Reloading

When the coaches and players went back to the drawing board during the off-season, they had to like what they saw. The 1995–96 team had a solid, if not spectacular, senior class and strong leadership from Steven Halko, Kevin Hilton, and junior Brendan Morrison. Still, most observers figured Michigan's best chance for the elusive grail would be the following year, when Morrison's gold-plated class became seniors.

But for Halko and his fellow seniors this was their last chance, and they played like it, ripping through the now familiar list of annual accomplishments in a businesslike fashion. They bowled over rivals the way Bo Jackson used to knock over defenders on his way to the end zone—straight ahead, without hesitation or mercy. Take the team's January 6, 1996, home game against Miami, in which the high-octane Wolverines scored a pair of goals within a minute of each other—four times. They scored on all four of their power-play chances, and they scored on three of *Miami's* four power-plays. Add it all up, and you get a 13-0 shellacking that no one there that night would forget.

They set school records for goals against average (2.15) and goal differential (+146), scoring 239 goals for and allowing a paltry 93 against. They dispatched opponents the way a world-class relay team might, during the qualifying heat, impatiently getting them out of the way without using up too much energy or emotion, keeping their eyes on the prize the entire time. The 1995–96 Wolverines took their team's eighth consecutive GLI championship, they claimed another CCHA regular-season title, they won the CCHA tournament by beating Lake Superior, and they finished the regular season with 27 wins, just 2 fewer than the record set by the 1990–91 team. But that's not what this bunch was playing for. Anything short of winning the NCAA title would be a disappointment.

The NCAA unwittingly aided the Wolverines by awarding the top two seeds that spring to eastern teams. Of course, the Wolverines should have recognized history was on their side. In 1992, 1994, and 1995, the NCAA seeded Michigan first, and each year ended in crushing disappointment. In 1996, the committee seeded them second. Turns out it's not just the Wolverines who fail to win the crown when they should, and win it when they shouldn't. The entire NCAA field does it, too. Since the NCAA started seeding teams in 1970, the first 66 seeds have gone a paltry 62-56 (.525)—which is atrocious, when you realize that first seeds can win up to three games per tournament, but can never lose more than one before being eliminated. Second seeds have faired much better, winning 85 games against 51 losses (.625). Likewise, those 66 top-seeded teams have won just 10 NCAA titles, compared to 15 for the second-seeded teams, 6 for the third seeds, and 2 for the fourth seeds. Clearly, being seeded first is not the prize most teams think it is.

Minnesota was one of only five teams to beat the Wolverines that season, ending Michigan's nine-game winning streak in the College Hockey Showcase the previous fall. After the Gophers dismembered Providence, 5-1, in the opening round in East Lansing, they earned a rendezvous with the Wolverines the next night at Munn Arena, the site of Lake Superior's upset of Michigan's 1993–94 squad, easily Michigan's greatest team never to win an NCAA playoff game. The Gophers were hardly awed by the '96 Wolverines, overwhelming them in the first period, outshooting them 13-3 and outscoring them 2-1, including a short-handed goal just four minutes into the game.

With 5:25 left in the second period, however, a Gopher defenseman took a roughing penalty in front of the Minnesota net, giving Michigan a chance to revive its title hopes. For the first 1:30 of the power play Michigan still couldn't muster a serious shot. With just 20 seconds left in the man advantage, John Madden tried to skate the puck around the Gopher cage but got tied up and left it there, taking his man out in the process. Mike Legg grabbed it behind the net and looked up to see what was available in front of him. If a miracle was a prerequisite to win an NCAA title, this would have been a good time for one.

At his London, Ontario high school, Mike Legg had mastered every sport from football to badminton. At Michigan he was a natural talent who needed the occasional kick in the pants to get going, but once motivated he could work wonders. He often stayed after practice to play shinny with his buddies or work on a few trick moves. He especially enjoyed playing around with a little maneuver he learned from a former summer teammate and future Detroit Viper named Bill Armstrong.

The move is so unusual it virtually defies description, but the photos on the following page will help. In the first frame, Legg starts by setting up shop behind the net, then lays his blade flat on the puck, and lifts the other end of his stick to squeeze the puck onto the blade. By itself this is a very deft move that few hockey players can execute smoothly. Next, Legg maintains enough centrifugal force to keep the puck from falling off his blade, which he holds vertically as he approaches the net—also impossible for most players. After he steps around the net, whipping it into the upper basket is actually the easiest part of the exercise, as simple as throwing snow from a shovel.

"I just kept doing it and doing it," he says. "I probably did it over a thousand times."

All great performers, be they musicians or actors, artists or athletes, work on their repertoire until they can perform their signature moves on autopilot. Then they let their instincts decide what movement to use and when. Legg told his father, Chuck, that he wanted to try *his* favorite move in a game just once before he graduated. Chuck understood but warned his son, "You don't want to be pulling that stuff unless there are no other options."

In the early evening of Sunday, March 24, 1996, Mike Legg—the same player who lost the face-off that led to Maine's overtime goal the year before—cradled the puck behind the net, looked around the zone, and saw no other options.

"It hit me when I turned around and no one was on me," he says, "and it just clicked in to do it."

He lowered his stick, scooped the puck up, and in one sweeping motion, swung the puck around to the front of the net. Minnesota goalie Steve DeBuss did what he was taught to do: he

The miracle goal
With his team down 2-1 in a do-or-die quarterfinal game, Mike Legg executed what ESPN's Keith Olbermann described as "the most amazing goal in college hockey history." The miracle goal tied the game and kept Michigan's 1996 NCAA title hopes alive.
(Courtesy of the U-M Athletic Department.)

moved to the attackers' side of the net, jammed his leg pad against the pipe, and stuck his stick out to block a pass or wrap-around attempt. But no books have instructions on how to stop Legg's play, because no one had ever pulled it off in a game before. While DeBuss watched Legg's feet and waited for an attacker who never materialized, Legg pitchforked the puck over the helpless goalie's shoulder, popping it off the top basket.

Four, five, six seconds passed. The Gophers still hadn't moved. They could only stand there, frozen, not believing what had just happened.

Eddie Kahn may have scored the first goal in Michigan hockey history, but Mike Legg scored the best.

In the Gophers' defense, the confused folks in the press box needed several slow-motion replays before they could begin to comprehend what they had just seen.

When the Wolverines discussed it after the game, the word *awe* came up with unusual frequency.

"I've seen him do it in practice five times a day, but it takes a lot of guts to try it in a game," Billy Muckalt said afterward. "Any time you get a tying goal it's a big lift, but we were in awe of that goal."

Even the best coach in the history of the game, Scotty Bowman, said, "I've never seen anything like it."

ESPN's Keith Olbermann didn't waste a second on any intellectual hand-wringing. He opened his broadcast that evening with an unequivocal statement: "This is the most amazing goal in college hockey history. We're not exaggerating."

By nightfall *CNN Headline News* was running the clip every half hour, and the announcers on ESPN's National Hockey Night had picked it for their MCI Play of the Night—even though the show doesn't cover college hockey. The next morning, *USA Today*, the *Washington Post*, and the *Boston Globe* all ran feature stories on it. When the season ended, Legg's move would win the ESPY Award for Most Outrageous Play and the Goal of the Year trophy from *Inside Hockey*, a magazine based in Stockholm that flew the Michigan star to Sweden for a banquet in his honor.

In their rush to flood Legg with accolades, however, the reporters ignored the *context* of the goal, which makes it far more impressive. Legg didn't debut his patented move in an exhibition game or some regular-season blowout, but in a do-or-die playoff game in which, if his stunt failed, his team might well have lost the game and joined the ranks of William Jennings Bryan, the Buffalo Bills, and Susan Lucci as perennial also-rans. The goal not only tied the game, 2-2, but it so shocked the Gophers, and so inspired the Wolverines, that it swung the momentum dramatically from Minnesota to Michigan in just a few seconds.

"That gave a big boost to the team," said Morrison, who knows something about big goals. "We fed off that goal. Minnesota was in awe. We always screw around with that kind of stuff after practice—but to do that in a big game . . ." Morrison finished his sentence by looking off into space and shaking his head.

"Before the goal I was playing terribly, and I wasn't putting forth the effort," Legg admitted later. "I needed something to get me going."

Legg's heroics snapped him and his teammates out of their slumber and reminded them that they, not the Gophers, were the better team. And from that point on, they were. They outshot Minnesota 7-0 in the first 14 minutes of the third period and took the lead on Warren Luhning's power-play goal. With just 5 minutes left, however, Minnesota got its first shot on net that period, a 40-footer from the left side, which was good enough to tie the game, 3-3.

The two teams seemed headed for another sudden death classic, something Michigan surely didn't welcome given its painful overtime history, when an electrified Brendan Morrison battled two Gophers behind the net, won the scrum, and dished a quick pass out to Billy Muckalt, cutting across the slot. Muckalt patiently waited for Minnesota's goalie to drop to the ice, then walked around him and slipped the puck into the net for a 4-3 lead. Two minutes later, Michigan had the victory.

It was a great college hockey game, a 4-3 playoff thriller. But afterward the coaches, the players, and the press could talk of only one thing. "I scored two goals and one assist in that game;

I was the MVP of the regional," Muckalt says today. "But at the press conference, nobody wanted to talk to me—and I can't say I blame 'em!"

Call it the shovel shot, the jai-alai move, or the Greatest Goal Ever Scored. A miracle by any other name is still a miracle.

Michigan was on its way.

Slaying the Dragon

In the semifinals in Cincinnati the Wolverines faced the defending NCAA champion, Boston University—the same Terriers that first upset the Wolverines 46 years earlier. But if the players on the '96 team had no knowledge of the 1950 Final Four or the Terrier Curse, they certainly had no trouble remembering their three most recent trips to the semifinals, two of which ended in wrenching overtime losses.

This time Michigan decided not even to make it sporting. In the same way the 1991 team made it a point to snatch the selection process from the NCAA committee's hands, the '96 squad was determined not to leave its chance at its first NCAA final in 19 years at the whims of sudden death. The Wolverines rushed the Terriers, outshooting them 18-7 in the first period alone, and nailed down a 2-0 lead in the game's first five minutes. They didn't let up the entire game, burying the Terriers, 4-0, in Michigan's most dominating performance of the season.

Terrier coach Jack Parker went farther. "It's hard to describe that game without talking about how well Michigan played," he said at the postgame press conference. "They blew us out of the building in the first four minutes. We were back on our heels quite a bit of the time. That team is as hungry and determined and well skilled and well prepared as any team I've ever seen play this game."

The Wolverines offered a more modest explanation. "We were ready," Greg Crozier said, "and BU wasn't."

"BU was a team of big names," added senior forward John Arnold. "But that's not what makes a championship team."

What does? Because no one on the team had been born within a decade of Michigan's last NCAA title, they couldn't be sure. They would have to figure it out for themselves—and do it in the next 48 hours, when they would take on Colorado College for the crown.

Of the 23 players on the 1995–96 roster, 9 walked on. In other words, almost half the team wanted to be at Michigan more than Michigan wanted them, which speaks volumes about their devotion to the school.

Take John Arnold. Several colleges expressed a strong interest in the Toronto native until he tore up his right elbow. He was all set to go to a Division III school when his dad told him, "You're better than that." So John started calling college coaches around the country until Michigan finally invited him down for a visit.

"I didn't know anything about Michigan," Arnold says, but they knew about him, since he was Steve Halko's teammate. "They asked me my SATs and grade-point average, then they called admissions, turned to me, and said, 'Welcome to the University of Michigan.'" Arnold didn't earn a full ride until his senior year—something several of his teammates could also say, which made the 1995–96 team unusually close. "No one was ever left out," Arnold says. "If someone said, 'Can I come along?' the answer was always yes."

Perhaps because they felt like they were all in it together, they had more grace under pressure than had previous Michigan teams. When Michigan made it to the Final Four in 1992, "Everyone had the death grip on their sticks," recalls Mark Sakala, who'd played for both teams. "This time we were dancing in the locker room before the game."

"The first year we went to the Final Four in '92, we may have had as good a team as we've had at Michigan," Berenson says. "But the earlier Final Four teams never played their best. They were distracted by all the hoopla of the Final Four. But [in 1996]

There wasn't a lot of jubilation after the BU semifinal game. This team just took it like another game, like they had done it before. They weren't happy just to get to the Final Four. This team expected to *win* it."

Berenson states flatly that the 1995–96 team was not his most talented. Of the eight seniors from 1993, for example, five played in the NHL the next season, and a sixth, forward Dave Roberts, played on the U.S. Olympic team before joining them in the pros. In contrast, only one player from the class of '96 would make it to the NHL.

But the 1995–96 team had something earlier teams didn't: a disregard for any title short of the NCAA crown, bordering on contempt. Thanks to the legacy of Kent Brothers, these guys were not content to take just one more step that year. They wanted the whole thing. Not the GLI silver bowl, not Showcase's golden skate, not the CCHA's square of glass—but the NCAA's unimposing, all-important slab of wood. And they wanted it now.

44

The Ghosts Are Gone

By March 30, 1996, only two college teams were still playing hockey. In the NCAA finals in Cincinnati Michigan faced a rejuvenated Colorado College program that had won 33 games and lost only 4, all by one goal. Both teams knew that, to win the NCAA title, they would have to beat their toughest opponent of the year. From the opening face-off the teams played an intense, tight-checking style, with the Tigers holding the highest-scoring team in hockey to just seven shots on net in the first two periods.

Michigan sophomore Billy Muckalt scratched the game's opening goal out of those limited chances midway through the first period, but the play was otherwise dictated by the Tigers. CC goalie Ryan Bach could have taken the first two periods off to go study in the stands, while Michigan's Marty Turco had to stare down 15 shots in the first two periods, most of them high-percentage chances from Colorado College's potent power play.

Early in the second period Colorado College went ahead on two goals less than two minutes apart. Late in the second, the Tigers appeared about to take a daunting 3-1 lead on yet another power-play opportunity. A CC forward held the puck near the left face-off circle, then sent it across the slot to Chad Remackel, who had set up on the right dot, uncovered. Remackel had enough time to walk in, find his spot, and fire a snap shot to the upper corner on the short side. But Turco slid across the crease to make a spectacular glove save, then held the puck defiantly right in front of Remackel, who couldn't help slumping his shoulders and staring at Turco in disbelief for several seconds.

"That could have put it away," Tiger forward Jay McNeill said after the game. "The crowd that wasn't cheering for Michigan was starting to cheer for us. We felt like we had the game in hand, and we didn't bury them when we had the chance. That save could have cost us the game tonight."

Berenson re-creates the play. "They work a nice play across the slot to get one of their forwards a perfect shot," he says. "Marty catches it like it was a basketball. He stops their best player on their best chance. They start thinking, 'What do we have to do?' Right there, we know we've got the goalie—and they know it, too."

Just as Legg's goal had awakened the Wolverines against Minnesota, Turco's save jolted the Wolverines out of their slumber, and inspired them to take the play to the Tigers. It was Legg himself who tied the game seven minutes into the third period, when he smacked a rebound out of mid-air and into the Tiger net. The Wolverines could muster no more, however, before the third period ended—a fact that should have concerned them, given their ugly overtime history since 1977, including three consecutive overtime losses in the NCAA playoffs.

"All the achievements, and all the obstacles we'd overcome, really weren't going to mean anything unless we won this game," Muckalt said afterward. "It was a once-in-a-lifetime chance."

Sometimes great things start with humble beginnings that are hard to remember after the fact. Sometimes one class quietly builds a strong foundation that allows another class to finish the job years later. And sometimes one player doing a little thing right can result in an entire team celebrating a big success just seconds later.

Almost four minutes into the first overtime, a Tiger player had the puck in his own corner and fired it along the boards to get it out. But Michigan captain Steven Halko boldly decided to make an extra effort to keep the puck in the Colorado zone, stopped it, then threw it back into the Tigers' corner. No one seems to remember it now—Halko's gutsy decision didn't make the score sheet or the papers—but that's where this play started.

A Tiger defenseman tried once again to clear the puck out of the zone, but this time Morrison snuffed the high pass with his glove, dropped the puck onto the ice, then zipped it to freshman Greg Crozier in the slot. Morrison then skated to the right circle, unnoticed. Crozier shot the puck low and on net. CC goalie Ryan Bach made the save but kicked the puck to the left face-off circle, where Billy Muckalt had camped out. Muckalt also shot low, and again Bach made the save, but this time he redirected it toward the right circle—exactly where Morrison had stationed himself after passing the puck to Crozier. In the chaos following Morrison's initial pass, no one had covered him. Now free, he skated toward the loose puck in front of Bach, who was scrambling to slide across the length of the crease. The two opponents performed a dance similar to the step rehearsed by Dan Hoene and Julian Baretta 19 years earlier.

Three years after Dan Stiver missed an open net against Maine in overtime, two years after a Lake Superior deflection sent a puck flipping over the shoulder of Steve Shields into the net, and one year to the day after Morrison himself hit the post against Maine in overtime, Brendan Morrison took a couple simple strides toward the sitting puck and snapped it past the fallen goalie into the vast open net behind him.

"It seemed to take forever," Berenson says. "But he scored, and then there was a pause. Everyone looks around to make sure no one was whistling it down, to make sure this has really happened. It is *in the net*. We've won this game. We've won the national championship."

Every team celebrates a national championship with enthusiasm, of course, especially a championship that ends in overtime. But there seemed to be an extra measure of joy, an additional dose of relief, a bonus shot of sheer ecstasy in the dancing and hugging and crying on the ice that day in Cincinnati. They were not merely rejoicing over a special game or a successful season, but the fruits of a dozen years of hard work, frustration, and determination. It was as if all the pain of the previous years had been justified by a single goal.

Just seconds after the players finished piling on each other, an ESPN announcer stuck a microphone in Morrison's face. Without any preparation and without missing a beat, Morrison said, "This is for all the guys who never had a chance to win it."

Vic Heyliger, '38, listened in Colorado Springs and let out a quick yelp. "We were really excited," he says. "That was *wonderful.*"

Rudy Reichert, '43, watched on TV at his home in Ann Arbor and felt proud "of the culmination of a long struggle"—something he knew something about.

Brendan Morrison's goal
"It seemed to take forever," Berenson recalls of Morrison's overtime goal against Colorado College for the 1996 NCAA title. Morrison said, "This is for all the guys who never had a chance to win it," causing dozens of former Michigan players to start weeping.
(Courtesy of the U-M Athletic Department.)

Al Renfrew, '49, and Wally Grant, '50, were in Cincinnati, where they "were just hugging and laughing," Grant says. "Anybody who wanted a hug, got one." When Morrison saw Grant from a distance, he raised his index finger, and yelled, "We did it, Wally!"

Mel Wakabayashi, '64, watched in Toronto, and was moved by the depth of the players' team spirit and their respect for those who came before, two values he holds dear.

Rob Palmer, '77, watched with his wife and two young children in their Michigan home. His wife, Giselle, was ecstatic, while Palmer felt a tremendous sense of relief that Berenson's insistence on doing things the right way—which the two had discussed on those soul-searching late nights in Berenson's basement a decade earlier—had been validated, the questions erased.

Alex Roberts, Mark Sorenson, and Billy Jaffe, all members of the Class of Heavy Lifting, 1990, had a section of tables staked out in a Chicago bar for Michigan fans. "When Brendan put it in the net, it was complete jubilation," Roberts says. "And when they interviewed Brendan afterward, and he said that—literally, I broke down crying. Everybody was bawling."

Kent Brothers, '91, watched far away in Newfoundland. "When you hear a kid like Morrison say something like that," Brothers says, "you know you've done something. Not too many things can make a grown man cry, but Michigan hockey is one of them."

David Harlock, '93, was playing that afternoon for Toronto's top farm club in Fredericton, New Brunswick, so he asked the team's radio broadcaster to keep his ears open for information on the game. Between the second and third periods of Harlock's game, the announcer came racing down to the locker room to tell Harlock Michigan had won in overtime. "Needless to say," Harlock says, "I went out and played my best third period of my season. Brendan's quote—that was probably one of the classiest things ever said. It meant as much to us as anything else about that game. For the guys who played in the lean years, it probably meant even more."

And in Orlando, Florida, Dan Hoene, '77, interrupted his vacation to root out a place to see the game. When he finally found one, he watched with his wife and two children, who could only guess what he was feeling as their father sat there, pleasantly surprised at what he was seeing and hearing.

Red Berenson, '62, the man whose few regrets in life include Michigan's failure to win the NCAA title his senior year, was there, of course, just a few feet away from his star forward. "Morrison's comment—my God," Berenson remarks. "It was just a wonderful thing to say."

Morrison's words meant something because they were true: the guys who won in it in 1996 came to Ann Arbor because of the guys who went before. And what Morrison gave them in that unrehearsed moment was recognition—and absolution.

"I was sick of hearing people say we couldn't win the big ones," Billy Muckalt said at the time. "This is the biggest, and we're the champions."

"The ghosts," Marty Turco said, "are gone."

And this time that ten inch by two foot slab of cherry wood was going on Michigan's bus.

45

The Guys Next Door

Shortly after winning the title, Berenson ran into Ken Kal, who had left U-M and WTKA to work for the Red Wings and WJR before the season began. "If I knew I could have won the national title without you," Ken Kal recalls Berenson saying, "I would've gotten rid of you a lot sooner."

"Red always said, never get too high or too low," Mark Sakala remembers, "but after this game, Red said you can get as excited as you want."

Certainly the Michigan fans did. Ann Arbor native Pete Uher, then a Huron high school student, was among the thousands of blue loyalists who made the trip to Cincinnati that spring, a trip he'll not soon forget. "Thirty minutes after the game, the Michigan fans were still in the stands, clapping," he says. "I remember driving home on I-75, and it was a freakin' caravan of cars with Michigan flags and signs, honking their horns all the way home. Go into any McDonald's in Nowhere, Ohio, and it'd be packed with Michigan fans—old and young people celebrating together, singing the 'Victors' and high-fiving each other. The workers behind the counters didn't know what was going on, but who cared? It was great."

But despite Berenson's go-ahead, relief, not rapture, was the predominant emotion on the team's bus ride home from Cincinnati. Everyone was more exhausted than elated. "People just wanted to be by themselves to think about it," Halko says.

John Arnold and Mark Sakala sat in the back of the bus with their new wooden trophy between them. "We were just looking out the window at a beautiful sunset," Arnold recalls. "Then the stars came out. Geez, how much nicer does it get?"

Later that night, back in Ann Arbor, some of the players made the obligatory stop at Rick's, a popular college hangout. Aside from a few pats on the back and a round of drinks from a Rick's owner who fancies himself a hockey player, you would have had no idea the small group of students in the corner had done something special by watching them. You wouldn't even think to ask.

The sense of eerie normality increased when the subdued celebration retired to the campus home of seniors Steve Halko, Kevin Hilton, Mark Sakala, and John Arnold—two blue chippers and two walk-ons who'd become close friends.

Relief and Rapture
Coach Berenson hugs a tearful Billy Muckalt, a ninth-round draft pick who proved the experts wrong by becoming a star. When the Wolverines finally won their first NCAA title in 32 years, they did not get wealth or fame, just a 10″ x 2′ slab of wood—but it was more than enough.
(Courtesy of the U-M Athletic Department.)

If the NCAA investigators ever decided to sniff around the Michigan hockey program for illegal payouts, the coaches would only have to take them to the seniors' house. Rest assured that the '96 bunch, like the other seniors before and since, never spent a dime on decent furniture, maid service, or commercial rug shampooers. Those guys could have filed for federal disaster relief—and gotten it. Their only extravagance was a pet African ridgeback frog, a softball-sized reptile that ate live mice. They got it from—surprise!—some frat guys.

"There are a lot of memories in this old house," John Arnold said at the time, and one suspected some of those crusty memories were still around, growing mold. Forget eating off the floor; you would have been advised not to eat off their plates. One players' bedroom was so heaped with clothes, books, papers, and other debris that it could have served as an archaeological dig. Their home was, in short, just like every other college house run by a half dozen guys. The only things tipping it off as a hockey haven were the broken sticks planted in the front lawn.

Perhaps nothing demonstrated better how low-key this high-flying team was than their fifth roommate, Tom Bersano, an Italian student whom Sakala met in an engineering class. When Sakala introduced Tom to his housemates the year before, Bersano spontaneously performed a headstand in front of the TV. "The idea," Halko said, "is that blood rushes to his head without him having to take a nap, which is supposed to help him concentrate."

Concentration is at a premium when you only sleep 10 hours a week, as Bersano did, in 15-minute intervals spread 4 hours apart. He didn't eat red meat or drink, and the only notes he'd taken in four years of engineering were contained in his well-worn 30-page, three-by-four-inch notebook, all scratched in microfilm-sized handwriting.

Bersano was as likable as he was eccentric. He knew as much about hockey as his housemates did about Turen, Italy, his hometown. He attended his first and only hockey game in January 1996—in shorts and a T-shirt, to strengthen his body against winter colds. For the 1996 NCAA title game, however,

Bersano was in the library, studying. When Steve Halko came home from Cincinnati that night with the championship trophy, he found Bersano at the top of the stairs. When Halko told him they'd won, Tom asked, "This was big game?"

Yes, Tom, this was Big Game, even if it was won by small names.

Class Acts

Just like two dozen other Michigan electrical engineering students, Mark Sakala woke up at 6 A.M. the following Monday morning, went up to North Campus, and took an engineering dynamics test. Well, there was *one* slight difference. As the professor passed out the exam, he stopped at Mark's seat, said, "Congratulations," then handed him the test. After the exam Sakala said he would have done better if he had studied more. Problem was, he and his teammates had been busy two days before winning the NCAA hockey title. Darn the luck, anyhow.

A few days earlier, in the middle of the playoffs, forward John Madden's English professor saw his letter jacket and asked if he played a sport. Captain Steve Halko's Euclidean geometry professor didn't even get that far. When Halko handed him a travel slip for an away game, the professor looked up, surprised. "They still have a hockey team?" he asked.

Things didn't change much after they won it all. Monday morning Halko showed up at 8:30 for his macroeconomics exam. Beyond a few whispered "Congratulations," the weekend's big event went unnoticed. "It was business as usual," Halko says. "And that was fine with me."

On campus, the hockey players are treated more like students than athletes. They don't weigh 300 pounds or stand 6'10", so they easily mix in with their average-sized classmates. They wear masks on the ice and are rarely recognized off it. According to assistant coach Billy Powers, "The kids waiting outside the locker room don't know who signed their program until after they sign it. They don't say, 'There's Brendan Morrison'; they read the autograph and say, 'That was Brendan Morrison.'"

Their personalities are as modest as is their appearance. Like most Michigan teams in the nineties, about half of the '96 players were Canadians, a breed not known for self-promotion. Just as well. In college hockey, there aren't many chances to sell oneself, anyway. There are fewer than 60 Division I college programs (compared to 260 in basketball and 114 in football), with no national network TV contract.

The attention Mike Legg got for his miracle lacrosse-style goal against Minnesota came as a shock to these players. "That was all brand new to us," Powers says. "Our kids still think it's fun, because we don't go through this every day."

After Mark Sakala's name was mentioned a dozen times on ESPN's broadcast of Saturday's title game, the following Monday one of his father's co-workers at Chrysler asked if he'd heard of this college kid on TV with the same last name. Yes, Vladimir Sakala replied, he'd heard of him.

One of Berenson's few concerns for his players was that they didn't spoil the joy of this accomplishment by embarking on a disillusioning minor-league stint. "Sakala's one of those kids I hope never plays again," he said at the time. "Why go through all the disappointment kids feel playing minors? He has nothing more to prove. You can't buy what we had here."

Sakala's father, a Czech immigrant, asked only that his son "do something with hockey." Mark may not have become an NHL prospect or a big name on campus, but he did do something with it: he became an NCAA champion.

Even without a pro contract or lucrative endorsements, that's still worth something.

"Thank You!"

When Michigan fans celebrated their previous NCAA hockey title 32 years earlier, Coach Red Berenson was 24, the 1995–96 players' parents were mere teenagers, and the site used for the 1996 pep rally, Matt Mann, was still a swimming pool, not a gymnastics venue.

They made up for lost time in grand style the Monday after winning the title. Twenty-five hundred zealous fans, plus the team's acclaimed pep band, filled the arena with their bodies and voices for a solid hour that Monday, while then president James Duderstadt, Coach Berenson, and the seniors addressed the fans.

The Michigan players walked on stage one by one, each welcomed by applause loud enough to drown out announcer Glen Williams. They wore their trademark yellow jerseys, baseball caps, and shy grins. A few even seemed pleasantly embarrassed by the attention, occasionally turning red-faced and sheepishly jamming their hands in their pockets.

"If someone would've told me it'd be 12 years before we won a national championship, I don't know if I'd be standing here today," Berenson cracked. "But I knew we'd win a national championship. You've stuck with us when we weren't even .500 and later when we went to the Final Four and came home empty handed, again and again."

The event was far from solemn. In praising assistant coaches Mel Pearson and Billy Powers, Berenson joked, "If my boss wasn't sitting over here, I'd tell you that if I wasn't around the players wouldn't even miss me. But since he is here, I won't say that."

The crowd reserved its biggest cheers for Brendan Morrison, the team's brightest star. In reference to his overtime goal, the crowd chanted, "O.T.! O.T.! O.T.!" when he came up to speak. The irony might have been lost on the crowd—it was Morrison who had missed the team's best chance the year before in triple overtime against Maine—but he got it and grinned. None of that mattered now.

Like his teammates, Morrison spent less time wallowing in the applause than he did thanking the fans and the pep band ("The best college hockey pep band in the nation!"). "When we rolled up to the rink," he said, "the parking lot looked like a football game, everyone tailgating. You were unbelievable."

When Morrison squelched speculation that he might jump to the NHL before his senior year, by adding, "I look forward to defending our title next year," the crowd erupted.

As they do near the end of each game, the fans yelled, "How much time is left?" Announcer Glen Williams played along. "There is *one minute* remaining in the pep rally." "Thaaaaaaank you!" the crowd responded, then walked on stage to congratulate the 1996 NCAA hockey champions in person. The band broke into "Hail to the Victors" one last time.

The fans were not merely thanking a talented team for a good weekend. They were celebrating the apotheosis of everything Berenson, his staff, and his players had been striving for, the realization of a vision that had been born a dozen years earlier.

"You feel cheated some seasons," Berenson says now, "but 1996 was a great relief."

46

The Sure Thing

Each class has its own obstacles to hurdle, its own demons to exorcise. Berenson's early teams had to develop character, then talent, then togetherness, until all that was left was to take home the slab of wood. But, because of the good work of those who came before, the class of 1997 had its own, unique challenge: What to do for an encore?

It was a nice problem to have, but a problem just the same. After some discussion among the players, two goals emerged: first, get all nine juniors—most of whom were being courted by the NHL—back on campus for their senior year. The seniors called each other that summer and quickly decided they would all return. The truth is, they didn't debate the issue too long, partly because the biggest stars were also the best students. Jason Botterill, whose dad is a college professor, is the only player to win the team's Academic Athlete Award three times; Luhning's father has a Ph.D.; and Morrison, an economics major, never seriously considered leaving, even though the New Jersey Devils were anxious to get the nation's two-time leading scorer on their team.

"There are a lot of good families behind those kids," Berenson said. "I'm not surprised when those kids make good decisions."

The second goal would be trickier: become the first college hockey team to win consecutive NCAA titles since—yep—Boston University, 25 years earlier. Although history stood in their way—when the Wolverines are supposed to win it, they can't—if any team could break the spell, this was the one. The '97 Wolverines had the national title in the cross-hairs from the moment their skates cut the ice that fall.

Juggernaut Defined

If the 1996 NCAA championship team was impressive, the '97 team was just plain scary. The '96 team attacked the castle. The '97 team *owned* it. To outsiders, the junior-dominated '96 team was a bit of a surprise, but everyone in college hockey saw the '97 team coming. There just wasn't anything they could do about it.

They had *defense*. The team would post a 2.26 goals-against average. They allowed their opponents to score two goals 9 times, one goal 12 times, and none at all 4 times. In 38 of their 43 games, they permitted their opponents fewer than 30 shots on net. When playing a man short, they allowed only 27 goals against, while scoring 19 shorthanded goals of their own, leaving them just minus-eight on the penalty kill for the year. For their opponents, going on the power play was barely worth the effort.

They had *offense*. While Morrison's men allowed only 98 total goals against them all season, they scored a staggering 91 goals themselves on the power play alone, more than two per game, for a success rate of over 30 percent. They scored 7 or more goals 14 times, which would have resulted in a lot of football scores if football rules allowed the losing team to score only one point. The team's 242 total goals—almost 6 per game—were the third most in school history, but the two teams that scored more, the 1976–77 and 1990–91 squads, let in 211 and 162 goals, respectively, compared to only 98 in 1996–97. You didn't go to Yost that season to watch two equally skilled teams battle down to the wire. You went to watch the Wolverines beat the stuffing out of their next hapless, hopeless victims—the same way Romans must have gone to the Coliseum to see lions maul Christians. The games weren't close, but it was enough to see one of the most ferocious hockey machines ever assembled rip its opponents limb to limb. "In '97, we didn't beat teams," Berenson says. "We tore teams *apart*."

"Michigan has the best group of forwards I've seen in college hockey in the last 10 years—maybe ever," said Wisconsin head coach Jeff Sauer, who'd been coaching in the WCHA since 1966. "They just keep coming at you."

The scoring leader, of course, was Brendan Morrison, who notched a point in 40 of the team's 43 games and was on the ice for over half the team's 242 goals. In the process of breaking the all-time Michigan marks for assists and total points, he won three GLI MVPs and two CCHA MVPs, the first-ever two-time winner in the league's 26-year history; he became Michigan's first three-time All-American since Wally Grant finished the trick in 1950; and he became the first Wolverine to win the Hobey Baker Award.

They had *balance.* Fifteen different players scored power-play goals, 13 scored game winners, and 6 scored hat tricks. Of the 23 players who appeared in three games or more, all but 3 had at least one point on Michigan's 35 game-winning goals, including goalie Marty Turco. "In any given game that year," Turco says, "three guys—*any* three guys—could've taken the night off and we'd still be the best team out there."

They had *teamwork.* The team set school records with 35 victories, an unbeaten streak of 23 games, a winning streak of 15, and its home record of 18-0-2 at Yost, where it outscored opponents 128-33. (Opponents did not enjoy playing there.) The Wolverines were ranked number one for all but 2 weeks of the 24-week season. Three of their four losses were by one goal, the fourth by two, including an empty netter. They did not lose more than *one game* in any month. And they didn't lose any in October, December, or January. In other words, Michigan's opponents went 0-for-winter against the Wolverines.

They had *brains.* Twelve members of that team carried a B average or better, qualifying them for the University's Athletic Achievement Award.

And they had *leadership.* The nine seniors on that team played 166 games in their careers and won 132 of them, both records at the time. Off the ice, they were as close as any class that Michigan's had. "That's the best senior class I've seen in 21 years of coaching," said Miami coach Mark Mazzoleni. "They've got it all."

Brown coach Bob Gaudet emerged from being swept at Yost, 7-2, 5-2, shaking his head. "This is the best team we'll ever play," he said. "You don't want to play them in this environment. Sometimes when you have a highly skilled team, they don't work quite as hard. Michigan plays hard."

The 1996–97 Wolverines were, quite simply, the best team in the history of Michigan hockey—even, perhaps, in the history of college hockey.

There was not a single thing this team wanted that it didn't get, including the College Hockey Showcase, the team's ninth consecutive GLI, its fourth consecutive CCHA regular-season title, its third CCHA playoff championship, its sixth consecutive first-round bye in the NCAA, and its third straight Final Four appearance. The steamroller showed no sign of letting up.

When Minnesota defeated Michigan State in their first-round NCAA playoff game, it looked as though Michigan might follow the exact same path to the title they did the year before, through Minnesota, Boston University, and Colorado College. But things don't always work out as planned.

Unlike the previous season, when Michigan needed Legg's miracle goal to put away the Gophers, in 1997 the Wolverines mounted a 5-0 lead just a minute into the second period. Game over.

Michigan traveled to the NCAA semifinals in Milwaukee, to face a team that should have gotten its attention: Boston University. While BU and Michigan had only played each other 15 times prior to the 1997 semifinals, 7 of those games were NCAA playoff contests, with BU winning three, including the 1950 upset that established the Terrier Curse.

Fifteen minutes into their 1997 semifinal, Warren Luhning drove to the Terrier net and buried the biscuit to give Michigan a 1-0 lead, which held up for the rest of the period. On paper, the game appeared to be already over. When they scored the first goal, the '97 Wolverines had gone 29-0-4 that year, and in such a tight-checking game, Michigan's tiny lead looked like it might be enough. But in the second period, BU attacked the defending champions the way Michigan had attacked BU the year before, outshooting U-M 11-5 while defusing the most explosive offense in the nation on the other end. The Terriers scored three unanswered goals that period, then dug in for the last 20 minutes.

In the six CCHA and NCAA playoff games Michigan had already played that season, its top line of Morrison, Jason Botterill, and Billy Muckalt had scored 20 goals and 24 assists—an absurd 7.5 points-per-game average. Botterill had been on the ice for just one opposing goal, while Morrison and Muckalt had not been on the ice for any. Yet there they were, down 3-1, and not getting anywhere near the BU net.

Realizing they had 20 minutes to save their golden season, the Wolverines went on the attack in the third. They outshot BU 9-5 and finally scored with 57 seconds left in the game to come within a goal of sending it to overtime. But they could manage no more, and—like their predecessors in 1950, 1962, and 1992 through 1995—they made an unexpectedly early exit.

After the game Wally Grant, the captain of the 1950 team that lost the initial heart-breaker to BU some 47 years earlier, approached Michigan's only other three-time All-American, Brendan Morrison, to console him. "I told him about our team and how you don't always win it when you're supposed to," Grant says. "It's just the way it is sometimes."

Despite falling short of their great expectations, a funny thing happened after the game. The players waited for the onset of the all-too-familiar heartache that followed Michigan's earlier playoff losses—but it never came. And why should it? They had already won the grail the year before, they had done everything asked of them on and off the ice all year, and they knew—they knew better than any other players in the country—that in the playoffs you need some breaks, and sometimes a miracle, to take the trophy home. Things don't always work out the way you'd expect.

"The importance of their career at Michigan would be hard to overstate," Berenson says of the class of '97. "Not just because of their success in college and pro hockey, but because all nine seniors came back, and eight got their degrees. It was an impressive bunch."

47

The Rocky Horror Hockey Show

The spectacle of a Michigan football Saturday has been celebrated ad infinitum, and justly so. Less well-known is the more
modest ritual that takes place on home hockey weekends, but
its devotees are at least as zealous as their football cousins.

Ann Arbor's winters lure few tourists. The months are bitter,
cold, and gray, with nightfall hiding the sun each day before
people can escape their jobs. There is, however, one diversion
that keeps at least six thousand people sane.

Unlike the crowds on football Saturdays, which are impossible for locals to ignore, the Michigan hockey contingent creates
only a minor buzz around town. On a Saturday night, at about
6:30, you might notice a few more drivers looking for spots in the
student ghetto off Packard and a few more pedestrians walking
down State Street—many popping into Pizza Bob's and Mr.
Spot's for some pre-game nutrition—but you might not be able
to tell what they're all up to just by looking at them, since their
shiny jerseys are covered by poofy winter coats. You'd have to
follow them to find out what this secret society is all about.

Standing outside Yost on game nights wouldn't give you many
clues, either, as no one is eager to linger outside breathing air so
cold it's opaque, standing under the moon-like floodlights on
snow so densely packed it squeaks like styrofoam under heavy
winter boots. In the dead of winter, all colors and smells have
been sucked out of the local scene.

But when you open the heavy wooden door to the regal Field
House, stamp your feet, and walk under the sign warning visi-

tors to WATCH OUT FOR FLYING PUCKS, your field of vision suddenly soars higher into the vast open space of the Field House, as if you're on a plane taking flight. You enter an almost magical world filled with all the sounds and smells and light the world outside the brick walls keeps buried until spring. People's voices rise as their bodies thaw; the scents of hot coffee, hot dogs, and hot almonds swirl under the stands; the bleachers are filled with thousands of dots of bright colors like a Seurat painting. And then the pep band announces its presence by blasting through the din of conversations, and you are transported from your daily work life into an electric experience shared with 6,000 like-minded souls.

Unlike walking into Michigan Stadium or Crisler Arena, when you walk into Yost the energy is all above you, not below you, and it's your job to climb up into it and become a part of it. Once you're in your seat, you're plugged directly into the surprising power of the place, and the only thing left to do is wait for the puck to drop.

The Michigan hockey team may not be as famous as its football or basketball counterparts, but the hockey fans feel like they're following the best team of the batch—and they show it every time they come to the rink. "We've got sort of a niche," Powers says. "The hockey fans are hockey fans, period. It's a tight, tight group."

The growing crowds were both a cause and an effect of the team's growing success. When Yost was empty, Berenson's teams had losing records four out of his first five years behind the bench. But from 1989–90 through 1997–98, they established an incredible home record of 143-19-16, with an .883 winning percentage, representing a substantial jump from the team's road average of .718.

The consistent sellouts, the band's wall of sound, and the unnerving chants the fans learned from Cornell's followers and then expanded on combine to create the unequaled energy of a Michigan hockey home game.

According to Blake Sloan, a former assistant captain and current Dallas Star, "When you play for Michigan, in their eyes, you can do no wrong." But if you play for the other team—well. . . .

Bob Uecker once cracked that Philadelphia fans would boo a blind man at an Easter egg hunt. Michigan hockey fans would, too, if he was wearing anything other than maize and blue. "It's a pretty ruthless crowd," Sloan adds. "The teams are already down two goals when they come into this place."

Like most modern athletic venues, Yost has scoreboards that tell the fans what to cheer and when, but this crowd hardly needs them—and besides, half of what they say couldn't go up on the screen anyway, for legal reasons. Compared to Yost, Crisler feels like a movie theater.

Thanks to years of diligent research and rehearsal, dating back to the infamous Cornell playoff series in 1991, the hockey fans have developed a dozen inside jokes they share at every game with enough ritualistic camp to rival *The Rocky Horror Picture Show*, a cult classic if ever there was one.

"We really didn't have any cheers before the Cornell series," Berenson says, referring to the 1991 weekend that reintroduced both sellouts and organized chants to the Field House. "There was no niche which made our building a tough place to play for opposing team. [That series] was great for our program. No question about it."

Nowadays when the game clock strikes 1:10 each period, the crowd asks, "How much time is left?"

"There is one minute remaining in the game," announcer Glen Williams says, right on cue.

"Thaaaaaank you," the crowd replies. If it's the third period of a feel-good Michigan blowout, Williams might add, "You're welcome."

The fans aren't as kind to opposing teams. When the teams go to their benches during time-outs, the crowd turns its attention to the opposing players' parents sitting right behind their sons, with the chant: "Ug-ly Pa-rents!" Likewise, if the enemy goaltender doesn't know enough not to lift his mask during breaks to cool off, the mob repeats the mantra, "Ug-ly Goal-ie!"

When a visitor gets a penalty, the fans start spinning their index fingers over their heads like umpires signaling home runs, while emitting a low "Oooooh" the way football fans do before the opening kickoff. The second the opposing offender enters the penalty box, the crowd caps its jeer with "C-Ya!" If the visiting team manages to escape being scored against, the crowd has an answer for that, too. After Williams announces the opposing team is at full strength, the crowd yells, "You still suck!"

If Michigan scores, however, it gets much worse. Woe is he who has to play goalie against Michigan at Yost Field House. It just can't be much fun for him—but it's a blast for everyone else in the old barn. The pep band counts off Michigan's total for the night, then the crowd sings, "We want moooooore goals," and points at the opposing goalie while chanting, "Sieve! Sieve! Sieve! It's all your fault! It's all your fault! It's all your fault! It's all your

The Rocky Horror Hockey Show
"Sieve! Sieve! Sieve!" The fans rocked the Coliseum in the fifties and Yost in the seventies but stayed away until Michigan's 1991 playoff series against Cornell. Now, Blake Sloan says, "It's a pretty ruthless crowd. The teams are already down two goals when they come into this place."
(Photo by Mark A. Hicks.)

fault!" These warm sentiments are followed by a progressive slur, which goes like this: "You're not a sieve, you're a funnel! You're not a funnel, you're a black hole! You're not a black hole, you just suck! You just suck! You just suck!"

The pièce de résistance occurs when a phone rings in the scorer's booth or press box during a lull in the action, prompting the crowd to yell, "Hey, Goalie! It's your mother! She just called to say: 'You suck!'" The audience enjoys this taunt so much they've become too impatient to wait for a real phone to ring, so now one fan brings his own white phone and holds it up toward the beleaguered netminder to cue his mates to initiate the insult.

Small wonder opposing goalies were pulled in 9 of 17 games at Yost during the 1995–96 title run, with a goals-against average two goals higher than Michigan's opposing goalies had in their home rinks.

"It's the greatest atmosphere," says Bowling Green head coach Buddy Powers, "and I would not trade it for anything."

Even when the Michigan goalie makes a great save at the other end of the rink, the poor opposing goalie still gets razzed, anyway. The members of the cheering section—which is to say, the entire crowd—point at the Wolverine netminder and yell, "Goalie!" then point to the opposing goalie and yell, "Sieve!" And they keep it up until the visitor's self-esteem is knocked down yet another peg.

Visiting teams just can't win—and that's the idea.

If you find yourself listening to a former college hockey player describe what he likes best about playing for his school and he doesn't mention the pep band in the first sentence, then you're not talking to a Michigan man. A Wolverine will invariably list team camaraderie, raucous fans, the old barn's electric atmosphere, and the pep band's contagious energy as the most enjoyable aspects of his playing days—and not necessarily in that order.

"One of the best things was getting ready all week for our games on the weekend," says Mike Knuble, "then stepping out onto the ice and hearing that band. That always got us going."

Doesn't matter if the guy went on to play for the Blackhawks or in a beer league, they all say the same thing: I never had more fun playing hockey than I did at Michigan, and the pep band was a big reason why.

"The band is so sweet," says Bubba Berenzweig, captain of the 1998–99 team. "Without them, Yost wouldn't be half as much fun, half as intimidating. They're incredible."

Although various ensembles played for the hockey team sporadically in the program's first four decades, the team didn't warrant a full-time hockey pep band until 1971, when William Revelli's successor, George Cavender, trained a small group of musicians for that express purpose. The fortunes of the band have often paralleled those of the team it plays for. Like the team, the band took a little while to gain momentum in the early seventies.

"It was a much smaller group in those days," says Dave Finn, who played with the hockey pep band from 1972 to 1975. "We used to have to beg people to play, and sometimes all we got was a trombone and a saxophone and nothing else."

Cavender put his hardened work ethic to bear on the hockey band, and soon got results. (When Bo Schembechler and he were still running their programs, they'd see each other at the same stoplight every morning when it was still dark out. They'd wave to each other, acknowledging the only other guy sufficiently obsessed with his work to be up so early.)

"Now it's a premier band, by far the most popular of the department's four pep groups," says John Wilkins, who conducted the hockey band from 1988 to 1990 and now conducts the alumni band when the students are on break. "They used to have 8 to 10 members, but now there are 80 to 90, as many as they can fit in that part of the stands. And you have to audition for it."

They have to work for it, too, practicing outside on Hill Street during the hockey season. Occasionally some hockey players will come by to listen to them practice, say thanks, and "be a part of the spirit," in the words of Berenzweig. When Berenzweig and teammate Bobby Hayes once visited band practice, they were enjoying the music when "the guy on the tower yells, 'Stop! Stop! What're you *doing?*'" Hayes recalls. "I look at Bubba, he looks at me, we're both surprised. We don't know what's wrong—it sounded good to *me*—but I guess they do."

The band's commitment to excellence is most obvious when the opposing team's band shows up, too. Such was the case in the 1999 CCHA playoffs at Joe Louis Arena, when Ohio State brought its band to take on the vaunted Michigan pep band.

After just five minutes of swapping songs back and forth, it was clear the Buckeyes had made a grave miscalculation. If this was truly a battle of the bands, it wouldn't have lasted two rounds. Compared to Michigan's wall of sound, Ohio State could offer only a nook of notes. The Buckeye band was twice as close to the press box as Michigan's, but half as loud, producing only enough energy to play for its section, while the Michigan band had enough power to play for the entire arena.

Michigan's band members wore their white gloves and shiny gold jerseys and put all their energy into their play, trying to push the notes out just a little farther. Michigan's repertoire allowed them to amuse, motivate, or rejoice with the players and the fans as the situation warranted—from their thumping renditions of "Temptation," "The Hawaiian War Chant," and, of course, "The Victors" to their whimsical versions of "Mr. Tallyman," "Bullwinkle," and "The Lone Ranger."

The Buckeye band members, on the other hand, were stuck in their seats and locked into a lame rehashing of stale seventies standards, including a version of "Soul Man" that had no soul and a "Takin' Care of Business" number that had been sanitized for your protection. Compared to the edgy strength of Michigan's band, the Buckeyes sounded like an "Up with People" troupe played by a chorus of kazoos at 33 rpm in a 45 rpm world. They rarely interacted with the crowd, opting instead to stay in the background as musical wallpaper.

And as soon as they finished, the blue band blew them away with a ripping rendition of "Live and Let Die."

After a few rounds of this imbalanced duel, the Buckeye drummers couldn't resist tapping their sticks in rhythm to the

Michigan band's infectious beat. The Buckeyes looked envious, as if they might have defection on their minds. The other members of the Buckeye band seemed to be waiting for a sympathetic referee to end the fight. If you've seen the classic photo of Muhammad Ali clenching his fist and yelling over a supine Sonny Liston, you have some idea how this particular fight ended. Not coincidentally, it mirrored the battle on the ice, one that Michigan won, 3-2, to advance to the conference finals.

"We appreciate playing for the best band in the best rink in the best program in the United States," says Marty Turco, who still holds the NCAA record for most victories. "And I think we make each other better."

"You're sitting on the bench, and you hear your band blowing theirs away," Turco's teammate Matt Herr adds. "You think, These guys are as into it as we are. And it gets to you. 'Our band's better than your band. Our school's better than your school. We're better than you are.'"

As Dizzy Dean would say, "It ain't bragging, if it's the truth." When it comes to college hockey pep bands, Michigan's remains unbowed and undefeated.

George Cavender, the pep band's founder, is now 80 years old and suffering from Parkinson's disease, a degenerative condition that gradually strips its victims of the ability to walk and talk. Some days the famed conductor can't connect to those around him, but on other days his former clarity returns like the sun breaking through a cloudy day. One of those days occurred recently when Florence, his wife of 54 years, showed her husband a picture of himself in his prime, leading the Michigan marching band in uniform, with all his vigor. When she asked him if he recognized the man in the photograph, Cavender didn't miss a beat. "The best damn conductor there ever was," he said, then grinned softly, closed his eyes, and nodded gently.

There is not a Michigan hockey player alive who would argue with that simple statement.

48

Keeping It Together

Every May the returning lettermen stay in town to take classes and work out with their teammates. For all but one year in the 1990s, spring marked the season of the players' discontent, as they licked their wounds from yet another agonizing end to their season, regroup, and try to regenerate their motivation for the coming fall. But in the spring of 1997, eight seniors had just graduated on time, another had left to play pro hockey, and 10 freshmen hadn't come in yet. "We were missing all our guys," recalls 1997–98 team captain Matt Herr, who's a ringer for Vic Heyliger, another upbeat New England prep school graduate. "There was no one here! That was eerie."

The class of '98 was tiny but powerful, including two first-team All-Americans, forward Billy Muckalt and goalie Marty Turco. It might have had a third if Matt Herr hadn't injured his groin muscle in the season opener and missed the next 15 games. On the other hand, the '98 team would have had only one All-American if Muckalt had not decided to return for his senior year.

Matt Herr was raised in New England, Marty Turco in Sault Ste. Marie, Ontario, and Billy Muckalt way out in British Columbia, but they all learned plenty about the University of Michigan growing up. "Even in British Columbia you see the Michigan football and basketball teams on TV all the time," says Muckalt, recalling the early days of his decision-making process. "I figured Michigan would give me the best opportunity to get a good education and play in the NHL. I was under Red's spell right from the start. If he told me to jump off a bridge, I'd do it—and do it twice. I was in awe of him."

He was also in awa of his teammates. "When you step on the ice for the first time as a freshman, you look around, and everybody's a great player. Look at the defense: you've got Steve Halko, Harold Schock, and Blake Sloan. At forward I'm going against Mike Knuble, Warren Luhning, Morrison, and Botterill. It's like, damn, where am I going to play?

"You gotta remember, I was drafted very late, 221st overall, in the ninth round by Vancouver, and I'm out there with these guys, and I know this guy was drafted in the first round, and that guy was drafted in the second round. But after a while I realized, Man, I can play here. Being a late pick just pushed me that much harder to prove people wrong."

He did. Muckalt joined Morrison and Butterill to form one of the most potent lines in Michigan history. Muckalt finished seventh on the team in scoring as a freshman, third as a sophomore and second as a junior, trailing only three-time All-American Brendan Morrison. He almost played too well. His surprisingly strong performance induced Vancouver's executives to solicit his services at the end of his junior year, and they made it tempting.

"I was going to leave before my senior year," Muckalt admits now. "Vancouver was telling me I was ready to go, and they offered me over a million a year for two years. And my line mates, Botterill and Morrison, had just left.

"But Red and I had a big talk. He said, 'You have a chance to be a senior, a leader, and a Michigan graduate. You want to finish what you start.' And my classmates kept calling me all summer. 'You better come back, man!'"

Muckalt ultimately chose to return to Ann Arbor. "I felt a big responsibility to Red, to honor my commitment, and to become more of a leader."

But that didn't mean he couldn't have a little fun. A few weeks before classes started Muckalt flew back to Michigan without his teammates' knowledge. After taking a cab back to the house on Packard that all five seniors shared, he decided to pull a prank by using the downstair's phone to call his teammates, who were hanging out upstairs. When they picked up the second line, Muckalt told them he'd given it a lot of thought, that it was a difficult decision, but he had decided to go pro. They were supportive, and said they understood.

"But when they hung up," Muckalt recalls, "they were just cursing the hell out of me, calling me a mercenary and a few other names. I was cracking up. So I went upstairs, told 'em I fooled 'em, and their reactions were so overwhelming, so appreciative, that right there, I knew in my heart I'd made the right decision."

Muckalt's return was necessary for the 1997–98 team to be successful, but it was hardly sufficient. "The expectations were kind of low for us," Herr says, in a considerable understatement. Berenson told his new boss, former athletic director Tom Goss, that it would be a "rebuilding year," a phrase that is splattered all over that season's media guide. "No one expected us to do anything," Herr adds. "But that wasn't all bad. When you have such a small class, you can all live with each other in one house and get really close. As seniors, that really helped us."

When the 10 freshmen arrived the following fall, the seniors had a lot of teaching to do. "It starts the instant they arrive on campus," Herr says. "They have to love Michigan as much as we do. The previous years we had such great seniors, I didn't want to let them down. That motivated us."

Despite the departure of the best class in Michigan history, Herr and his classmates conceded nothing. "My first two years, we hadn't won it yet," he explains. "That made us work harder. So I told all the returning players at our first team meeting, 'I don't want to see your [1996 NCAA championship] rings. Put them away until the spring. We have to earn our own.'"

Growing Pains

The notion that this team might win its own championship rings seemed absurd once the 1997–98 season began. While Michigan did manage to win the College Hockey Showcase, held at Yost over Thanksgiving weekend, it failed to win everything else.

The team lost two of its first five games, including Michigan's first home loss to Michigan State since 1994. (Morrison's class hadn't lost that many games until mid-February the previous year.) Two weeks after that home loss to Michigan State, Michigan was shut out for the first time since the Lakers administered their infamous 10-0 shellacking in 1991. These setbacks were disappointing, but the boys knew they would be forgotten if they could stretch the string of GLI titles to 10.

"A joke starts every year: who's going to be the first senior class to break the run of GLIs?" Turco says. "We put up seven fingers as freshmen, nine as juniors. We weren't around for the first six GLI titles, but we felt like we had to keep the string going."

The tournament's longest winning string snapped after Michigan advanced to the finals against Michigan State and lost to its in-state rival yet again, 5-3. A month later Herr's team got swept in a weekend series for the first time since February 1994, and followed that up a month later by suffering another sweep—this one at the hands of Michigan State, for the first time since 1989. Against the arch-rival Spartans, the 1997–98 Wolverines had gone 0-4 and never finished within two goals.

The worst setback for the seniors, however, was becoming the first Berenson-coached team to kick a player off. "We actually gave the guy more chances than he deserved," Turco said of freshman Troy Kahler, "so the whole thing dragged on all season."

The '98 team seemed determined to snap every winning streak the '97 team had established or extended. All told, Michigan had 10 losses by mid-March, the first time its losses had reached double digits since 1991. By the end of the regular season Michigan had broken another streak, that of four straight CCHA regular-season titles. You get the idea. This truly *was* a rebuilding year.

In fairness, to say the 1997–98 team wasn't the equal of the unprecedented '97 bunch is not to say the '98 team had nothing going for it. "We had the best goalie in college hockey and two of the best forwards," Muckalt points out. "So right there you've got three of the best players around. Not many teams had that." Muckalt was also impressed by how well fellow seniors Chris Fox and Greg Malicke played when it mattered most, and how quickly the large group of underclassmen came along.

"It was evident early on that we'd have to lead these guys and help them develop if we were going to become a decent team," Muckalt says. "Unlike some other years, when we were so loaded with seniors, that year we *needed* the freshmen. We didn't want to hold them back. To watch them improve over the course of the year was really gratifying."

The team also had good timing. Although Michigan failed to score 200 goals that season for the first time in the nineties—the '98 team scored only 163 goals all year, almost a third less than the previous squad's 242—no team in Michigan history ever squeezed more out of the goals it scored. Of Michigan's 46 games in 1997–98, a record 19 were decided by one goal, and Michigan won 17 of them. Five of those games went into overtime—formerly Michigan's Achilles' heel—but the '98 Wolverines were 4-0-1 in O.T. going into the CCHA playoffs. The 1997–98 season, in almost every way, was the exact opposite of the previous six—for better and for worse.

"I'm pullin' my hair out every night," Turco says. "But we had to learn team defense, and in the end we did."

"We'd go back to Marty during a game and say, 'Turcs, just hold us in it, and we'll get you one,'" Muckalt recalls. " 'Keep kickin', baby.'"

Both sides held up their ends of the bargain. Against Ferris State, for example, Turco "stood on his head," in Muckalt's words, knocking back 29 shots, including a point-blank wrister in overtime. Seconds later Muckalt ended the game with his second goal of the night. "We were so excited, Marty and I ran into each other at mid-ice," Muckalt recalls. "But he had his goalie equipment on, so I fell down."

"Don't forget," Herr points out, "the guys in front of us had already taught us how to win."

* * *

345

For all their missed opportunities to shine, Herr's class still had one final chance to make a lasting mark in the CCHA playoffs. Michigan's first-round opponent, Notre Dame, had only beaten Michigan once in 15 years. But on the opening night of their best-of-three series, the Fightin' Irish built a 4-0 lead by midgame and held on for a 4-2 victory.

The Irish seemed determined to get rid of the defending league champions the following night, going up 1-0 in the first period, before Billy Muckalt tied the game with seven seconds left in the second period. The game was beautifully played, with the shots all but even—34 for Notre Dame and 35 for Michigan—and plenty of good chances at both ends. When the game went into overtime, Michigan stood on the brink of elimination from the CCHA playoffs—and, in all likelihood, the NCAA's as well. But neither side could break through during the first 19 minutes of the first overtime period, until junior Bobby Hayes buried the goal that won the game, tied the series, and kept the team's far-fetched dreams alive.

The third and final game matched the drama of the first two. Because Michigan defensemen Sean Peach and Mike Van Ryn were both out with concussions suffered earlier in the hard-hitting but clean series, junior Bubba Berenzweig had to step up and play over half the game. The Wolverines recognized the urgency of their situation and rifled 15 shots at the Notre Dame net in the first period, while allowing only 3 at their end—but still entered the locker room down 1-0. Notre Dame doubled the deficit five minutes into the second period, but Michigan again outshot the Irish, 8-3, and eventually got goals from Mark Kosick, a freshman flyer, and Berenzweig, the junior workhorse, to tie it up.

Michigan continued to outshoot the Irish in the third period, 14-7, and squeezed two more goals out of that batch to go ahead, 4-3. Both were set up by upperclassmen and buried by freshmen. The lessons Herr and company sought to pass down in September seemed to have been absorbed by March.

Turco made the 4-3 lead stand, leaving only Ohio State between the Wolverines and the CCHA finals. Because they had not lost to the Buckeyes in 34 games, dating back to November 1989, the Wolverines figured they had a straight shot to their third straight playoff finals. But with the score tied 2-2 in the third period, both Hayes and Turco made uncharacteristic mistakes, giving the puck away in their own zone on three occasions, all of which the Buckeyes turned into goals to beat Michigan 4-2. The Wolverines had left themselves at the NCAA committee's mercy for the first time since 1990.

"Basically, you don't lose to Ohio State, and we lost," Herr says. "That hurt. After that game, we didn't know if we were ever going to put on a Michigan uniform again."

"Red said, 'I feel sorry for the seniors if you don't get a bid,'" Turco recalls. "In other words, if you *do* get in the tournament, make the most of it."

During the nineties it had become a Michigan tradition for the team to gather on the Sunday before the NCAA tournament to watch the ESPN selection show. Since the Wolverines got a first-round bye six of those years, the only suspense was finding out whom they would play and where.

But on Sunday, March 22, 1998, the question was not where but *if* the Wolverines would be playing again that season. A decade earlier, when Berenson was struggling to bring his team up to snuff, this was exactly the kind of break they couldn't get. The NCAA committee snubbed them in 1990—but made up for it in 1998, not only inviting them to the party but letting them play in the Midwest regional at Yost.

"Home ice was going to be huge," Berenson says. "This was the last chance to redeem ourselves for the GLI and CCHA losses."

On Friday night, March 27, the third-seeded Wolverines took on the sixth-seeded Princeton Tigers. After their upside-down season, the Michigan players knew better than to take anyone lightly. With the score tied at 1-1, Mark Kosick had the puck while facing the boards in the right corner, and threw a blind pass to the slot. Instead of finding any teammates, however, the puck rattled off a Tiger defenseman and bounced over the goalie's stick into the net for the game's final score.

"Luckiest goal ever," Berenson confessed after the game.

It was as if the hockey gods were trying to pay Michigan back for all the breaks they denied the great Michigan teams of the early nineties in a single season. The '98 Wolverines could only hope the debt was not yet fully paid.

Beating Princeton meant Michigan had to face defending NCAA champion North Dakota, ranked second heading into the 1998 playoffs. The Sioux were having the kind of season Michigan had the previous year and looked virtually unstoppable.

But the hockey gods apparently decided to go overboard with reparations. The Michigan–North Dakota game was the second half of a doubleheader, with Ohio State playing Michigan State beforehand. The fourth-seeded Buckeyes took the number one ranked Spartans into overtime, pushing the Michigan–North Dakota game well past its 9:00 P.M. scheduled start.

"We're watching the game on TV from the training room under the stands," Herr recalls, "and we hear the crowd going nuts above us. We had our pregame meal at two, and now it's nine o'clock. Rick Bancroft, our trainer, was bringing up bananas, fruit, some soft pretzels, anything, to keep us from starving without filling us up."

A few minutes into overtime of the OSU-MSU game, the Buckeyes put the Spartans away. "We hadn't beaten State all year, and now they were gone, out of the way," Turco says. "Our fans go berserk."

Because of the late start—the puck didn't drop until 10:15 that night—the stands were already packed and jacked for warmups—"And that *never* happens," Turco says.

"When we come out the place is going nuts, and the band is going ballistic. For motivation, that's better than the NCAA title, the GLI, and the CCHA combined. We were jacked. That place was rockin'! Best game I ever played in, in my entire life."

Home crowd or not, the Sioux were the returning champions and quickly showed the Wolverines why, going up 2-0 in the first period. In the final minute of the opening period, the official gave Herr a minor penalty for slashing and Andrew Merrick a major penalty and a game misconduct for checking from behind. With two people needed to serve Merrick's penalties, Herr recalls, "I'm in the box with so many guys we could've had a party in there. It didn't look good."

If North Dakota could score on the ensuing 5-on-3 power play to go up 3-0—which was the smart bet—it likely would have spelled the end for Michigan's season. But the Michigan penalty killers turned in a heroic performance and kept the Sioux from scoring. Shortly into the second period, right as Herr jumped out of the penalty box, Turco made an acrobatic save. Justin Clark collected the rebound and cleared it off the boards, right to the area Herr was skating into, all alone. The setup virtually duplicated Joe Lockwood's famous goal against the Soviets in Berenson's first season.

"I see this play in my sleep," Herr says, meditating on the memory. "When I dream of a goal, this is what I dream of. I jump out of the box, and the puck comes off the boards, right to me. You usually have to settle it down, but the puck lays flat for me. It just sits down. I come in on net, I fake to my backhand, I fake to my forehand. But the goalie's really back in the net, almost falling in it. I look at him and see what he's giving me, and the five hole is open. I shoot it right there, it goes straight through—and I'm numb."

In just a few heartbeats, the Wolverines had swapped a season-ending 3-0 deficit for a 2-1 game they didn't deserve to be in, but were. "Twenty seconds after Matt scores his goal the crowd was *still* going nuts," Turco says. "I thought the roof was coming off."

The returning champions regained their composure and, a few minutes after Herr's goal, went ahead 3-1 on a shot from the far boards that just squeezed inside the far post. But midway through the second period, on a Michigan power play, Herr got the puck to freshman Mark Kosick, who passed it to Muckalt in the slot. Without taking any time to look, Muckalt whipped a backhand toward the net, which found its way through Sioux goalie Aaron Schweitzer to pull Michigan within one, 3-2.

Seconds after the horn sounded to end the second period, a

North Dakota player took an amazingly stupid penalty by hitting a Michigan player after the whistle. When play resumed in the third period, Michigan took full advantage of the power play when Greg Crozier buried the puck to tie the game at 3-3.

After being outshot 18-11 in the second period, Michigan outshot the Sioux 11-8 in the third, and the crowd started to believe that maybe, just maybe, its baby-faced team could beat the defending champions. With three minutes left in the game Herr and Bobby Hayes broke loose on a two-on-one break, which Hayes finished by firing a one-timer past Schweitzer's left shoulder, good for Michigan's fourth goal and its first lead of the game, 4-3.

The already roiling crowd exploded. For the games' remaining two minutes, the players could barely hear each other yell for the puck. When the buzzer sounded, Berenson was actually seen smiling, clapping, and hugging Mel Pearson—his first official hug outside of senior night or the Final Four.

"You don't realize what's happened until you sit down in your stall afterward," Herr says. "Whew! We're going to the dance!"

"Best game ever," insists Turco, who's played in a few. "Best game ever."

49

Back to the Dance

"When we were ending all those winning streaks during the season," Herr says, "we told the team, 'What we go through now doesn't matter. What we're going to be remembered for is what we do at the end.' We weren't the best team at Christmas or March first, but at the end, yes."

"They should have never let us get to Boston," Muckalt said afterward, "because once we were there we could smell it."

Boston's Fleet Center hosted the 1998 Final Four, where Michigan's first opponent would be the University of New Hampshire, located just a few hours northwest of Boston. Even though it was practically a home game for the Wildcats; even though Turco made two huge errors trying to handle the puck from the net; and even though this team really had no business being in the Final Four to begin with, the boys in blue handled the whole thing like they'd been there before, which of course, they had, for four straight years. Michigan took it to New Hampshire on the strength of Berenzweig's two-goal effort and dismissed the Wildcats, 4-0.

That spring's top seeds, Michigan State and the infamous Terriers of Boston University, had been knocked out by lesser teams, who themselves had since departed. But Boston College, which had a 25-8-5 record and had breezed past Colorado College and Ohio State, was still standing. With a home crowd of 18,276 boisterous Bostonians screaming for their Eagles, it's safe to say the Wolverines weren't the most popular team in the arena that night.

The Eagles jumped ahead, 1-0, on a long shot that froze

Turco, but being behind was nothing new for this group. Of Michigan's eight CCHA and NCAA playoff games, the Wolverines had trailed in six and been tied in another. With Boston College up 2-1 in the third, an attacking Eagle forward burned Berenzweig, but Turco's able goaltending erased the mistake—just as Bubba's two goals in the previous game covered Turco's miscues. Although Michigan was still behind 2-1 with just six minutes to go, the Wolverines' 16-2 record in one-goal games precluded any impulse to panic. No one got too low, and, when Mark Kosick scored on a freak rebound to tie the game, 2-2, no one got too high, either.

When Michigan came out for overtime, the Hex of Julian

1998 Celebration
Of Michigan's 46 games in 1997–98, a record 19 were decided by one goal, and Michigan won 17 of them—including the NCAA finals. "They should have never let us get to the Final Four," Muckalt said afterward, "because once we were there we could smell it."
(Courtesy of the U-M Athletic Department.)

Baretta was but a distant memory. The Eagles fired one shot off the left post and another off the crossbar—but the hockey gods were clearly wearing maize and blue that night. Michigan out-shot the Eagles 10-3 in 14 minutes of overtime, but it was Josh Langfeld's simple afterthought of a shot, after he skated around the Eagles' net, that slipped in between the BC goalie's leg pad and the pipe that put the game away. It was just the kind of half-baked goal that had beaten Michigan repeatedly in years past.

Needless to say, the hometown crowd wasn't thrilled with the outcome. When the Michigan bus pulled out of the Fleet Center, "we've got the lights on in the bus, the trophy in the back, and all of Boston is giving us the finger," says Herr, a native of New York State. "We loved it! It was awesome!"

These overachievers might have stumbled through most of the

Berenson and Muckalt
"I was under Red's spell right from the start," Muckalt says. "If he had told me to jump off a bridge, I'd do it—and do it twice. I was in awe of him."
(Courtesy of the U-M Athletic Department.)

season, but their improbable playoff run gave them 34 wins for
the season—just one off the school record set the year before—
and a total of 133 victories for the class of '98, one more than the
storied class of '97 collected.

"Without the other classes losing overtime heartbreakers and
learning," Herr says, "without them teaching us what it takes to
win, it's fair to say we couldn't have won in '98."

50

Character

Although 91 percent of Berenson's players get degrees, compared to 84 percent of the student body at large, naturally not every Michigan player is bound for NASA. And while the vast majority are upstanding citizens, a few have been in no danger of sainthood, and a few have made unflattering headlines over the years. Several years into the Berenson era, one player was justly arrested for throwing a brick through a sorority house window after learning his former girlfriend was dating another student.

Brian Wiseman, however, seems to have been unfairly tried in the local papers, even as the Canadian court system readily exonerated him of any wrongdoing. In early 1994, as Wiseman was winding up his college career in grand style, leading a star-studded team in scoring, he received a call from a police investigator in Ontario, informing him that he'd been accused of sexual assault. In accordance with Canadian law, however, the investigator could not tell him who had filed the complaint, nor even where or when the alleged encounter had taken place. Likewise, neither the investigators nor the judges are allowed to throw out frivolous cases during the 'discovery' phase of the investigation, as they can in the U.S., because Canadian law does not allow for a discovery phase. Thus, any case brought by anyone for any reason automatically goes to trial, regardless of its merits.

"The investigator flat out told me, 'I'm going through these records with these statements, and there's not enough evidence, but my hands are tied,'" Wiseman recalls. "I said, that's fine, I'm not asking for special favors."

But the phone call left Wiseman reeling. For a month afterward he left his home only to go to class, to the rink, and to student-teach in Saline, a nearby community. He remained in a state of limbo for two years while the case wound through the Canadian court system. Eventually he learned the incident that the plaintiff was addressing had occurred three years earlier, when Wiseman, then a 19-year-old freshman, and the woman—someone that he'd known for a few years, then 16-years-old—had had sex in his hometown, which Wiseman readily admitted. In hindsight, Wiseman feels he used poor judgment sleeping with a 16-year-old, but poor judgment does not constitute a crime, especially since the age of consent in Canada is 15.

Dave Shand served as an assistant under Berenson from 1989 to 1993 and as one of Wiseman's legal advisers during the trial. After the *Ann Arbor News* caught wind of the case, Shand and Wiseman requested a meeting with the paper's publisher, sports editor, and the reporter assigned to the story. While Canada's gag-order laws prohibited discussing the case on the record, Wiseman wanted to give his side of the story and let the journalists ask any questions they wished.

"Wiseman pulled no punches," Shand says, "and he never did. In the entire process, he was never caught in a lie or even a half-truth because he was always completely honest, even about sleeping with her."

The next day the *News* ran a front-page story entirely from the plaintiff's point of view as presented in the complaint, without any counter-information. "None of them had the guts to put their name on it," Shand says, "just 'contributions by staff reporters.' It was a joke."

Among other facts, the paper failed to mention that the couple had spent the entire night together, and the two were seen leaving together the following morning by her friends. Between that day and the time Wiseman received the fateful phone call from the Ontario police, the woman had been bragging that Wiseman, who was a big fish in this small city, was her boyfriend. (The woman's friends confirmed all of this during the trial.)

When Wiseman became a senior, however, and it was clear he

might sign a lucrative professional contract, her story changed. She claimed in her brief that she'd seen Wiseman in a number of local bars, and each time she suffered mental anguish, often breaking down and crying on the spot. But Wiseman was not in the country at the times she claimed to have run into him, and her friends testified that they'd never seen him again in her presence.

Likewise, her counselor testified that his client had never mentioned Wiseman's name during therapy—although she did claim to have been assaulted by 17 other men, up to and including Santa Claus. (We are not making this up.) When the jury retired to chambers to deliberate the verdict, the judge felt compelled to tell the others that if it were up to him, the trial would be over immediately. The jury returned shortly thereafter to give their answer: not guilty.

But the damage was done. "I never had any doubt that I'd eventually get by it and get through it," Wiseman says today, "but it was a heavy weight that I carried around for an awful long time, from the first phone call until I was acquitted two years later. Seemed like every few months there was a turn to it, and I had to file something or provide more testimony. It was always hanging over my head.

"The hardest thing was when the news first hit the stands. They didn't get my account, just the information from the complaint: A person has been charged with sexual assault. It was a hard time, and difficult for the people who care about me."

Although speedily acquitted, the drawn-out process probably hurt Wiseman's appeal to NHL teams, who, like the press, didn't know his side of the story for two years, until the trial itself. Although he did get a cup of coffee in the NHL, "I'm sure there were teams that maybe shied away," he says. He also paid out well over $50,000 in legal fees.

On the positive side, Wiseman's reputation among those who knew him in Ann Arbor and throughout the minor leagues, where he often served as team captain, remained sterling, and his conduct was above reproach. But a few painful lessons had been learned about the justice system, the press, and life in the spotlight. Wiseman's acquittal, incidentally, was covered in a small blurb buried deep in the local sports section.

"I knew the whole story from the beginning," Steve Shields says. "To see someone you're that close to have to go through all that, the misperceptions, the whole thing—it was painful to watch. I really admire the way he handled everything. If it were me, I probably would've snapped a few times."

"It was horrible," Shand adds, "but I think Brian handled the whole thing extraordinarily well." Shand is less impressed, however, with the local paper. "I haven't bought an *Ann Arbor News* since."

But probably the most well-known incident during the Berenson era involved Coach Berenson himself. In the spring of 1994, shortly after his team won a school record 33 games and took its second league title in three years, Berenson taped his weekly radio show at Banfield's Bar and Grill on Packard. When it was time to go home, Berenson walked outside and relieved himself in the back lot of a nearby library branch before getting into his car. Once he put the keys in the ignition, a local policeman who had watched him leave the bar arrested him for drunken driving.

Although others were willing to excuse his behavior, Berenson is having none of it. Former *Ann Arbor News* hockey beat writer Doug Hill insists Berenson was not drunk when he left the bar, but Berenson says, "Legally, I was." Likewise, Bo Schembechler suggests that any man who judges Berenson too harshly for going to the bathroom outside is probably being hypocritical, but Berenson replies, "Well, it doesn't look good in the papers."

When former football coach Gary Moeller was arrested for public drunkenness, by all accounts an entirely atypical event for the mild-mannered coach, he followed the disastrous advice of an attorney who knew nothing about defending public figures, who told him to hide from the press, not realizing that his case would be tried in the papers, not in the courts.

Berenson took the opposite approach. Knowing he had made an embarrassing mistake, as soon as he returned home that night he called up his assistant coaches to warn them about what they were going to hear the next day, then he called CCHA commissioner Bill Beagan first thing in the morning. Making matters worse for him, Berenson was to be named the CCHA Coach of the Year the following night at the annual league banquet.

"Red called me," Beagan recalls, "and said, 'I wanted you to be first to know that the CCHA Coach of the Year has been called a drunk.' Red just totally disarmed himself; he was humiliated. He was just so remorseful for the stigma associated with what had happened. What am I going to say to him? If we all look in the mirror, everyone has something that we can say, 'Boy I wish I could erase that!' But, it's there. And it ain't going away."

Berenson then asked Beagan if he should address the incident that night at the awards banquet. Beagan says that he replied, "Red, I would face it head on. I would bring it up and say what you have to say. And he did."

"It was a learning experience for me," Berenson says. "And I tried to turn it into a learning experience for the team, too. I'm always preaching to the players not to do anything to embarrass your team, your school, your family, so I felt terrible that I put everyone in that predicament. It was a low point, and it came at a bad time.

"Well, everyone at the banquet knew what had happened the night before. There wasn't any point, I felt, in trying to act like it didn't happen. I tried to turn it into a constructive lesson. I told them that I felt I let the college hockey community down. I said we are more vulnerable, and more visible, than other people on campus, so we have to be extra careful."

"I thought he addressed it quite well," Beagan said. "But I think the bottom line is, it would take a helluva lot more than that to destroy Red Berenson's credibility. He's the furthest thing from a bad actor you can get."

Apparently the university leadership agreed, concluding that the evening's events were an aberration. They decided not to punish Berenson any more than he already had been by the local police and press.

Berenson proved their faith was not misplaced in the following years. The best evidence that these incidents were not representative of the hockey program has been the conduct and character of its coaches and players on and off the ice.

It's fair to say the hockey players tend to be more inconspicuous and articulate than most big-time athletes. Perhaps that's because, unlike football or basketball, hockey has a viable minor league system, so players interested only in playing hockey can go elsewhere. That's not to say they're all so polished you'd invite them for tea with Miss Manners, but you wouldn't be embarrassed to have them meet, say, the vice president, which they did twice in the 1990s.

Having high behavioral and academic standards comes at a price, of course, but Berenson doesn't flinch when it's time to pay. Right before a crucial series against Michigan State in February 1998, for example, Berenson decided to bench Marty Turco, still the winningest goalie in NCAA history, because he had missed a class. Turco hadn't violated NCAA rules or even university rules, but he'd violated Berenson's rules, and that was enough. The Spartans swept Michigan for the first time since 1989, but Berenson had no second thoughts about his decision.

"What you see on the ice tells you this guy is a whale of a coach," Schembechler says of Berenson. "I have enormous respect for him as a person. You talk about fundamental values—honesty, integrity, hard work—he's got 'em. You can't be a laissez-faire coach."

A Mellow Red

"Red Berenson is the greatest friend you could ever have," says longtime equipment manager Ian Hume. "It just takes some players longer to figure that out than others."

During the winter of 2000, Rob Brown, a member of the class of '90, stopped by Yost to watch the team practice for a bit, but the school was on spring break so the schedule was scrambled. Instead of finding the team on the ice, Brown went up to Berenson's office to find the coach putting on his coat and grabbing his briefcase, ready to go home. But when he saw Brown coming up the stairs, he set his briefcase down, took his coat off, sat down on the couch, and said, "Have a seat." The two talked a few minutes about hockey, but devoted most of their half-hour chat to Brown's career, his life, and how things were going in general.

"I think he's just as proud of the guys who've gone on to start business careers or go to med school as he is of the pro players," Brown says. "There's a certain distance a coach has to keep from his players. Everyone who played for Red would probably tell you they have a different relationship with him now than they did when they played. At the time I played for him he wasn't so far removed from coaching in the NHL, so that might have added an extra distance there. And he had to teach us how to be winners, too. But seeing the relationship he has with current players shows me that he's closed some of that distance.

"Here's a busy guy who's about to go home at the end of the day, and a guy he coached 10 years ago, a guy he still sees quite often, really, comes up the stairs, and he drops everything just to catch up," Brown says. "What a great feeling."

Berenson's implacable expression behind the bench makes a serious poker player look like a circus clown. Whether his team's ahead by 10 or behind by 10, he looks about as lighthearted as a man filing his tax return.

"Some people can switch their personalities to accommodate a situation—and Red's not one of those people," assistant coach Billy Powers says. "He's a very consistent person."

But in 1996–97, with things going so well on and off the ice— five Michigan players would receive academic awards that year, and eight of nine would graduate on time—the relentless Berenson finally allowed himself to enjoy the moment. During that glorious season, in which there never was heard a discouraging word, Red Berenson started smiling in private and—get this— even showed his sense of humor in public. Okay, you're not likely to hear him tell jokes that begin with "Three guys walk into a bar," but you will get a steady stream of wry one-liners. Those who've been around him the past decade have also noticed he's warmed up considerably to the young charges who have put the Michigan program back on the map.

Berenson had finally gotten his program where he had envisioned it being years earlier. He had two top-notch assistant coaches, his school had become the first choice of many blue-chippers, and, of course, the team was winning. "It's a lot more fun for the coaches, the players, the fans," Powers says. "That changes everything."

"Red came from pro hockey," Powers adds, "where there's a lot of distance between the players and the coach. It's a big adjustment to college, where you have to be more hands on. I know the guys I played with would probably be surprised at how he's really become more of a player's coach."

"I've seen him change," Pearson says. "He's a very proud guy, and he wasn't happy with the situation before. It was harder to be relaxed around the players when we were losing. But now he's much more relaxed with the players away from the rink."

Berenson's hard-nosed reputation was still intact when some of the '97 seniors signed on. "I'd heard stories," says Morrison. "I'd heard that he's hard on the players, that he blows up. I think he's more of a mellow guy now. He picks his spots and knows when to slip a joke in."

"I'm closer to the players now," Berenson concedes. "I don't think I need to be as much of a driving force on the team as I used to be. You start by pulling your team out of the mud. Now that things are going well, I've become more of a shepherd, just picking up the strays lagging behind."

For all the changes the program and the coach have undergone the past decade, a lot has remained consistent—which is, incidentally, one of Berenson's favorite words. (Berenson's been happily married for over four decades and even his cars outlast two-term presidents.) Hard work, dedication, and loyalty are still in fashion. The coach still cajoles his players to prepare for life after hockey—although, ironically, he hasn't had one.

"Upperclassmen have continued to carry the torch, echoing the messages that Red's been sending," Powers says. "It takes time to get your personality meshed with the team's. The last decade the kids have done such a good job, it's given Red a chance to get to know the kids a whole lot better. But there is nothing that I see that's laid back about him. He still expects the kids to do their part and the team to win."

Schembechler, summing up Berenson, says "He's not buddy buddy with his players, but they know he's in their corner. He's been extremely loyal to Michigan and what it represents. Red's just a class act, all the way."

Part IX

Passing the Torch
1999–Present

51

The Forgotten Class

When the 1998–99 University of Michigan team gathered for the first time at a newly renovated Yost Arena on September 14, the players and coaches were surrounded by their program's success. They met in a locker room so plush—with thick blue carpeting, a juice machine on the counter, and a fancy nameplate above each player's lacquered wooden locker—that no one who played for Michigan before 1996, or for almost any other college in the country, would recognize it as a college hockey locker room. If not for the gumball-colored practice jerseys in each stall, it would be more living room than locker room.

The room was just the most tangible sign of the program's health, which at that time already included a nation-leading 272 victories in the 1990s—setting the school record for a decade, with a year and a half left to go—two NCAA titles in the past three seasons, and eight straight seasons of sellouts. The CCHA coaches that fall picked Michigan to take another title.

Waiting for the coaches to address them were six wide-eyed but highly touted freshmen who had had nothing to do with that success; sitting among them, though less quietly, were seven determined seniors who already owned two NCAA title rings but felt they hadn't made a name for themselves. Captain Bubba Berenzweig, the only senior with a realistic chance to play in the NHL, called himself and his peers "the forgotten class."

"Everyone was talking about Mike Comrie this and Mike Comrie that," Berenzweig said, referring to the celebrated freshman who stood just 5'8" but led all Canadian junior players with 138 points in just 58 games the previous year. If one man's face represented the precociousness of the class of '02, it was surely Comrie's.

"I walk in the room that day," senior Greg Crozier recalls, "and I see a number 39 hanging from one of the freshman stalls, Comrie's number. 'What's this about?' When we made the team, we were told to pick a number between 1 and 35. The times they are a-changin', I guess. I see that jersey, I figure the kid's a superstar."

Berenson also had some misgivings when he walked in a few minutes later. "You look around the room, and you realize it's true: Matt Herr's gone, Billy Muckalt's gone, Marty Turco's gone. So you ask yourself, 'Who's going to score 20 goals in here? Who's going to keep the other team from scoring?'

"This senior class has always had a cloud over it," Berenson added. "They'd been an important class, but always a kind of overlooked class. They never had to lead the team, but they also hadn't had the chance to have a leadership role.

"The tension between seniors and freshmen is always a challenge for coaches. You have to make goals for the freshmen, who don't know what they can do at this level, and you need to have your seniors become leaders and have their best seasons. If not, you're not going to succeed."

The seniors included Berenzweig and Crozier, both eastern prep school stars who had logged 243 games at Michigan between them; Justin Clark, whose mom sent in a video of her son four years before to get the Michigan coaches' attention; Bobby Hayes and Dale Rominski, two walk-ons from suburban Detroit who worked so hard and contributed so much that their teammates elected them assistant captains their senior years; and Greg Daddario, Berenzweig's best friend from Connecticut's Loomis-Chaffee prep school, a third-string goalie who had walked into Berenson's office the previous spring to tell him that, as a student with a 3.9 grade-point average double-majoring in English and economics, he had decided it was time to quit.

Although Berenson doesn't always try to talk players out of such decisions, he urged Daddario to return for his senior season, explaining that the highly respected player's value to the team couldn't be measured on paper and that he would always regret not finishing what he'd started and being a part of his senior year. Daddario thought about it, and eventually agreed to return for his last season.

In his first address in front of the 1998–99 team, Berenson let his charges know they had the unique challenge to avoid slipping backward—something no other team he'd coached had faced before.

"We have a lot of challenges here. Your jobs aren't set. We don't know whose job it is to lead the team in scoring, who's going to kill the penalties, who's going to step up in big games. Winning isn't just about being the best players; it's about being the best team."

Berenson talked about the importance of upholding the expectations of the players—on the ice, off the ice, and in the classroom—expectations dozens of seniors have established before them.

Then he closed by saying, "So now it's day to day. Let's see who's going to step up. Let's see how good we are. We could take a huge step backward this year, or we can keep it going forward. It all depends on what you guys decide."

The Wolverines started the season tripping over themselves. In their second game, the defending national champions took on the University of Niagara Purple Eagles—yes, that's correct—and needed all but the last 1.7 seconds of overtime to win, 6-5. Instead of waking up for the next game, they lost 2-1.

"We had raised the bar so high, anything short of an NCAA title seemed like a disappointment," Berenzweig said, "but now you see how difficult it is."

"It looked like it could be a long season," remembered assistant coach Billy Powers.

But the team improved its record to a respectable 7-2-1 before its big fall weekend: Michigan State on November 20, with Notre Dame the next night.

Michigan beat the Spartans in a slugfest match, 2-1, on Dale Rominski's shorthanded drive to the net, then sent the Fighting Irish home the next night with a 1-0 loss. "In one weekend," Billy Powers said, "we went from 'Anyone can beat us' to 'We can beat anyone.'"

By late January, Michigan's record stood at 18-5-2, and any fear of a post-title collapse during a "rebuilding year" was the farthest thing from the Wolverines' minds.

Michigan entered its rematch with Michigan State just two points behind the Spartans, 29 to 27, with a game in hand. It left the game with a disheartening 3-3 tie, after giving up a third-period lead for only the third time in the last 101 times they'd had it.

"In our situation," Berenzweig said, "this takes a lot out of you. Of all the games I ever lost or tied, this one hurt the most."

Apparently it hurt everyone. The Wolverines embarked on the worst stretch of Michigan hockey in over a decade, going 0-4-4 over their next eight games.

"The strange thing is, I still feel our team is playing pretty well," Berenson said at the time. "This has been a tough season for everyone, but our guys have kept their heads. Bubba's classmates are all finding their roles, and Bubba has really become a man. I still think our best hockey is ahead of us."

Sure enough, Michigan exploded like an overagitated bottle of champagne, going 3-1 over its remaining 4 regular-season games, including a 9-4 thrashing of Miami on senior night. Almost magically, all six members of the forgotten class who skated out had scored goals by then, and the seventh senior, goalie Greg Daddario, got into the game with six minutes left.

When he made his first save, his teammates banged the boards with their sticks, the crowd gave him a standing ovation, and the band broke into a stirring rendition of "Temptation," a song they usually reserve for game-winning goals and clutch third-down conversions. At the final buzzer, Berenzweig aad his classmates mobbed Daddario as if he'd just beaten the Spartans.

"That night," Clark says, "was the best feeling I had since the '98 championship."

The Wolverines put their March momentum to good use going

into their do-or-die regular-season finale against Northern Michigan. "This is the whole season as far as I'm concerned," Berenson told them. "We simply have to come through."

They did. The Wolverines beat the Wildcats, 5-2, and they kept it up straight through the CCHA finals, where they blew past Northern Michigan, 5-1, to give them a 24-10-6 record and their ninth consecutive NCAA invitation.

"We're all the same guys," said sophomore Mark Kosick, "but something about Michigan, we get up this time of year, like we're different guys."

"Once you get to the playoffs, you know your time's coming," Bobby Hayes said, "but you don't know when. It's like playing Russian roulette with your hockey career."

The gun seemed to have a few extra bullets in it on March 26, 1999, in Michigan's opening-round NCAA playoff game with Denver. Playing "the single worst period of hockey we've played since I've been coaching—bar none," in Billy Powers's words, Michigan all but rolled over for the Pioneers. By the midpoint of the second period, Denver had outshot Michigan by the unheard of margin of 17-2 and had built a 3-0 lead.

"It could've been 5-0, just a massacre," Powers added. "They were outskating us, out-hitting us, out-thinking us. We started feeling desperate just to get it past our own blue line. You gotta give 'em credit—Denver looked awesome, and we just couldn't get anything going."

"I couldn't believe how poorly we played, especially for a seasoned team," Berenson says. "It was like we'd never been there before. On five of our six power plays, we didn't even get a shot. We weren't doing anything right."

After Denver's third goal, 7:34 into the second period, Berenson called an unorthodox midgame time-out.

"This was Mel's decision," Berenson said, "and it was the right one." Although the coaching staff typically uses most of its time-outs for Mel Pearson to draw up a play for the extra attacker, during this time-out x's and o's were the farthest things from the agenda.

Berenson, punctuating each point with his index finger, told them, "We didn't come here to embarrass ourselves. So forget about the score, just forecheck and play the way Michigan can play.

"Now, look at me, in the eyes, so I can tell if you're ready to play." Berenson then looked at his players, one by one, and said, "Okay. You're ready. Now go do it."

Berenson's boys did as instructed: They forgot about the score, they ignored the trash talking, they got back to playing Michigan hockey. And from that point on they outshot the cocky, trash-talking Pioneers 22-1 to win 5-3, in one of the most incredible turnarounds in NCAA playoff history.

"I've never seen a game like that," Pearson said.

The players' adrenaline prevented most of them from falling asleep before three in the morning, but they needed their rest. In less than 24 hours, they would be taking the ice against New Hampshire, the best team in the nation.

The Wildcats outshot the Wolverines 34-21, but thanks to Josh Blackburn's goaltending, they could only manage a single goal in regulation off a fluke play with 75 seconds left in the first period, which Hayes matched in the third period.

"The guys still felt, going into overtime, that we were going to win," Pearson says. It is a testament to the program's accrued confidence, developed over a decade by those who went before, that Michigan probably had more confidence than New Hampshire when overtime started. In the early nineties Michigan had lost to less talented but more poised teams, and now they were in a position to be that type of team, and ruin someone else's season.

Just three minutes into overtime, however, Michigan botched a reverse behind its own net, and the Wildcats scored their second fluke goal of the evening to end the Wolverines' year.

"It was a huge shock. A huge shock," Berenzweig said. "I didn't think it was real. And I've never seen Clark that choked up in my entire life. Crozier couldn't move. We loved each other as teammates. It was nothing more than that. That was by far the lowest point of my career. I won't ever feel that way again in my life. I know it."

Back in Ann Arbor, the team still had the ice available for the next two weeks, so each day a few of the guys would walk down to the rink after class, get suited up, and hop on the ice to play a little shinny—something no professional players would ever do at season's end.

After all the fans, the press, and the pressure of playing for the best college hockey team in the nineties had disappeared, the guys on the 1998–99 Michigan hockey team were doing exactly what their ancestors in the Huron Hockey Club were doing out on the frozen river more than eight decades earlier.

They were just playing hockey for the sheer love of the game and the joy of playing together.

The last official function of every Michigan hockey season is the Deker Awards Banquet, held that year on April 11. "The thing that makes the Michigan program special," Berenson explained from the dais, "is not the wins and losses but the camaraderie and experiences that culminate at the banquet."

The banquet's final component is always the "Senior Reflections"; that year, Greg Daddario led off. Berenson introduced him by saying, "Nobody worked harder. I don't think there's a player on this team who wouldn't sell his soul to have Greg be a part of this program."

Daddario, who could barely see over the podium, said, "My first Michigan memory, I came out to Ann Arbor with Bubba on his recruiting trip. Bubba was in the office with Red, and I was waiting outside. Billy Powers comes by and says, 'You wanna go for a ride, see the campus?' I say sure, and he takes two hours to show me the campus. It's that kind of program.

"Halfway through my junior year, I went into Red's office and say it's time for me to quit. Well, you talked me out of it, Coach, and I can't thank you enough for that."

Daddario clutched the podium and breathed deeply, to keep from crying, but it was already too late for Bobby Hayes's mother and Sue Shand, the academic adviser for the team. "Having the respect of your teammates is so important," Daddario continued. "It's something I'll never forget, something I'll always take with me." He thanked the supporters, he thanked his coaches, he thanked his teammates, he thanked his family.

"I'm going to work for BankOne in Chicago," he said. "This pleases my mom because she always saw me going the business route, but I've got this letter from the Charlotte Wheelers. I was planning to go to BankOne, but they're offering me $400 a week. Charlotte Wheelers, here I come."

After the laughter died down, Daddario turned serious. "I had experiences here I wouldn't have had anywhere else. I thank you."

With that, Greg Daddario had officially spent more time at the podium than between the pipes.

Like every other member of the forgotten class, Sean Ritchlin got teary-eyed at the podium, then finished with words all of them would have agreed with: "It's not the championships I'll remember, it's the guys who won them. Thanks for everything."

A few weeks later, after all seven seniors had graduated on time and moved away, Berenson sat in his office and reflected on the season just past.

"1999 was a good season—not far off the mark. But the highlight of this season was the banquet, where they communicated their experience so well. We didn't win the whole thing, but the seniors spoke well, and when I walked out I felt really good about what they'd done and where the program was going."

52

The Future Is Now

It's a testament to the continued success of the Michigan hockey program that the 1999–2000 team didn't draw much attention. Yes, the Wolverines were the CCHA regular-season champions, and they would have returned to the Frozen Four if they had been able to hold their third-period lead against Maine in the NCAA quarterfinals. And true, all four seniors graduated on time. But these things have come to be expected in Ann Arbor. It was business as usual.

Because Michigan hockey had already established itself as the nation's preeminent college hockey program in the nineties, it would take a lot to turn heads. But heading into the 2000–2001 campaign, it looked like that team might have what it took to do so. Although super sophomore Mike Comrie decided not to return for his junior year, the rest of the roster remained virtually intact.

Even the normally circumspect Berenson had to admit the outlook was bright. "I think we could be a good team if we continue to get strong senior leadership, maintain a strong work ethic, and get a little luck," he said a few months before play began. "I like our depth. On paper, we should be one of the better teams."

If they weren't, the Wolverines' schedule—one of the toughest in the country, with 7 of the nation's top 12 teams on the slate—would tear them to pieces. Michigan opened the season at the Icebreaker Tournament against a strong Colgate team and defending NCAA champion North Dakota, and emerged with two respectable ties. That tournament propelled the Wolverines to a

13-3-3 record by December 9, but they would have to cool their heels for twenty days before playing their next game at the GLI on Dec. 29.

"We were on a roll," Berenson recalled after the season's end, "and we were disappointed we had a long break."

Michigan ended the respite with its worst weekend of the season, enduring drubbings by a weak Michigan Tech team and Boston College. Granted, several Michigan stars were off in Russia playing for national all-star teams, but Michigan had surmounted that same problem almost every year of its nine-year run of GLI titles.

"We really bottomed out at the GLI," Berenson said. "The worst GLI I can remember in a long, long time. You can make excuses, but there it is."

The GLI setback sent Michigan sliding into a patch of inconsistency, exacerbated by injuries that cost vital players like Dave Huntzicker, Jay Vancik, and Jed Ortmeyer over four dozen games after the break. "Our team never seemed to get 100 percent healthy," Berenson said. "That put a big hole in our line-up. We'd split weekends—we'd get a win and a loss, a loss and a win—so when we approached the year-end tournaments, our team just didn't have the momentum that we've typically had. We were a lot more vulnerable than we usually are."

Perhaps more troubling than Michigan's 1-4-1 regular season finish was the team's shaky senior leadership.

Before the season, Berenson had warned, "You're only as good as your seniors. Josh Langfeld, Mark Kosick, Scotty Matzka, and Geoff Koch—these seniors have to have their best years. If they do that, that will make a huge difference."

At the end of the year, however, only one of the team's nine seniors—forward Bill Trainor—could say he'd had his best season, with 12 points. The senior class could not seem to rally the underclassmen the way the '98 seniors had inspired them. Sometimes the seniors couldn't even get along with each other either—a stark contrast with the remarkably unified seniors of the previous decade, who had lived, vacationed, and stayed in close contact with each other years after graduating.

In some ways the team was a victim of its own success. With the endless waves of blue-chip players washing up on Michigan's shores year after year, it had become easy to take for granted that Michigan would always have enough talent to battle with the best, and that ability alone would guarantee them a place among the nation's elite teams. There were times the 2000–01 team forgot just how hard their predecessors had worked together to get to that level.

All that talent naturally enticed NHL teams to tempt Michigan's players to leave school early for the pros. This wasn't a new problem, of course, but it was a new generation, one that seemed more inclined to view Michigan as a training camp than as an experience to be valued on its own terms. Berenson never had to worry about David Harlock, Steve Halko, or Brendan Morrison turning pro, but throughout the 2000–01 season, every month another player was rumored to be preparing to make the jump.

But something magical stirs in Michigan men in March. In the first round of the CCHA playoffs, they mopped up on Ferris State, 8-3 and 3-0, then found a way to win against Nebraska-Omaha in the league semifinals at Joe Louis, exacting revenge for UN-O's semifinal upset the previous year. Although the Wolverines lost 2-0 to Michigan State in the CCHA finals, they had skated well and proven that they could play with the nation's number one team.

"It wasn't a season of firsts for us," Berenson assessed. "We couldn't win the GLI, the regular season title, or the league playoffs. But then we had a chance to redeem ourselves in the NCAA—and we were still ranked pretty high [fifth], all things considered."

The Wolverines also had the intangible Michigan mystique on its side, dating back to the days when Coach Barss's team upset Minnesota for the league title in 1927, Coach Heyliger's troops upended a string of favorites in the early NCAA tournaments, and Matt Herr's gutsy squad dropped by heavyweight after heavyweight en route to its unlikely title in 1998. The coaching staff drew on the team's rich history by quoting Kent Brothers' infamous speech during the 1991 Cornell series: "My hockey career ends when we lose our next game," he'd said. "But I'm not ready to finish. We need to pull it together. Either I'll do it all by myself, or you'll join me."

The 2001 team, like Brothers' '91 edition, pulled it all together at the eleventh hour, coming from behind in the first round of the NCAA tournament against upstart Mercyhurst, 4-3, and making an early lead against WCHA champion St. Cloud State stick the next day for another 4-3 victory.

"We went into the NCAA's and really put our best foot forward," Berenson said. "We played probably the best game of the season against St. Cloud, as good a team as anyone we'd faced. We got it all together when it mattered."

The victories also secured the school's first Frozen Four berth since the current seniors were freshmen on the 1998 NCAA title team. The similarities to that team were becoming clearer with each victory: both were promising but uncertain squads that had to overcome numerous obstacles, and suddenly had a chance to win it all. And once again, Michigan would face Boston College.

The coaching staff tapped the team's tradition by asking more than a dozen former Michigan players to give a few words on a video, or a fax, or a phone call—and despite the short notice, every one of them, from 1989 Captain Myles O'Connor to 2000 Captain Sean Peach, came through, sending their support from the farthest corners of the continent. Some of Red's first players, like David Harlock and Steve Shields, reflected on their missed opportunity to take home that slab of wood; more recent players like Brendan Morrison, Matt Herr, and Marty Turco recalled how exhilarating it was to get their hands on it after thrilling overtime triumphs.

The players also received a call from a lawyer in Newfoundland named Kent Brothers, and a fax from a New York Islander named Billy Muckalt, who had boldly declared in 1998—when the current seniors were freshmen and the current freshmen were high school sophomores—"They should have never let us get to [the Frozen Four], because once we were there we could smell it."

Michigan started out slowly against Boston College, falling behind 3-0, but seemed to remember who they were and what they were representing midway through the game. John Shouneyia ended BC's shut-out in the middle stanza, followed by Michigan leading scorer Andy Hilbert's near miss on a break-way. Mike Cammalleri scored Michigan's second goal just a few minutes into the third period, which left the Wolverines down just 3-2 with about 15 minutes left and more than enough momentum to blow past the wide-eyed Eagles. It seemed almost inevitable that Michigan would find a way to beat the snake-bitten BC boys, who had failed in the three previous Frozen Fours, extending their school's NCAA dry spell to 51 years, a streak that dated back to the Eagles' first and only NCAA title in 1949.

The inspired Wolverines kept firing the puck on the Eagles' net, including high-percentage shots by Langfeld, Kosick, and Jillson, but just couldn't get the rubber thing to go in.

"We had the scoring chances and we had the goaltending, and we nearly did it," Berenson said, "but we just couldn't get back in it."

The 2000–01 team ultimately lost the game, 4-2, on an empty-net goal, but it had won something else in the bargain: an identity, and the respect of those who came before.

"A lot of people questioned this team's leadership and character," said Brian Wiseman, '94, who had returned to the program as an administrative assistant the previous fall. "But I think in the end, you saw a lot of people exemplify what Michigan is all about. When push came to shove, the seniors stepped up and came through, like true Michigan men."

Some perspective is called for. A record of 27-13-5, especially with Michigan's masochistic schedule, is one all but a few teams would have killed for. And with its Frozen Four appearance, the class of 2001 became the seventh group of Michigan seniors to make it to the NCAA semifinals in the last 11 years. Ted Barss, the grandson of Dr. Joseph Barss, Michigan's first coach and inspiration for the Team Player Award given at the annual banquet, reflected on the team's success, saying "I have to tell you, if he saw what the program has become today, he'd be so impressed, so pleased."

As Berenson had said at his first Michigan press conference in 1984, his goal was not merely to build a good team, but a good program, one that would stand the test of time. He echoed those words a few days after the conclusion of his 17th season. "Seven out of eleven final fours, that's the mark of a good program, not just a good team," he philosophized. "That's been our guiding light. The Michigan hockey program is on the map. And that's the thing that makes me feel most proud."

If the near future of the team looks bright, the long-term future of the program looks even brighter. Interest in Michigan hockey has never been higher. With over 500 fans already on the waiting list for season tickets, there is plenty of demand to justify adding a balcony to the east side of Yost across from the press box, replete with nearly 300 movie-theater-style seats that are expected to go fast.

Demand is so high, in fact, that Berenson predicts the team to move into a new facility in the next 10 to 20 years. One possibility is Crisler Arena, but with its very un-Yost-like atmosphere, and $12 million already needed in repairs just to return it to its original condition, Berenson believes the team will settle elsewhere. More likely, he says, the school will build a new arena on campus.

Berenson's improved squads also helped restore Deker club membership, year by year. After bottoming out at 60 members during the depths of the Giordano years, Deker membership today totals over 600 boosters who not only sponsor the fall team picnic, blue-white game, and the banquet, but they also contribute each year to the endowed scholarships for the hockey team, currently at eight and rising.

Berenson and the Dekers have also been at work for several years on a different kind of infrastructure: endowed scholarships. They have already raised enough for eight scholarships. Raising $5 million more would ensure the funding of the entire roster of scholarships, sparing the program from being at the mercy of any financial winds of change the athletic department might experience in the future.

Berenson expects those scholarships will go increasingly to native-born players. While the teams he played on rarely had more than one American on the roster, the current Wolverines have only three Canadians. With the growth of American junior hockey programs and national all-star camps, Berenson expects even more U.S. players to fill college rosters nationwide.

This, in turn, will help more schools start their own programs and generate more interest in college hockey. From the time Vic Heyliger organized the first NCAA tournament in 1948 to the mid-1970s, the number of Division I college teams grew from 20 to over 40 but stalled there for two decades. In the 1990s, however, the number has exploded to almost 60 schools sponsoring Division I hockey teams, with at least a half dozen others on the verge of doing so.

"The CCHA is strong and will expand," Berenson predicts. "The momentum [former CCHA commissioner] Bill Beagan started has continued. College hockey is going in the right direction right now, and I'm confident it will continue in the right direction. It's growing in numbers and popularity, for the right reasons. I think the biggest growth spurt of college hockey is still in front of us."

"I still think the future of college hockey is extremely bright," former commissioner Bill Beagan says, "but unfortunately the greatest benefactor is the NHL. The NHL wants to kill the NCAA's rule 12.2.3.2.4.1 and make Major Junior A players eligible to play Division I college hockey—something the most conscientious people in college hockey are against. The future of college hockey depends a lot on how much distance they can keep between themselves and the NHL. If college hockey lets the NHL's tentacles get in to college hockey, they'll screw it up."

Assuming they don't, however, Beagan believes the game's best years lie ahead. "If I was still the commissioner of the CCHA," Beagan adds, "I would send some more wagons west to get USC, Berkeley, and other western schools playing hockey. The future of college hockey is not going to put any more people in Yost or Munn. Those places are already packed and probably will be for a while."

And how much longer will Berenson be behind the Michigan bench? "I don't have a plan," he says. "I'm going year by year. I don't see myself as a career coach, someone who can't give it up. I'm not going to keep going on just to break records. I'm not worried about that. I don't know who will follow me—I think Mel Pearson deserves a shot and would do an excellent job—but I'm not worried about the future of this program, either."

A good model for Michigan's hockey program in the post-Berenson years might be found down the road in the Michigan football program. Schembechler's successors, Gary Moeller and Lloyd Carr, may not have had Schembechler's stature or charisma, but they both have run successful and clean programs—which is probably what you can expect from Berenson's descendants, too.

"I think the Michigan athletic department is going in the right direction," Berenson adds. "The Michigan hockey team will continue to compete nationally and will be as well thought of in the next 20 years as it is right now. You can always slip, of course—we've seen that—but things are in place for a bright future."

Homegrown

The lifeblood of any hockey program is its players. Michigan has received infusions from some unlikely places, starting with Calumet and Eveleth; then moving west to Regina, Calgary, and British Columbia; and finally tapping New England prep schools. But while Michigan's principle sources of talent have shifted every decade or so, there has been one steady stream of players running throughout the program's existence, located right under the coaches' noses: Ann Arbor.

They grew up running around the Coliseum and the Field House, playing on local ponds and in local parks, and dreaming of playing for the maize and blue.

They weren't drafted by NHL teams. They weren't offered full rides at Michigan—or anywhere else. Most of them weren't recruited at all.

But in every decade that Michigan has had a varsity hockey team, Ann Arbor players have been on it—and once they make it, they generally make the most of it.

In the twentieth century, exactly two dozen local players realized their dream of playing for Michigan, from faculty son Waldeck Levi on the inaugural 1923 team right up to David Huntzicker on the 2000–2001 squad. Once they pull on their first Michigan sweater, these underrated players seem magically transformed into overachievers.

Of Michigan's 24 native sons, 2 have become captains and 4 have been voted into the Deker Hall of Fame. Eight of those 24 players have suited up since 1981, 6 of whom have earned a league or team honor, including the CCHA player of the week award and a total of eight team trophies, for being the most improved, the top academic athlete, the most sportsmanlike, and the most valuable player.

On paper, the success of the local players makes little sense. The Upper Peninsula opened its first professional league in 1903; Eveleth christened its high school varsity team in 1922, about the same time as the eastern prep schools formed theirs; and the Canadian cities have been playing organized hockey since time eternal. Ann Arbor, in contrast, didn't form its first little league until 1954 and didn't sponsor a high school hockey team until 1962. Yet six local players who never played anything more sophisticated than pond hockey were able to make UM's varsity squad—their first organized hockey team.

The local boys beat the odds partly because, unlike their out-of-town teammates, playing for Michigan is all they ever dreamed of. What they've lacked in ability they've made up for in passion.

The most celebrated of Michigan's first local players was Art Schlanderer, whose grandfather came to Ann Arbor with the first wave of German immigrants and died in the line of duty as a volunteer fireman sometime in the 1870s. Art Schlanderer was born in 1910 and grew up on Hamilton Street, just a few blocks from his old friends Kip Taylor and Nate Weinberg. Art and his pals trudged through the snow to skate on the Huron River, the flooded tennis courts and, on special days, at the shiny new Coliseum. Schlanderer's mother would drop two nickels into his mitten, enough for a full day of fun with his friends. "I was sort of a rink rat," he wrote late in life.

As Schlanderer grew up, he and his buddies would occasionally skate with the Michigan team. In the mid-1920s he attended the old Ann Arbor High School, in what is now the Frieze Building, when Ann Arbor's streets were dirt roads and the fire department still used horse-drawn wagons. By then Schlanderer was already a three-sport star, "but when the ice was ready at the Coliseum," he wrote, "all I wanted to do was play hockey."

Schlanderer was a smart enough student to be accepted by

the Michigan business school in 1927, and a good enough player to attract Coach Lowrey's attention, too. Said to be "the fastest guy in town," Schlanderer was named team captain in 1930–31. He led his team to their second straight Big Ten title and he qualified for the 1932 Olympic team, but in those days players had to pay their own way. The Depression kept Schlanderer from

Arthur Schlanderer '31
Initiated 3-16-28
Hockey Captain of 1930
Conference Champions

Art Schlanderer
"In high school I played golf and basketball," said Ann Arbor native Art Schlanderer. "But when the ice was ready at the Coliseum, all I wanted to do was play hockey." He captained the 1930–31 team and saw every Michigan team play until he died in 1995.
(Courtesy of the Schlanderer family.)

going to Lake Placid, and also forced him to forgo law school to help out with the family's then-45-year-old jewelry store, where he worked the rest of his life.

On January 28, 1995, Schlanderer and the other aging hockey alums watched the current crop of Wolverines beat the University of Illinois-Chicago, 5-4, in overtime. The team was 19-4-1, and on its way to its second straight league title. Schlanderer and his mates rejoiced in the program's renaissance, which would culminate in the school's eighth NCAA title fourteen months later. But the next day, when he and his wife went to his son Mark's house for Sunday dinner, all he could talk about was how good it was to see all his old hockey friends again, and make some new ones, too.

Two days later, on January 31, 1995, Art Schlanderer passed away. He was 85 years old.

When Mark Schlanderer was sorting through his father's papers a week later, he came across the fresh ink his father had put down a few days before seeing his final Michigan hockey game. His father's graceful, patient penmanship filled two sheets of yellow legal paper, which he clipped to a copy of an old yearbook photo of the Michigan hockey team. At the top of the first page he wrote, simply, "Michigan Hockey" and ended his notes as follows:

"I have seen every team play that Michigan has ever had and Ann Arbor has supported them all the way. I played for Michigan, missed three games because of injuries in that time, was captain in 1931."

Perhaps it says enough about Michigan hockey that a successful, respected businessman would feel compelled, at age 85, to record not his business career but his college hockey memories, and define himself primarily as a former Michigan hockey captain.

Fred Heddle and Burt Stodden played on the team before World War II. Rudy Reichert walked onto the team shortly after they left.

"I've had a one-track life," he says today. "Undergrad, grad school, med school, and raising my family, all in Ann Arbor."

Reichert grew up on the corner of Baldwin Avenue, three doors down from Burns Park. He is the grandson of the minister of Bethlehem Lutheran Church on Fourth Avenue and the son of a banker at Ann Arbor Bank. Like most kids in Burns Park, Reichert skated every day he could on the frozen tennis courts. "We'd start playing after school, go home to have supper without taking our skates off, then go back out," he says. "We probably cut up the rugs, but our moms didn't complain."

Ann Arbor kids have been doing the same things ever since, and a few lucky ones did them well enough to follow Reichert's footsteps to the university.

During the team's first three decades, Ann Arbor players made significant contributions to the university team, but in 1954–55 and 1955–56 not one American made the roster, let alone anyone from Ann Arbor. Just one local player, Jay Katz, joined the varsity during the entire decade, and only for one season, 1957–58.

While Wolverine hockey was at an all-time high in the fifties, the number of local players on the U-M roster was at an all-time low. A few local hockey boosters met at Colonial Lanes in July 1962 to discuss how they might help promote amateur hockey in the city, from the Michigan hockey team to the recently formed Ann Arbor Amateur Hockey Association (AAAHA). The twelve charter members, including such local luminaries as Gus Crouch, Doug Barnett, Howard Wikel, Bill Stegath, and Carl Isaacson, decreed that dues would be ten dollars a year, then started mulling over possible names.

Bob Knapp, Michigan's skate sharpener, asked Al Renfrew what it means when a player dekes the goalie. "That means," Renfrew replied, "that you fake him out."

"Great!" Knapp said. "That's us—a bunch of fakers." And that's how the Dekers picked their name.

In 1954–55, former Michigan goalie John MacInnes and hockey trainer Carl Isaacson started the AAAHA, which immediately attracted 112 players skating in three divisions, the oldest being "Juvenile," a name the league later reconsidered. Since the little league was already up and running, the Dekers' first order of business was to convince the Ann Arbor school board to fund a hockey team for Ann Arbor High. A few months after the Dekers' inception the school board approved their proposal. The Pioneers played their first season in 1962–63, won their first state title the next year, and won it again in 1966, 1967, 1971, 1984, and 1985, while the cross-town Huron River Rats have made it to the Final Four three times.

Mission accomplished.

The Dekers' work on behalf of the AAAHA and the two high school programs started bearing fruit in the late sixties, when the first generation of little league players began graduating from high school. Of the two dozen Ann Arborites who have made Michigan's team, three-quarters of them did so after the Dekers pumped life into the local scene. After the AAAHA and high school teams were established the town produced eight Wolverines from 1965 to 1973, and four more who made the roster but did not earn varsity letters.

Two of them were Don Fardig, '76, who finished second in scoring his first two seasons, and Don Dufek, '76, a two-sport star at Michigan who went on to play football for the Seattle Seahawks.

"Dufek, the Duke, the Bullett," Bo Schembechler ruminates. "One of the toughest S.O.B.s I ever coached. He was one of those swashbuckling, ass-kicking guys, and I bet he played hockey that way, too."

Oh, yes, he did.

"Doof, one of my favorite guys," Farrell says, taking up Schembechler's meditation. "He had a reputation around the league as being a ferocious player. He used to make the glass rattle when he hit guys, just crushed 'em. He was not a dirty player, but he'd get penalties for roughing just because he'd wipe guys out. I had to explain to the refs he's not doing anything wrong, he's just one tough guy. But they felt like they had to give him something when the other guy's still lying on the ice."

When future Badger Mike Eaves made his first college recruiting visit to Michigan, he saw Dufek in the locker room. "My god, the guy was cut like paper," Eaves remembers. "The guy ran about 220, with 3 percent body fat. Oh, man, could he hit. I saw him hit a few people, just put 'em into next week."

"He was disciplined, he knew what it took to win," Farrell adds, "but it took a great effort to come back into the lineup midseason after football was done. But his teammates knew that when he came back, he would play. They loved 'im."

Because of football, Dufek could never participate in hockey's preseason conditioning or the first third of the season. By his senior year, 1975–76, the Big Ten's new rules allowed the Michigan football team to go to the Orange Bowl, extending the season another six weeks. Meanwhile, the hockey team had gotten better, so it was even harder for Dufek to earn his spot back when he returned to the ice his senior year, when he only got into 14 hockey games.

"As a great fan of Doof's, it kind of pained me," Farrell says. "I tell ya, if he had played more hockey, he could've been a pro player without any question."

But Dufek, who enjoyed a solid career in the NFL, has no regrets. His hockey memories are good ones. "They used to freeze Burns Park, and we all went down there and went to the Coliseum to watch the college guys play," he says. "Hockey's kind of a cult sport. Making that team is an accomplishment I'll never forget. Needless to say, it was a total thrill."

Just as Dufek grew up watching local players like Bucky Straub play for the Wolverines, Roger Bourne watched Dufek.

"Growing up here in town, I always wanted to play for Michigan, not the Red Wings," says Bourne. "I'd go down to the old Coliseum on Thursday to see if they needed a stick boy for the weekend, and sometimes it worked. I'd get a stick and a roll of tape for it. They had a rough team back then. Didn't win a lot of games, but they did a lot of brawling."

Although Bourne set the Pioneer record for total points at 200 in 1977, he never shopped around for colleges. "It would have been tough for me [emotionally] to go anywhere else," Bourne says. "I didn't even look. Farrell only promised to get me in the school and give me a chance. That's all I wanted. They didn't have to do a whole lot of coaxing to get me to come to Michigan."

Bourne came to Michigan despite the fact that he'd have to walk on to the number-one-ranked team in the country. "I think I got into three games that first year," he says. "I wasn't contributing much, but the guys never made me feel like I wasn't part of the team."

Bourne scored his first goal his sophomore season against Wisconsin's great goalie, Julian Baretta, and notched 18 more points that year, 18 more the next, and 47 in his senior season, good for third on the team behind two future NHLers. Nonetheless, Bourne played without a scholarship until midway through his junior year, and finished his career with a half scholarship. "We never pushed it," Bourne explains. "I wouldn't trade it, my whole hockey career, for anything."

By Bourne's senior year, 1980–81, Michigan had four former Pioneer players on the team—an unofficial team record—including Mark Perry, Dave Fardig, and Ted Speers, '83.

Speers finished his career ninth on Michigan's all-time school scoring list, with 172 points, but like every other Ann Arbor native, he had to walk on. Speers quickly found his place, winning both the team's MVP and scoring titles his last two seasons, and set the National Sports Festival scoring record along the way.

"The Ann Arbor kids do better than they should because of two things," Speers philosophizes. "You've been told all your life you're not good enough to play here, so you have the determination in your gut to prove them wrong. And you're playing in front of your home town, which you've been dreaming of since you were nine. You don't want to fail. You want to prove you belong. The full-ride guys from Canada, you think they're better than you, then a week later you realize, they put on their skates the same way you do."

Speers was followed by Brad McCaughey, '88, the only Wolverine who played his hockey at Huron High, home of the River Rats. "The kids from western Canada, those guys are first- and second-round draft choices," he says. "They're expecting to play for some major college, where the Ann Arbor guys are a little more unsure. We're just hoping to make the team.

"The coaches at MSU were trying to get me to go up there as a recruited walk-on," he recalls, "so they would send me clippings about how deep they were. I thought that was a funny method of recruitment. 'We're loaded with talented—come walk on!'"

McCaughey declined State's overtures and Western's promise of tuition in his sophomore year to walk on at Michigan with no promises whatsoever. "You've gotta say, it's very easy for Michigan to recruit us local guys," McCaughey says. "They say, 'Come to camp,' and we say, 'Okay! You got it! I'll be there! I'll even bring my own stuff!'"

Despite a stellar high school career, in which he scored 100 goals and 75 assists in 73 games (he still holds every school scoring record), McCaughey had a lot to learn. "I came out of high school a straight-legged skater," he says. "The first year Red put me on a line with Brad Jones and Tom Stiles, and I spent all practice just trying to keep up. I'm pretty sure I was the only player in Michigan history to take power skating all four years—and not because I wanted to."

Like Rudy Reichert before him, McCaughey's desire to wear the maize and blue compelled him to put in a lot of extra practice time—and for both of them, it worked. McCaughey's skating skills improved significantly and, coupled with his already keen scoring touch, produced great results. He finished fifth in scoring his freshman year, then second, second, and fifth as a senior on a much better team, ranking thirteenth on Michigan's career scoring list when he finished.

Midway through McCaughey's explosive sophomore year, Berenson offered him a full ride—but asked him to continue living at home. "I'm probably the only player in college hockey history who was grounded for an entire semester," McCaughey cracks. "But you don't care. As an Ann Arbor kid, playing for Michigan—that's your NHL."

Tim Helber, '90, sacrificed more than McCaughey and received less for it—at least initially. As a member of the first family of Ann Arbor hockey, one that produced five Pioneer captains (and a daughter who captained the field hockey team), Helber grew up surrounded by the game. Their father, Paul, supervised the WCHA refs, which got the boys into the Coliseum and Yost Field House, where young Tim and his mates would horse around under the stands during the games.

"I always remember looking up to the Michigan players," Helber says, "but especially looking up to Roger Bourne and Ted Speers." Helber did something they never did, however, and that was lead the Pioneers to state titles in 1984 and 1985. Nonetheless, after scoring a couple goals in the 1985 blue-white game, Helber was cut. On the eve of Michigan's tryouts during his sophomore year, Helber and former Pioneer goalie Tim Genyk decided on a lark to give it a second shot. Lo and behold, they both made it.

Helber's career didn't go as smoothly as McCaughey's, Speers's, or Bourne's. He played in half the team's games as a sophomore and got in all but four of them as a junior, scoring nine points, but was scaled back to 11 games in his final season, 1989–90, the year the team narrowly missed getting its first NCAA bid in 13 years. But Helber's collegiate career didn't end on a sour note, for two reasons.

"Unlike the other guys on the team, I never once felt I would play beyond my days at Michigan," he says, "so it really was an honor to play every time I put the Michigan sweater on. I knew playing for Michigan was the ultimate goal I could have attained, and I'm proud of that." Helber is even more proud of the fact that Berenson, Pearson, and Shand had enough respect for him to make him the team's graduate assistant the following year.

"I do have a great deal of pride knowing that I played and coached for one of the greatest players of all time, and one of the greatest coaches," Helber says, summing up his college career. "That's pretty good, for a no-name player out of Ann Arbor, to be a part of that. As Red always says, you look in the mirror and you'll always be a Michigan hockey player."

Helber's younger brother Mike, '92, failed to win any state high school hockey titles—his team lost in overtime to Marquette in 1988—but he did win the state's Mr. Hockey award in his junior and senior seasons, broke his hero Roger Bourne's Pioneer scoring record of 200 points, with 235, and even topped the national mark for goals in a season, with 65. You might think he would have gotten lots of attention from serious college programs, but you'd be wrong.

Berenson would occasionally watch Helber's Pioneer team practice at Yost, and former assistant coach Larry Pedrie once called Helber up to his office after practice, tossed him an application, and said, "Fill this out and give it back to me," no one had talked seriously with him about playing at Michigan.

"I had no idea where I was going to go," Helber recalls, "and it was getting scary because all my friends around school are saying, 'I've gotten into there, I'm going there.' I'm thinking, maybe no one's interested."

Helber's courtship didn't begin until the *Detroit Free Press* ran a story in January about Helber's assault on the national scoring record, and mentioned the dearth of calls he'd received from colleges. A couple days later Michigan Tech called up, curious. "You mean you're not going to follow your brother to Michigan?" they asked, surprised.

"They haven't even talked to me," Helber replied. Tech invited him up for a visit. Helber liked what he saw, and the Huskies offered him a half scholarship. The next week Berenson called Helber into his office and asked, "What do you think about Tech?"

"Nice place," Helber said, poker faced.

"What do you think about Michigan?"

"I like Michigan, but it doesn't seem like you're all that interested."

"Well, we've been busy," Berenson responded. "What'd they give you?"

"A half ride."

"Well, we can do that too," Berenson said. And that's how Mike Helber became the only player in Ann Arbor history to receive any scholarship money before playing his first game.

"You know, I'm sure I would have gone to Michigan either way," Helber admits. "But I would have been really, really disappointed if they hadn't shown any interest. I don't think there's anyone else on that team who could say that when they were 10 years old, they dreamed of playing for Michigan."

Mike Helber scored his first goal in his second game and passed to his older brother the next night for Tim's first collegiate goal—all in front of their grandparents, who rarely saw them play. Mike finished among the top third in team scoring his last two seasons at Michigan and became an effective penalty killer, too. Although he never received more than a partial scholarship he, like the other Ann Arborites who preceded him, has no regrets.

"I don't think I've ever felt anything as good in hockey as hopping onto the ice at Yost with 7,000 fans up there and the band playing full blast," says Helber, who went on to play professional hockey in Sweden for a decade. "Sometimes I'd get gassed in warm-ups from getting so revved up. Two or three laps, and you're just flying. There's nothing that compares to it. Nothing."

Since Mike Helber left Pioneer for Michigan in 1988, the gap between high school hockey and college hockey has grown to the point where few, if any, Ann Arbor high school players will be able to cross that chasm in the future. Lifelong Ann Arbor native Dave Huntzicker started playing hockey in the AAAHA and attended countless Michigan games, but decided to play junior hockey prior to becoming a stellar defenseman on Michigan's team. Like all Ann Arbor-born Wolverines, however, he knows how inspiring it is to play for the team he idolized when he wasn't tall enough to see over the boards.

"You grow up all your life watching them; it's what you want," he says, echoing the sentiment of Ann Arbor players since Art Schlanderer. "It'll be a sad day when I leave this place."

But when Huntzicker does, he will have joined Dave Newton, '65, the only other Ann Arbor native to win an NCAA title.

"They're always a step behind when they come in," Berenson says of the Ann Arbor players, "but they all ended up playing on a regular basis. They've all become solid players and a credit to Ann Arbor."

54

Passing the Torch

What is Michigan hockey?

It starts when the players arrive in Ann Arbor. Since almost all hockey Wolverines come from small towns—the only consistent big-city source of talent over the years has been Toronto—most players are initially awed by Michigan's football stadium, the size of the campus, and the energy generated by the fans at the Field House.

"You come from junior hockey in Kelowna, BC, where you've got 8,000 people in the whole town," Muckalt explains, "and all of a sudden you come to Ann Arbor where there are 8,000 people in the rink. It makes an impression."

The effect is just as powerful coming from the other side of the continent. "When you're from Newfoundland," Kent Brothers says, "and you see this place—wow!"

The players adjust, of course, and come to love the school spirit, the informal student life, and the family feel of the hockey team. And before they know it, it's over.

"Red always said this'll be the best four years of your life," Brad McCaughey says, "and it's true. But he also said you won't realize that until four years out of college. And that's true, too." In college hockey, whether you're an All-American or an also-ran, four years is all you get. It's the great equalizer—but also one of the elements that bond the players together.

Like most hockey alums, Kent Brothers had to give up playing competitive hockey after leaving Michigan to pursue a more conventional career. "I went to law school back in Newfoundland,

and I was just bored as hell," he admits during an alumni weekend. "No friends, no identity. Here, I've got 25 friends who'll do anything for me. Guys are always happy to see you. In law school, everyone just wants to get a job."

Surprisingly, perhaps, the alums who make it to the NHL feel about the same way Brothers does about life after college.

"I'm much closer to my college buddies," says Mike Knuble, who has played with Steve Yzerman in Detroit, Wayne Gretzky in New York, and Ray Bourque in Boston. "Everyone's on the same page in college. You're all single, you're all students, you're all doing the same things.

"The NHL guys ask about it sometimes—how things were in college—out of curiosity, maybe a little envy. They ask about going to football games, and living with your teammates. Most of them want their kids to go to college. And the guys who see they're going to be lifetime minor league players, they really regret it."

"Rink to rink, it's exactly the same routines," says NHL veteran David Harlock. "The morning skate, the afternoon naps, the same songs during the games for each situation. It's redundant, overkill. You see it 82 times a season, it gets to you."

The year after leaving Michigan in 1993, three-time captain David Harlock played for the Canadian Olympic team in Norway, earning a silver medal, then joined the Toronto Maple Leafs for one game before being sent down to the minors. In between he had five days off, so he decided to drive to East Lansing to see the 1994 NCAA quarterfinal game between Michigan and Lake Superior, which ended in another stunning loss for the Wolverines. But that's not what Harlock noticed.

"When I saw that game, I couldn't believe how much I missed college hockey," he says. "The atmosphere, the band, the rival schools. Each college rink is different—a lot of the buildings have quite a bit of character to them—and they give you a lot of different things to pay attention to. You just don't run into that at the professional level.

"The most fun I've ever had playing hockey was during my college days. We were all going through the same experiences—academics, social life, hockey—and you can all relate very easily to each other. In the NHL, everyone has entirely different backgrounds, totally different approaches to the game and what they want to get out of it. When we were in college, no one was going to get traded or get a raise. The primary concern we had was to do the best we could for Michigan. We had a lot more of a team-type atmosphere there. You know, I've already played for seven pro teams, but I'll always see myself as a Michigan player, a Michigan man."

With that summation, Harlock unwittingly echoes the exact phrase Berenson used while recruiting Harlock that irritated him so much: "It's an easy decision," Berenson had told him. "You're either a Michigan man or you're not."

Thomas Wolfe's famous warning, You can never go home again, does not seem to apply to Michigan hockey players. True, the four years go quickly, and when they're over everyone has to move on to the next phase of their lives. But that doesn't mean they can't visit their old town, their old times, their old friends—and they do, the first weekend in August for the alumni hockey games and golf scramble.

When Berenson hatched the idea years ago they didn't draw enough alums to complete a golf outing, but these days over 100 alums return to fill the rosters for three hockey games, with a waiting list for tee times. "I don't think you'll see this anywhere else," says 1998 captain Matt Herr.

Like high school homecomings, the hockey reunions can make the guests a little anxious. Brothers, for one, hadn't returned to Ann Arbor since he left in 1992 before coming back in 1998. "I was so nervous," he confessed, "I felt like I was preparing for a Broadway play." He wasn't concerned about his reception—Pink Floyd partner Don Stone picked him up at the airport, without Brothers ever asking—but about being overwhelmed by emotions.

"It means so much," he says. "The sense of identity is so strong. I walk back to the rink and see the first alumni game, and the band is playing 'The Victors,' there are a thousand people in the stands, and it fills you right up—where you came from, who you are. And I'm crying.

"Red could've gone out and gotten someone else, but he stood by me. In 20 lifetimes, I'll never be able to give back what it gave me. I'm so appreciative."

Whenever the former Michigan teammates meet up in the Field House lobby, the scene is the same: their eyebrows go up, their grins grow big, and their hands jut out, ready to give enthusiastic handshakes. The younger guys add a hug.

But it's not all hearts and flowers. The players have also come back for another taste of the locker room ribbing they enjoyed as players. When Steve Shields, who became a starting NHL goalie in 1999, entered the locker room filled with players 50 and over, getting dressed for the first alumni game, they take more shots at him than the Bruins do.

"Too bad you're not in the other net tonight," one elder says, "or we'd fire it up."

Shields gives as good as he gets. "I've never seen guys sweat so much," he replies, "just getting dressed."

When the former gladiators take to the ice, they wear nameless practice sweaters on their backs, square hats on their heads and thick glasses on their noses. The old hierarchy no longer applies. There is a new world order on the ice, creating the kind of game where Steve Shields can find himself in a goaltending duel with his old backup, Al Loges, and Mike Knuble can lose the puck on a penalty shot while a former fourth-line player like Tim Helber scores a hat trick.

But the band is playing like it matters, and 2,000 fans have shown up to buttress the illusion. Those players from the program's nadir in the early eighties are particularly impressed. "I didn't play in front of this many people," Ted Speers says, "when I was in college."

The second leg of the Alumni Weekend Triathlon (hockey, beer, and golf) takes place at Fraser's, a sports bar since before the term existed. The players order beers en masse—"Who needs one? Put it on my tab"—and slip a few dollars into the jukebox to hear some Lynyrd Skynyrd, Marvin Gaye, and Bob Seger.

No one seems to notice, but on the far wall hang pictures of a half dozen of these guys from their salad days. In addition to a large photo of the 1996 NCAA championship team, there's Dave Shand as a Washington Capital, Dave Debol as a Hartford Whaler, and Rob Palmer as a Los Angeles King—all of them sporting outdated uniforms as outdated as their haircuts. And there's a priceless shot of Pat Hughes in an Edmonton Oilers sweater, standing behind Montreal Hall of Famer Steve Shutt, with Hughes's stick pulled up so hard against Shutt's throat that Shutt is leaving his feet. When you look at those photos, then back at the guys talking at the bar about their day jobs, the pictures feel like they were taken in another lifetime.

An unwritten rule dictates that everyone, from the most celebrated NHL star to the most anonymous fourth-line player, checks his hockey card at the door. For one weekend, everyone's just a former Michigan hockey player, and that's how they like it. Each year the alums broaden their circle of friends beyond their own class, until the common experience of being a Michigan Wolverine blurs the decades. The older players lit the torch, the younger ones took good care of it, and both recognize the contributions of the other. If there's a generation gap afoot, you won't find evidence of it here. Whatever separates them is easily bridged by what connects them: They're all Wolverines.

It's Nine O'Clock, and No One's Watching

It's nine o'clock at Yost Field House. Michigan stars Pat Hughes and Rob Palmer, Kris Manery and Dave Debol, Alex Roberts and Bobby Hayes are wearing their maize and blue jerseys, preparing to take the ice. But there are no referees at these games, no fans, and the scoreboard keeps track only of the time remaining in their hour of rented ice.

Keep looking and you realize why: This is a mere pickup game, one featuring a full spectrum of socks, one played strictly for the love of the sport.

The players start filing into the locker room every Tuesday night at about 8:30 and get dressed in the same seat every week. The rules of the pickup game are few and simple: The first team to score five goals "wins," after which the goalies change ends. They keep going until the Zamboni comes back on at 10:00. There are no face-offs, no penalties—courtesy and common sense govern play—and offsides is called by committee. Three players yelling "Off!" seem to be the threshold.

If anybody accidentally drops another player, the guy who did it stops to see if the other guy's all right and helps him to the locker room if necessary. If the victim goes to the hospital, he can expect a call the next day from the perpetrator.

"Out here you never get a hack, you never get a whack," says Dave Shand, which explains why the players don't wear masks. "When we played in the pros we were paid to take s—— and give it back. Now we just want to have fun."

The weekly skate started out 20 years ago as preseason conditioning for the players' senior league team, "until finally," one recalls, "one year we said, 'Why can't we just skip the league and keep doing what we're doing?'"

Take away the play-stopping whistles, the dangerous stick work, and the erratic game times that run from 7:00 to 11:00 in the city league, and you've got the hockey equivalent of boneless chicken: all the best parts of the game and none of the gristle.

Even if no one else is watching, sometimes the guys can't help but sit back and admire the skills in front of them. Rob Palmer, '77, the assistant captain on Michigan's 1977 NCAA runner-up team, still plays his position with textbook perfection, never cutting corners on his footwork, his back-checking, or his defensive rotations. They say the first time you skate in on him is a nerve-racking experience, because his eyes bore right through your chest, as if Coach Farrell were watching him from the bench and his scholarship still depended on stopping you. Needless to say, he does.

In Pat Hughes's 10 NHL seasons—in which he won three Stanley Cups with the Montreal Canadiens and Edmonton Oilers, playing alongside Guy Lafleur and Wayne Gretzky—he scored on an impressive 14 percent of his shots, just 3 percentage points behind Gretzky himself. When you see Hughes's shot, you understand why. Actually, you don't *see* Hughes's shot; you hear it bang off the inside of the pipe, you watch the net billow behind it, and you finally see the puck roll out on its side, like Marie Antoinette's head from the guillotine. It has the same effect, too: A Hughes shot pops all the game's pent-up energy and action in an instant, forcing guys to slouch their shoulders and glide to the bench.

Kip Maurer, '78, relies not on size, speed, or strength but on his head and hands, quietly leading the crowd in scoring most nights. He has the Gretzky-like confidence to wait a split second longer before making his move; when the defenders can't take it anymore and commit to one direction or the other, the sea parts, and Maurer is free to do what he will.

The alums might have lost a step, but their hands and heads are as quick as ever. Roger Bourne, '81 likes to dangle the puck out in front of his body, tempting defenders to bite, and when they invariably do he yanks it back like a yo-yo with the toe of his stick, whisks it over to the left side of his body, and skates right by them. He then gives the poor goalie the same treatment, finally tossing a backhand shot to the top pocket of the net, knocking the goalie's water bottle onto the ice, just for effect. Bourne can score goals that make even the former NHLers lean back and emit a quiet "Whoa. . . ."

Of course, a young speedster like Brian Wiseman, '94, fresh out of pro hockey, can make everyone go "whoa" just by turning on his wheels, or his hands, or his shot—his option—but he chooses instead to pass, leaving the scoring to guys who need the goals a lot more than he does.

The games are played for fun, but the intensity builds as the teams approach five goals. "These are highly competitive personalities," Mark Miller observes, "and you're not going to change that." When a team gets to four, therefore, both squads get serious about hustling back on defense, clearing opponents out of the slot, and blocking shots. Even the former NHLers can't help but lean around the glass partition between the two benches to ask what the score is. "You gotta win at least one game each night," Miller says. "You don't want to get shut out."

And for good reason. Unlike league games, after these contests you have to share the same locker room with the same guys you just played against, not to mention sharing the same end of the bar that night. Get swept and you're going to hear about it.

Although these guys have graduate degrees, thriving careers and good families, if you press them, most will admit this is their favorite night of their week, when they can shed all the identities they've acquired since they left Michigan and return to the simple days when all they needed was a little black puck and some buddies to play with.

"This is the best skate around," Bourne says in the locker room afterward. "When this ends, I'm done."

But when Bourne's done, another Michigan alum will replace him. And that's how the game goes on.

If you were to step outside that locker room filled with aging Michigan hockey players and walk a few blocks toward Burns Park, you'd find a bunch of local kids playing shinny on the frozen tennis courts—the same game Roger Bourne played in a quarter century ago, the same game Rudy Reichert skated in before World War II, and the same game Art Schlanderer joined before World War I.

The boys on the ice don't wear Red Wings paraphernalia, and they don't dream of playing in Joe Louis Arena with the rock music blaring before face-offs. No, like their predecessors, who passed away before these kids were born, these young skaters wear Michigan sweatshirts and jerseys, and they dream of playing for the Wolverines with the stands packed and the pep band blasting "The Victors." And for a lucky one or two, their dreams will come true, and the torch first lit by Joseph Barss and Eddie Kahn will be passed on to them.

And that's the story of Michigan hockey.

Appendixes

Michigan's Head Coaches

Coach	Years	Seasons	Games	W	L	T	Pct.
Joseph Barss	1922–23 to 1926–27	5	51	26	21	4	.553
Edward Lowrey	1927–28 to 1943–44	17	281	124	136	21	.476
Vic Heyliger	1944–45 to 1956–57	13	302	228	61	13	.789
Al Renfrew	1957–58 to 1972–73	16	440	223	206	11	.520
Dan Farrell	1973–74 to 1979–80	7	270	135	129	6	.513
Wilf Martin	1980	1	2	1	1	0	.500
John Giordano	1980–81 to 1983–84	4	149	68	75	6	.476
Red Berenson	1984–85 to Present	17	713	448	220	45	.671
Totals		79	2,208	1,253	849	106	.596

Team History

Season	Overall Record	Conference Place	Postseason
Coach Barss			
1922–23	4-7-0	—	—
1923–24	6-4-1	—	—
1924–25	4-1-1	1st	—
1925–26	3-5-2	3rd	—
1926–27	9-4-0	T1st	—
Coach Lowry			
1927–28	2-10-1	3rd	—
1928–29	5-11-1	T2nd	—
1929–30	12-7-2	1st	—
1930–31	10-5-2	1st	—
1931–32	9-6-2	2nd	—
1932–33	10-4-2	2nd	—
1933–34	10-6-0	2nd	—
1934–35	12-3-2	1st	—
1935–36	7-9-0	2nd	—
1936–37	11-6-1	T1st	—
1937–38	13-6-0	T1st	—
1938–39	8-8-2	2nd	—
1939–40	5-14-1	2nd	—
1940–41	2-14-1	3rd	—
1941–42	2-14-2	3rd	—
1942–43	1-10-2	3rd	—
1943–44	5-3-0	—	—
Coach Heyliger			
1944–45	3-6-0	—	—
1945–46	17-7-1	—	—
1946–47	13-7-1	—	—

(*continues*)

Team History (continued)

Season	Overall Record	Conference Place	Postseason
1947–48	20-2-1	—	**NCAA Champion**
1948–49	20-2-3	—	NCAA Third Place
1949–50	23-4-0	—	NCAA Third Place
1950–51	22-4-1	—	**NCAA Champion**
1951–52	22-4-0	2nd	**NCAA Champion**
1952–53	17-7-0	2nd	**NCAA Champion**
1953–54	15-6-2	2nd	NCAA Third Place
1954–55	18-5-1	2nd	**NCAA Champion**
1955–56	20-2-1	1st	**NCAA Champion**
1956–57	18-5-2	2nd	NCAA Finalist
Coach Renfrew			
1957–58	8-13-0	6th	—
1958–59	8-13-1	3rd	—
1959–60	12-12-0	5th	—
1960–61	16-10-2	3rd	—
1961–62	22-5-0	3rd	NCAA Semifinalist
1962–63	7-14-3	7th	—
1963–64	24-4-1	1st	**NCAA Champion**
1964–65	13-12-1	5th	—
1965–66	14-14-0	5th	—
1966–67	19-7-2	4th	—
1967–68	18-9-0	4th	—
1968–69	16-12-0	4th	—
1969–70	15-15-0	6th	—
1970–71	9-21-0	9th	—
1971–72	16-18-0	6th	—
1972–73	6-27-1	10th	—
Coach Farrell			
1973–74	18-17-1	7th	—
1974–75	22-17-1	6th	—
1975–76	21-18-0	4th	—
1976–77	28-17-0	3rd	NCAA Finalist
1977–78	15-20-1	9th	—
1978–79	8-27-1	10th	—
1979–80	23-13-2	4th	—
Coach Martin			
Coach Giordano			
1980–81	23-17-0	5th	—
1981–82	18-15-5	4th	—
1982–83	14-22-0	9th	—
1983–84	14-22-1	9th	—

Season	Overall Record	Conference Place	Postseason
Coach Berenson			
1984–85	13-26-1	9th	—
1985–86	12-26-0	8th	—
1986–87	14-25-1	7th	—
1987–88	22-19-0	5th	—
1988–89	22-15-4	4th	—
1989–90	24-12-6	4th	—
1990–91	34-10-3	2nd	NCAA Quarterfinalist
1991–92	32-9-3	1st	CCHA Reg. Season Champion/ NCAA Semifinalist
1992–93	30-7-3	2nd	NCAA Semifinalist
1993–94	33-7-1	1st	CCHA Reg. Season & Trny. Champion/ NCAA Second Round
1994–95	30-8-1	1st	CCHA Reg. Season Champion/ NCAA Semifinalist
1995–96	34-7-2	T1st	CCHA Reg. Season & Trny. Champion/ **NCAA Champion**
1996–97	35-4-4	1st	CCHA Reg. Season & Trny. Champion/ NCAA Semifinalist
1997–98	34-11-1	2nd	**NCAA Champion**
1998–99	25-11-6	2nd	CCHA Tournament Champion/NCAA Second Round
1999–00	27-10-4	1st	CCHA Reg. Season Champion/NCAA Second Round
2000–01	27-13-5	T2nd	NCAA Semifinalist

Captains

Year	Captains	Year	Captains
1922–23	Kyle R. Macduff	1962–63	Lawrence Babcock
1923–24	Edgar A. Kahn	1963–64	Gordon Wilkie
1924–25	Dan Peterman	1964–65	Wilf Martin
1925–26	Irving Reynolds	1965–66	Mel Wakabayashi
1926–27	Stephen Jones	1966–67	Mike Martilla
1927–28	William Maney	1967–68	William Lord
1928–29	Mortimer Fisher	1968–69	Paul Domm
1929–30	Clarence Bryant	1969–70	David Perrin
1930–31	Art Schlanderer	1970–71	Paul Gamsby
1931–32	John Tompkins	1971–72	Brian Skinner
1932–33	Emerson Reid,	1972–73	Rick Mallette
	Keith Crossman	1973–74	Randy Trudeau
1933–34	George David, Jr.	1974–75	Randy Trudeau
1934–35	John Sherf, John Jewell	1975–76	Angie Moretto, Greg Fox,
1935–36	Lawrence David		Tom Lindskog
1936–37	Victor Heyliger	1976–77	Kris Manery
1937–38	Robert Simpson	1977–78	John McCahill
1938–39	Leslie Hillberg	1978–79	Mark Miller
1939–40	Elden James	1979–80	Doug Todd
1940–41	Charlie Ross	1980–81	Tim Manning
1941–42	Paul Goldsmith	1981–82	Steve Richmond, David Richter
1942–43	Henry Loud	1982–83	Ted Speers, David Tippett
1943–44	Bob Derleth	1993–84	Jim McCauley,
1944–45	Ted Greer		Kelly McCrimmon
1945–46	Conrad Hill	1984–85	Ray Dries
1946–47	Conrad Hill	1985–86	Frank Downing
1947–48	Conrad Hill	1986–87	Jeff Norton
1948–49	Allan Renfrew	1987–88	Todd Brost
1949–50	Wally Grant	1988–89	Todd Brost, Myles O'Connor
1950–51	Gilbert Burford	1989–90	Alex Roberts, Mike Moes
1951–52	Earl Keyes	1990–91	David Harlock, Don Stone
1952–53	John Matchefts	1991–92	David Harlock
1953–54	James Haas	1992–93	David Harlock
1954–55	William MacFarland	1993–94	Brian Wiseman
1955–56	William MacFarland	1994–95	Rick Willis
1956–57	Robert Pitts	1995–96	Steven Halko
1957–58	Neil McDonald	1996–97	Brendan Morrison
1958–59	Robert Watt	1997–98	Matt Herr
1959–60	Robert Watt	1998–99	Bubba Berenzweig
1960–61	Dale MacDonald	1999–00	Sean Peach
1961–62	Red Berenson	2000–01	Geoff Koch

Michigan in the NCAA Tournament

Year-by-Year in the NCAA Tournament
(24 years in the tournament, 38-17 record, .691 winning percentage)

Year	Round	Result
1947–48	Semifinal	defeated Boston College, 6-4 (OT)
	Championship	defeated Dartmouth, 8-4
1948–49	Semifinal	lost to Dartmouth, 4-2
	Consolation	defeated Colorado College, 10-4
1949–50	Semifinal	lost to Boston University, 4-3
	Consolation	defeated Boston College, 10-6
1950–51	Semifinal	defeated Boston University, 8-2
	Championship	defeated Brown, 7-1
1951–52	Semifinal	defeated St. Lawrence, 9-3
	Championship	defeated Colorado College, 4-1
1952–53	Semifinal	defeated Boston University, 14-2
	Championship	defeated Minnesota, 7-3
1953–54	Semifinal	lost to RPI, 6-4
	Consolation	defeated Boston College, 7-2
1954–55	Semifinal	defeated Harvard, 7-3
	Championship	defeated Colorado College, 5-3
1955–56	Semifinal	defeated St. Lawrence, 2-1
	Championship	defeated Michigan Tech, 7-5
1956–57	Semifinal	defeated Harvard, 6-1
	Championship	lost to Colorado College, 13-6
1961–62	Semifinal	lost to Clarkson, 5-4
	Consolation	defeated St. Lawrence, 5-1
1963–64	Semifinal	defeated Providence, 3-2
	Championship	defeated Denver, 6-3
1976–77	First Round	defeated Bowling Green, 7-5
	Semifinal	defeated Boston University, 6-4
	Championship	lost to Wisconsin, 6-5 (OT)
1990–91	First Round	defeated Cornell, 2 games to 1 (4-5 [OT], 6-4, 9-3)
	Quarterfinal	lost to Boston University, 2 games to 0 (5-1, 8-1)
1991–92	West Regional	defeated Northern Michigan, 7-6
	Semifinal	lost to Wisconsin, 4-2
1992–93	West Regional	defeated Wisconsin, 4-3 (OT)
	Semifinal	lost to Maine, 4-3 (OT)
1993–94	West Regional	lost to Lake Superior State, 5-4 (OT)

(continues)

Michigan in the NCAA Tournament (continued)

Year	Round	Result
1994–95	West Regional	defeated Wisconsin, 4-3
	Semifinal	lost to Maine, 4-3 (3 OT)
1995–96	West Regional	defeated Minnesota, 4-3
	Semifinal	defeated Boston University, 4-0
	Championship	defeated Colorado College, 3-2 (OT)
1996–97	West Regional	defeated Minnesota, 7-4
	Semifinal	lost to Boston University, 3-2
1997–98	West Regional	defeated Princeton, 2-1
	West Regional	defeated North Dakota, 4-3
	Semifinal	defeated New Hampshire, 4-0
	Championship	defeated Boston College, 3-2 (OT)
1998–99	East Regional	defeated Denver, 5-3
	East Regional	lost to New Hampshire, 2-1 (OT)
1999–00	East Regional	defeated Colgate, 4-3 (OT)
	East Regional	lost to Maine, 5-2
2000–01	West Regional	defeated Mercyhurst, 4-3
	West Regional	defeated St. Cloud State, 4-3
	Semifinal	lost to Boston College, 4-2

All-Americans

First Team (44 players)

Wally Gacek	1948–49	Tom Polonic	1964
Connie Hill	1948–49	Gordon Wilkie	1964
Wally Grant	1948–49-50	Mel Wakabayashi	1965
Ross Smith	1949–50	James Keough	1968
Dick Starrak	1949	Robbie Moore	1974
Gil Burford	1951	Dave Debol	1977
Neil Celley	1951	Murray Eaves	1980
Hal Downes	1951	Paul Fricker	1981
Bob Heathcott	1951	Myles O'Connor	1989
John Matchefts	1951–53	David Oliver	1994
Jim Haas	1952	Brian Wiseman	1994
Earl Keyes	1952	Brendan Morrison	1995–96–97
John MacKennell	1952	John Madden	1997
Doug Philpott	1952	Marty Turco	1997
George Chin	1952–53	Bill Muckalt	1998
Willard Ikola	1953	Jeff Jillson	2000
Alex MacLellan	1953	Andy Hilbert	2001
Reggie Shave	1953		
Mike Buchanan	1955		

Second Team (8 players)

Dick Dunnigan	1955	Brad Jones	1987
Tom Rendall	1955	David Roberts	1991
Lorne Howes	1955–56	Denny Felsner	1991–92
Bill McFarland	1955–56	Steve Shields	1993–94
Bob Schiller	1955–56	Mike Knuble	1995
Bob White	1958–59	Kevin Hilton	1996
Bob Watt	1959	Jason Botterill	1997
Red Berenson	1961–62	Mike Comrie	2000

All-Time Series Summary (1923–2001)

Air Force	1-0-0	Marquette H.C.	1-0-0
Alabama-Huntsville	1-0-0	Massachusetts-Lowell	2-0-0
Alaska-Anchorage	2-0-1	McGill	11-4-0
Alaska-Fairbanks	20-2-0	McMaster	12-1-2
Alberta, University of	1-0-1	Mercyhurst	1-0-0
American School of Osteopathy	0-1-0	Merrimack	1-0-0
Amherstberg	1-0-0	Miami (Ohio)	54-14-2
Beck College	1-0-0	Michigan-Dearborn	1-0-0
Boston College	8-4-0	Michigan State	119-105-8
Boston University	10-7-0	Michigan Tech	112-89-4
Bowling Green	57-29-2	Middlesex-Huron	0-1-0
Brantford H.C.	4-3-0	Minnesota	114-119-14
Brown	7-0-0	Minnesota-Duluth	23-16-1
California	5-0-0	Montreal, University of	8-4-2
Chatham A.C.	2-6-1	Nebraska Omaha	4-2-0
Chatham Juniors	3-1-0	New Brunswick	1-0-0
Clarkson	2-1-0	New Hampshire	4-2-0
Colgate	4-1-1	Niagara	1-1-0
Colorado College	56-34-3	North Dakota	45-35-4
Cornell	3-2-1	Northeastern	2-0-0
Dartmouth	3-3-0	Northern Michigan	15-10-3
Dearborn A.C.	2-0-0	Notre Dame	54-39-4
De LaSalle Juniors	1-0-0	Ohio State	49-22-9
Denver	35-46-1	Ohio University	1-0-0
Detroit A.C.	1-0-0	Olympic Club	1-0-0
Detroit Vickers	1-3-0	Ontario Agriculture	8-3-0
Essex Frontiers	1-0-0	Owen Sound Juniors	1-0-0
Ferris State	46-22-2	Paris A.C.	6-3-1
Fingal A.F.	1-0-0	Pennsylvania	1-0-0
Grand Rapids Rockets - IHL	0-1-0	Point Edward	4-4-0
Guelph	1-0-0	Port Dover	1-1-1
Haley A.C.	2-0-1	Princeton	5-1-0
Hamilton	1-0-0	Providence	1-0-0
Harvard	5-2-0	Queens	7-0-0
Iderton A.C.	1-0-0	Rensselaer Polytechnic	
Illinois	6-13-0	Institute (RPI)	3-6-1
Illinois-Chicago	32-16-2	Sarnia	5-2-0
Kent State	9-0-0	Sault Ste. Marie	1-0-0
Kitchener A.C.	1-0-0	St. Cloud State	1-0-0
L'Assumption	0-2-0	St. Lawrence	8-2-1
Lake Superior State	35-43-6	St. Louis	2-0-0
London H.C.	3-9-0	St. Mary's	0-0-1
Loyola-Montreal	2-0-0	St. Michael's	1-1-0
Maine	3-3-0	St. Thomas A.C.	2-0-0
Marquette	7-8-0	Toledo Mercurys - IHL	0-1-1

Individual Single Season

Team Scoring Leaders

Year	Name	Games	Goals	Assists	Points
2000–01	Andy Hilbert	42	26	38	64
1999–00	Mike Comrie	40	24	35	59
1998–99	Mike Comrie	42	19	25	44
1997–98	Bill Muckalt	46	32	35	67
1996–97	Brendan Morrison	43	31	57	88
1995–96	Brendan Morrison	35	28	44	72
1994–95	Brendan Morrison	39	23	53	76
1993–94	Brian Wiseman	40	19	50	69
1992–93	David Roberts	40	27	38	65
1991–92	Denny Felsner	44	42	52	94
1990–91	Denny Felsner	46	40	35	75
1989–90	David Roberts	42	21	32	53
1988–89	Todd Brost	40	20	30	50
1987–88	Rob Brown	41	21	23	44
1986–87	Brad Jones	40	32	46	78
1985–86	Brad Jones	36	28	39	67
1984–85	Brad Jones	34	21	27	48
1983–84	Jim McCauley	36	17	26	43
1982–83	Brad Tippett	36	19	40	59
	Ted Speers	36	18	41	59
1981–82	Ted Speers	38	23	16	39
1980–81	Steve Richmond	39	22	32	54
1979–80	Murray Eaves	33	36	49	85
1978–79	Mark Miller	36	23	26	49
1977–78	Dave Debol	36	20	38	58
1976–77	Dave Debol	45	43	56	99
1975–76	Kris Manery	42	37	24	61
1974–75	Angie Moretto	38	39	28	67
1973–74	Angie Moretto	34	25	22	47
1972–73	Rick Mallette	31	7	28	35
1971–72	Bernard Gagnon	34	35	26	61
1970–71	Bernard Gagnon	29	26	22	48
1969–70	Dave Perrin	30	19	15	34
1968–69	Dave Perrin	27	28	16	44
1967–68	Doug Galbraith	25	21	15	36
1966–67	Bob Baird	26	21	25	46
1965–66	Mel Wakabayashi	28	19	33	52
1964–65	Mel Wakabayashi	26	17	21	41
1963–64	Gary Butler	29	38	30	68
1962–63	Gary Butler	24	25	20	45
1961–62	Gordon Berenson	29	43	27	70

1960–61	Gordon Berenson	28	24	25	49
1959–60	Bob White	24	6	27	33
1958–59	John Hutton	24	10	27	37
1957–58	Neil McDonald	21	11	14	25
1956–57	Tom Rendall	25	22	18	40
1955–56	Bill McFarland	23	19	28	47
1954–55	Bill McFarland	24	33	23	56
1953–54	Doug Mullen	23	22	39	61
1952–53	John Matchefts	24	18	30	48
1951–52	Bob Heathcott	24	13	31	44
1950–51	Neil Celley	27	40	39	79
1949–50	Gilbert Burford	27	40	29	69
1948–49	Gordon McMillan	25	24	36	60
1947–48	Gordon McMillan	21	30	29	59
1946–47	Al Renfrew	20	19	16	35
	Gordon McMillan	21	14	21	35
1945–46	Gordon McMillan	23	29	27	56

Goals

Red Berenson	1961–62	43
Dave Debol	1976–77	43
Denny Felsner	1991–92	42
Gil Burford	1949–50	40
Neil Celley	1950–51	40

Assists

Brendan Morrison	1996–97	57
Dave Debol	1976–77	56
Brendan Morrison	1994–95	53
Denny Felsner	1991–92	52
Gordon Wilkie	1963–64	51
Kevin Hilton	1995–96	51
Brian Wiseman	1993–94	50

Points

Dave Debol	1976–77	99
Denny Felsner	1991–92	94
Brendan Morrison	1996–97	88
Murray Eaves	1979–80	85

Points by a Defenseman

Steve Richmond	1980–81	54
John Blum	1980–81	52
Tim Manning	1979–80	51
John Blum	1979–80	50
Jeff Norton	1986–87	48

Yost Ice Arena

Attendance Records at Yost Ice Arena

Year	Games	Att.	Avg.	Rec.
1973–74	17	74,339	4,373	12-5-0
1974–75	18	88,725	4,929	13-5-0
1975–76	22	106,090	4,822	13-9-0
1976–77	21	96,077	4,613	16-5-0
1977–78	17	85,052	5,003	10-7-0
1978–79	17	64,775	3,810	5-12-0
1979–80	23	106,926	4,649	18-3-2
1980–81	18	93,230	5,179	12-6-0
1981–82	19	76,902	4,047	12-6-1
1982–83	19	68,519	3,606	10-9-0
1983–84	18	54,579	3,032	10-8-0
1984–85	16	48,669	3,042	7-8-1
1985–86	18	72,873	4,048	8-10-0
1986–87	18	78,036	4,335	8-10-0
1987–88	18	87,739	4,874	11-7-0
1988–89	20	90,941	4,547	7-10-3
1989–90	22	100,317	4,559	14-5-3
1990–91	22	105,054	4,775	17-3-2
1991–92	20	110,266	5,513	17-1-2
1992–93	19	114,720	6,037	16-1-2
1993–94	16	106,168	6,636	14-2-0
1994–95	17	114,778	6,752	14-2-1
1995–96	17	115,786	6,811	15-1-1
1996–97	20	128,133	6,407	18-0-2
1997–98	22	140,760	6,399	18-4-0
1998–99	19	120,662	6,351	15-4-0
1999–00	21	134,365	6,398	15-5-1
2000–01	19	121,339	6,386	13-3-3
Totals	533	2,705,820	4,941	358-151-24

Note: Capacity 8,100 from 1973–74 to 1990–91, 7,235 from 1991–92 to 1995–96, and 6,343 from 1997–2001.

Top Single Game Crowds

8,411	Michigan State	1/29/88
8,404	Michigan State	2/18/89
8,396	Michigan State	2/17/90
8,392	Michigan State	12/9/89

Top Weekend Crowds

19,114	Cornell	3/15–16–17, 1991
15,528	Michigan Tech	2/27–28, 1981
15,240	Lake Superior	1/31–2/1, 1992
15,206	Michigan Tech	11/21–22, 1975

Top Single-Game Post-Renovation Crowds (1996–97 to Present)

6,738	Ohio State	1/29/00
6,711	Ohio State	2/6/99
6,703	Michigan State	2/25/00
6,694	Michigan State	11/20/98

Dekers Hall of Fame

Avon Artz
Larry Babcock
Red Berenson
Gil Burford
Todd Brost
David Burns
Gary Butler
Don Canham
Neil Celley
Ross Childs
George Chin
Keith Crossman
Warren Crouch
Dave Debol
Paul Domm
Dick Dunnigan
Merle Falk
Greg Fox
Neil Gabler
Wally Gacek
Bernie Gagnon
Doug Galbraith
Paul Gamsby
Wally Grant
Bob Gray
James Haas
Bob Heathcott
Vic Heyliger
Connie Hill
Lorne Howes
Pat Hughes
Willard Ikola

Carl Isaacson
Eldon James
John Jewell
Brad Jones
Steve Jones
Edgar Kahn
Jim Keough
Earl Keys
Dan Lerg
Tom Lindskog
William Lord
Eddie Lowrey
Dean Lucier
Joe Lunghamer
Dale MacDonald
Bill MacFarland
John MacInnes
Alex MacLellan
Kris Manery
Tim Manning
Joe Marmo
Mike Martilla
Will Martin
John Matchefts
Kip Mauer
John McDonald
John McKennell
Gordon McMillan
Mark Miller
Robbie Moore
Angie Moretto
Doug Mullen

Jeff Norton
Myles O'Connor
John Palenstein
Rob Palmer
Dan Petermann
Doug Philpott
Albert Pickus
Bob Pitts
Rudy Reichert
Emerson Reid
Tom Rendall
Al Renfrew
Bob Schiller
Art Schlanderer
Reggie Shave
John Sherf
George Sibilsky
Lois Simmons
Brian Skinner
Ross Smith
Ted Speers
Dick Starrak
Leonard Teitelbaum
Jack Tompkins
Randy Trudeau
Herb Upton
Mel Wakabayashi
Bob Watt
Bob White
Gordon Wilkie
Glenn Williams

Hockey M-Men

Each year listed for an individual represents a full season. For example, 95–96 means the player earned a letter for both the 1994–95 and 1995–96 seasons.

Abbett, John   1928–29
Abbey, Vincent   1944
Allen, Edwin   1938
Allman, Albert   1945
Anderson, Gordon   1943–44
Anderson, Robert   1923
Arman, Krikor 1998–99–00–01
Arnold, John   1993–94–95–96
Artz, Avon   1933–34
Ashworth, Roy   1972–73
Athens, John   1943–44
Augimeri, Vincent   1981

Babcock, Larry   1961–62–63
Bagnell, Karl   1970–71–72
Bahrych, Maximillian   1941–42
Baird, Robert   1965–66–67
Baker, Sean   1985–86–87–88
Balestri, George   1947
Ballantine, James   1988–89–90–91
Baseotto, Bruno   1980
Bassey, Albert   1949–51
Bayless, Tom   1949
Beach, David   1938
Berenson, Gordon   1960–61–62
Berenzweig, Andrew   1996–97–98–99
Beresford, James   1923–24
Berryman, Richard   1935
Bieber, William   1963–64
Binnie, Randall   1967–68–69
Bjorkman, John   1984–85–87
Blackburn, Josh   1999–00–01
Blanzy, Russell   1974–75–76–77
Blum, John   1978–79–80–81
Bochen, Steve   1958–59–60
Bolles, Roy   1973
Bondy, Scott   1975
Botterill, Jason   1994–95–96–97
Bourke, Peter   1994–95–96–97
Bourne, Roger   1979–80–81
Boysen, Robert   1965–66–67

Bradley, Roy   1942–43
Brand, Hendrikus   1965–66
Brandrup, Paul   1979–80–81–82
Brauer, William   1983–84–85–86
Brietmeyer, Philip   1944
Brennan, David   1977–78–79–80
Brook, Allan   1967–68–69
Brost, Todd   1986–87–88–89
Brothers, Kenneth   1988–89–90–91
Brown, Richard   1956
Brown, Robert 1975–76
Brown, Robert   1987–88–89–90
Brumm, Leonard   1948–49–50
Bryant, Clarence   1928–29–30
Buchanan, Michael   1955–57
Buchanan, Neil   1954–55–56
Burford, Gilbert   1949–50–51
Burgett, Michael   1973–74
Burnes, Andy   2001
Burns, Richard   1968
Busch, William   1969
Butler, Gary   1963–64
Butts, William   1961–62–63

Calvert, Lawrence   1939–40
Cammalleri, Mike   2000–01
Canfield, William   1940
Carlile, Todd   1983–84–85–86
Carter, Keith   1981
Cartier, Jean-Yves   1970–71–72
Celley, Neil   1949–50–51
Chadwick, Alfred   1938–39
Chaffee, Donald   1932
Chapman, Harvey   1932–33–34
Chase, Edward   1937
Chase, William   1935–37–38
Chiamp, Mark   1982–83–84–85
Childs, Ross   1957–58–59
Chin, George   1952–53–54
Clark, Justin   1996–97–98–99
Coffman, Michael   1976–77–78–79

Cole, John   1963–64
Coleman, Robert   1964
Collins, Robert   1940–41–42
Comb, Raymond   1927
Comb, Walter   1923
Connelly, Gary   1971
Cooke, George   1937–38–39
Comrie, Mike   1999–00
Cooney, Patrick   1952–53–54
Copeland, Glenn   1927–28
Copeland, John Todd
   1987–88–89–90
Coristine, Ronald   1962–63–64
Cormier, Daniel   1976
Corson, John   1940–42
Cosby, Baden   1955–56
Cossalter, Clement   1946–48
Courtis, Thomas   1929–30–31
Courtis, Walter   1935
Coventry, Markham   1933
Coyle, James   1959–60–61
Cragg, Graham   1950–51–52
Crawford, Scott   1998–99
Crossland, Hugh   1962
Crossman, Keith   1931–32–33
Crozier, Greg   1996–97–98–99
Cullen, Gordon   1973–74
Cullen, Terry   1979
Curtis, Thomas   1929–30–31
Cusack, Michael   1986
Cushing, Patrick   1959–61
Cutler, Barry   1960

Daddario, Greg   1998–99
Dance, William   1942–43
David, George   1932–33–34
David, Lawrence   1934–35–36
Day, Richard   1964
Deasley, Bryan   1987–88
Debol, David   1975–76–77–78
Dechaine, Pierre   1964–65
Deeks, Donald   1968–69–70
DeMartino, John   1983–84
Denton, John   1927
Derleth, Robert   1943–44
Desmarais, Rene   1971
Domm, Paul   1967–68–69

Downes, Harold   1950–51
Downing, Franklin   1983–84–85–86
Downing, Matthew   1987–88–89
Dozzi, Delky   1958
Dries, Raymond   1983–84–85
Dufek, Donald   1973–74–75–76
Dunbar, Peter   1972–73–74
Dunn, Douglas   1953–54
Dunnigan, G. Richard   1955–56–57

Eaves, Murray   1979–80
Elliot, Irwin   1936
Elliot, Jonathan   1982–83–84–85
Evans, Douglas   1989–90–91–92

Fabello, John   1936–37–38
Falconer, Robert   1971–72–73–74
Falk, Merle   1969–70
Fardig, David   1981
Fardig, Don   1973–74
Fedorov, Anton   1994
Felsner, Denny   1989–90–91–92
Ferguson, Robert   1964–65–66
Fife, Robert   1941
Fisher, James   1926–28–29
Fleming, Robert   1949
Fletcher, Owen   1974
Forrest, George   1963–64
Fox, Chris   1995–96–97–98
Fox, Gregory   1973–74–75–76
Fraser, Brad   2000–01
Freeman, Ernest   1933
Frescoln, Chris   1994–95–96–97
Fricker, Paul   1980–81
Frumkes, Joseph   1932

Gabler, Cornelius   1926–27–33
Gacek, Walter   1946–47–48–49
Gagnon, Bernard   1970–71–72
Galbraith, Douglas   1967–68–69
Galipeau, Roger   1964
Gamsby, Paul   1969–70–71
Gassoff, Bob   1998–99–00–01
Gaynor, Michael   1989
Gibson, E. Clark   1955
Giles, Gregory   1969
Gillis, John   1941–42

Glendinning, Wil   1968–69
Goff, Daniel   1984–85–86
Goff, Patrick   1983–84–85
Goldman, Edward   1920–21
Goldsmith, Paul   1940–41
Gordon, Chris   1991–92–93–94
Gordon, Robb   1995
Gould, Jay   1954–55–56
Gourley, Donald   1957–58–59
Grace, Charles   1929
Grade, Jeffrey   1982
Graham, Robert   1945
Grant, Wallace   1946–48–49–50
Gray, Robert   1962–63–64
Greening, Charles   1959
Greer, Ted   1944–45–46–47
Griffin, John   1949
Gross, Phllip   1967–68–69
Gubow, David   1971

Haas, James   1952–53–54
Halko, Steven   1993–94–95–96
Hampson, Gordon 1978–79–80–81
Handel, Michael   1987–88–89
Hanna, Bernard   1955–56–57
Hansen, Lars   1967–68–69
Harlock, David   1990–91–92–93
Hart, Samuel   1928–29–30
Hartman, Gerald   1967–68
Hastings, Douglas   1970
Hawkins, John   1982
Hawley, Arthur   1942
Hayes, Bobby   1996–97–98–99
Hayton, Barrie   1957–58–59
Heathcott, Robert   1950–51–52
Hebert, Yves   1954–55
Heddle, Frederick   1940–41
Helber, Michael   1989–90–91–92
Helber, Timothy   1988–89–90
Henchel, Jeffrey   1985–86–87
Henderson, Charles   1944–45
Henderson, Clayton   1923
Henderson, Edward   1964–65–66
Herman, Harold   1966–67–68
Herr, Matt   1995–96–97–98
Heyliger, Donald   1969–70
Heyliger, Douglas   1969–70

Heyliger, Victor   1935–36–37
Hilbert, Andy   2000–01
Hill, Conrad   1946–47–48–49
Hillberg, Leslie   1938–39
Hillman, Douglas   1942
Hilton, Kevin   1993–94–95–96
Hinnegan, Kenneth   1960–61–62
Hoene, Daniel   1975–76–77–78
Hogan, Timothy   1992–93–94–95
Hood, Alexander   1964
Hooper, William   1925–26–27
Howes, Lorne   1955–56–57
Howland, George   1946–47
Howland, Glenn   1947
Hudas, Gregory   1984–85
Hughes, Patrick   1974–75–76
Huntzicker, Dave   1998–99–00–01
Hutton, John   1957–58–59
Hyman, Charles   1952

Ikola, Willard   1952–53–54

Jackson, Eric   1971
Jacobson,William   1946–47–48
Jaffe, William   1988
James, Eldon   1938–39–40
James, Gilbert   1936–37–38–39
Jarry, Michael   1970–71–72–73
Jenswold, Hohn   1944–45
Jewell, John   1933–34–35
Jillson, Jeff   1999–00
Jones, Bradley   1984–85–86–87
Jones, Stephen   1927–28–29
Joseph, Gabriel   1928–29–30

Kahn, Edgar   1923–24
Kardos, Gary   1972–73–74–75
Karpinka, Jerry   1955–56–57
Kartusch, Wayne   1962–63
Katz, Jay   1958–59
Kaufman, Lee   1951
Kautz, Joe   2001
Kawa, Ben   1975–76–77–78
Kelly, Peter   1958
Kelly, William   1961–62
Kemp, Robert   1942–43
Kennedy, Donald   1955

Keough, James   1967–68–69
Keough, Timothy   1989–90
Keyes, Earl   1950–51–52–53
Kise, Scott   1987–88
Knuble, Michael   1992–93–94–95
Kobylarz, Paul   1982–83–84–85
Koch, Geoff   1998–99–00–01
Kolb, Gerald   1960–62
Komisarek, Mike   2001
Kosick, Mark   1998–99–00–01
Koviak, Bruce   1966–67–68
Kramer, Ted   1989–90–91–92
Krussman, Donald   1981–82–83
Kuzniar, Chester   1946
Kwong, Randall   1987–88–89–90

LaJeunesse, Terrance   1973
Langen, Wilho   1930
Langfeld, Josh   1998–99–00–01
Larson, Roberts   1927
LeFebvre, Jerry   1970–71–72
Legg, Michael   1994–95–96–97
Lerg, Daniel   1977–78–79–80
Levi, Waldeck   1925
Lilienfield, Robert   1945
Lindskog, Douglas   1974–75–76
Lindskog, Thomas   1973–74–75–76
Lindstrom, Carlton   1924–25
Lockwood, Joseph   1985–86–87–88
Loges, Al   1993–94–95
Lord, William   1966–67–68
Lorden, Gary   1985–86–87–88
Loud, Henry   1941–42–43
Lounsberry, Fred   1945
Lovett, James   1939–40–41
Low, E. Reed   1936
Lowe, John   1957
Lucier, Dean   1965–66–67
Luhning, Warren   1994–95–96–97
Lundberg, Brian   1979–80–81–82
Lunghamer, Joseph   1960–61
Luongo, Stephen   1978

MacCollum, Donald   1934–35
MacDonald, J. Barry   1964–65–66
MacDonald, L. Dale   1959–60–61
MacDuff, Harry   1925–26

MacDuff, Kunle   1923
MacFarland, William   1954–55–56
MacInnes, John   1946–50
MacLellan, Alexander   1951–52–53
Macnab, Bruce   1984–85–86–87
Madden, John   1994–95–96–97
Magnuson, Kevin   1997–98–99–00
Makris, Timothy   1985–86
Malcolmson, Craig   1968–69
Malicke, Gregg   1996–97–98
Mallette, Richard   1970–71–72–73
Manery, Kris   1974–75–76–77
Manning, Timothy   1978–79–80–81
Mans, James   1983–84
Marich, David   1981–82–83–84
Marks, Harold   1929
Marmo, Joseph   1949–50–51
Marra, Thomas   1969–70–71
Mars, Jeffrey   1978–79–80–81
Marshall, John   1927–28
Marshall, Robert   1946–47
Martin, Wilfrid   1964–65
Martinson, Ronald   1952–53
Martila, C. Lee   1966–67–68
Martilla, Michael   1965–66–67
Mascarin, Telly   1953
Mason, Peter   1979–81–82
Matchefts, John   1951–53
Mateka, Edward   1959–60
Mattson, Gary   1958–59–60
Matzka, Scott   1998–99–00–01
Maurer, Clifford   1975–76–77–78
Maxwell, D., Wallace   1957
May, Dennis   1979–80–81–82
May, Douglas   1982–83–84–85
May, Edward   1950–51–52
McArdel, Owen   1948–49
McCahill, John   1975–76–77–78
McCaughey, Bradley
   1985–86–87–88
McCauley, James   1981–82–83–84
McCrimmon, Kelly   1981–82–83–84
McDonald, John   1947–48–49–50
McDonald, Neil   1956–57–58
McGonigal, John   1961–62–63
McIntosh, Donald   1956–58
McIntyre, David   1982–83–84

421

McKennell, John   1951–52
McMillan, Gordon   1946–47–48–49
Merrick, Andrew   1997–98–99–00
Merrill, Jack   1936–37
Messinger, Thomas   1944
Milanowski, Paul   1950
Milburn, Joe   1980–81–82–83
Miller, Mark   1976–77–78–79
Mink, Mark   2000–01
Mixer, Richard   1944
Moes, Michael   1987–88–89–90
Moore, Robert   1973–74–75–76
Moretto, Angelo   1973–74–75–76
Morrison, Arnold   1986
Morrison, Brendan   1994–95–96–97
Morrison, Gary   1974–75–76–77
Morrison, Ross   1962
Muckalt, Bill   1995–96–97–98
Mullen, Doug 1952–53–54
Munich, Anthony   1978
Murray, Craig   1999–00–01

Natale, Gregory   1974–75–76–77
Naylor, Gordon   1951
Neal, Randall   1972–73–74–75
Neary, Glen   1987–88
Neaton, Patrick   1990–91–92–93
Nedomansky, Vaclav   1990
Neff, Michael   1982–83–84–85
Newton, David   1963–64–65
Nielsen, Bernard   1959–60–62
Nieberg, Michael   1989
Norton, Jeffrey   1985–86–87
Nygord, Albert   1928–30

O'Connor, John   1985
O'Connor, Myles   1986–87–88–89
O'Dell, John   1934
O'Malley, Kevin   1999–00–01
Olsen, William   1937
Oliver, David   1991–92–93–94
Olver, John   1978–79
Ortmeyer, Jed   2000–01
Ouimet, Mark   1990–91–92–93

Pacholzuk, Rodney   1977–78–79
Page, Gregory   1965–66–67

Palenstein, John   1960–61
Palinski, Ambrose   1938
Palmer, Robert   1974–75–76–77
Palmer, Richard   1975–76–77–78
Paolatto, Louis   1950–53
Pardoski, Ryan   1987–88–89–90
Paris, Paul   1972–73–74–75
Parrish, James   1976–77–78–79
Pashak, Bernard   1968–69–70
Peach, Sean   1997–98–99–00
Pelow, Paul   1950–52
Pendlebury, Thomas 1961–62–63
Perrin, David   1968–69–70
Perry, Mark   1979–80–81–82
Petermann, Daniel   1923–24–25
Peugeot, George   1947
Philpott, Douglas   1952–53–54
Pickus, Albert   1953
Pitts, Robert   1955–56–57
Polonic, Thomas   1964–65
Porte, Thomas   1932
Powers, William   1986–87–88
Precious, Robert   1945
Prouse, Thomas   1931

Quirk, Daniel   1923–24

Rane, John   1940
Read, G. Martin   1964–65
Reichert, R. Edward   1942–43
Reid, Emerson   1931–32–33
Reid, William   1980–81–82–83
Rendall, Thomas   1955–56–57
Renfrew, Allan   1946–47–48–49
Reynolds, Irving   1924–25–26
Rhode, Dennis   1961
Richmond, Steve,   1979–80–81–82
Richter, David   1979–80–81–82
Ritchlin, Sean   1996–97–98–99
Roach, Bernard   1925–26–27
Roberts, David   1990–91–92–93
Roberts, Alex   1987–88–89–90
Rodgers, Donald   1961–62–63
Roemensky, Mike   2000–01
Rominski, Dale   1996–97–98–99
Ross, Charles   1939–40–41
Rossi, Michael   1986–87

Rossi, Paul   1985–86

Sacka, Ron   1992–93–94–95
Sakala, Mark   1993–94–95–96
Samuelson, Gilbert   1939–40–41
Sarazin, Pierr   1973
Scarpace, L.J.   2000–01
Schiller, Thomas   1955–56
Schlanderer, Arthur   1930–31
Schock, Harold   1994–95–96–97
Seychel, Chris   1983–84–85–86
Shand, David   1974
Sharples, Warren   1987–88–89–90
Shave, Reginald   1952–53
Shaver, Verne   1977–78
Shaw, Murray   1970
Shea, Francis   1928
Sherf, John   1933–34–35
Shields, Steve   1991–92–93–94
Shouneyia, John   2000–01
Sibilsky, George   1926–27
Sinclair, Alan   1992–93–94–95
Sindles, Harold   1934
Sippola, Alvin   1930
Sittler, Ryan   1993–94
Skinner, Brian   1970–71–72
Slack, Brian   1969–70–71
Sloan, Blake   1994–95–96–97
Smith, D. Ross   1946–48–50
Smith, James   1937–38
Smith, Sampson   1935
Sorensen, Mark   1988–89–90–91
Speers, Ted   1980–81–82–83
Spitzberg, Eric   1976–77–78–79
Spring, Paul   1983–84–85
Starr, Gary   1957–58
Starrak, Richard   1946–47–48–49
Staub, Robert   1970–71–72
Stedman, Sam   1946–47–48–49
Sternberg, Robert   1943
Stephenson, H. Howard   1950
Stewart, Cam   1991–92–93
Stewart, Thomas   1934
Stiles, Thomas   1983–84–85–86
Stiver, Daniel   1990–91–92–93
Stodden, Richard   1939–40–41
Stone, Donald   1988–89–90–91

Stone, Mike   1991–92–93–94
Stuhldreher, Harry   1951
Sulentich, Karl   1945
Sutton, Robert   1979–80–81
Sweet, Arthur   1954
Swistak, J.J.   2000–01
Switzer, Edward   1956–57–58
Switzer, James   1984

Tamer, Chris   1990–91–92–93
Tessier, Jeff   1979–80–81–82
Thayer, William   1976–77–78
Thompson, Mark   1965–66–67
Thrun, Thomas   1974
Tippett, Bradley   1980–81–82–83
Tobin, James   1939
Todd, Douglas   1977–78–79–80
Todd, John   1923–24
Tompkins, Jack   1930–31–32
Trainor, Bill   1998–99–00–01
Trudeau, W. Randall
   1972–73–74–75
Turco, Marty   1995–96–97–98
Turner, Bradley   1987–88–89–90
Turner, Dean   1977–78

Ullyot, Ronald   1966–67–68
Unsworth, Gary   1958
Unsworth, Herbert   1931
Upton, Herbert   1944–45–47
Urban, Jeffrey   1986–87–88–89

Van Biesbrouck, Julian   1980
Van Ryn, Mike   1998–99
Vancik, Jay   1999–00–01
Varvari, Rudy   1978–79–80–81

Wagner, George   1974
Wakabayashi, Mel   1964–65–66
Waldron, Sherwood   1928
Walter, Daniel   1965–66–67
Ward, Aaron   1991–92–93
Watt, Robert   1958–59–60
Waymann, John   1976–77–78–79
Weitzel, Gorege   1924–25–26
Wenzell, Peter   1977
Werner, Frank   1972–73–74–75

Wheeler, William   1976–77–78–79
White, James   1986–87–88–89
White, Robert   1958–59–60
White, William   1960–61–62
Wilkie, Gordon   1962–63–64
Williams, William   1931–32
Willis, Richard   1992–93–94–95
Wills, Warren   1958
Wilmot, Francis   1927

Wilson, Thomas   1959–61
Wiseman, Brian   1991–92–93–94
Wreford, Charles   1961
Wright, David   1991
Wyzgowski, David   2001

Yoxheimer, Steven   1981–82

Zimmerman, Frank   1975–76–77–78

Bibliography

Bacon, John U. "The Gipper." *Detroit News*, January 5, 1997.

———. "Puck-emon: Hockey in Japan Is Serious Business. Just Ask the Bunnies." *ESPN Magazine*, December 13, 1999, 104–10.

———. "Undercover Champions." *Detroit News*, April 7, 1996.

———. "Fielding Yost: The Tradition Maker," In *A Legacy of Champions: The Story of the Men Who Built University of Michigan Football.* Farmington Hills, MI: CTC Productions and Sports, 1996.

Bak, Richard. "Blueprint for Detroit." *Hour Detroit Magazine*, May 2000, 86–90.

Behee, John. *Fielding Yost's Legacy.* Ann Arbor: Ulrich's Books, 1971.

———. *Hail to the Victors.* Ann Arbor: Ulrich's Books, 1974.

Bertozzi-Villa, Elena. *Broadmoor Memories: The History of the Broadmoor.* Missoula, MT: Pictorial Histories Publishing, 1998.

Betts, Diane Lynn. *The Broadmoor World Arena: Pictorial History Book.* Colorado Springs: Broadmoor Publishing, 1988.

Bird, Michael J. *The Town That Died.* Toronto: McGraw-Hill Ryerson, 1962.

Brooks, David. "The Organization Kid." *Atlantic Monthly*, April 2001, 40–54.

Brown, Gerry, and Michael Morrison. *ESPN 1999 Sports Almanac.* New York: Hyperion, 1999.

Canham, Don. *From the Inside.* Ann Arbor: Olympia Sports Press, 1996.

Cohen, Richard M. *The University of Michigan Football Scrapbook.* Indianapolis: Bobbs-Merrill, 1978.

Dekers Hall of Fame Biographies, located in the concourse of Yost Field House.

Diamond, Dan. *Total Hockey*. New York: Total Sports, 1998.

Dicther, Heather. "The Road to Excellence: A History of the Michigan Hockey Program." Undergraduate term paper, University of Michigan, April 27, 1998.

Dinger, Ralph. *The National Hockey League Official Guide and Record Book, 2000*. Kingston, NY: Total Sports Publishing, 1999.

Dryden, Ken, and Roy MacGregor. *Home Game: Hockey and Life in Canada*. Toronto: McLelland and Stewart, 1989.

Dunbar, Willis F. *Michigan: A History of the Wolverine State*. Grand Rapids: Wm. B. Eerdmans, 1966.

Gordon, Lois, and Alan Gordon. *American Chronicle*. New Haven: Yale University Press, 1999.

Hilton, John. "Don Canham's Empire." *Ann Arbor Observer*, September 1983.

Hirsh, E. D., Jr., Joseph F. Kett, and James Trefil. *The Dictionary of Cultural Literacy*. New York: Houghton Mifflin, 1988.

Hollander, Zander. *The Complete Encyclopedia of Hockey*. Detroit: Gale Research, 1983.

Jennings, Peter, and Todd Brewster. *The Century*. New York: Doubleday, 1998.

Kahn, Edgar A. "Albert Kahn: His Son Remembers." *Michigan History Magazine,* July–August, year unknown, 24–31.

———. *Journal of a Neurosurgeon*. Springfield, IL: Charles C. Thomas, 1972.

Keegan, John. *The First World War*. New York: Vintage Books, 1998.

Kryk, John. *Natural Enemies*. Kansas City: Andrews and McMeel, 1994.

MacNeil, Robert. *Burden of Desire*. New York: Bantam Doubleday, 1992.

Madej, Bruce. *Michigan: Champions of the West*. Champaign, IL: Sports Publishing, 1997.

Manchester, William. *Winston Spencer Churchill: The Last Lion*. New York: Bantam, Doubleday, Dell, 1983.

Maritime Museum of the Atlantic. Various Web pages from <http://museum.gov.ns.ca/mma/>.

Marwil, Jonathan L. *A History of Ann Arbor*. Ann Arbor: Ann Arbor Observer Press, 1987.

McCambridge, Michael, ed. *ESPN SportsCentury*. New York: Hyperion, 1999.

Media Guides from the University of Michigan hockey team, 1937–present, plus the 1999–2000 media guides of the University of Michigan football team; the Notre Dame football team; and the hockey teams of Colorado College, the University of Denver, the University of North Dakota, the University of Minnesota, the University of Wisconsin, Michigan Tech University, Northern Michigan University, Lake Superior State University, Michigan State University, Boston University, Boston College, and Dartmouth; and the league guides for the WCHA, the CCHA, Hockey East, and the NCAA Frozen Four, plus those of the Detroit Red Wings and Detroit Lions.

Peckham, Howard H. *The Making of the University of Michigan: 1817–1992.* Ann Arbor: Bentley Historical Library, University of Michigan, 1994.

Perry, Will. *The Wolverines.* Huntsville, AL: Strode, 1974.

Power, John. *One Goal: A Chronicle of the 1980 U.S. Olympic Hockey Team.* New York: Harper and Row, 1984.

Schembechler, Bo, and Mitch Albom. *Bo.* New York: Warner Books, 1989.

Schreiber, Penny. "The Heroic Life and Tragic Fate of Raoul Wallenberg." *Ann Arbor Observer,* May 1995, 31–37.

Searle, Caroline, and Bryn Vaile. *The Official Olympic Games Companion.* Herndon, VA: Brassey's Sports, 1998.

Shackman, Grace. "Weinberg's Coliseum." *Ann Arbor Observer,* February 1983, 101–2.

Swift, E. M. "Sportsmen of the Year: The 1980 U.S. Olympic Hockey Team." *Sports Illustrated,* December 22–29, 1980.

Time/CBS News. *People of the Century.* New York: Simon and Schuster, 1999.

University of Michigan. Bentley Historical Library. Clip book of the *Michigan Daily,* the *Ann Arbor News,* the *Detroit News,* and the *Detroit Free Press,* 1911–present.

University of Michigan. Minutes of the Board in Control of Intercollegiate Athletics, 1910 to the present.

University of Michigan. Sports Information Department. Media Guides for ice hockey, football, and basketball.

Wallechinsky, David. *The Complete Book of the Winter Olympics.* New York: Overlook Press, 1998.

Yost, Fielding H. *Football for Player and Spectator.* 1905. Reprint, 1992.

Index

Numbers in italics refer to photographs.